Dumfries House

Dumfries House

An Architectural Story

Simon Green
Edited by Jane Thomas

First published in 2014
Re-printed in paperback in 2016 by
Historic Environment Scotland.

Historic Environment Scotland
John Sinclair House
16 Bernard Terrace
Edinburgh EH8 9NX

Registered Charity SC045925

British Library Cataloguing-in-Publication Data.
A catalogue record for this book is available from
the British Library.

ISBN 978 1 902419 95 4

Printed in Poland by Perfekt, Warsaw

Frontispiece: Dumfries House *HES 2010 DP083152*

End papers: Plate XIX and Plate VIII from Robert Wood's
Ruins of Palmyra 1753 *HES DP149862 & DP149863*

Contents

Acknowledgements

The author wishes to acknowledge the assistance of all the individuals who contributed to the preparation of this volume.

This book would not have been possible without the generous support of John Crichton-Stuart 7th Marquess of Bute who through his archivist and curator Andrew Maclean and subsequently Lynsey Nairn have made the wealth of information held in the Mount Stuart Archives available. Their expert guidance has enabled this exhaustive study to come to fruition. The contributions made by Jennifer Dowager Marchioness of Bute, Peregrine Bertie and Ninian Crichton-Stuart are also much appreciated.

Charlotte Rostek and the staff of The Great Steward of Scotland's Dumfries House Trust provided continued support, advice and open access to Dumfries House and its estate throughout the preparation of the volume.

Many others have contributed including Orlando Rock and Christies; Simpson and Brown Architects Jen Armstrong, Tom Addyman and James Simpson; John Batty, Peter Burman and Ian Gow of The National Trust for Scotland; Andrew Martindale of Historic Scotland; Stephen Astley and Frances Sands at Sir John Soane's Museum; Historic Environment Scotland staff Heather Stoddart, John Borland, Angus Lamb, James Mackie, Steve Wallace, Derek Smart, Zoe Gibson, Neil Gregory, Jane Thomas, Alasdair Burns, Oliver Brookes, Rebecca Bailey, Clare Sorensen, Diane Watters, David Cowley, Robert Adam; Mairi Sutherland, proofreading. Linda Sutherland, indexing; Charles Hind of RIBA Drawings Collection; Bob Heath; John Gifford; Tristram Clark; Sir Robert Clerk of Penicuik; Christopher Dingwall; Iain Gordon Brown; Elizabeth Graham; Matthew Williams; Stewart Smith; Kristina Taylor; Mr & Mrs Keith Adam; Michael Davies; Anne Riches; Catherine Cruft; Gavin Stamp.

Family Trees

The Crichton Earls of Dumfries & The Dalrymple Earls of Stair

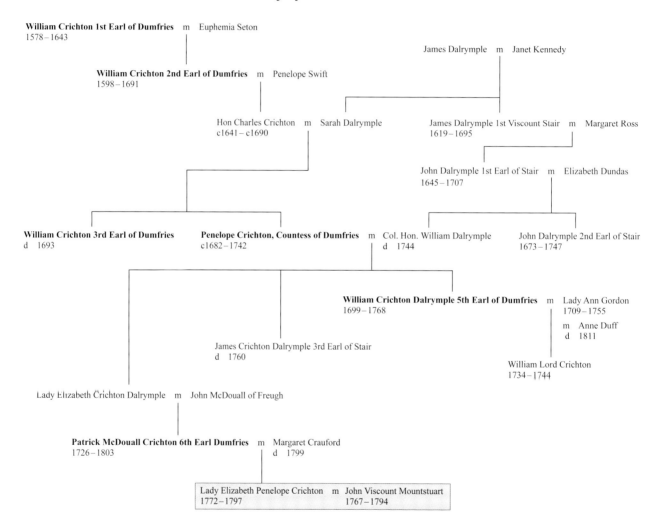

William Crichton 1st Earl of Dumfries m Euphemia Seton
1578 – 1643

James Dalrymple m Janet Kennedy

William Crichton 2nd Earl of Dumfries m Penelope Swift
1598 – 1691

Hon Charles Crichton m Sarah Dalrymple
c1641 – c1690

James Dalrymple 1st Viscount Stair m Margaret Ross
1619 – 1695

John Dalrymple 1st Earl of Stair m Elizabeth Dundas
1645 – 1707

William Crichton 3rd Earl of Dumfries
d 1693

Penelope Crichton, Countess of Dumfries m Col. Hon. William Dalrymple
c1682 – 1742   d 1744

John Dalrymple 2nd Earl of Stair
1673 – 1747

William Crichton Dalrymple 5th Earl of Dumfries m Lady Ann Gordon
1699 – 1768   1709 – 1755

m Anne Duff
d 1811

James Crichton Dalrymple 3rd Earl of Stair
d 1760

William Lord Crichton
1734 – 1744

Lady Elizabeth Crichton Dalrymple m John McDouall of Freugh

Patrick McDouall Crichton 6th Earl Dumfries m Margaret Crauford
1726 – 1803   d 1799

Lady Elizabeth Penelope Crichton m John Viscount Mountstuart
1772 – 1797   1767 – 1794

Stuarts of Bute

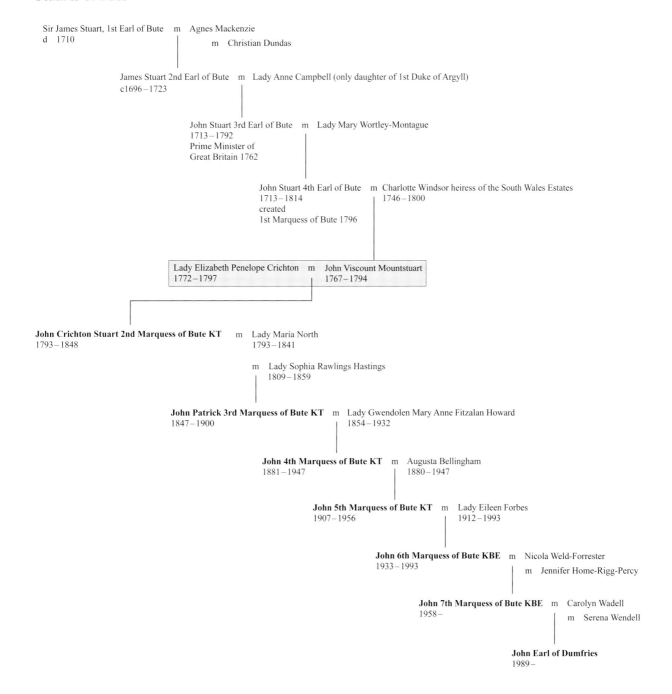

Sir James Stuart, 1st Earl of Bute   m   Agnes Mackenzie
d   1710

                      m   Christian Dundas

James Stuart 2nd Earl of Bute   m   Lady Anne Campbell (only daughter of 1st Duke of Argyll)
c1696–1723

John Stuart 3rd Earl of Bute   m   Lady Mary Wortley-Montague
1713–1792
Prime Minister of
Great Britain 1762

John Stuart 4th Earl of Bute   m   Charlotte Windsor heiress of the South Wales Estates
1713–1814   1746–1800
created
1st Marquess of Bute 1796

Lady Elizabeth Penelope Crichton   m   John Viscount Mountstuart
1772–1797   1767–1794

John Crichton Stuart 2nd Marquess of Bute KT   m   Lady Maria North
1793–1848   1793–1841

                      m   Lady Sophia Rawlings Hastings
                           1809–1859

John Patrick 3rd Marquess of Bute KT   m   Lady Gwendolen Mary Anne Fitzalan Howard
1847–1900   1854–1932

John 4th Marquess of Bute KT   m   Augusta Bellingham
1881–1947   1880–1947

John 5th Marquess of Bute KT   m   Lady Eileen Forbes
1907–1956   1912–1993

John 6th Marquess of Bute KBE   m   Nicola Weld-Forrester
1933–1993

                      m   Jennifer Home-Rigg-Percy

John 7th Marquess of Bute KBE   m   Carolyn Wadell
1958–

                      m   Serena Wendell

John Earl of Dumfries
1989–

Introduction

William Crichton-Dalrymple, 5th Earl of Dumfries, laid the foundation stone of Dumfries House on 18 July 1754. He had commissioned the design from the young architects John, Robert and James Adam who were also to act as contractors for the building. It is the earliest country house designed and built by the Adam brothers whose fame was to eclipse that of their father William, the most prominent Scottish architect of his day. Robert Adam was heavily involved in the design but left his brothers John and James to see the building through to completion when he left for Europe on the Grand Tour. The House was saved for the nation in 2007 in recognition of the importance not only of the building but also of its original furnishings. This spectacular and well documented collection not only includes works by Thomas Chippendale but also by three important Edinburgh furniture makers: Francis Brodie, Alexander Peter and William Mathie.

The House lies in rolling farmland to the west of Cumnock on the south bank of the Lugar Water. Its origins lie in the relatively modest estate of Leifnorris, a towerhouse of which nothing now survives. William Crichton, 7th Lord Crichton of Sanquhar and 1st Earl of Dumfries, bought the estate in 1635 from the Crawford family.[1] In 1643 he sold Sanquhar Castle, the Crichton family seat, to the Earl of Queensberry, seemingly out of financial necessity.[2] The Crichtons extended and consolidated their Ayrshire estates during the 17th century, acquiring various lands including the barony of Cumnock and Glenmure, Waterside to the north of the Lugar Water and the ancient castle of Terringzean to the east. In the early 18th century they purchased further lands including the Sherrifdom and Estate of Clackmannan and the Mochrum estates in Dumfriesshire.

The neo-Palladian design of Dumfries House with its central block, quadrant wings and pavilions is still clearly visible, later alterations having respected the form of the original house. At a discreet distance, the Coach House and Stable do not compete with the 5th Earl of Dumfries' new home. HES 2008 DP040168

The Earls of Dumfries were closely related to the Dalrymple Earls of Stair. The 5th Earl of Dumfries' mother, Countess of Dumfries, in her own right[3] married William Dalrymple a younger son of the 1st Earl of Stair and appears to have lived mostly in Clackmannanshire.[4] The 5th Earl served in the army under his uncle, 2nd Earl of Stair, most notably at the Battle of Dettingen. Leifnorris was made available for the 5th Earl when his mother died in 1742 whilst his father was still living in Clackmannanshire. This close connection between the Stair and Crichton families is now most clearly expressed through the tapestries in the Tapestry Room, which were acquired by the 2nd Earl of Stair when he was an ambassador in Paris. On 17 November 1760, the Earl inherited the title of the 3rd Earl of Stair from his elder brother; on his death, the Stair title passed to his cousin John Dalrymple.[5]

The Earl's first wife died in 1755, soon after building had begun, and the house was largely complete before the Earl could find a longed for second wife. His letters to the Earl of Loudoun are peppered with phrases such as 'sound and single'.[6] The 5th Earl eventually married the much younger Anne Duff on 19 June 1762. She was the daughter of William Duff of Crombie, Fife, and Elizabeth Dalrymple, daughter of Robert Dalrymple of North Berwick, and hence a distant cousin. She appears not to have been the great heiress that he believed his two earldoms should have attracted[7] but she was young and attractive as the Thomas Hudson portrait commissioned by her husband in 1763 shows.[8] The marriage was not without its difficulties; the Countess of Northumberland's diary entry for 15 October 1762 reads, 'Colonel Montgomery expelled fr. Dumfries House for being behind the window curtain with the Countess.'[9] Three years after the union there was still no heir, a fact which almost certainly prompted the 66 year old Earl to join the title and the Estate into an entail.[10] This was a legally binding way to

The principal evidence of the extensive late 19th century alterations to the House on the entrance front are the domed pepperpot turrets. HES 2010 DP083185

ensure that whoever inherited the title as 6th Earl of Dumfries would also receive both the Ayrshire and the Wigtownshire Estates. The entail was drawn up on 14 December 1765 and lists all the lands and properties.[11] His nephew Patrick McDouall, son of his sister Elizabeth, was being groomed, somewhat reluctantly, to take over and had to be persuaded to give up his career in the Army in order to inherit these substantial estates.[12]

The 5th Earl died only eight years after the House was completed and, as planned, the Estates passed to his nephew Patrick McDouall who added Crichton to his name when he succeeded to the Earldom. Along with his industrious wife, he further developed and embellished the Estate. Their daughter and sole heir, Lady Elizabeth, married John, Lord Mount Stuart, the eldest son of John Stuart 1st Marquess of Bute. John, 2nd Marquess of Bute, was the eldest son of this union which brought together the Estates and titles of the Stuarts and the Crichtons; the family names were amalgamated to Crichton-Stuart and the title of Earl of Dumfries was adopted as the courtesy title of the heir.

Dumfries House now became an integral part of the extensive Bute Estates. While the family's ancestral seat was Mount Stuart on Bute, Dumfries House remained in use as a treasured family property, well maintained, periodically redecorated and rarely let.[13] The 2nd Marquess of Bute lived at Dumfries House during part of his childhood and in later life continued to spend time there despite having extensive properties

and business interests elsewhere, most notably in South Wales. He proposed some major alterations which were not realised and so it was left to his son to make the biggest, albeit sympathetic, changes to the House. In the last decade of his life, the 3rd Marquess, having already commissioned a myriad of building projects including the rebuilding of Cardiff Castle, Castell Coch and Mount Stuart, turned to Dumfries House, which had always been a favourite residence and where both his grandmothers had spent their childhoods. As soon as he came of age he had carried out various minor alterations and re-decorations but in later life he took a more dramatic course of action.

In his twenties and thirties he had worked closely with his friend the architect William Burges on numerous projects, most notably in South Wales. In later life he had a similarly fruitful friendship with Arts and Crafts architect Robert Weir Schultz with whom he masterminded the transformation of Dumfries House. The sophistication and subtlety of this scheme is one of the glories of Dumfries House. The technicolour bombast of Cardiff Castle was here traded for careful additions and alterations that respect the balance and poise of the 18th century house. After his death in 1900, his son, the 4th Marquess, continued working closely with Schultz to finish the exterior elements of his father's scheme as originally intended while

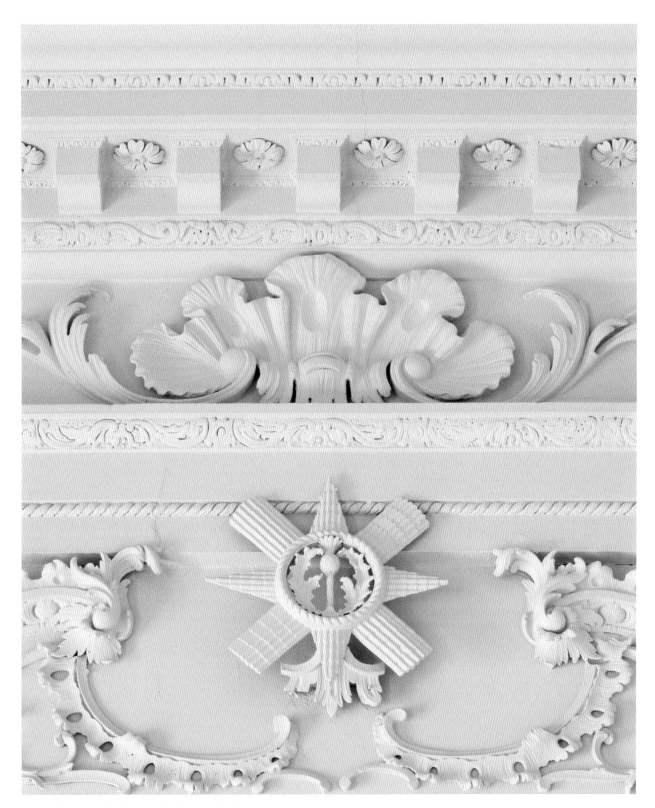

internally embellishing and altering the House to meet his requirements.

In 1934 Dumfries House became the principal home of John Earl of Dumfries, heir to the 4th Marquess of Bute. For the first time in over 130 years it became the principal residence of a young family, rather than one amongst many Bute residences. This prompted further alterations including the creation of a new dining

The 5th Earl of Dumfries celebrated his elevation to the Order of The Thistle in the plasterwork of the Dining Room, the most important room in his new House. HES 2007 DP033724

room. On the death of the 4th Marquess in 1947, the family moved to Mount Stuart but the 5th Marquess died only seven years later and Dowager Marchioness Eileen returned to Dumfries House in 1956, living there until her death in 1993. Although some of the original furniture had been distributed around other Bute properties, she reunited the collection in the twentieth century; her careful stewardship ensured that the integrity of the original Adam house as built and furnished could be appreciated.

The Bute family archive held at Mount Stuart is the most important and extensive source of information about the family and their buildings. It not only holds the papers of the respective Earls and Marquesses but also the papers of various related families such as the Earls of Loudoun and so the House can be better understood within the context of its time. Most importantly however, the combination of the sympathetically maintained house with most of its original contents along with the cornucopia of information held in the Archive enables a detailed examination of its architectural development.

Dumfries House has always been a treasured family home as opposed to a great house of parade and this is what differentiates it from the houses of the 5th Earl's contemporaries such as Lord Hopetoun. This book explores the fascinating history of Dumfries House from its inception in the mid 18th century to the death of Dowager Marchioness Eileen in 1993. In 2007, after many deliberations, John Crichton-Stuart, 7th Marquess of Bute, decided to put the House, its historic contents and the immediate Estate up for sale. A consortium led by HRH Prince Charles, Duke of Rothesay, bought the House, the contents and the land with the express aim of making it more accessible to the public. The House and its Estate have now entered a very different and exciting period as they are developed and restored to show their glories to a wider public under the careful guidance of the Great Steward of Scotland's Dumfries House Trust.

1   William 7th Lord Crichton of Sanquhar had been created Viscount of Air on 2 February 1622 for his services to the crown and on 12 June 1633 during Charles I's visit to Scotland he was created Earl of Dumfries, Viscount of Air, Lord Crichton of Air and Cumnock. This reference to Air and Cumnock in the new titles suggests that the Crichtons had already acquired lands in Cumnock prior to the acquisition of the Leifnorris Estate; however Paterson states that it was the 2nd Earl who acquired the barony of Cumnock from the Dunbars of Cumnock during the reign of Charles II, for whom he was a privy councillor. The heavily mortgaged estate of Sanquhar Castle and its barony were sold to the 1st Earl of Queensberry between 1642 and 1643 to ease the family's finances. The 1st Earl died at an unconfirmed date during this period but both the 1st Earl and his heir were signatories to the sale of the ancestral seat of Sanquhar. Paterson 1863, 332

2   William Crichton 7th Lord Crichton lavishly entertained James VI & I at Sanquhar Castle in 1617 and contributed greatly to the expenses of Charles I, Scottish Coronation after which he received the Earldom of Dumfries. These costly events are cited by Wilson and McMillan 1931, 101, who in turn reference Spottiswoode as the reason for the sale of Sanquhar Castle and estate.

3   She inherited the title and estates from her brother, the 3rd Earl, at the age of 11.

4   In 1708 Col William Dalrymple, husband of the Countess of Dumfries bought the Clackmannan Estate and the Sherriffdom from David Bruce as a result of his bankruptcy. Crouther 1936, 100. William Dalrymple developed the colliery, installing a water powered drainage wheel, and lined the Pow at the mouth of the Black Devon with stone blocks to improve the landing place for loading coal into flat bottomed boats a modest precursor of the activities of his great-grandson the 2nd Marquess of Bute's work at Cardiff. The 5th Earl's mother died at Clackmannan in 1742. Clackmannan Tower was a much more substantial building than we see, consisting of a large late 16th century mansion house attached to the ancient tower. Swan 1987, 6

5   The illustrations of Dumfries House in *Vitruvius Scoticus* are inscribed, 'The seat of the Earl of Dumfries and Stair' which shows that these engravings were made between 1760 and 1768, after the House was completed.

6   Earl of Dumfries at Leifnorris 19 June 1758 writing to Earl of Loudoun. Bute Archives LO/2/105/1

7   Dumfries House Sale Catalogue, Christie's, 2007

8   Now in the Royal Albert Museum Exeter, it originally hung on the west wall of the dining room.

9   Greig, H 1926, 25–6

10   On 26 July 1769, a year and a day after her first husband's death, Anne married Hon Alexander Gordon Lord Rockville, son of the 2nd Earl of Aberdeen. The timing would suggest that the marriage was held as soon as possible after a suitable period of mourning had been observed. Her second husband was her first husband's first wife's half brother. She died on 21 August 1811 having produced at least nine children.

11   Deed of Entail of the Earl of Dumfries 14 December 1765.
Lands mentioned:
Barony of Cumnock, Dalhanny, Nether Garrieve, Garclaugh, Templelands with Burgh of Barony and regality of Cumnock
Leiffnorris, Waird, Blackwoodhill
Templelands & clachan of Cumnock, Lowes, Over Sherrington & Blackhall, Crocklar, Boylston and Grierston, Blacklands, Broad meadow of Logan Clockloghair and Cubbs Cloon
Auchencross
Barony of Glenmuir, Glenmuir, Pepperthill, Schaw, Castle Coole, Dornall
Little Chang, Over Glaisnock, Shiell and Powhapple
Mossmark, Brunston, Craigman, Knockdons
Waterside, Pennyland, Kirkland, Glasshead, Glenside, Hapland, Old Byre, Ballanceholm
Fauld and Bank, Writing Acre, Hundred Merkland, Waterside, Pennyfadzeoch Easter
Barony of Mochrum
May Brae, Upper and Nether Gleulings, Airilick, Corval, Grlchrew, Shallochglass, Drumdrew, Drummatt, Gargarries-Hither and Nether, Craigach, Craiglary, Half Merk, Kirriehallock, Parkhill
Lochronald, Mains of Lochronald, Ballineinoch, Drummalloch, Merks, Airieligg, Arriesses
Sleudonnan, Craigarrie, Derries, Monandorie-Over &Nether, Alterkinross, Craigenadie, Kilgallick, Dennycarsh, Eldrack, Lewisland, Kilglassoch, Inshank, Erriolglassals, Deroachline and Drummaine
Bute Archives DU/5/2

12   Information from Charlotte Rostek from unpublished McDouall family letters, copies of which are held at Dumfries House.

13   After the death of the 6th Earl in 1803, Dumfries House was occupied by his brother John McDouall who unfortunately died five months later. The House was then looked after by a small staff until the 2nd Marquess came of age in 1814. During the minority of the 3rd Marquess and after the death of his mother in 1859 the House was lived in by his guardian Sir Charles Fergusson.

Principal Plans and Survey Drawings

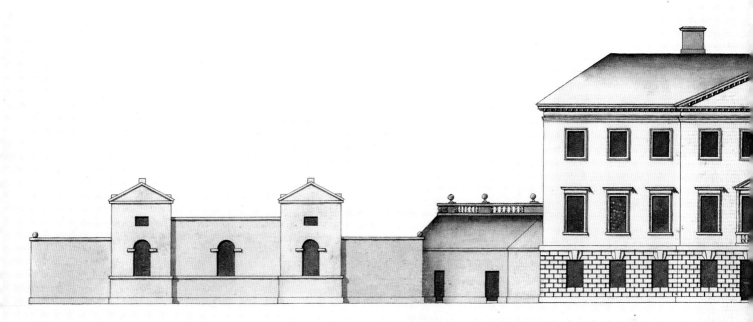

Scale of

This is The Elevation referr'd to in
Honble The Earl of Dumfries &

FRONT

the Contract between The Right
In. Rob.t & Ja.s Adams Architects.

Dumfries.

In.s Rob.t & Ja.s Adam.

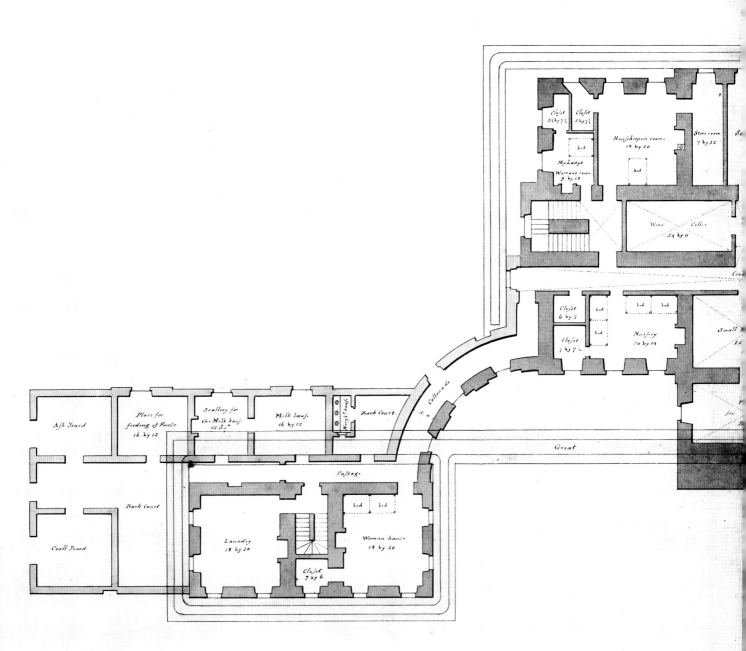

Ash Yeard

Place for feeding of Fowls 16 by 12

Scullery for the Milk house 12 3"

Milk house 16 by 12

Back Court

Great

Back Court

Coall Yeard

Laundry 18 by 20

Passage

Woman house 18 by 20

Closet 7 by 6

bed bed

Collonade

Back Court

Closet 3 by 7½

Closet 5 by 7½

My Lady

Womans room 9 by 13

bed

Housekeepers room 18 by 20

bed

Store room 7 by 22

Wine Cellar 24 by 11

Closet 6 by 7

Closet 7 by 7½

bed

bed

Nursery 20 by 14

bed   bed

Small

Scale of

Plan referr'd to by

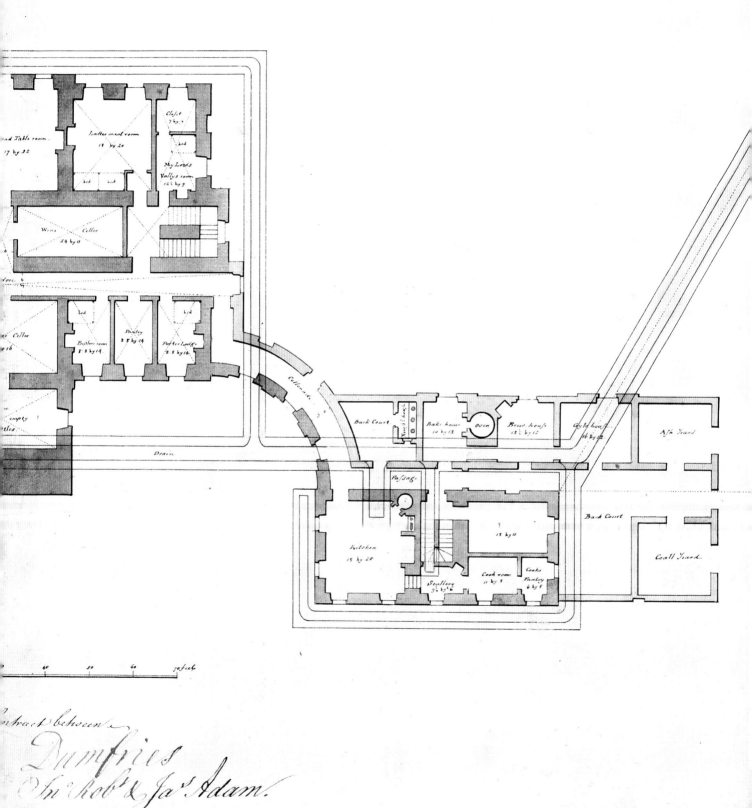

Plan 3 Adam 1754 Contract Drawing – Ground Floor Plan Bute Archives DHP/1/4

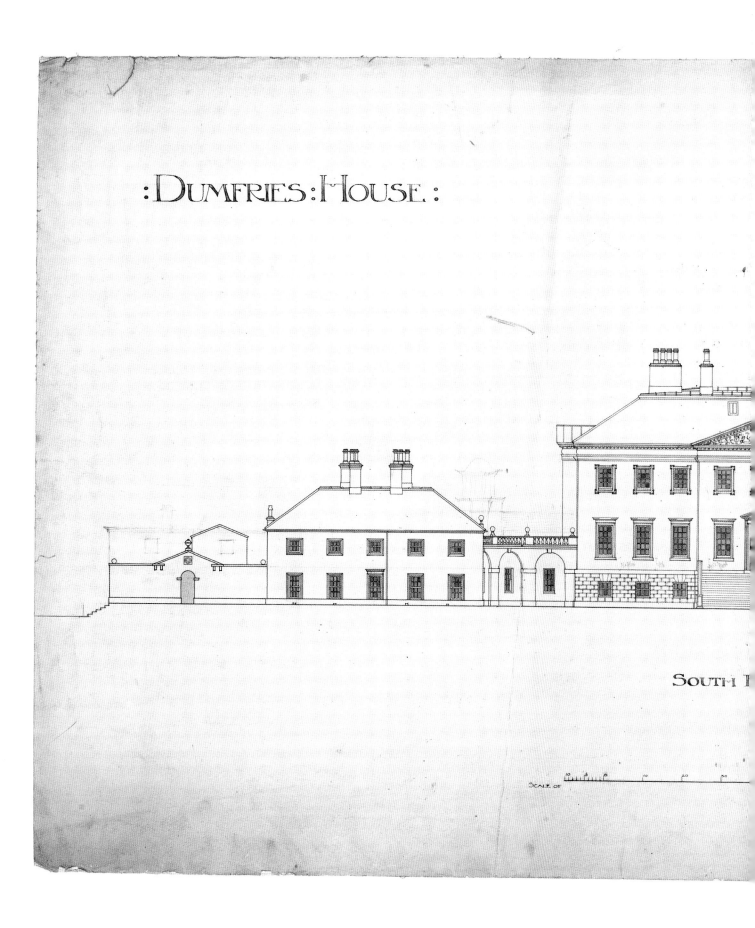

:DUMFRIES:HOUSE.:

SOUTH

SCALE OF

Plan 7 Weir Schultz 1894 Survey – South Elevation Bute Archives DHP 11/9

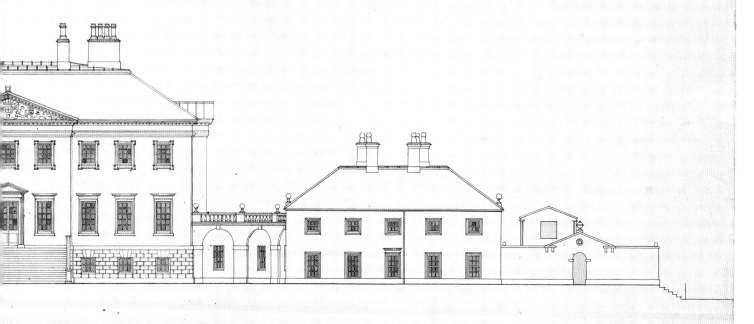

ELEVATION

14 Gray's Inn Square.
London W.C. Jan 1894.

FEET

:DUMFRIES:HOUSE:

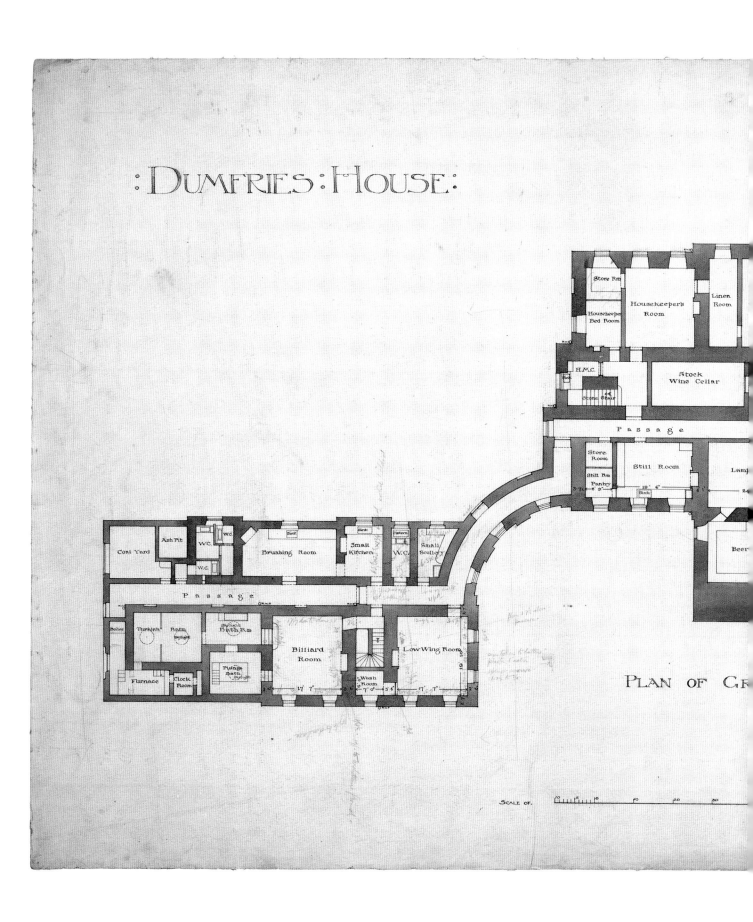

Store Rm

Housekeeper's Room

Linen Room.

Housekeepers Bed Room

H.M.C.

Stock Wine Cellar

Stone Stair

Passage

Store Room

Still Room

Lamp

Still Rm Pantry

Beer

Coal Yard

Ash Pit

W.C.

W.C.

W.C.

Brushing Room

Sink

Small Kitchen

Sink

Cistern

W.C.

Small Scullery

Passage

Boiler

Turkish Bath

Bath Rm

Billiard Room

Wash Room

Low Wing Room

Plunge Bath

Furnace

Clock Room

PLAN OF GR

SCALE OF.

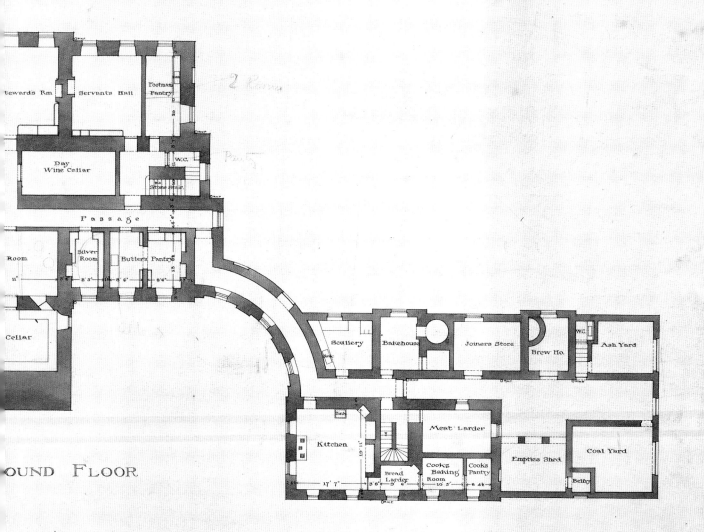

No 1.

tewards Rm   Servants Hall   Footman Pantry

Day
Wine Cellar   W.C.

Stone Stair

P a s s a g e

Room   Silver
              Room   Butlers Pantry

11"   3'6"   8'5"   16" 8' 6"   8'6"   3' 7½"

Cellar

Scullery   Bakehouse   Joiners Store   Brew Ho.   W.C.   Ash Yard

OUND   FLOOR

Kitchen   Meat Larder   Empties Shed   Coal Yard

Bread
Larder   Cooks
Baking   Cooks
Room   Pantry   Belfry

2'6"   17' 7"   3'6"   5' 6"   10 5"   6 4½"

2 Rooms

Party

19' 11"

Bink

40   50   60   70   80   90 FEET.

:14 Gray's Inn Square:
:London .W.C. Jan. 1894:

:DUMFRIES :HOUSE:

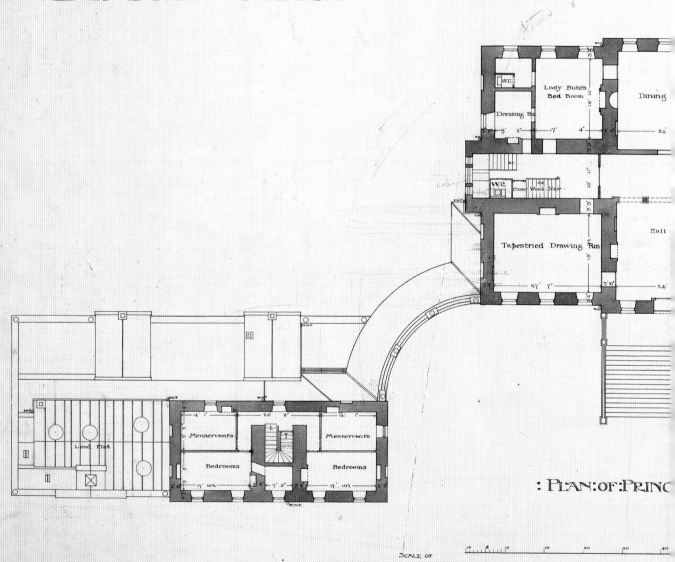

WC

Lady Bute's
Bed Room

Dining

Dressing Rm

9' 5'   17'   4'   3' 0'   24'

WC   Closet Wood Stair

Tapestried Drawing Rm

Hall

27'   7'   3' 0'   24'

Lead Flat

14' 1'   20' 8'   14' 1'

Menservants   Menservants

Bedrooms   Bedrooms

2' 6'   17' 10½'   3' 6' 7' 0' 3' 6'   17' 10½'   2' 6'

: PLAN :OF :PRINC

SCALE OF   10 5   0   10   20   30   40

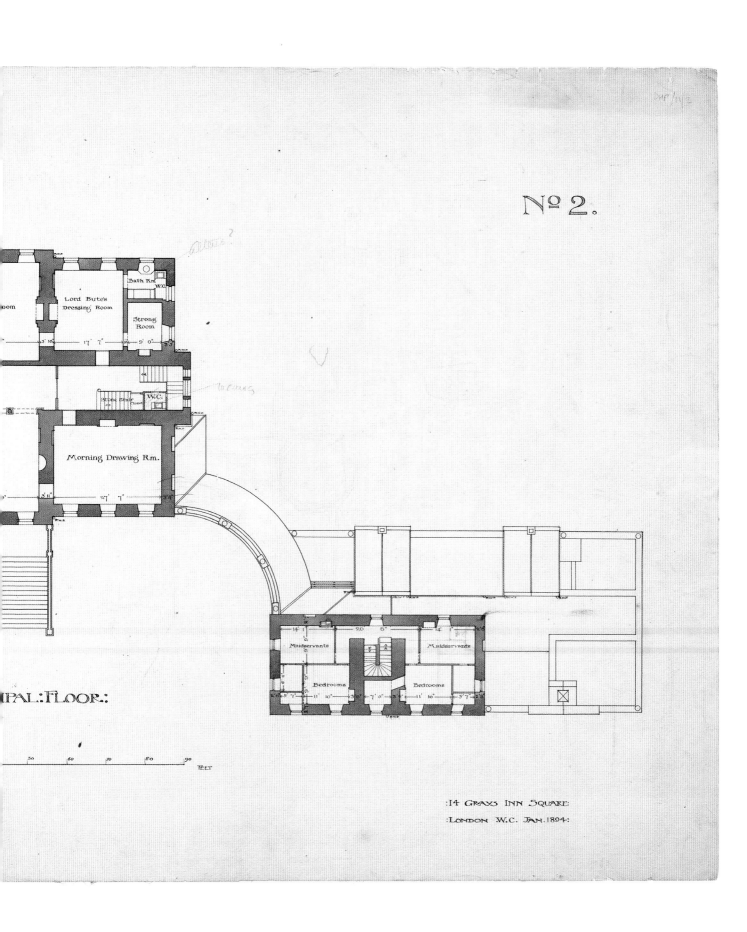

№ 2.

altois?

Bath Rm.
W.C.

Lord Bute's
Dressing Room

Strong
Room

worns

W.C.

Stone Stair
Closet

W.C.

Morning Drawing Rm.

PAL: FLOOR:

50   60   70   80   90
FEET

Maidservants   Maidservants

Bedrooms   Bedrooms

:14 Grays Inn Square:
:London W.C. Jan. 1894:

DVMFRIES HOVSE

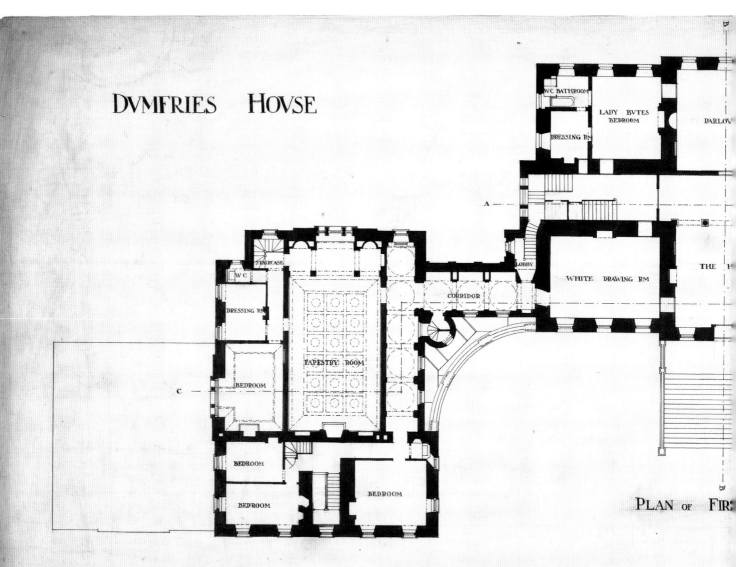

WC BATHROOM

LADY BVTES BEDROOM

PARLOV

DRESSING RM

A

LOBBY

WHITE DRAWING RM

THE H

STAIRCASE

WC

CORRIDOR

DRESSING RM

TAPESTRY ROOM

C

BEDROOM

BEDROOM

BEDROOM

BEDROOM

PLAN OF FIRS

SCALE

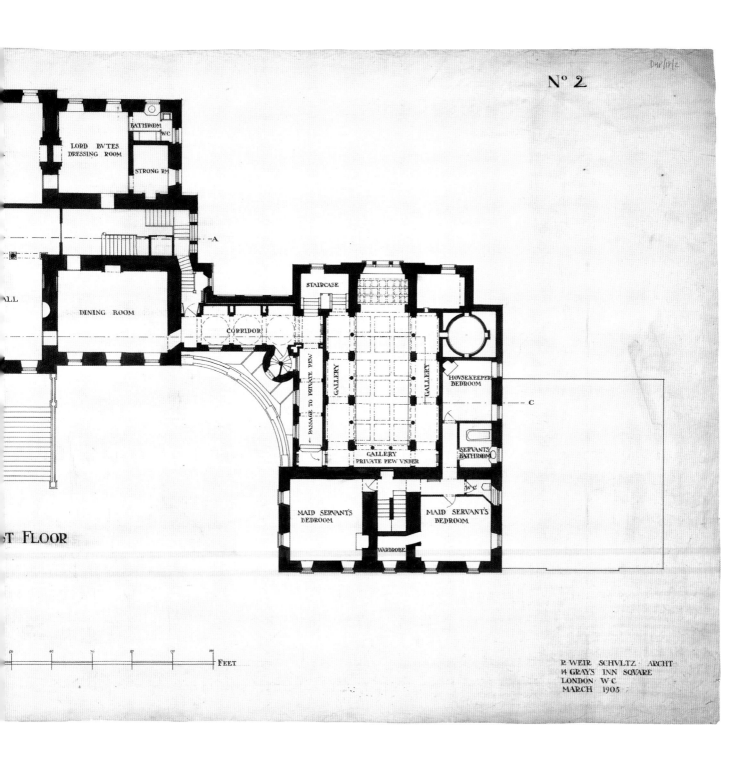

N° 2

BATHROOM
WC

LORD BVTES
DRESSING ROOM

STRONG RM

LORD BVTES DRESSING ROOM ...

A

HALL

DINING ROOM

CORRIDOR

STAIRCASE

PASSAGE TO PRIVATE PEW

GALLERY

GALLERY

GALLERY
PRIVATE PEW VNDER

HOVSEKEEPERS
BEDROOM

C

SERVANTS
BATHROOM

WC

MAID SERVANTS
BEDROOM

MAID SERVANT'S
BEDROOM

WARDROBE

ST FLOOR

FEET

R. WEIR SCHVLTZ ARCHT
14 GRAYS INN SQVARE
LONDON W C
MARCH 1905

Plan 12 Weir Schultz 1905 Survey – Bedroom Floor Plan Bute Archives DHP 18/2

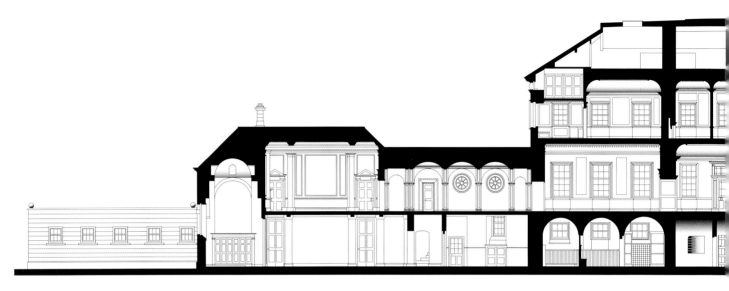

Section X–X'

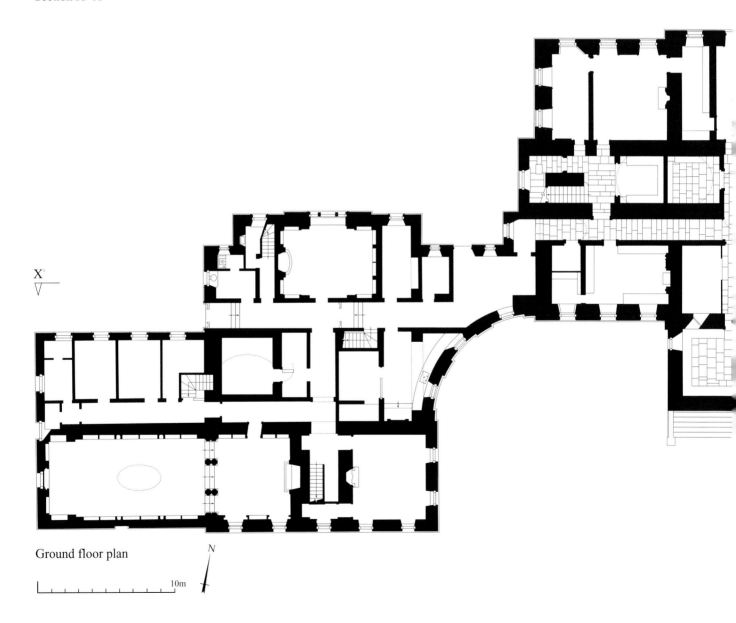

X'

Ground floor plan

N

10m

Plan 15 RCAHMS 2008 Survey – Ground Floor Plan HES GV005214

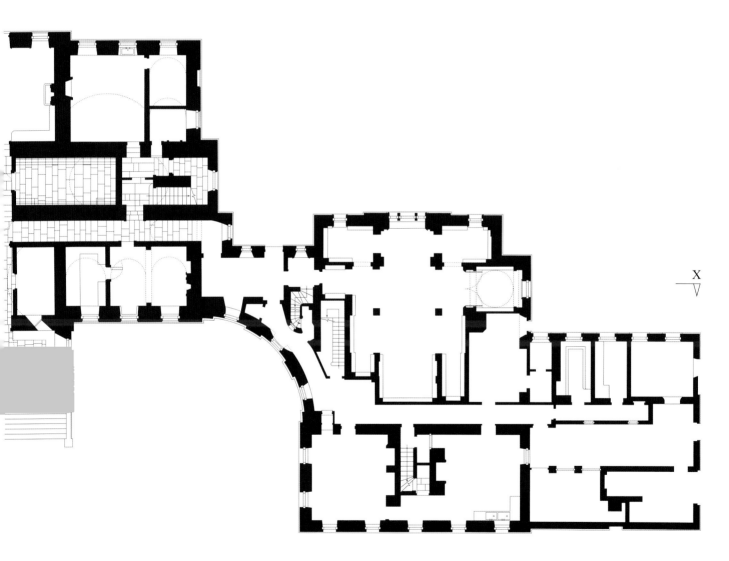

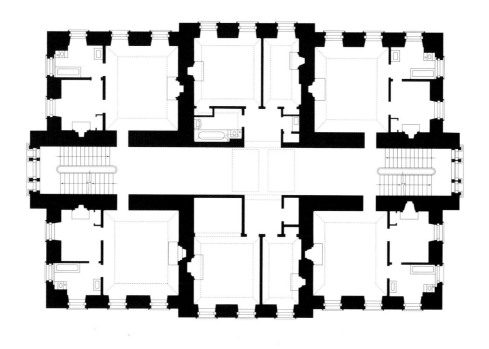

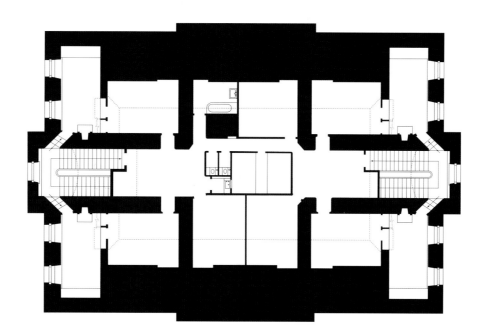

Plan 17 RCAHMS 2008 Survey – Bedroom Floor Plan HES GV005216

WILLIAM. EARL d DUMFRIE

Chapter 1: Designing the House 1742–1754

Is the house to go or not?

Andrew Hunter to the 5th Earl of Dumfries, 7 June 1750[1]

The Decision is Taken to Build a New House

William Crichton-Dalrymple was created 5th Earl of Dumfries on the death of his mother, the Countess of Dumfries, in 1742. He was, at the time of his succession, aide-de-camp to his father's elder brother, John 2nd Earl of Stair (1673–1747), commander of the allied forces under George II in the War of the Austrian Succession.

His inheritance principally comprised the Estate of Leifnorris[2] and the lands surrounding it, which included the barony of Cumnock and Glenmure.[3] The new Earl waited until the death of his uncle to resign his commission, immediately moving into Leifnorris to begin the development of his Ayrshire estate with the planning of an impressive new seat for his family at its centre.[4]

The historic core of the Leifnorris Estate occupies a relatively small area bounded to the north by the Lugar Water; all the buildings that pre-date the construction of Dumfries House lie here close to the Polcalk Burn. Nothing survives of Leifnorris itself, once the seat of the Crawfurds of Leifnorris, which occupied a prominent site north-west of the present house on a knoll between the stable block and the Adam Bridge.[5] The 3rd Marquess of Bute commissioned an archaeological investigation of the site in 1897 (Fig 5.9) the results of which are not particularly informative[6] while Robert Gordon's manuscript map of Ayrshire[7] of 1634 simply marks 'Lefno' on the southern bank of the Lugar.[8] However, Blaeu's map of 1654 schematically depicts the 'Cast of Lefno' as two linked towers, one larger than the other.[9]

Fig 1.1 Portrait of William Crichton-Dalrymple 5th Earl of Dumfries by Thomas Hudson, 1757. The Earl's coronet is sitting on the designs for Dumfries House. Great Steward of Scotland's Dumfries House Trust

Roy's map[10] illustrates the building as a U-plan, open to the south with the western wing bigger than the eastern one (Fig 1.2). This relates closely in form to a drawing on a 1756 estate map[11] on which Leifnorris is drawn in elevation as a three-bay, three-storey tower linked by a two-storey bay to a two-bay, three-storey tower (Fig 1.3). A single-storey, three-bay ancillary building is shown to the west, another three-bay building lies to the south-east with an attached walled enclosure and a small pavilion with a conical roof is shown to the south. Formal gardens are shown to the north of Leifnorris with walks marked on the plan as 'old garden'.

It is not known if the 5th Earl contemplated extending and altering Leifnorris as an alternative to building a new house. This was often the preferred option in Scotland at the time as can be seen in other Ayrshire houses for example at Cassillis, Culzean and Sorn. The fact that the towerhouse was not the ancient seat of the Crichtons may have been a factor in the decision not to extend it since the new Earl almost certainly would have wished to establish himself in the area. The Boswells, his close neighbours at Auchinleck, had also chosen to build a brand new house on a virgin site while preserving their old castle as a ruin in the landscape. The building of Auchinleck (Fig 1.4) occurred at the same time as Dumfries House but the complexity of the plan and the elaboration of the main facade of the former are in stark contrast to the restrained simplicity and logic of Dumfries House, suggesting a very different series of influences and aspirations.

The Site

Dumfries House was sited to the south-east of Leifnorris on higher ground at the centre of a pre-existing designed landscape which had been laid out on a bluff above

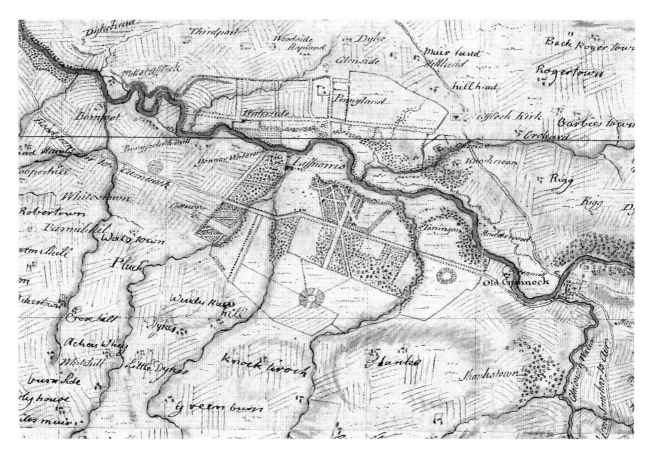

Fig 1.2 Roy's map (1747–55) shows the old house of Leifnorris with mounts, radiating avenues and rides that focus on the proposed site for the Earl's new house in an arrangement which is closely related to that of the gardens at Newliston. The British Library. Licensor Scran

Fig 1.3 A rare depiction of the old house of Leifnorris on an estate plan of 1756 shows its linked towers and subsidiary buildings including the block that is now the stable to the west, the Lady's Well by the river to the north and the incomplete new house to the south-east. Bute Archives DHP/24

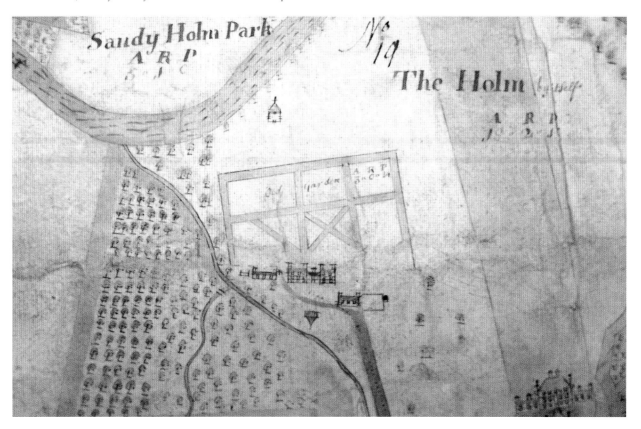

Fig 1.4 Auchinleck House, Ayrshire. The richly ornamented elevation looks back to the work of William Adam but is almost contemporary with Dumfries House. HES 2009 DP063724

Fig 1.5 Newliston Garden Plan. The Earl of Stair, probably with William Adam, laid out these gardens whilst living in the old tower of Newliston although the new house, which Adam proposed to site at the centre of the garden to the east, was not built. Mrs C E Maclachlan, Newliston House

the flood plain of the Lugar Water.[12] It sits on an axis between the Pennyfadzeoch D's, a circular plantation dissected by a ride to the west and Terringzean Castle to the east.[13] In laying out the landscape before work had begun on building a new house, the Earl was following the Earl of Stair's example at Newliston, West Lothian.[14] The famous victory his uncle had won at the Battle of Dettingen is commemorated both in the gardens of Stair's house at Newliston and in a man-made commemorative wooded mount at Dumfries House.[15] In August 1760 the Countess of Northumberland visited the newly completed Dumfries House; her description of the established grounds gives some sense of a landscape that has since been largely swept away:[16]

> Dumfries House stands in the midst of a Park of 1200 acre wch has in it 600 Acre of well grown wood, the outside of all which are planted with Roses & Honeysuckle. There are near the house

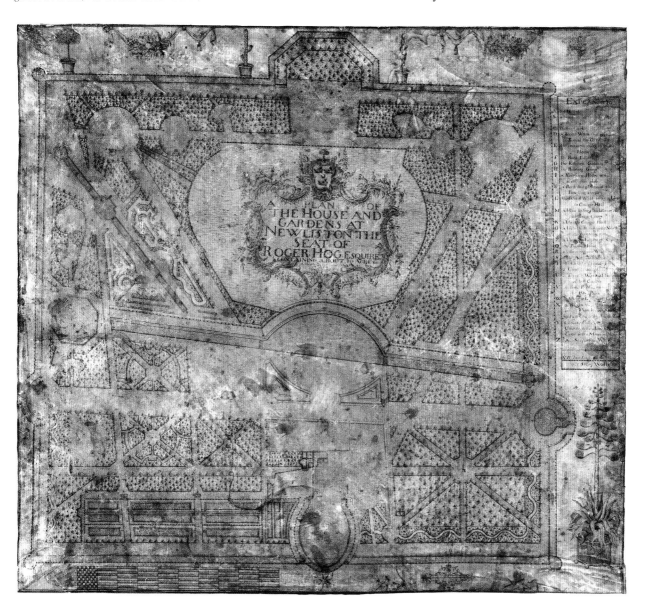

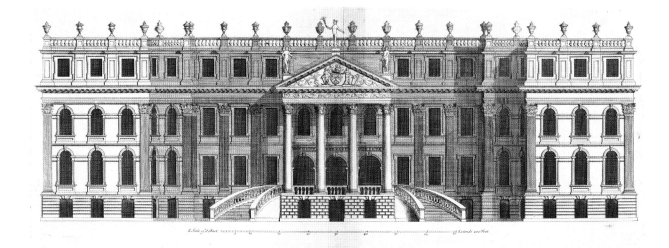

The East Front of Hopton House toward the Court

some fine grown Oaks & the River Lugar runs thro the park. Beech & Oak grow very well here. All the rising grounds are planted wch he call'd Mounts & most of them are named after his friends that have been at the place (at) (Stair) Mount Bland & Northumberland Mount.

The Stair and Bland Mounts lay to the south of the House. They were circular in form with stone-faced ditches and appear to have been well established by the time Roy's map was surveyed.[17] Although of different sizes, they were all planted to a similar design with a central circular clearing surrounded by a deep ring of trees through which rides or views were cut. Each mount afforded views of the House and other features on the Estate. Similar commemorative mounts were created at nearby Auchincruive and at Loudoun Castle in the 1730s suggesting that their creation here was following a local trend.[18] An 18th century working drawing for constructing a circular mount surrounded by a ditch[19] is the only design that has survived for the formal landscape that was created before the building of Dumfries House (Fig 5.21).

Fig 1.6 The great palace front of Hopetoun House, West Lothian, seat of the Earls of Hopetoun . A grand scheme to enlarge William Bruce's original design was begun by William Adam and completed by his sons during the time that Dumfries House was under construction. Plate engraved for Vitruvius Scoticus *in the 1760s. HES DP144173*

A complex arrangement of rides leads out into the landscape from the site of the proposed new house. 'They are most of them cut for views & his best objects are the Isle of Arran and the Hills of Cunningham a little ruin'd Octagon Tower[20] wch stands on a hill with detach'd Trees on it in the Park.' 'The Old House call'd Castle of Loch Norris' (Leifnorris) is also mentioned as a feature of the landscape.

No records survive regarding the designer of this elaborate landscape plan. However, the Earl was almost certainly influenced by the extensive scheme that the Earl of Stair, inspired by French examples, was laying out around Newliston from the 1720s

Fig 1.7 The exquisite villa of Mavisbank, Midlothian, which was designed by William Adam and Sir John Clerk of Penicuik, reflects the general form of Dumfries House with its central block and linked pavilions. Plate engraved for Vitruvius Scoticus *in the 1760s. HES DP029439*

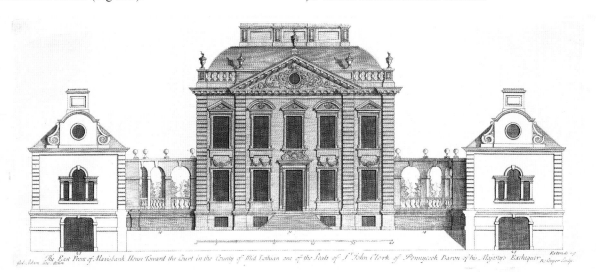

The East Front of Mavisbank House toward the Court in the County of Mid Lothian one of the Seats of S.r John Clerk of Pennycook Baron of his Majesty's Exchequer

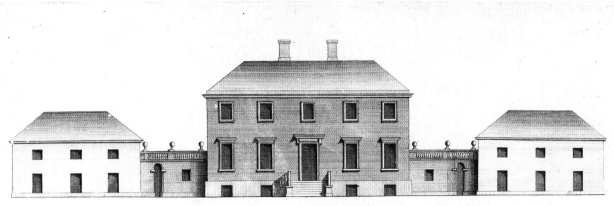

West Front of *BALLOCH MYLE HOUSE* The Seat of *ALLAN WHITEFOORD* Esq.ʳ
in the County of Ayr.

Fig 1.8 Alan Whitfoorde, a friend and neighbour of the 5th Earl of Dumfries, commissioned Ballochmyle from John Adam when Dumfries House was nearing completion. HES DP144215

onwards to the designs of his friend William Adam, Scotland's premier architect of the time.[21] In particular, both landscapes include elements that celebrate the Battle of Dettingen at which they fought together.[22]

In the case of both these estates, their designed landscapes were laid out before building work began on either of the houses which were designed to lie at their hearts[23] and from which a number of rides would radiate out with views to distant hills and monuments.[24] Since this was the concept behind the laying out of several early 18th century Scottish estates, such as Taymouth Castle in Perthshire, of itself this does not prove that William Adam had any hand in the design of the Dumfries House policies. However, Adam's connection with the Earl's powerful uncle is interesting in view of the fact that they both employed Adam to design houses for them.

The main approach to the Estate appears always to have been intended as being from the north across the Lugar Water although this was only possible by means of a ford until John Adam's bridge was built in 1760. The drive meanders picturesquely through the Estate at the back of the House and in order that this elevation should be suitably impressive it was finely detailed and given an interesting silhouette through the use of toofalls, a feature that was not entirely successful in the House as built (Fig 1.21). As the House disappeared from view, the drive swept over the bridge, around past the ruin of Leifnorris to give an oblique view of the south front that emphasised the elegant composition of the main block and advanced pavilions before arriving at the front door. The approach from the south was considered a secondary drive, running as it did via the Mains Farm entrance. The fact that the early 19th century Stockiehill Gate Lodges are on the line of the original public road indicates how close the road came to the south front of the house. Although it was

a relatively narrow road, it was nevertheless the main route linking Cumnock to Ochiltree and thence to Ayr.[25] Clearly the House was deliberately placed in order that it should be fully visible to passers-by as the impressive new seat of a major peer.[26]

While a more bucolic effect would have been gained by placing the house on the north bank of the Lugar where the prospect from the principal rooms would have been more attractive, there was insufficient estate owned land on which to build to the north of the river at this period.

Choice of an Architect

Nothing within the Earl's extensive correspondence records any discussion about the choice of an architect for his new house which is perhaps surprising given that he sought the advice of his fellow Scottish peers, lawyers and neighbours on a myriad of other subjects.[27] However, William Adam was an obvious choice because notwithstanding his link with the Earl of Stair, his was undoubtedly the most successful architectural practice in Scotland at the time. Adam had an enviable client list that included the Earls of Hopetoun and Roxburgh, Robert Dundas of Arniston, Sir John Clerk of Penicuik and Lord Braco.[28] He had built a number of major country houses such as Duff House, Banffshire (1735–9) and the House of Dun, Angus (1730) and was in the process of carrying out major alterations at Hopetoun House, West Lothian (from 1721).[29] By the time the Earl had resolved to build his new house, however, William Adam was elderly and increasingly infirm[30] and he died not long after the commission for Dumfries House was received, leaving his eldest son John not only in charge of the job but also of the practice along with his brothers Robert and James. The continued success of the practice was assured by the ongoing patronage of country house clients such as the Earl of Hopetoun, Alan Whitefoord (Ballochmyle House, Ayrshire) and Patrick Hume of Billie (Paxton House, Berwickshire).

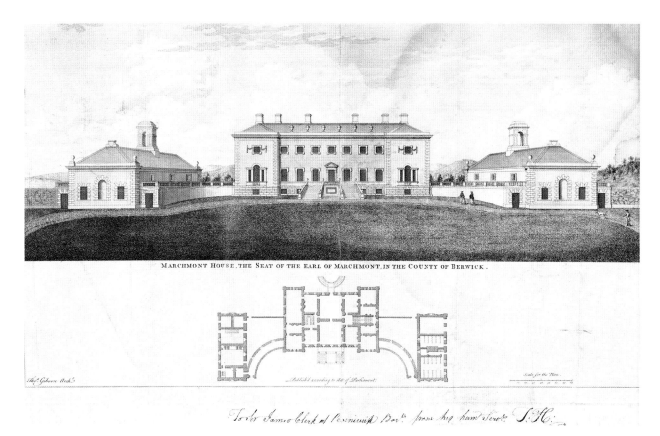

MARCHMONT HOUSE, THE SEAT OF THE EARL OF MARCHMONT, IN THE COUNTY OF BERWICK.

Building a New House

The first recorded reference regarding the possibility of building a new house is on 19 November 1748 when Andrew Hunter, the Earl's lawyer in Edinburgh, wrote to him saying; 'Mr Adam who I see now in town will wait your Lo[rdshi]p whenever you desire.'[31] This refers presumably to John Adam who had been running the business since his father's death on 24 June that year. John would have been extremely busy at this time because the firm was heavily involved with the building of Fort George in Inverness, a massive project which had recently begun on site. The next reference occurs in the Earl's account book for 4 June 1750, 'given Mr Adam and his servant £22.1/0.'[32] This possibly refers to a visit to Leifnorris for a measured survey of the site which would have required an assistant. Three days later on 7 June, Andrew Hunter wrote, 'I hope Mr Adam has given your Lordship full satisfaction. Is the house to go or not.'[33] The reply is lost but it cannot have been very positive and it appears that the Earl was asking for more advice from his fellow peers. On 27 June 1750 Hunter wrote 'your lop seems undetermined yet as to the House at least until the Earle of Hopetoun and Mr Adams be of one mind. I wish the E[arl] of Dumfries had equal estates and then we should have a good House.'[34] This is the first mention of the Earl of Hopetoun in relation to the building of the new house. Andrew Hunter was acutely aware of the Earl's finances, which were not always commensurate with his aspirations. On 27 July 1750 he wrote, 'I understand My Lord Hopetoun had finished his observations

Fig 1.9 In 1750 the Earl of Marchmont designed a new house for himself in consultation with his friends Alexander Pope and the Earl of Burlington. Architect Thomas Gibson constructed Marchmont House, the relatively austere exterior of which has similarities with the second design for Dumfries House. HES SC1034196

upon the plan and that Mr Adam is to send your Lop the estimates soon. I agree with your Lop that you need a new House, but would not have your Lop go into an expense that would shorten your living comfortablie.'[35] The plan to which the Earl of Hopetoun is referring has not been identified. The discussions continued in a letter he wrote to the Earl of Dumfries on 12 April 1751:

My Lord. Messers Adams have at different times shown me various drawings for the Principal Front of your intended house and they carry one with them that I do think is nothing inferior to the first tho' that's having received the sanction of Lord Burlington's approbation puts it above exception. As to the Garden Front after several attempts to get free of the Beau window we found it impossible without altering the whole disposition that is in effect making a new plan which we thought would not be agreeable to your Lords' and might have occasioned greater inconvenience.

I have also seen the estimate of the expenses which I could not pretend to examine particularly that being a long and laborious work but doubt not your Lo'p will find exact as they assure me

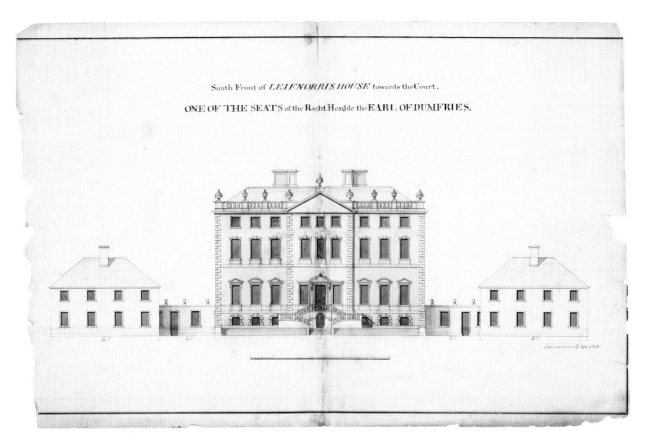

South Front of *LEIFNORRIS HOUSE* towards the Court.

ONE OF THE SEATS of the Right Honble the EARL OF DUMFRIES.

they have taken all possible pains to make it so. If your Lo'p determines to go on with your plan I most heartily wish it may prove to your satisfaction. I beg my most humble compliments may be acceptable to my Lady and am with great respect My Lord your Lo'ps most obedient and most humble servant. Hopetoun[36]

This letter is of great significance in that it is the first mention of the involvement of one of the most important arbiters of taste and architecture in mid 18th century Britain, Richard Boyle 3rd Earl of Burlington (1694–1753). Burlington was not only an architect in his own right, he also collaborated with architects and designers such as William Kent and advised his fellow peers on matters of design. More detailed analysis of the influence of Burlington on the proposals for Dumfries House is problematic since we have no evidence as to the precise drawings and estimates that he was shown.

The First Elevation

The principal source of information about the evolution of the design for Dumfries House comes from a series of estimates and drawings in the Mount Stuart Archives. Despite the wealth of detail contained in the estimates, the documentation of the building is not complete for the entire three year building period.[37] John Adam's 'Estimate of a House for the Right Honble the Earl of Dumfries propos'd to be built at Leifnorris' is dated 1751. It gives an exhaustive specification of the proposed works stretching to eleven pages including stonework,

Fig 1.10 The earliest surviving design elevation for Dumfries House c1751 shows the Adam office continuing to work in the manner of William Adam.
Bute Archives DHP/2

wright work, slater work, lead work, window sashing, plaster work and hardware of the proposed building.[38] The estimate is clearly divided into three sections dealing with the main block, the pavilions and offices, and the 'Great Drain'. The last shows the importance of water supply and waste management, a constant theme in the history of Dumfries House. This estimate relates closely to the elevation entitled 'South Front of LEIFNORRIS HOUSE towards the Court. ONE OF THE SEATS of the Right Honble the EARL OF DUMFRIES'[39] (Fig 1.10).

The first elevation is a presentation drawing of the south front and shows a tall three-storey block over a basement. The central three bays under the pediment are narrowed to emphasise the height of the facade. Nothing is known of the plan or the detail of the other elevations for this scheme because this is the only design drawing that survives. Furthermore, there is no information about the exact site for this proposal other than that it appears to be intended for a new building on a level site because the rocky outcrop on which Leifnorris stood would not have been big enough to accommodate it.[40] The style of the proposed new house is redolent of the designs of William Adam in their complexity of detail including the narrowing of the central three bays (eg Buchanan House of c1745[41]) and in scale (Haddo House of 1731–6[42]) but since the Adam office carried on producing drawings in the house style after William Adam's death, it is not possible to reach a definitive conclusion from the evidence of this elevation alone.[43] However, the lack of any reference to William Adam in the archives of the Earl, who was particularly conscious of his status and would seem likely to have mentioned his appointment of the pre-eminent architect in Scotland, tends to suggest that he was not personally involved and, in any event, the timescale would have meant that Dumfries House was designed right at the end of his life when he is recorded as being increasingly unwell.

Despite the lack of documentary evidence that William Adam had a hand in the design for Dumfries House beyond the fact that this, presumably first, scheme has some stylistic similarities with his late works, architectural historians continue to debate the possibility of his involvement.[44] The earliest published attribution was by Sir John Stirling Maxwell in 1938.[45] Stirling Maxwell was a recognised champion of William Adam having attributed his own house Pollok House, Glasgow, to him.[46] Previous historians, such as A H Millar, author of *The Castles and Mansions of Ayrshire*, 1885, make no mention of William Adam. In Millar's case, his text clearly shows that he examined the original drawings that were then held at Dumfries House.

One undated sketch plan (Fig 1.13) survives in the Mount Stuart Archives which may relate either to the earliest elevation, or to the Hopetoun and Burlington letter mentioned above.[47] The plan, which is inscribed 'Plan of Dumfries House Ground flat', is drawn on six

Fig 1.11 *A Venetian window lights the west stair of Dumfries House.* HES 2013 DP151646

sheets of paper spot glued together and, in its hatched style, is very similar to John Adam's working drawings for Inveraray.[48] However, the use of 'Dumfries House' in the title is problematic because the name of the house was only changed from Leifnorris to Dumfries

Fig 1.12 *A Palladian window (a Venetian window set within a relieving arch) on the front facade of Edinburgh's Register House, designed by Robert Adam in 1771.* HES DP095277

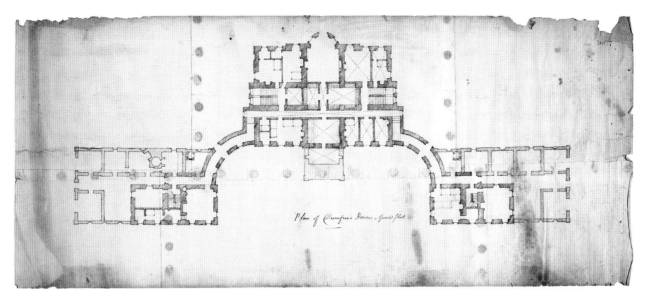

Fig 1.13 The earliest plan for Dumfries House dates from c1751. The arrangement of the lower floor is very similar to what was built apart from the large projecting bow on the north front. Bute Archives DHP/7

House at the laying of the foundation stone on 18 July 1754.[49] The drawing must predate this since the plans of the house were finalised and agreed by this time. It is perhaps shorthand for Lord Dumfries' house on what was very much a sketch rather than a finished drawing or the title may have been added later when papers were being organised.

The plan is almost identical to the house as constructed, describing a nine-bay central block with a three-bay advanced centre linked by quadrant wings to five-bay pavilions with attendant service courts, the main difference being the large central bow on the north front. The close similarity between this sketch plan which shows the straight flight of entrance steps, the twin staircases as well as details of the vaulting as executed in the main block and the pavilions as being of five bays with service courts proves that this relates not to the first elevation but to the later estimates and schemes. What differentiates this plan is the north facade with its prominent central bow window (as mentioned by Lord Hopetoun); this is the only plan in the Bute family archives that shows this feature. The north front is composed of nine bays with a slightly advanced five-bay centre of which the bow occupies the central three bays which creates a substantial ground floor room with a fireplace and niche opposite with an external door. This room is of a scale of the principal reception rooms on the floor above.

The form of the proposed north elevation is not entirely successful: the five-bay advanced central portion requires thicker walls to balance the facade which results in uncomfortably uneven window reveals in the adjacent rooms; while possibly acceptable in service rooms, this would not have been the case in principal rooms. Extrapolating this plan suggests that,

on the floor above, the central North Parlour would be flanked by closets and that the bed chambers would have been at the ends of the block. A remnant of this arrangement can be seen in the c1753 plans[50] discussed below. This sketch plan shows that the plan of the house was not finalised until much later in the design process than has been previously thought.[51]

The first estimate describes a facade of greater richness and complexity than that which was ultimately built. The walls were to be finished in broached ashlar in contrast with the 'plain polished free stone in the Base, beltings & strings of both fronts & ends, in all the Rustick corners, in all the Solls (sills), lintels & blocks … Pediments of the windows … Great Cornish and Pediments … Ballustrades.' '204 stone balusters for the top of the house & beau on the back front' at 5 shillings each are specified along with '19 vases for the top of the House' at £3.00 each. Two enriched pediments are specified for the main fronts at £21.00 each. The south pediment is to contain 'My Lord's Coat of Arms … impaled with My Lady's and the angles to be filled up with foliage'. The north pediment's decoration is less specific containing 'a compartment round a window & foliage in the angles'.[52]

The rather unusual combination of 'a Festoon & Scrolled Key to the paladian window in the North Front' may derive from an illustration in Isaac Ware's *Designs of Inigo Jones* of 1731[53] which shows such an arrangement flanking the fireplace in the Dining Room at Houghton, Norfolk, by William Kent. The terms 'paladian' and 'venetian' are used in different parts of the estimate referring presumably to different types of window; this is confusing in that the terms are now often interchangeable. In the final design Venetian[54] windows light both staircases at Dumfries House.

Early in 1748 William Adam dispatched his eldest son John to London to discuss urgent business with the Board of Ordnance and also to discuss works

Fig 1.14 *The relative austerity of the north front of Dumfries House.* HES 2007 DP033625

Fig 1.15 *The unusual combination of a Palladian window set above a projecting bow beneath a pediment in Thomas Wright's 1754 design for Nuthall Temple is the closest parallel to the arrangement described in the first estimate for Dumfries House.* RIBA Library Drawings Collection RIBA 29773

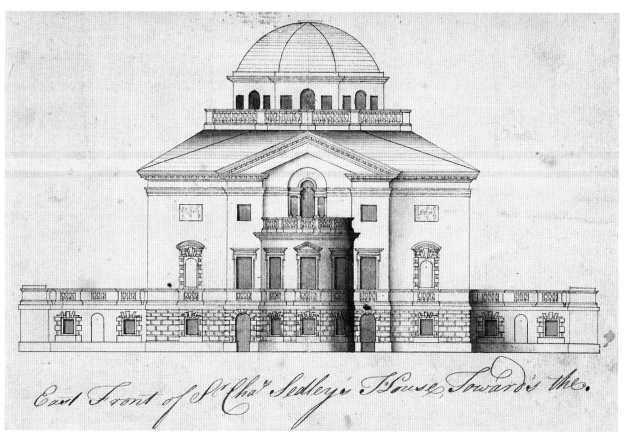

Fig 1.16 The Saloon on the first floor of Yester House, East Lothian, which rises up into a deeply coved, coffered ceiling is comparable with the first floor gallery that was originally proposed for Dumfries House. HES SC737102

underway at Inveraray with Duke of Argyll and Roger Morris.[55] While he was in London, he sketched a Venetian window set within a relieving archway in the Drawing Room at 18 Bruton Street, a house designed by Lord Burlington for the Earl of Granville.[56] Lord Burlington owned a drawing by Andrea Palladio of a palazzo facade with this feature at its centre.[57] He had first used this device on a house he designed for General Wade in London and, most famously, on his villa at Chiswick. This connection suggests that the use of the term 'paladian' in the Dumfries House estimate refers specifically to a Venetian window set within a blind arch. This feature would, it is thought, have gained 'Lord Burlington's approbation.'[58] Without a drawing showing this feature it is impossible to determine if this nuance of design was intentional or whether John Adam when writing the estimate was aware of its significance. If so, this represents the earliest use of this particular form of Venetian window in Scotland. The earliest extant example dates from much later; Robert Adam featured it prominently in his design for Edinburgh's Register House, 1771 (Fig 1.12).

Putting the different features of the north front recorded in the Estimate together and relating it to the undated sketch plan showing the 'beau' window produces a curiously idiosyncratic elevation. The combination of the balustrade topped 'beau,' window,[59] the 'paladian' window, the pediment with its window and the balustrade topped with urns is difficult to imagine especially when seen in relation to what was

eventually built. However, a number of these elements were combined at Nuthall Temple, Nottinghamshire, designed by Thomas Wright for Sir Charles Sedley, 1754,[60] a drawing for which[61] shows just such an arrangement, the east front of a central three-windowed balustrade topped bow window rises through two storeys with a Palladian window above; this is set within a five-bay advanced, pedimented centre. It is unlikely that the Adam brothers saw this design but the similarities are striking. The sole vestige of this elaborate scheme for the north front of Dumfries House is the central window on the principal floor with its pediment above and balustraded panel below.

The Dumfries House estimate describes the proposed plan in some detail. The ground floor contains the service accommodation including extensive cellars. The principal floor appears to provide accommodation similar to that which was eventually built. It details the proposed finishes including 'Rich Stucco Ornaments in the ceilings of the Dining Room and Drawing Room, And in the coves, ceilings & side walls of the Hall & Parlour'. Finishes for 'My Lady's bed chamber', 'My Lord' and 'My Lady's dressing rooms', attendant closets and the paired stone staircases are also specified.[62] On the lodging storey above, the most striking feature is the gallery which was intended to run across the building from front to back occupying the three central bays. The Estimate details the arrangement with the stairs rising to 'lobbies' which serve the pairs of bedrooms with closets at the east and west ends. This gallery lit presumably at the north end by the 'paladian' window described above and by the central three windows to the south would have been the largest room in the house. For it not to appear cramped or oppressive, it would have needed a higher ceiling than those of the adjacent bedrooms so it perhaps rose though both the lodging storey and the 'attick' storey. This seems likely given that the only rooms mentioned on the 'attick' floor are the further four 'principall' bedrooms with closets in the same arrangement as the floor below. The structural walls of the present house allow for this double height space to be accommodated within the main structural walls running north to south whereas the east to west structural walls only flank the staircases.

At 60 ft long, the Gallery would have provided an impressive space that may have been intended to display the set of four Gobelins tapestries acquired by Lord Dumfries from his uncle, Lord Stair.[63] In the house as built, the only space that could accommodate even two of them was the Drawing Room. The arrangement of the first floor Saloon and Drawing Room at Yester, Midlothian, created by William Adam in 1729, parallels the proposed Gallery arrangement at Dumfries House.[64] At Yester, as was common in late 17th and early 18th century country houses in Scotland, the reception rooms are on different levels whereas at Dumfries House as built, the Drawing Room and Dining Room were always intended to be on the principal floor along with the family bedroom suite. This demonstrates that Dumfries House was designed in line with contemporary fashion, albeit on a relatively modest scale. Prominent examples of this modern arrangement were being built on a much grander scale at the same time at Hopetoun House and also at Marchmont House. To conform with this fashion, John Adam was also adapting his father's design at Arniston, Midlothian, so that the most important rooms, the Drawing Room and Dining Room, were both located on the principal floor.

The absence of a dedicated library at Dumfries House is surprising because in the early 18th century libraries were regarded as an essential component of the country house. *Vitruvius Scoticus* records a great number of libraries which are never part of the suite of principal rooms but are instead located at one remove. This does not mean they were not lavishly decorated, the most notable example being the library in the attic at Arniston House, Midlothian,[65] designed by William Adam for Sir Robert Dundas. At Yester House, East Lothian, and the Drum, Midlothian, the libraries were designed to be accommodated in one of the pavilions as was also proposed at Hopetoun.[66] The absence of a reference to a designated library in any of the designs for Dumfries House suggests changing attitudes and

requirements rather than an item that was removed because of cost. Bookcases were distributed throughout the house and the Earl's Dressing Room probably contained the principal volumes.

The Second Estimate
The first estimate of 1751 came to a total of £9182 10s 9d which was broken down as 'Estimate of the body of the house £6851.14/11; Ditto of the offices £2174.19/-; Ditto of the Drains £155.16/0'. The resulting discussions and revised estimates all relate to cutting the cost rather than altering the overall scheme. This is why the first estimate is of considerable importance to the understanding of the development of the design. On 19 March 1753 Lord Dumfries wrote from Leifnorris to his great friend and neighbour the Earl of Loudoun,

> Mr Adam has at last finished the plans & estimates for the new house, but I have not yet seen them and of consequence have taken no resolution about them. I know yr Lop is much for the building.[67]

The letter also shows that the Earl was becoming impatient with the whole process. The length of time between the first estimate of 1751 and the second of March 1753 suggests that a dramatic rethink of the design was taking place. The Earl is recorded as collecting books, for example two volumes of 'Paladios Architecture' were bought from Alexander Donald & Son, Edinburgh on 19 July 1753.[68] He also paid in full in advance for a copy of 'The RUINS of the Emperor DIOCLESIAN's Palace at SPALATRO in DALMATIA' which was to be delivered as soon as it was published. The printed receipt is signed by Robert Adam.[69] It may be that these acquisitions were prompted by Robert or his brothers in order to encourage their patron to adopt the fashionable design they were proposing; the acqustion of the Palladio in July 1753, just as the estimates and the design were being finalised, seems more than a coincidence.

In 1752 George II conferred the Order of the Thistle on the Earl of Dumfries, an event of great significance for the development of Dumfries House. The celebration of this title permeates the interior design of the new house and must have spurred the Earl's desire to commence building. The second estimate,[70] like the first, is in the hand of John Adam and makes a dramatic alteration to the plan by omitting the lodging storey whilst retaining the ground, 'principall' and 'attick' storeys. The accompanying set of plans[71] (Figs 1.17–1.20) show the form of the house virtually as built, the main difference on the ground floor being that the functions of the pavilions are reversed, ie the Kitchen and larders etc are in the west pavilion and the Laundry etc is in the east pavilion. On the 'principall' floor (Fig 1.17) the Hall, staircases, Drawing Room

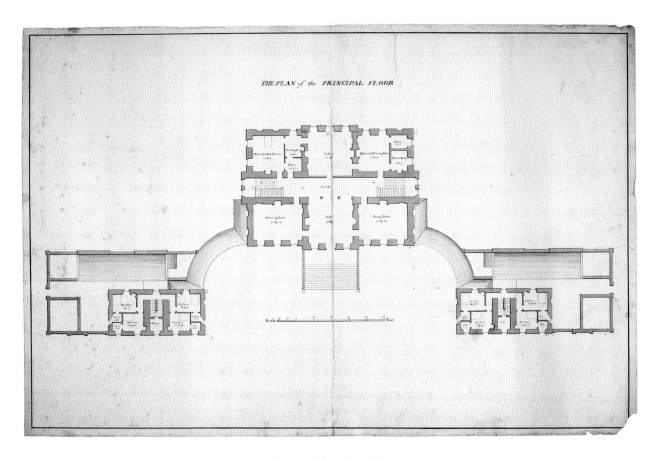

Fig 1.17 Plan of Principal Floor of a 'New Design for Leifnorris' for the Earl of Dumfries c1753. *Bute Archives DHP/4/4*

Fig 1.18 Plan of Ground floor of a 'New Design for Leifnorris' the Earl of Dumfries c1753. *Bute Archives DHP/4/3*

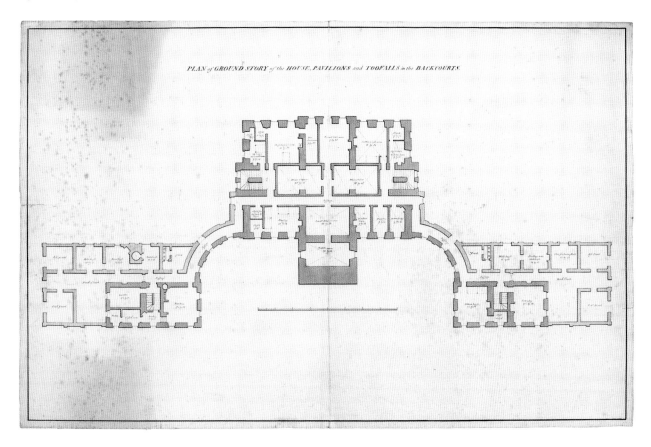

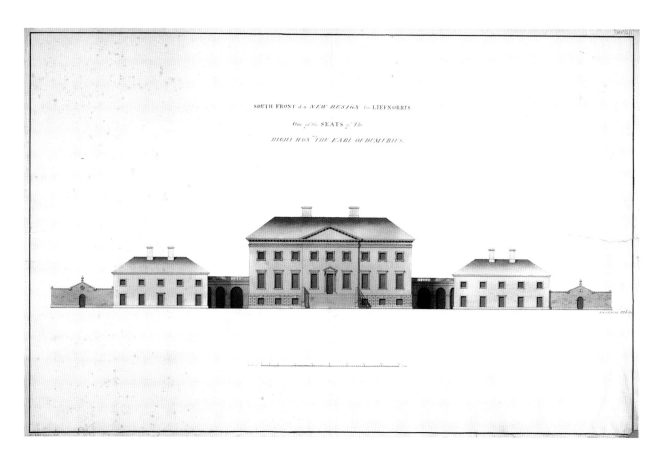

Fig 1.19 South Elevation of a 'New Design for Leifnorris' for the Earl of Dumfries signed RA (Robert Adam) c1753. Bute Archives DHP/4/1

Fig 1.20 North Elevation of a 'New Design for Leifnorris' for the Earl of Dumfries signed RA (Robert Adam) c1753. Bute Archives DHP/4/2

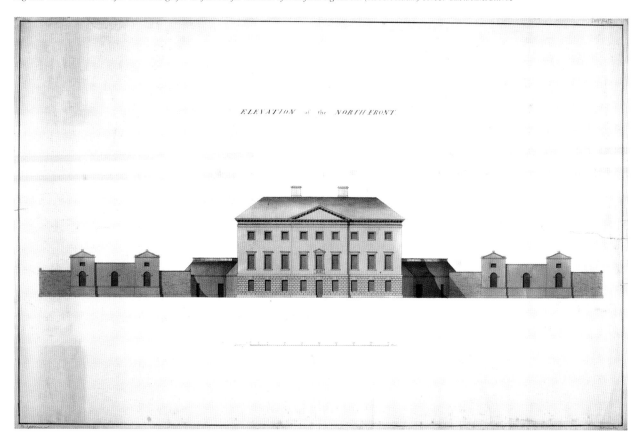

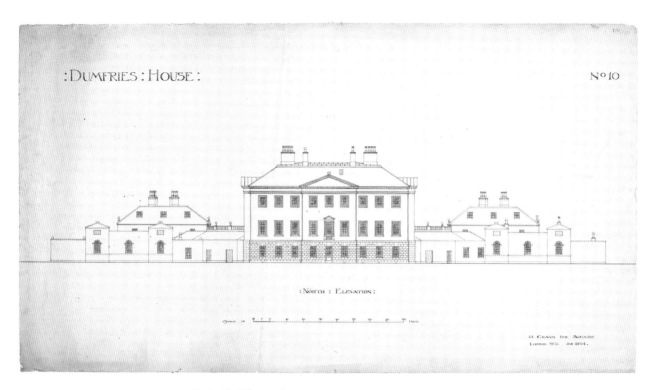

: DUMFRIES : HOUSE : Nº 10

: NORTH : ELEVATION :

Fig 1.21 The north elevation of Dumfries House as constructed was surveyed by Robert Weir Schultz in 1894. It is somewhat different to the design in the 1754 Adam contract in showing in reality the way in which the bulk of the pavilions interrupted the modulated silhouette created by the toofalls.
Bute Archives DHP/11/10

and Dining Room are as eventually built. The main difference occurs in 'My Lady's chamber', the family bedroom, which is positioned at the north-west corner looking west with the two closets between this bed chamber and the North Parlour. This room has blank windows to the north, an arrangement that may well be a survival of the scheme described in the early sketch plan in which the north front had a five-bay advanced front. The Parlour and 'My Lords dressing room' remain exactly as built, complete with the Charter Room, the only other change being that the Earl's closet has a window facing east rather than north as built. The other difference is that the staircases are lit by simple paired windows rather than the more elaborate Diocletian and Venetian windows that were eventually chosen. We do not have drawn plans for the upper floor but in the revised estimate, the 'attick' storey of the first estimate became the bedroom floor of the new scheme with the staircases linked by a corridor while the four 'principall' bedrooms with their paired closets are located at the corners as in the earlier plan. The transverse gallery is replaced by four smaller bedrooms, with internal closets providing the bedroom accommodation lost with the omission of the lodging storey.

The elevations (Figs 1.19–1.20) are a revelation, showing the transformation of an old fashioned design that was rooted in the work of William Adam and his contemporaries into something far more pared down: a simplification of his neo-Palladianism signalling the direction that Robert Adam's creative impulse was to take. The elevations are signed by Robert Adam, who appears to have been the principal draftsman during this period;[72] they are the earliest surviving signed drawings from the design process. The removal of the lodging

storey and the simplification of the external decoration rationalises and strengthens the design. The central three bays are now the same width as the flanking three bays thereby increasing the horizontality of the facade, an emphasis that is further reinforced by its termination in five-bay pavilions with walled courts at either end. The main block is given a 'Rustick Basement' and the linking quadrants are drawn as open arched arcades topped with balustrades.

The elaborate entrance staircase shown on the first estimate is simplified into a large straight flight, very similar to that designed by John Adam for Hopetoun House in 1751.[73] Both the north and south elevations are given greater syncopation, modulating in height from the main block down to the quadrants, up to the pavilions and then further down to the courtyard walls. Strangely, the projecting bays containing the staircases shown on the plans do not appear on the elevations but we do not have the east and west elevations that might help to explain this anomaly. The windows of the principal floor are the largest as befitting their importance in lighting the principal rooms and are all fitted with 'Architraves, Freezes, Corniches'.[74] The square windows described in the first estimate as lighting the 'attick' storey now light the bedroom floor; they have lugged architraves but only on the entrance elevation, those at this level on the other elevations having simpler architraves. The resultant design reflects the order and repose sought by Palladio and British architects of the Palladian revival,

15

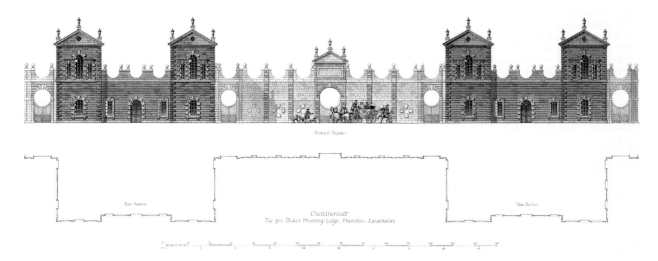

Principal Façade

Chatelherault
The 5th Duke's Hunting-Lodge, Hamilton, Lanarkshire

where the importance of particular rooms is reflected in the proportions of each element including the windows. A possible Scottish influence on the design is Thomas Gibson's Marchmont House (Fig 1.9) of 1750 which demonstrates the same clearly defined hierarchy between the windows of the *piano nobile* and bedroom floor above[75] and which was reputedly designed with the advice of the Earl of Burlington and Alexander Pope.[76] It is clear from a letter that Lord Dumfries wrote to the Earl of Loudoun on 26 July 1758 that he was familiar with Marchmont House.[77] John Adam's Ballochmyle House, Ayrshire, of 1760 for Alan Whitefforde has a similar arrangement on a smaller scale.[78]

These drawings are the first that survive for the north front. The austerity of the main block shows

Fig 1.22 William Adam's design for the façade of the ornamental dog kennels at Chatelherault, Lanarkshire, consisted of a series of toofall type blocks which created a dramatic silhouette. HES SC428575

the influence of James Paine at, for example, Belford Hall, Northumberland.[79] The most distinctive feature of this façade is a pair of toofalls: small, classical pavilions which take the form of pedimented single-bay blocks linked by a high screen wall, each with an arched window flanked by lower screen walls.[80] These elements may be derived from Holkham Hall, Norfolk, which had, in effect, been designed by a committee comprising the client, the Earl of Leicester, the Earl of Burlington and the architects,

Fig 1.23 The form of nearby Ballochmyle, Ayrshire, is similar to that of Dumfries House with a similarly proportioned Palladian façade, if on a more modest scale. HES SC742518

William Kent and Mathew Brettingham from 1724.[81] A Scottish precedent is the ornamental dog kennels and banqueting house at Chatelherault which was designed by William Adam for the Duke of Hamilton in 1731.[82] Chatelherault works as a silhouette but at Dumfries House this would not have been the case since the south pavilions, which are not on the same axis and are larger, would have interrupted the silhouette on the skyline, hence the sleight of hand (or deliberate omission) in the presentation elevation. The discordant effect that was actually produced can be seen in the Robert Weir Schultz survey elevations of 1894 (Fig 1.21).[83] While the 1753 elevational drawing is skilfully handled to produce a dramatic elevation, in reality, the effect would have been greatly reduced, something that reflects the inexperience and youth of the designers.

A memorandum from the Earl of Dumfries dated 8 August 1753[84] makes clear that he had resolved to begin building the house before he had finalised the contract with the Adam brothers. It suggests that he felt that the negotiations over the estimates were reaching a conclusion and that he was more or less settled on the design. This confirms the importance of the second estimate and of the drawings signed by Robert Adam in the design for Dumfries House. The memorandum outlines the works to be carried out during the 'following season', presumably 1754, which includes digging the Great Drain and opening quarries on the estate and 'outside the parks'.

Fig 1.24 John Adam introduced the idea of using a straight set of steps to create a grand entrance at Hopetoun House in 1751, a feature he was to use again soon after at Dumfries House. HES SC1336432

Third Estimate

The third estimate is entitled 'Estimate of a House for the Right Honble the Earl of Dumfries shewing what articles are performable by my Lord & what by John and Robert Adam'.[85] This estimate is undated but appears to have been presented to the Earl in December 1753 since Andrew Hunter, the Earl's Edinburgh lawyer, wrote to him on the 11th of that month stating that, 'Mr Whiteforde told me the other day that he had the night before a visit from Mr John Adams who left with him the Scroll or draught of the contract for your house which he was to look over and send to me.'[86] This estimate seems to have been produced in order that the works could be phased with the Earl taking responsibility for completing the interior, presumably over a longer period, whilst living in the old house of Leifnorris. His neighbour Lord Auchinleck adopted a similar tactic, building his mansion 'so slowly and prudently, that he hardly felt the expense'.[87] The fitting out costs for the central block or 'body of the house' represented a significant proportion of the budget, coming to £2,205 9s 10d out of a total of £5,839 9s 10d for the construction of the entire central building. The total cost of the revised scheme, the central block and the offices including the pavilions and toofalls etc was £7,971 9s 2d as opposed to the £9,181 10s 9d of the first estimate showing a saving of £1,211 1s 7d.[88] This saving was largely due to the omission of an entire floor of accommodation and restraint in the finishing of all the rooms save for the plasterwork in the four reception rooms and the elaborate carving in the Dining Room.

Fourth Estimate, Contract Drawings and Contract, 1754

On 9 February 1754 Andrew Hunter wrote to the Earl:

> On Thursday last at Mr Whitefoords He and I with Mr John Adam revised the draught of the contract between your Lop and John and Robert Adam as to building your new house some alterations were made on it and a clean coppie to be made and sent to your Lo next post.[89]

11 days later he reported that a 'Coppie of the contract to be sent by carrier tomorrow morning' because it was 'too bulkie' for the post.[90] This appears to be the fourth and final estimate which was virtually identical to the third estimate and which formed the basis for the contract.[91] The contract was drafted by John McHaffie, Andrew Hunter's clerk, signed by John, Robert and James Adam in Edinburgh on 24 April 1754 and witnessed by Andrew Hunter and Alan Whitefoord of Ballochmyle. On 19 May the Earl signed the contract at Leifnorris as witnessed by his servant Joseph Wilson and Andrew Hunter. The contract drawings[92] provide a wealth of information and appear to have been adhered

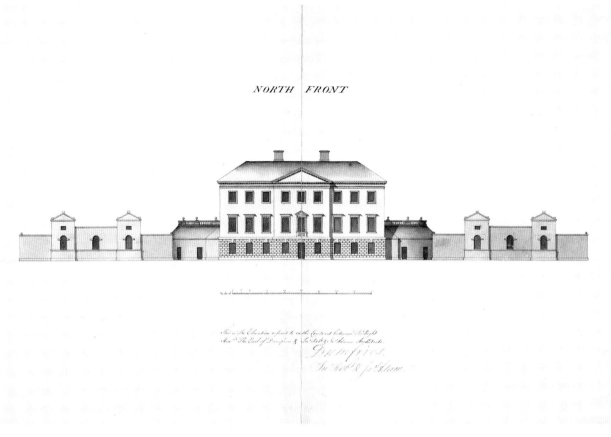

Fig 1.25 Contract Drawing of North Elevation signed by the Earl of Dumfries, John, Robert and James Adam 1754. Bute Archives DHP/I/2

Fig 1.26 Contract Drawing of South Elevation signed by Earl of Dumfries, John, Robert and James Adam 1754. Bute Archives DHP/I/I

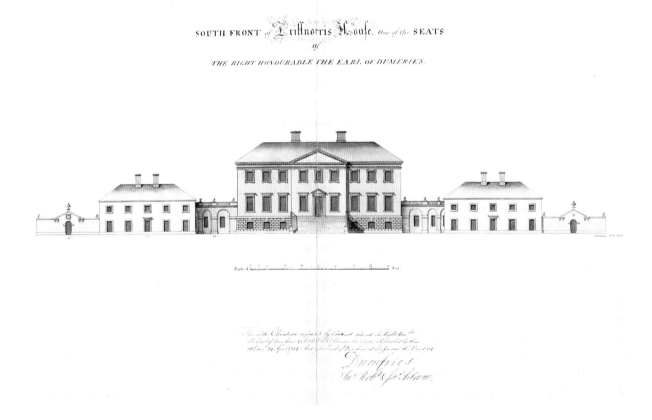

ELEVATION of one of the ENDS

Fig 1.27 Contract Drawing of East Elevation of main block signed by the Earl of Dumfries, John, Robert and James Adam 1754. Bute Archives DHP/1/3

to very closely. There have only been relatively minor and subtle alterations and additions to the main block which can still be experienced very much as the Earl and the Adam brothers intended.

The plan as drawn in the contract (Figs 1.28–1.30, Plans 1–6) is well considered, the rooms are well proportioned, they connect with each other easily where required and there is a logical hierarchy in terms of the relative arrangement of the rooms according to their function. This refined simplicity is clearly evident in the house as built. Adherence to an almost totally symmetrical plan on each level produces a sense of all-pervading order that disguises the subtlety of the plan. A similar if more elaborate sense of order and an over-arching quality of design can be seen for example in the Earl of Burlington's Chiswick House but whereas Lord Burlington was designing a private retreat for which an overriding aesthetic could take precedent over practical considerations, at Dumfries House the Adams were designing a house that needed to work on a daily, functional basis. The fact that the plan has been so little altered over the centuries shows that it works well. The lack of discreet access for the servants to each floor in a house built without internal plumbing is the principal issue and one that betrays perhaps the relative inexperience of the Adam brothers.[93] Two houses that John Adam went

on to design after Dumfries House, Ballochmyle and Paxton, contain secondary staircases that allow the houses to be serviced discreetly but this is provided through asymmetry in the plans, something that was not allowed for in the Dumfries House design.

In terms of alterations, in addition to the swapping of the pavilion functions, the paired windows that were intended to light the lower flights of the staircase are now replaced with a single window. On the principal floor the staircases are lit by tripartite Diocletian windows and the suite of family rooms either side of the North Parlour is arranged symmetrically. 'My Lady's bed chamber' and closet look north whilst the dressing room looks to the west. The 'Attick' (bedroom floor) remained as suggested in the earlier estimate with four 'principall' bedrooms at the corners, each with adjacent dressing rooms and closets. Four smaller bedrooms, each with an internal closet, occupy the central section of the plan. The staircases are lit by Venetian windows. An entresol is inserted above the dressing rooms and closets of the four principal bedrooms to accommodate a further four bedrooms with closets. These rooms are accessed via narrow stairs off the top half landing of each of the staircases and are lit by narrow windows inserted into the east and west elevations of the 'Great Entablature' which is the band of masonry encircling the house beneath the roof. The use of an entresol, while an effective way of providing further bedrooms without affecting the envelope of the house, could be interpreted as an old fashioned feature given that Sir William Bruce often used them, for example at Kinross House, Kinross-shire (Fig 1.31), begun in 1685 and Harden House (now called Mertoun) Scottish Borders begun in 1703, as did William Adam, most notably at Duff House, Banffshire, of 1735. Other solutions could have been found such as using the attic for further accommodation, as at Hopetoun House where the dormer windows are hidden behind the parapet, but with no parapet at Dumfries House, this option was not possible. The use of the attic level as accommodation seems to have been resisted from the first estimate where the ceiling of the upper gallery would have probably risen to occupy a third of it.

The Elevations

Three elevations are included in the contract: the 'South Front', the 'North Front' and 'Elevation of One of the Ends'. The last is in fact the east elevation with a section through the quadrant wing passage and the truncated blind windows of the Dining Room. The most striking alteration to the elevation is the enlargement of the bedroom floor windows from square to rectangular; they are still smaller than the windows on the principal floor but the clear hierarchy that characterised the earlier elevation is somewhat reduced. The whole design as built appears to be

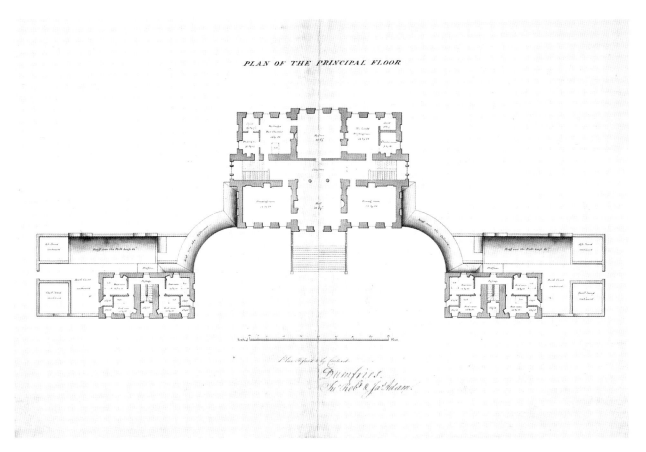

Fig 1.28 Contract Drawing of plan of Principal Floor signed by the Earl of Dumfries, John, Robert and James Adam 1754. *Bute Archives DHP/1/5*

Fig 1.29 Contract Drawing of plan of Ground floor signed by the Earl of Dumfries, John, Robert and James Adam 1754. *Bute Archives DHP/1/4*

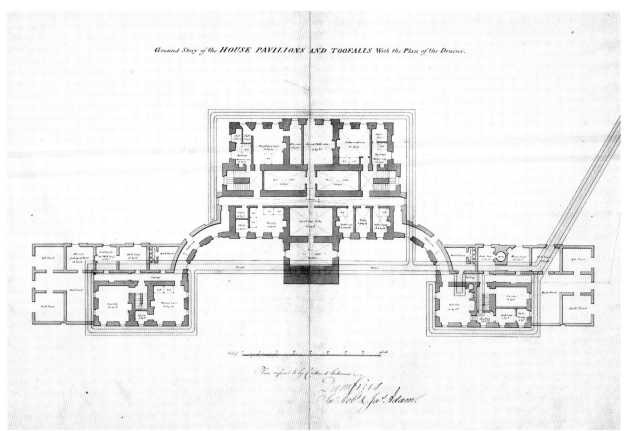

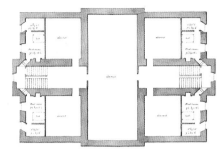

PLAN of the INTERSOLLS and GARRETS

Plan of the LODGEING or ATTICK Story.

raised; in the 1754 South Front contract drawing the architraves of the upper windows are shown as almost touching the great entablature whereas on the side and North Front there is a much clearer gap which allows for the entresol rooms and their windows to function. The anomaly is amended during the construction so that the area between the upper windows and the great entablature that we see today has proportions closer to the Robert Adam drawn scheme of 1753. This improves the proportions and while the upper windows become larger than those drawn in 1753, the greater size of the principal floor windows continues to emphasise their importance. This subtle change gives a much more assured and well mannered facade than that actually shown in the contract drawing. The end elevation is quite elaborate with both Diocletian and Venetian windows and the windows in the Great Entablature lighting the entresol. Clearly the disjunction between the toofalls on the symmetrical north and pavillions on the south fronts was not regarded as a problem, even though it would have been apparent on the approach to the house. This disjunction can be seen in the c1900 photograph where the western toofal on the north front can be clearly seen when approaching the house from the south (Fig 1.37).[94]

Fig 1.30 Contract Drawing of Bedroom and Attic Floors 1754. Bute Archives DHP/1/6

Fig 1.31 At Kinross House, Kinross-shire, William Bruce inserted windows into the cornice to light the entresole floor, an arrangement used seventy years later at Dumfries House. HES SC702624

The Staircases

An issue that remains unresolved is: why plan two identical staircases but omit any form of subsidiary stair from the main block of a substantial country house? The main stair at Paxton is adjacent to the Entrance Hall whilst the spiral service stair is close to the family apartments. The two staircases at Dumfries House were originally designed to be open to the Hall (Plan 4) and are unusual in that they have equal status both being similarly finished and decorated and each visible from the other. The glazed doors at the rear corners of the Entrance Hall were inserted in the early 19th century but the stairs are still open to each other on the first floor. This was one of the unique features of the plan in which the Hall flows into both stair halls, thereby creating a T-shaped space which was lit from three directions. The lack of a service stair has always been problematic. Why one stair is built of stone and the other of timber has also prompted a great deal of debate but the adaptation of the design for reasons of economy is clear in the changes to the treatment of the staircases given in the estimates. The design of the house appears to have been largely settled and agreed when the second estimate was presented to the Earl in 1753 and so while a more modest secondary stair could have been inserted at this stage it would have altered the design thereby necessitating another cost cutting solution. The first estimate had included stone staircases 'bottled steps of the two inner stairs which are proposed hanging stairs'[95] rising from the ground floor to the garret whereas the second estimate only mentions stone stairs from the ground floor to the principal floor. The third estimate states that only one stair was to be of 'stone with bottled steps and hanging'.[96] The fourth estimate and contract states that both stairs will be of stone from the ground floor to principal floor, and that one stair will continue as a hanging stair to the garret whilst the other will be of 'Wainscot steps and plats in a hanging timber stair from the principal story to be framed upon solid firr to

prevent noise.'[97] This suggests that the reason why one stair is of stone and other is of wood is purely a matter of cost. It was prudent for reasons of fire prevention to have at least one stone stair but a second stair could be made of wood to save money. A main staircase with separate enclosed subsidiary stairs is the most common arrangement in country houses of this period. However, at Dumfries House both staircases are open to the Entrance Hall and of equal importance which, whilst maintaining the beautiful symmetry of the plan, created problems for the day to day running of the house.

James Gibbs and the Sources of the Design[98]

One of the sources that appears to have been used by the Adam office when planning Dumfries House was James Gibbs' *Book of Architecture*, an illustrated description of the architect's work to which William Adam subscribed in 1728. Two years later Adam designed Balgreggan House, Wigtonshire,[99] for John McDouall of Freugh, who was married to the sister of William Crichton Dalrymple, future 5th Earl of Dumfries. The principal floor of Balgreggan (Fig 1.36) is very similar to Gibbs' design for Kelmarsh Hall, Northamptonshire,[100] with paired, identically scaled and enclosed staircases flanking a central hall and a suite of rooms linked across the building opposite the Hall.[101] Not only was William Adam's design influenced by Gibbs, it is a matter of record that the Earl visited his sister's house.[102] William Adam's unbuilt design for Lord Dumfries' uncle at Newliston, West Lothian, also features a pair of principal staircases flanking a central hall.[103] The design shows a central tribune between the Entrance Hall and saloon with the pair of staircases rising behind arcades on either side. Dumfries House remains unique in Britain as the only built example of a mid 18th century house with a pair of principal staircases open to the Entrance Hall without any other staircase within the main block or even access to the pavilions above ground level.[104]

There are a number of designs in Gibbs' *Book of Architecture* that have features redolent of Dumfries House,[105] a house for a 'Gentleman in the Country,' shows a nine-bay house with an advanced pedimented three-bay centre with a central hall approached by a straight flight of steps. The Hall is flanked by rooms behind which are paired staircases in exactly the same arrangement as that used at Dumfries House. The plan contains paired closets in the end bays and arched linking colonnades which are also found at Dumfries House. Plate 46[106] shows the design for 'Sir Gregory Page's house, Park Terrace Greenwich, London' where a central hall with a columned screen leads to a flanking pair of staircases. Kelmarsh Hall has quadrant

Fig 1.32 The plan of Paxton, Scottish Borders, with its spiral service staircase is perhaps more convenient than that of Dumfries House but is complicated by corridors and angled doorways in marked contrast to the simplicity and clarity of Dumfries House. HES 2013

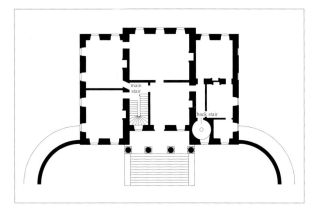

Fig 1.33 The view from the west staircase of Dumfries House gives an impression of how the gallery on the principal floor, as described by the Countess of Northumberland, must have originally looked. HES 2007 GV005219

Fig 1.34 *The south front of Dumfries House.* HES 2010 DP083187

Fig 1.35 *The design of a house for a gentleman in Yorkshire, as published by James Gibbs in his* Book of Architecture, *Plate 63 1728, closely parallels the design for Dumfries House both in terms of its facade but also its plan. The principal floors of both have twin staircases, although in the Gibbs design the stair halls are enclosed.* HES DP149870

Fig 1.36 *Balgreggan House was designed by William Adam for the 5th Earl of Dumfries' sister and her husband McDouall of Freugh. Its paired staircases suggest the influence of James Gibbs but, unlike the staircases at Dumfries House, they were both enclosed. From plates engraved for* Vitruvius Scoticus *in the 1760s.* HES DP144158 & DP144159

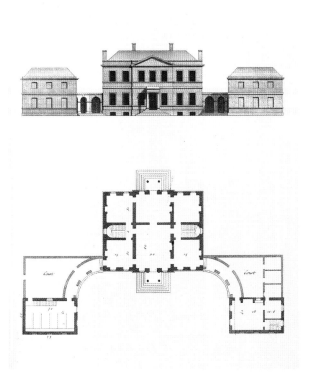

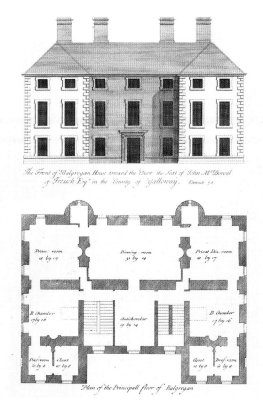

Fig 1.37 A rare photographic view of Dumfries House c1900 that shows the toofalls, smoke rising from the western one, before both were demolished.
HES SC1342633

wings leading to two-storey five-bay pavilions with paired chimney stacks and the square windows of the attic storey have lugged architraves. The description of plate 42 'Plan and Upright of a House 100 feet in Front' states 'There are two staircases leading up to two Rooms of the same dimensions with the Hall and Salon, but double the height, cov'd and adorn'd with fretwork. On each side of these rooms are alcov'd Bed chambers, and over them four other apartments.' This appears to relate very closely to the supposed arrangement of the bedrooms in the first scheme for Dumfries House as outlined in the first estimate.[107] Plate 63 (Fig 1.35) is of a house very similar to Dumfries House, if smaller, with paired staircases and a strictly symmetrical plan complete with quadrant links to pavilions with enclosed courtyards.[108]

The evolution of the Dumfries House design is intriguing in that, whilst the general plan and form appear to have been settled upon early on in the process, realising the design without compromising the concept was a protracted process. The translation of the estimate and the contract drawings into such a

dynamic building took detailed planning and involved numerous specialist craftsmen. The estimates show that although it took over three years from the initial suggestion to the signing of the contract this lengthy design stage combined with the need for financial restraint resulted in a building of great beauty and architectural importance.

The final design for Dumfries House is extremely accomplished and recognisably the work of Robert Adam, ably assisted by his brothers. The symmetry and simplicity that gives the exterior of Dumfries House its grandeur is tempered with restraint, something that is reflected in the planning of each floor. A sense of order and seemliness is all pervading with the occasional exuberant, if carefully controlled, flourish, especially in the plasterwork. The design is by no means revolutionary in a British context but, while it is not ground breaking, it is highly refined. Dumfries House can rightly be regarded as the 'pinnacle of mid 18th century country house design in Scotland'[109] in the light of which it is interesting that Robert Adam was, on his return from Italy, to be so influential in taking British architecture, and especially country house design, in a different direction.[110]

1   Quotation from a letter from Andrew Hunter to the 5th Earl of Dumfries dated 7 June 1750.

2   On 17 January 1635 a charter was drawn up that outlined the sale of Leifnorris by Mathew Crawfurd and his wife Anne Kennedye to the 1st Earl of Dumfries, 9th Lord Crichton of Sanquhar. It consisted of 'Tower, fortresse, mansion place, orchards, yards and pertynences'. Bute Archives DU/2/31/1

3   The Crichtons arrival in Ayrshire is recorded in writs concerning the acquisition of the lands of Cumnock and Glenmure including a contract of sale by Sir William Cunningham of Caprington to William Crichton, Viscount Air, afterwards 1st Earl of Dumfries, of the lands and barony of Cumnock and Glenmure. These lands were bought for the sum £66,600 Scots on 24 June 1629. There is also a disposition by Sir William to Viscount Air of part of the Templeland lying between the kirklands of Cumnock and the water of Lugar dated 26 December 1629. A further charter was drawn up on 29 January with the consent of Sir George Crawfurd of Leifnorris confirming the transfer of the lands. On 18 July 1635 a royal charter by King Charles I records the Precept of sasine of the same date and an instrument dated 27 January 1635 to William 1st Earl of Dumfries of lands of Leifnorris, the Ward and Blackwoodhill. No documents survive for the actual value of the estate. 29 January 1635 is the date of the 'literae obligitoriae' granted therein of the ownership of Liefnorris by William 1st Earl of Dumfries. Once the Crichtons had a suitable residence at Leifnorris they could contemplate selling Sanquhar Castle, their previous residence. Bute Archives DU/2/25 & DU/2/31/1

4   The 5th Earl had bought a house in 1745 at the top of the Lawnmarket close to Castle Hill in Edinburgh. His father Col Hon William Dalrymple of Glenmure remained on his estates in Clackmannanshire. Bute Archives Bundle A 719

5   The first recorded mention of this site is found in 1440 when a 'Craufurd of Lochnorris, whose daughter, Elizabeth, was married, probably about 1440, to Sir Robert Hamilton of Brentwood'. The family were probably descended from the Craufurds of Loudoun. By 1511 they were known as the Craufurds of Lefnoreis confirmed as such in a charter from James IV. The tower at Lefnoreis was known as the Ward hence the Ward of Lefnoreis refers to the building rather than to a person. Paterson 1863, 326

6   Bute Archives DHP/ADD/11

7   Robert Gordon (1636–52). Manuscript map held by the NLS.

8   Bute Archives DHP/25

9   Blaeu Atlas NLS Map.Fac.b.C18 (1654)

10 Roy Military Survey of Scotland 1747–1755 British Library Maps C.9.b

11 Bute Archives DHP/22

12 Leifnorris stood near the present stable block. It has been completely demolished.

13 Roy Military Survey of Scotland 1747–1755. British Library Maps C.9.b

14 Brown 2012, 321. Although William Adam designed a new house at Newliston in 1723, to be built in the centre of the elaborate designed landscape, it was never built and the 2nd Earl of Stair continued to live in his old towerhouse.

15 The Dettingen Mount lies about 100 metres west of the roundabout on the A70 at the junction of the A70 and A76 trunk roads.

16 Unpublished extract from the diary of Duchess of Northumberland, transcript held at Dumfries House.

17 Roy Military Survey of Scotland 1747–1755. British Library Maps C.9.b

18 The landscape at Auchincruive, Ayrshire, was laid out by William Boutcher from 1723 and three commemorative mounts can still be seen, Mount Stairs, Scarburgh and Loudoun. The circular woods and landscape at Loudoun Castle, Ayrshire, were planted by the 4th Earl of Loudoun from the 1730s to a design possibly by the Earl of Mar. *An Inventory of Gardens and Designed Landscapes*. Vol.2 1985, 156, 325

19 The mount on the drawing has dimensions of a diameter of '615 feet' which relate almost exactly to the existing Stair Mount. This is shown on both Roy and Smiths maps which would suggest that this drawing is dated prior to the building of Dumfries house. The total estimate was for £58 2s 6d and this document with its scaled plan and section gives enough information for the construction. Uncatalogued drawing, Bute Archives

20 This is the ruined Terringzean Castle to the west of the House visible to the west of the A76: it remains in the ownership of the Marquess of Bute.

21 The great landscape gardens designed by Le Notre at Vaux-Le-Vicomte and Versailles seem likely to have influenced the Earl of Stair, who was well acquainted with the French Court.

22 A 1759 copy of a design for the landscape at Newliston by William Adam of c1725. Drawing at Newliston.

23 Adam 1980, plates 32–36

24 McWilliam 1978

25 The road was moved further south and sunk into its present cutting in the 19th century.

26 A vignette drawn in 1772 shows the House clearly visible from the road. Bute Archives DHP/24

27 Bute Archives Loudoun Papers contain numerous examples of the 5th Earl requesting advice which are referred to below.

28 John Clerk of Eldin wrote that William Adam was 'a man of distinguished genius, inventive enterprise and persevering application', who commanded 'respect from his equals and uncommon attachment from those of the highest rank among whom the great Earl of Stair was one, who seemed by a sympathy of character to be peculiarly destined for the friend and patron of such a man'. Fleming J, 7

29 The Earl of Hopetoun was in the process of completing the large additions to his own house, his father having commissioned William Adam in 1721 to transform the house Sir William Bruce had designed for his mother and which was being completed by William's sons. Rowan 1984, 190

30 Gifford 1989, 184

31 Bute Archives DU/5/37/8

32 *Ibid* DU/5/19/19

33 *Ibid* DU/5/19/8

34 *Ibid* DU/5/37/9

35 *Ibid* DU/5/19/9

36 *Ibid* DU/5/29/1

37 Maclean 2007, 9–10

38 Bute Archives DU 5/29/2

39 *Ibid* DHP/2

40 18th century drawing conventions often disguise or ignore the vagaries of the landscape.

41 Adam 1980, plate 135

42 *Ibid*, plate 56

43 As William Kay points out 'The non-cursive title to the Leifnorris design is problematic as a diagnostic tool as it is indistinguishable in the drawings known to be by William Adam and those to be by John before and after his father's death in 1748.' Simpson & Brown 2008, 43

44 John Gifford in his authoritative biography *William Adam 1689–1748: A Life and Times of Scotland's Universal Architect* makes no mention of either Leifnorris or Dumfries House but James Simpson in *Vitruvius Scoticus: a study* 1980 describes 'A design for Dumfries House first commissioned by the 4th Earl of Dumfries before his death in 1748'.

45 Stirling Maxwell 1938, 193

46 Glasgow Corporation 1967, 3

47 Bute Archives DHP/7

48 For example the drawing for the proposed dairy at Tombreac of 1753. Lindsay & Cosh 1973, 139

49 The *Edinburgh Evening Courant* Tuesday 23 July 1754 reports that at the laying of the foundation stone the name of the new house was to be Dumfries House.

50 Bute Archives DHP/4

51 Maclean 2007, 10

52 Bute Archives DU 5/29/2

53 Ware 1731, plate 35

54 The Venetian window is sometimes called a Serliana since it was published in 1537 in Serlio's *L'Architettura* although it probably originated with Bramante. A Venetian window is 'a tripartite window consisting of a central opening with a semicircular arch over it springing from two entablatures of narrower flat topped openings on either side'.

55 Fleming 1962, 82

56   RIBA Library Sketchbook SE 16/3

57   RIBA Drawings Collection. Inigo Jones had purchased the drawing in Italy; it had passed to his heir and pupil John Webb, who sold it to Burlington.

58   Simpson & Brown 2008, 38

59   Bute Archives DU 5/29/2

60   The four 18th century villas inspired by Palladio's Villa Rotunda were Mereworth, Chiswick House, Footscray Place and Nuthall Temple. Nuthall Temple was the last of four, the only survival being Chiswick House by the Earl of Burlington. Summerson 1969, 199

61   The drawing is held in the BAL Drawings collection. John Harris describes Wright's unusual arrangement 'His attitude to composition, being that of an amateur, was less trammelled by precedent than would have been the case with a professional architect.' Harris 1995, 98, fig. 101

62   Bute Archives DU/5/29/16

63   These were subsequently hung together in the late 19th century Tapestry Gallery.

64   James Smith and Alexander MacGill built Yester between 1699 and 1728,: a year after they completed their work William Adam was called in to make alterations.

65   Adam 1980, plate 41

66   Hopetoun House Seminar 23 June 2011. Detailed discussions about the library at Hopetoun.

67   The extensive Loudoun papers at Mount Stuart include the correspondence between the 5th Earl and Lord Loudoun. Bute Archives LO/2/78/24

68   Bute Archives DU/5/31/5

69   Received from the Rt Hon Three guineas in full of a work intitled, The RUINS of the Emperor DIOCLESIAN's Palace at SPALATRO in DALMATIA which I promise to deliver how soon it is published Signed Robert Adam part printed receipt Undated. Bute Archives DU/5/31/7

70   Bute Archives DU/5/29/16

71   Bute Archives DHP/4/1–4

72   Bute Archives LO/2/86/11

73   Rowan 1984, 195

74   Bute Archives DU/5/29/16

75   Strang 1994, 103

76   Cruft, Dunbar and Fawcett 2006, 520

77   Bute Archives LO/2/105/2

78   HES photographs AY 2333. View from south-west of Ballochmyle House, 1883

79   Belford Hall elevation drawing dated 1754. Leach 1988, 63–4

80   The term 'toofall' appears in each of the Dumfries House estimates and in a description of an out building at the 5th Earl's townhouse in Edinburgh (ref. Bute Archives letter bundle A 719). The outer ones were not demolished until the early 20th century.

81   Worsley 1995, 139

82   This in turn was influenced by the screen at Queen's College Oxford then under construction. Gifford 1989, 147

83   Bute Archives DHP 11/10

84   Bute Archives DU/5/20

85   Bute Archives DU/5/20/3

86   Bute Archives DU/5/37/24

87   Only the Dining Room at Auchinleck appears to have been initially completed with its elaborate plasterwork, the rest of the interior being left plain. John Cornforth, *Country Life* 18 July 1991 p.78 Allardyce 1888, 165–6

88   Bute Archives DU/5/29/16

89   Bute Archives DU/5/37/27

90   Bute Archives DU/5/37/28

91   Bute Archives DU/5/29/7

92   Bute Archives DHP/4/1–4

93   Notes from discussions at the Society of Architectural Historians of Great Britain Study day at Dumfries House 2008.

94   Bute Archives Lady Margaret's Photograph Album

95   Bute Archives DU 5/29/2

96   Bute Archives DU/5/29/16

97   Bute Archives DU/5/29/7

98   Thanks to Andrew Martindale for pointing me in this direction.

99   Adam 1980, plate 128 and photographic view HES WG/426

100 Gibbs 1728, plate 38

101 The enclosing or separating of the staircases meant that the servicing of the house could be carried out discreetly.

102 Uncatalogued family private letters of the 5th Earl of Dumfries, Bute Archives

103 Adam 1980, plates 32–36

104 The east stone stair became by default the service stair providing access from the Kitchen pavilion to the Dining Room and was made more discreet by the insertion of the screen walls and doors in the early 19th century.

105 Gibbs 1728, plate 57

106 *Ibid*, plate 46

107 This was influential on the design of Yester House, Midlothian, with its magnificent saloon with its deeply coved ceiling and Drawing Room stretching from the front to the back of the first floor flanked by bedrooms suites and staircases. *Ibid,* plate 42

108 The Adam brothers continued to use published designs as sources of inspiration, such as Isaac Ware's *Complete Body of Architecture*, which provided for John a model for the south front of Paxton House, Berwickshire. A Rowan, Paxton House Berwickshire II, *Country Life* August 1967, 423

109 Conversation with James Simpson at Dumfries House September 2008

110 A comparison with houses such as Cottesbroke Hall, Northamptonshire, of c1702 and James Gibbs' Ditcheley Park, Oxfordshire, of 1722–26 which have main blocks with quadrant wings linking to pavilions is constructive showing that the built form of Dumfries House was not particularly innovatory but that it was superbly executed with a restraint that emphasises the richness within.

Chapter 2: Building the House 1753–1761

To the great work here

Lord Dumfries to Lord Loudoun, 6 June 1754[1]

The Building of the House

With the design agreed and the Contract signed by the 5th Earl on 19 May 1754, construction of the House could begin in earnest. The Adam brothers were not only responsible for the design aspects of the project but also acted as contractor for the building works, an approach which had made their entrepreneurial father William extremely successful.[2] In the Contract the respective responsibilities of client and contractor were clearly set out:

> It is understood that My Lord is to dig the foundations; Furnish all Materials for the Masons & Plaisterer's work & Lyme for the Sclaters work, And to lay them down on the Spot; To perform all the Carriages of every kind; Furnish Scaffolding, Cooms, Mortar Mares, Troughs &ca.; Sower the whole lyme; and pay the trades peoples Travelling days.[3]

The architects were responsible for almost everything else relating to the construction of the exterior and finishing of the interior including all the plasterwork. The Earl was responsible for commissioning elaborate elements such as marble chimneypieces and carved decoration for the interior walls. In 1753, Robert Neilson, the Earl's gardener, was appointed as Overseer[4] with responsibility for carrying out the Earl's part of the works. The Adam brothers appointed John Mitchell as foreman of the masons. The precise responsibilities of both men were detailed in the Contract.

Fig 2.1 Portrait of Robert Adam by George Willison, 1773.
National Portrait Gallery NPG2953

Before building work could begin, there was a considerable amount of preparatory work to be done such as the appointment of tradesmen and the procurement of materials. Transportation of building materials for large projects such as Dumfries House was always an issue; the closer that suitable stone and wood could be found relative to the site the better and so the sourcing of materials from the Earl's estate was prioritised in order to reduce costs to a minimum.[5] In particular, stone quarries had to be identified and opened up in order to provide the different types of stone required, especially the high quality stone needed for the exterior. Access roads were constructed and the means by which to convey materials and men across the Lugar Water was resolved, this being seven years prior to the construction of the Adam bridge. Accommodation close to the site also had to be found for the large workforce.

No details survive regarding the craftsmen employed by the Adam brothers to carry out the building and fitting out of the House. A trusted and highly skilled workforce probably moved with them from job to job but in the absence of documentary evidence it is not possible to identify the individuals who worked at Dumfries House beyond the two foremen, Neilson and Mitchell, and one of the masons, William Naismith. There are, however, very detailed accounts of the work done under Neilson's direction such as the recruitment of local labourers at 6d per day for the digging of the Great Drain.

Construction of the Great Drain began with the preparation of the ground in 1753, sometime before the Contract for the building was signed, thereby demonstrating the Earl's impatience to get things started.[6] As part of the Earl's responsibility the Drain

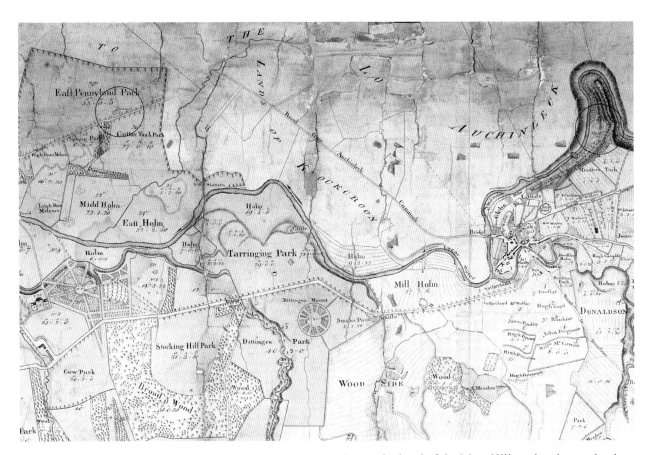

Fig 2.2 Detail of the 1772 Home Estate Plan showing the Templand and Pennyland Quarries (circled) that were dug to provide building stone for Dumfries House. Bute Archives DHP/24

was not included in the Adam office estimates, instead appearing in Neilson's accounts for 1753–4 which make clear that at £557 3s 4d, this element represented a large item in terms of the overall building costs of £2,670 6s 11d[7] The Drain was a large conduit which ran beneath the House removing all the waste water from the Laundry in the west wing and the Kitchen and sculleries in the east wing and was crucial to the form and functioning of the new building as can be seen from the ground floor plan (Plan 3).[8]

The sourcing of building stone from the Dumfries House Estate was not without its problems. It is unclear who was responsible for the important matter of selecting the different types of stone required but it is likely that the Adam brothers were directly involved, given that Neilson was responsible for the quarrying itself, and that the Earl would have been consulted. It is not known how much stone was quarried before the building operations were begun but the Dumfries House Contract contains an extensive listing of the precise requirements to be supplied from the Templand Quarry.[9] A distinctive, wavy-bedded sandstone with pronounced worm-casts was chosen for the exterior walls of the main block. The British Geological Survey identifies at least three quarries in the Templand Wood area[10] and suggests that either the Logan Quarry on the bank of the Lugar Water, now filled in, or one at

the nearby head of the Mote Hill peninsula may be the source. A quarry is shown on a 1772 estate plan.[11] A new road to the Templand Quarry was formed to avoid flooding of the existing road when the river was high, which suggests that this quarry was close to the Lugar Water.[12]

Of this locally quarried stone, the best was reserved for the principal north and south elevations; inferior stone from the same source was used on the less prominent east and west elevations. The latter was riddled with holes originally formed by worm-casts when the stone was being formed and was plugged with iron; these plugs are particularly visible where the stone has become stained. It is probable that the iron plugs were painted to match the surrounding stonework since this unusual feature escaped the notice of the otherwise acutely observant Countess of Northumberland who documented her visit to the House.[13] The compromise over the imperfect stone was a pragmatic one given that the extra cost of finding and opening up a new source of suitably high quality stone would have been prohibitive and the consequential delay unacceptable.

Red stone for the internal walls was taken from a quarry at the corner of the 'clump of firrs at Pennyland.'[14] It lay to the south of the East Pennyland Park near the Pennyland Lodge which lies on the Estate's north drive to the east of the Gothic Temple Lodge. The quarry at the 'outside of the parks', noted

Fig 2.3 This aerial view of the site of Pennyland Quarry (now bisected by the A76) shows its proximity to Dumfries House. HES 2013 DP153670

Fig 2.4 Good quality, unblemished sandstone from the Templand Quarry was used on the most important, front elevation. HES 2010 DP083194

as 'probably Woodhead Quarry', was only to be used when the river was high and workers were unable to cross to the Pennyland side.[15]

The large quantity of timber required for scaffolding was provided by the Estate. Fir was chosen for formwork of the vaults on the ground floor, the inside arches of doors and windows and for lath to support the plaster. The larger birch trees from Shaw Wood to the east of the site were used for trusses while the timber required for the servants' accommodation was found from a variety of sources such as the packing cases from the old house of Leifnorris which had been partially dismantled. Despite having being culled for building materials, the old house was clearly still habitable because the Earl continued to use it as his Ayrshire home until the new house was ready.[16]

In terms of accommodating the workforce, some were housed at the Nest, a long, low thatched cottage which stood to the south-east of the present house, close to the Nest Burn, until the late 19th century. The rest were accommodated in Pennyland House on the other side of the Lugar Water, which has since been demolished but which was presumably located close to the quarry of the same name. The Earl's Memorandum[17] noted that a rope and pulley system should be erected to ensure that when the river was too high for the ford, the workmen could always get to

work. It also recommended that a masons' shed was built about 20 or 30 feet to the south-east of the west pavilion, approximately where the sunken garden is now.

The foundation stone was laid on 18 July 1754 with great ceremony. Two reports were published; the first was in the *Scots Magazine*, which stated that the new house was to be called Dumfries House and that the Earl had laid the foundation stone in the 'presence of many persons of distinction of both sexes, who were invited to witness the solemnity'.[18] Robert Adam's concern to publicise the event in more detail is apparent in the Earl's lawyer, Andrew Hunter's, account of an exchange between the two:

> Mr Robert Adam called here on Monday last and informed me of the Company your Lop had and the proceedings at Laying the foundation of Dumfries House, and at the same time showed me a letter containing a different account of it which he said he had shown to Mr Whitefoord and desired that I might get it published in the Courant.[19]

The report that was consequently published in the *Edinburgh Evening Courant*[20] is much fuller than that in the *Scots Magazine* although, interestingly, no reference is made to the architect of the new house. It describes how those invited, including 'Her Grace Catherine Duchess of Gordon, His Excellency General

Fig 2.5 The Pennyland Quarry provided the stone for the pavilions and also for the bridge designed by John Adam. HES 2010 DP151649

Fig 2.6 Detail of the west elevation showing the inferior stone from the Templand Quarry. Worm-cast holes in the sandstone were in-filled with iron and then probably originally painted over. HES 2013 DP151647

Bland and the Honorable Mr Wemyss', supported the new name of the house.[21] The party went the short distance, 'from the House of Leifnorris, to the field where the new house is to be built, through a crowd of people who lined the road. Tents were pitched for the reception of the company, who witnessed the foundation stone's being carried from the principal tent and laid attended by a band of music.' The scale of the festivities was lavish and numerous healths and toasts were drunk including those to 'The King, the Royal Family and the Lord Chancellor,' the latter demonstrating the Earl's firm allegiance to the anti-Jacobite establishment, something that was to be celebrated prominently within the new house with the placing of his portrait above the Drawing Room chimneypiece.[22] In addition, 'Handsome presents were made to the workmen', presumably in the hope of ensuring the quality of their workmanship and efficient completion of the building. The celebrations continued into the evening when, 'the trees were illuminated with lamps, and the whole ceremony concluded with a ball'.

With the laying of the foundations and the installation of the Great Drain, the influence of the Earl and his overseer on the building operations was greatly reduced. The architects and their foreman now had more of a say over the day to day operation of the site. The first clue that the Earl was perhaps feeling that the building process was beyond his control is hinted at in a letter to the Earl of Loudoun written from Leifnorris on 6 June 1754 during a description of another of his building projects, 'Mathew Gray is engaged to finish the church & school house at Cumnock … I know not if he's engaged to the great work here which is not yet begun and when it may be finished no man can tell.'[23]

Within a year of the laying of the foundation stone for Dumfries House, Lady Anne Gordon, Countess of Dumfries, was dead. Although her loss was felt deeply by the Earl,[24] he resolved to complete the House and

also to remarry, not least because his heir, his only child, William, had died in 1744 at the age of nine.[25]

Progress at Dumfries House is recorded both in the certificates of completion issued jointly by Robert Neilson and John Mitchell and in the payments made by the Earl's lawyer to the Adam brothers who administered payments for the contracted building works. The increasingly tardy settlement of the bills illustrates that, although the project appears to have run according to budget, the Earl and his lawyer had to be extremely mindful of cashflow because the project was financed primarily out of income from the Earl's estates rather than from existing capital.[26]

The building programme began with the main block, followed by the pavilions and back courts and lastly the fitting out of the interior. The first and largest instalment of £1,500 was due on the laying of the foundation stone. Presumably this represented the costs incurred in setting up the site as well as those relating to the preparation of the Contract and associated drawings (Plans 1–6). Robert Adam asked Andrew Hunter for the settlement of this first bill on his return to Edinburgh following the foundation laying ceremony. The payment was made on 26 July for which Hunter had called in various debts and interest payments due to the Earl. Construction of the ground floor began in earnest with the second stage payment of £1,000 which was paid on completion of the extensive vaulting and the third for £800 on completion of the joisting over the principal storey. The walls of the main block were largely constructed, the entablature completed and the joists of the garret laid and a further £800 paid on 18 December 1756. By the following August, the timber and lead work of the roof were completed and the fifth instalment of £800 paid. This marked the completion of the shell of the main block.

The sixth and seventh instalments of £900 each were due once the roofing of the east and west pavilions

Fig 2.7 *The South Pediment was richly carved with the 5th Earl's coat of arms flanked by the Order of the Thistle and the Crichton Wyvern.* HES 2010 DP083206

and their linking colonnades had been completed.[27] However, there was a long delay between the finishing of the work for the seventh instalment and its settlement; a certificate of completion was issued on 22 December 1757 but the bill was not paid until nine months later.[28]

The toofalls on the north front and the courtyard walls of both pavilions, were completed[29] and £700 due on 3 February 1759 although the payment was not received until 2 June 1759.[30] The ninth and final instalment of £579 11s 2d which included the fitting out of the interior and the snagging, about which there was much discussion, was due to be paid sometime between 1759 and 1760 but was not settled until 1764. The total cost of building the House given in these accounts is £7,979 11s 2d. The fact that this concords precisely with the estimate on the Contract demonstrates that the payments outlined above were no more than a way of staging the payments to coincide with the requirements for the different stages of the building process. This methodical approach no doubt reflects the experience that the Adam brothers had gained both as architects and contractors whilst working for their father.

The principal element of the exterior that was detailed in the Contract but not included in the contract drawings was the carving of the 5th Earl's coat of arms in the south pediment. In the Contract it states that the Adam brothers are 'Also to perform the carv'd work of a coat of arms and pieces of foliage to be putt in the pediment of the south front.'[31] John Mitchell, foreman

of the masons, would have overseen the carving but who executed it is not recorded. It comprises a central heraldic shield with supporters flanked by the badge of the Order of the Thistle and the Crichton Wyvern identical to that in the Entrance Hall, except for the fact that the wyvern and thistle badge are on the opposite sides in that arrangement.

Letters in the Mount Stuart Archives add a personal dimension to the building process. The Earl was clearly keen to keep an eye on the building works, especially during the period when the House was beginning to appear out of the ground; on 15 February 1755 he wrote to the Earl of Loudoun from his Edinburgh townhouse,

I propose to set out for Clackmannan[32] the beginning of March, to settle my affairs there to enable me to be at Leifnorris earlier in April to attend the building.[33]

On 25 May 1755 he writes again,

the new house advances very fast tis to be roofed in and sashed before the end of summer and they talk of the house warming in August 1758. I should think myself extremely happy to have the honour and pleasure of your lordships company on the occasion.[34]

The complexity of transporting, installing and weighting numerous sash windows is discussed in a letter John Adam wrote to his brother James from the building site:

I have spoken to My Lord Dumfries about the transportation of the sashes. Both he & Mr Neilson agree that it is impossible for the horses here to do it. My Lord desires that we will get them sent. Will you for that purpose, desire Alex Gowan to enquire if any retour carts from Leadhills can be had and let Alex Whyte also endeavour to by Billery who brought the deals here last year, or any other carter & see what they will perform off cart. I wish John Paterson may get the weights ready, that they may come at the same time, and he must have a man to travel along with the sashes, to take care that no accident happens to them. I believe that the carts must also have a covering of sail clothes in case of rain.[35]

The Adams had mining interests at Leadhills and although all transportation of materials was the responsibility of the Earl, they were willing to help devise a practical solution in this case. The fact that it was cost effective to have the sash windows prefabricated off site shows the highly developed nature of some aspects of the building trades in the mid 18th century. John Adam, like his father, was an astute businessman and probably had an interest in the workshop, the location of which is unknown, in which the sashes were made.

An insight into the working practices of John Adam at this period is an aspect that is missing from the extensive archives relating to Dumfries House. However, a detailed set of accounts and measurements for the mason work for another country house that he had designed and was building at the time, Paxton House, Berwickshire, are held in the National Archives of Scotland.[36] James Nisbet[37] acted both as mason and superintendent of works at Paxton,[38] thereby removing John Adam from direct involvement as contractor, something that appears to have caused some tension between Adam and his client at Dumfries House. A detailed agreement was drawn up to which Nisbet makes reference which suggests that, as at Dumfries House, each aspect of the building process was subject to contractual agreement.[39] The mason work, an aspect that we have little record of at Dumfries House, is examined in great detail with 198 different items listed under the main house alone. The Great Drain is listed separately and given some importance along with the Pavements and the Brick Partitions, most of which appear to have been concentrated in the attics.

We have little information about the day to day building process at Dumfries House other than that it was a heavily labour intensive operation with the potential for a wide variety of accidents and injuries. There was, in fact, only one recorded fatality in the creation of Dumfries House, that of William Naismith, one of the masons, whose epitaph was written by his nephews Thomas and Robert Naismith:

Here lyeth, The body of William Naismith Mason, Well excellent liked in his Profession of an agreeable temper and disposition, religious without affectation, he dyed by a fall from Dumfries House the 3rd day of November 1756 in the 40 year of his age, Unanimously regretted by the brotherhood, his remaining relations his brothers or acquaintances implied in the building, Payed their last duty to his memory with a very uncommon sympathy and affection and erected this tombstone at their expense[40]

The rest of the building operation appears to have run relatively smoothly, albeit in the Earl's eyes at times very slowly.[41] The last major element of external work to be carried out in 1760 was the construction and connection of the water supply to the House which cost £90 18s 9d.[42] This was not included in the Contract and was therefore the Earl's responsibility. Robert Selby, an Edinburgh plumber, was employed to lay on the water supply, the route of which is unknown although, given the topography, it must have been piped in from the higher ground that lay to the south of the new house.[43] The supply presumably fed the Kitchen and sculleries in the east wing and the Laundry in the west wing but no reference is made to the existing supply on the drawings for the complete replacement of the system in the 19th century. Not all the amendments to the original specification were made for reasons of economy. London Crown Glass was used on the south front instead of Newcastle Crown Glass which had been the original, less costly, choice.[44]

As the building works drew to a close there were various outstanding jobs to be completed that had not been accounted for in the original Contract. John Neilson's account for the extra building works that were undertaken are not itemised but over the period 1759–63, £2,146 2s 5d was spent on these works out of a total of £4,170 0s 7d spent on extras.[45] These amounted to a considerable sum but John Adam having gained considerable experience working with his father was most probably able to execute a workable contract. It is not possible to determine the precise works carried out by John Neilson but John Adam issued an account for additional wright work carried out in 1760–61 which included supplying garret doors, roofing of the clock and bell towers in the courtyards and sawing up of old packing cases for lath, at a cost of £132 8s 11d.[46] This not only illustrates the thrifty nature of the building operations but also that there was still work to be done on making the building habitable despite the fact that it had been built according to the signed Contract and completed on budget.

The Earl of Dumfries and the Adams

The relationship between the client and the architect is a very important one and the expectations that each has at the outset and the status of the relationship during and after the contract is always interesting. There are numerous instances of the total breakdown in this working relationship between architect and patron, indeed the most celebrated is that between William Adam and Lord Braco over the building of Duff House, Banffshire, which culminated in a vitriolic and protracted lawsuit that lasted from 1743 until 1747. While the lawsuit was found in favour of William Adam, Lord Braco contested the judgement and it has been suggested that this contributed to the 'long and severe indisposition' that was to prove Adam's final illness.[47] By contrast, the friendship between William Adam and the Earl of Stair led to a collaboration that resulted in a number of garden schemes, as described in the previous chapter, although few of the architectural schemes proposed by the pair reached fruition.[48]

The Earl of Dumfries seems to have treated the Adam brothers as a combination of protégés, family friends and business associates. Their relationship appears to have been very cordial although there were

tensions over the final settlement of the bills and some of the final details.[49] An unpublished manuscript 'A life of RA'[50] by John Clerk of Eldin, who was married to Susannah Adam, sister of the Adam brothers, together with correspondence held in the Clerk of Penicuik papers,[51] make it clear that the friendship between the Earl and the Adams embraced the whole family, a fact that must have been a key factor in the choice of the brothers to design the new house.[52] Robert Adam wrote a letter to his mother on Wednesday 11 August 1754[53] whilst staying at Leifnorris during the early stages of the construction of the new house in what appears to be as much a social as professional capacity:

My dearest Mother

I thought to have wrote you by Tuesday's post from this place but realy was so occupi'd with Drinking and doing nothing that it was not in my power to fulfil my intentions. We arrived here on Sunday afternoon, were we found no strangers but all the family in good Health & top humour. Since that time Mr Alex Gordon my Lady's Brother returned from Bargany, where he had with Mr Charteris & Mr Wemyss who returned last week to Newmiln.[54] He has been here ever since & is a very fine Boy So that we are always merry and laughing.

Fig 2.8 Portrait of John Adam by Francis Cotes, c1750. Mr and Mrs Keith Adam, Blair Adam

Fig 2.9 Portrait of James Adam by Allan Ramsay, 1754. Bridgeman Fine Art TW426951

I have since given my Lord an account of my
Travels who is not very fond of C…H [Charles
Hope] as he thinks him a vast Scrub & says he
imagines I must stay awhile after him in order
to make my acquaintances. I often give hints
about letters or recommendation but find that he
does not choose to give any where Hope is to be
introducer & I suppose thinks them needless on
that account & you know you cannot insist for
that on their own behalf. I told my Lord that I
propos'd writing the Duchess of Gordon & ask
her commands which he approves of greatly so
that if I have time I will do it by the same post.
My Lord & the Ladys took notice of My giving
them an invitation to our house & then going
away to leave them. I excused myself the best
way I could but at the same time told him, that I
hoped would do you & the rest of the family the
honour of a visit on Jamie as landlord. He said he
was determined to wait on you as he promised &
to have you with him as he had a great desire to
be acquainted with you & had heard much of your
character which lost nothing on that occasion…

We expect to get away from this tomorrow & to
reach Glasgow tomorrow night & Inveraray on
Friday if possible.

The Earl does not at this point seem to have any
problems with Robert going away and, in effect,
abandoning the building project just as construction
began, which suggests that his contribution as
designer was finished and that he was leaving his more
experienced elder brother John to take responsibility for
the practical matters. The first reference to Robert Adam
as the designer of Dumfries House is by John Clerk of
Eldin who wrote in his biography, 'Dumfries House
was planned, and more particularly superintended by
Robert as a favourite of the Earl.'[55] We know that the
latter cannot be the case because Robert left for Italy
soon after the building work got underway but his direct
contribution to the design of the House is corroborated
by the fact that he alone signed the elevations for the
second estimate.
   A letter[56] from John Adam to his brother James
written at Leifnorris on 14 May 1757 gives a clue to
the relationship between the client and architect. The
exterior of the building was well advanced by this time
with the main block roofed and the completion of the
pavilions well advanced. In this letter is the clearest
explanation of the different roles taken by the three
Adam brothers John, Robert and James in the creation of
Dumfries House. John wrote:

Since my arrival here my Lord has had many
enquiries about the time of Bob's being home &
seemed always to expect that he was to return

Fig 2.10 John Adam designed this Mausoleum in Greyfriars Churchyard,
Edinburgh, for his father William in 1753 when the designs for Dumfries
House were being finalised. Sir John Soane's Museum (Photography Hugh Kelly)

to Scotland. I therefore resolved to undeceive
him & have accordingly done so this afternoon.
He said that for some time past he suspected
it would land in him settling in London & was
of the opinion it was a very right thing; that he
wished him well wherever he was & he hoped he
should have success.

This informal exchange implies that Robert had
no involvement in the completion of Dumfries House.
He left for London with James in October 1754 en
route to meet up with Charles Hope, second son of the
1st Earl of Hopetoun, in Brussels. James returned to
Scotland via Antwerp later that year and Robert went
on to Rome, eventually returning to London in January
1758.[57]
   John Adam's role in the creation of Dumfries House
should not be under estimated or eclipsed by the later
fame of his younger brothers. The pivotal role he played
in the winning of the contract and the creation of
Dumfries House is evident:

When I found him [Lord Dumfries] in this
humour I opin'd my own intention of going
abroad, but you cannot conceive how much he
was confounded. However he soon recovered
himself & said that it appeared to himself most

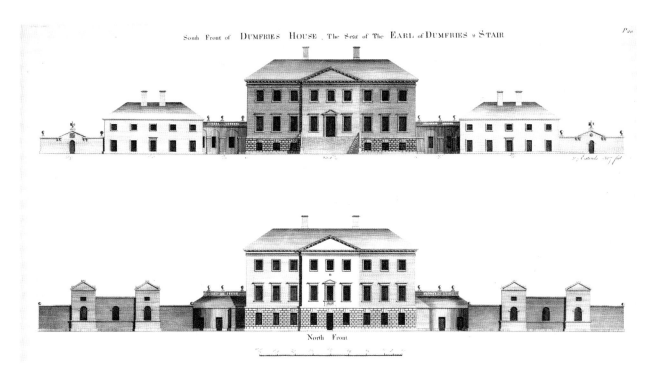

Fig 2.11 A set of drawings for Dumfries House were engraved in the 1760s with the intention of publishing them in Vitruvius Scoticus, *a volume of architectural designs that had been begun by William Adam but was unrealised on his death. John Adam attempted to revive the publication in the 1760s.* HES DP144162

Fig 2.12 Ground and principal floor plans of Dumfries House. HES DP144371

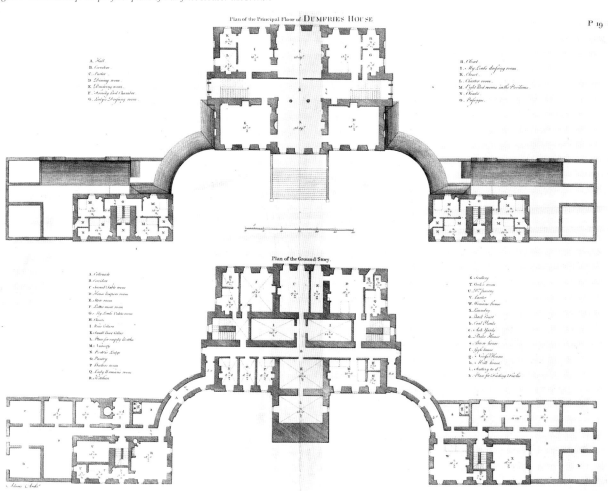

extraordinary that we should undertake peoples works & then go one by one & leave it. That for his part he was an ignorant man in all these matters & I must be sensible it was to me that he had trusted, as both my brothers were young when he began, and that it was in my experience that he trusted still, so that it was a thing he could by no means consent to.

This letter also makes clear the Earl's leap of faith in following the example of his friend and fellow peer, Lord Hopetoun, who had employed the youthful Adam brothers to complete Hopetoun House (1750–54). One wonders if the Earl took on the brothers thinking that as they had newly taken over the running of the family firm on the death of their father in 1748 that they would be less expensive. The letter goes on:

I urged for answer your being at home, who made it your endeavour to satisfie his Lop in every particular & would visit the works as often as was necessary, and that the situation of

Fig 2.13 Bedroom floor plan and west elevation of Dumfries House. HES DP144174

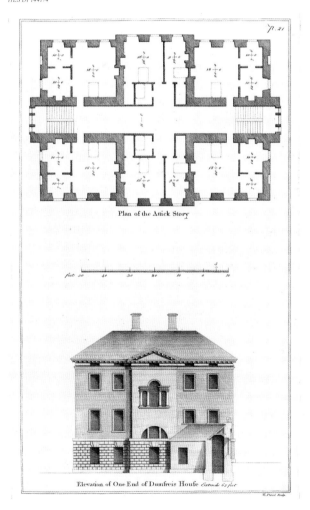

our affairs at present were such that it was ten to one if I could ever have such an opportunity & from the friendship he had always shown to our family I had flatter'd myself with his indulgence to put a thing in practice that I thought would be of such advantage to me. He said that his friendship for me & for us all was real but that Charity must begin at home; and tho' he had a very great regard for you & thought extremely well of your abilitys yet it could not be expected your experience should exceed your years & that therefore he could by no means agree to my going away.

This goes some way to explain the different roles of John and James in the building process. James was regarded as being perfectly capable of dealing with the day to day problems, although this suggests that he was not resident on the site but was instead directing matters from Edinburgh, whilst John was responsible for larger issues and the contract overall. The letter concludes:

I then told him that this was not a scheme hatched of yesterday but had been the result of much deliberation and consultation among us & when the resolution was taken we had both endeavour'd to put everything in such forwardness with respect to his house that it was impossible anything amiss should happen. That all the drawings were finished, the moulds ready & everything as much done as if I were to be on the spot all of my life. But in short it was beating the air to say anything to him. He was deaf & inexorable so that I was obliged to promise him at present I should not go. John Adam

John therefore had to give up the opportunity of travel abroad and the advantages it gave to his younger brothers. How his architectural career would have been developed had this longed for trip been possible can only be guessed at.

1   Quotation from a letter written by the 5th Earl to Earl of Loudoun dated 6 June 1754. Bute Archives LO/2/86/9

2   Francis Smith of Warwick (1672–1738) was a contemporary of William Adam and the two are compared in Gomme's biography of Smith (Gomme 2000). The Adam brothers and Smith offered a similar service as both architect and contractor. Smith specified for 'each site a team of essential master-craftsmen; a mason and or a bricklayer, carpenter, joiner, plumber and glazier, sometimes a slater or tiler, later joined by painter, plasterer and perhaps a carver'. These different master craftsmen would have had apprentices and assistants. There would also have been day labourers, carters and quarrymen making up a substantial workforce. Gomme 2000, 49

3   Dumfries House Contract, 1754. Bute Archives DU/5/26/16

4   Overseer Robert Neilson's Account (among Estate accounts) 1st year 1753–4, £557.3.4. Bute Archives DU/5/29/16

5   Where money was less of an issue, quality stone was transported a considerable distance, for example William Adam supplied the stone for Duff House from his own quarry at South Queensferry near Edinburgh and shipped the already cut and finished stone up to the site in north-east Scotland. Clifford & Gow 1995, 33

6   Labourers' receipts, May 1753–October 1754. Bute Archives DU/5/71/108 Labourers' wages June–October 1754. Bute Archives DU5/71/15–23

7   On 8 August 1753 the 'Requirements of the Great Drain' were set out. The Drain was specified to be 3½ feet wide with side walls 18 inches thick. The floor of the Drain, which was to be 6½ feet deep at the west end of the west pavilion, was to slope down 7 feet to the east end of the east pavilion and then a further 5 feet into the ditch at the Ha-ha. This sunk fence is still visible in the woods to the east of the House. Bute Archives DU/5/29/6

8   Bute Archives DHP1/4

9   The stone required from the Templand Quarry was listed with very specific requirements as: '66 Feet running of Base 1′ 3″ thick and at least 1′ broad on the bed; 190 feet running of the base 1′ 6″ thick and same breadth on the bed; 140 pieces of Rustick 2′ long, 1′ thick and from 10–12″ broad on the bed; 30 pieces of Rustick 2′ 9″ inches long and same breadth; 600 pieces Rustick 2′ long, 1′ 3″ inches thick and same breadth; 60 pieces 2′ 9″ long, 1′ 3″ thick and same breadth; 200 pieces Rustick 1′ 9″ long, same thickness and breadth; 300 feet running of Bell, 1′ thick, 1′ 6″ broad at bed; 30 stones for steps from 5 to 6 feet long, 15″ broad, 7″ thick; 20 stones for newal steps and plats from 5½ to 8 feet long, 2½′ broad at one end and 1′ broad at the other 7″ thick.' The stone that was required from the Quarry at the back of the parks is much less specific in that it would not be seen and was listed as: '400 pieces of ashlar for rebates and corners to doors and chimneys within the ground floor from 15–20″ long, 1′ high and 9–12″ broad on the head; 30 stone for lintels to doors from 4′3″ to 5′6″ long, about 14″ broad and 7–8″ thick.' Bute Archives DU/5/20

10 BGS Report OR/10/015 Draft. A Resource Assessment of Building Stone and other Construction Geo-materials on the Dumfries House Estate. E K Hyslop, E A Tracy, P A Everett & LJ Alornoz-Parra BGS 2010

11 The 1756 Smith and 1772 Home Estate maps in the Mount Stuart Archives show that the site of the Templand Railway viaduct and thus the possible quarry site would have been within the 5th Earl's estate. The First Edition Ordnance Survey Map is dated 1859.

12 A new road was to be made from Templand Quarry to the High Road near the old cemetery and also up the bank on the west side of the Shaw Wood to the site of the house. Hand written narrative bound in with a copy of the Contract, Dumfries House Contract, 1754. Bute Archives DU/5/29/16

13 Countess of Northumberland's Diary of a visit to Dumfries House in August 1760, unpublished manuscript. Alnwick Castle Archives

14 Ibid

15 Ibid

16 '281 days of a wright taking down old lyning & fitting it up for surbase lyning in the Housekeepers room, My Ladys womans room, nursery & lyning above the chimneys & mouldings round them, taking up old floors for sarking to the Coach house (the rest) was afterwards used by Mr Neilson for other purposes'. Bute Archives DU/5/30/13.

17 The 5th Earl's Memorandum Book and Accounts 1756–63. Bute Archives DU/5/20

18 Scots Magazine, XVI, 1754, 353

19 Andrew Hunter writing to Earl of Dumfries on 27 July 1754. Bute Archives DU/5/37/29

20 Edinburgh Evening Courant, Tuesday 23 July 1754

21 Catherine Duchess of Gordon, the principal guest at the laying of the foundation stone, was the half sister of Anne Countess of Dumfries; both were daughters of the 1st Earl of Aberdeen. It should be noted that none of the Earl's fellow peers with whom he corresponded regularly were able to attend, especially his near neighbour the Earl of Loudoun.

22 Lord Chancellor Hardwicke played a leading role in the suppression of the Jacobite cause after the 1745 rebellion and is now perhaps most famous for his legislation of 1746 The Disarming Act which prohibited the wearing of tartan and the confiscation of the highlander's military arms. Cheape 1995, 32

23 Lord Dumfries to Lord Loudoun writing from Leifnorris on 6 June, 'Mathew Gray is engaged to finish the church & school house at Cumnock, but I know not if he's engaged to the great work here which is not yet begun and when it may be finished no man can tell.' Mathew Gray was presumably a mason, the church was rebuilt in Cumnock in 1754; there is a drawing for a new gallery in the Mount Stuart Archives (HES A 27304). This shows that the Earl as a Heritor of the Cumnock Church had on-going building projects at the time of the 'great work'. The Earl of Dumfries' papers mention various minor works at the church which has since been demolished. Bute Archives LO/2/86/9.

24 On 18 June 1755 the Earl writes to the Earl of Loudoun that he is 'mourning the death of his wife very deeply'. Bute Archives LO/2/93/15

25 William Crichton, Lord Crichton son of 5th Earl and Lady Anne Gordon, was born on 12 December 1734 and died on 9 September 1744.

26 A great number of 18th century country houses were paid for by debt. Conversation with A Martindale June 2013

27 Receipt of £900 dated Edinburgh 16 December 1757, 'being the sixth payment due by contract for building Dumfries House and that at roofing in & sashing the East Pavilion & Collonade'. Signed John Robert and James Adam. Bute Archives DU/5/46/12

28 'We Robert Nilson overseer of the Rt. Honourable the Earl of Dumfries, and John Mitchell foreman of the masons at Dumfries House, do hereby Certifie that the East Pavillion and Collonade of Dumfries House was roofed in about 8th November 1757. The sashes were all in about the 26th November, the covered passage is all paved straight into the kitchen, the kitchen scullery Cooks roome and closet are all paved, the Covered passage is all lathe ready for the plastering.' Signed Robert Neilson and John Mitchell 22 December 1757. Bute Archives DU/5/46/11

29 'Mr Robert Neilson overseer of the Rt Hon E of D's buildings and John Mitchel Foreman of the masons at Dumfries House do hereby certifie that the Toofalls were all roofed in and flashed, and the walls of the Back Courts, Coale and ashyeards are fully built and compleated on the 3rd February 1759.' Signed 'Robert Nilson and John Mitchel'. Bute Archives DU/5/47/31

30 Receipt of £900 signed John, Robert and James Adam and dated Edinburgh 29 August 1758, 'being payment due by contract when the West Pavilion & Collonade of Dumfries House are roofed in & sashed.' Bute Archives DU/5/46/44

31 Dumfries House Contract p.3. Bute Archives DU 5/20

32 His parents had lived at Clackmannan where his father had had various business interests including coal mining which the 5th Earl continued to manage after his father's death.

33 Letter of the 5th Earl of Dumfries to Lord Loudoun. Bute Archives LO/2/104/2

34 Bute Archives LO/2/102/25

35 NRS GD18/8436

36 Mason work accounts for Paxton House, where work was begun in 1758, before Dumfries House was complete. The accounts are dated 9 May 1767. NRS GD267/16/9/21

37 James Nisbet went on to work as the executant architect for Robert Adam on a number of projects including the castles at Wedderburn and Dalquharran. Colvin 1995, 706

38 Cruft, Dunbar and Fawcett 2006, 607

39 'A note of the whole forgoing sums in so far as they are calculated for the prices fixed by our agreement.' NRS GD267/16/9

40 Naismith Gravestone Cumnock Church.

41 Slow progress with the building was due, in part at least, to poor weather. The Earl wrote to the Earl of Loudoun on 27 October 1758 from Leifnorris complaining about the bad weather and the fact that the masons were going to have to stop and that the leading might have to cease. Bute Archives LO/2/105/4

42 Cost of the Extras or Accessories of Dumfries House

		TOTAL
1760 laying on water to house		£90.18.9
1761 laying on water to house		£19.3.6
1761 laying on water to wash house	£18.16.6	£128.18.9
Coach house, Wash house etc		£558.6.7
1760–1 Coach house, Wash house etc painting	£14.5.6	£572.12.1
Bridge		£430.16.2
1760–2 Bridge Balustrades and obelisks	£112.4.8	£543.0.10
1760–2 Gateway or Temple		£279.17.7

Bute Archives DU/5/29/16

43 Bute Archives DU5/30/7–8

44 'London Crown Glass to be put in the sashes on the south front in place of the Newcastle Crown Glass specified in the third estimate.' Bute Archives DU/5/29/1

45 In Overseers account various 'accessories'

7th year 1759–60		£641.18.3
8th year 1760–1		£505.11.6
9th year 1761–2		£545.15.10
10th year 1762–3	£452.16.10	£2146.2.5
TOTAL		£4170.0.7

John Adam's notes of 'THE EXTRAS' in the Dumfries House Contract. Bute Archives DU 5/29/16

46 Bute Archives DU/5/30/13

47 Gifford 1989, 181

48 William Adam is attributed with the design of the Stables and offices at Newliston, Midlothian, 1725–35, and possibly the pair of lodges that survive south of the present house. Colvin 1995, 64

49 Lord Dumfries writing from the house on 18 May 1760, 'Mr Adam has used me shamefully, as to the stairs, locks, and backs of grates that were all broke down or cracked before we came into the house which will I'm afraid never give me real satisfaction.' Bute Archives DU/5/33/11

50 This unpublished manuscript appears to have been written shortly after Robert Adam's death as part of an unrealised publication; see 'A Retrospective View of John Clerk of Eldin with Some Comments on Adam's Castle Style' by John Fleming in *Concerning Architecture*, 1968, ed. John Summerson. NRS GD18/4981

51 NRS GB234/GD18

52 In *Robert Adam and his Circle*, 1962, John Fleming used these documents to explain the friendship between the Earl and Robert but further documentary research has shown that the Earl and Countess of Dumfries befriended the whole Adam family.

53 NRS GD/18/4744

54 Later called Amisfield, East Lothian (demolished).

55 NRS GD18/4981

56 NRS GD18/4836

57 Rykwert & Rykwert 1985, 37

DVMFRIES HOVSE
CVMNOCK · AYRSHIRE ✦ Nº 3
Details ½ Full Size of Hall Ceiling·
Adams Bros, Architects 1755

Note·Cove Pieces are···
Extended in True Elevation

Finale in Centre
of Side Cove···

Corner Piece·
at Mitre of Cove

Corner Piece
on Ceiling··

Band round
Centre Piece·

Centre Piece.

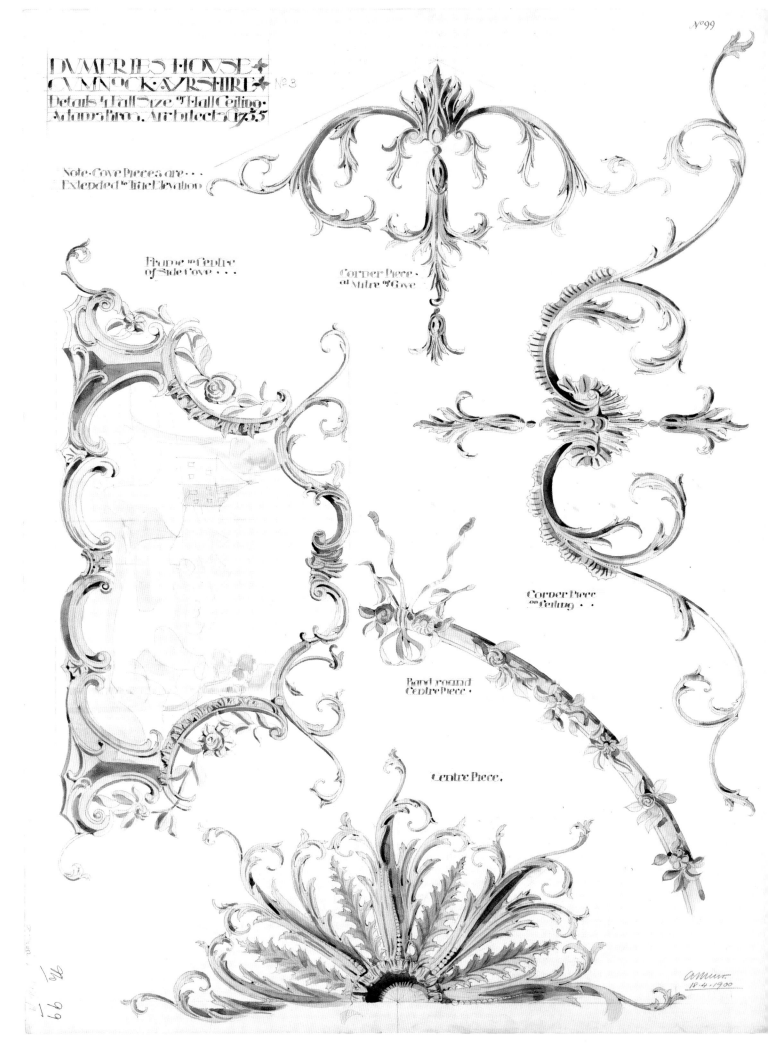

A Muir.
18·4·1900

Chapter 3: Fitting out the House 1756–1762

The inside of the house is handsome and thoroughly convenient

Countess of Northumberland, 1760[1]

The Fitting Out of the Interior

With the shell of the house complete and water-tight, the fitting out of the interior could begin. The relative austerity of the exterior, save for the heraldic flourish of the pediment, was designed to contrast with the richness of the interiors. A sophisticated programme of plaster decoration was created to give a unique character to each of the four reception rooms, the Entrance Hall, Drawing Room, Dining Room and North Parlour. This magnificent celebration of the plasterer's art survives with remarkably little alteration; the Entrance Hall plasterwork is the only area that bears later schemes of gilding and colouring. This rich plasterwork, combined with panelled rooms and two expensive London chimneypieces, made the new Dumfries House a suitable setting in which the 5th Earl could entertain but took far longer to complete than the Earl had anticipated.

He had begun contemplating the furnishing and decoration of his new home in 1756 but housewarming celebrations were not held until 4 June 1760. His first action was to commission Samuel Smith of Compton Street, London, to mend and clean the set of four Gobelins tapestries which he had acquired from his uncle, the 2nd Earl of Stair.[2] Smith backed the tapestries with 78 yards of canvas, provided 73 yards of 'Girtwebb & lining the same' and supplied a packing case at a total cost of £9 5s.[3] It is perhaps curious that the Earl only ever

proposed hanging two out of the set of four tapestries. He was clear from the start about where the tapestries were to hang, as his memorandum of 3 November 1755 demonstrates:

> There is to be a piece of hanging for the West end of the Drawing Room which is to occupy the whole space in breadth and the whole height from surbase up to the astragal. There is to be another on the East end of the same height with the former and as broad as the space between the two doors will admit for. The dimensions of the first will be 18ft 7in long by 9ft 10in high and of the second 7ft 4in long (or broad) and 9ft 10in high besides selvage or border to fix them by.[4]

This implies that once the architectural proportions of the house had been agreed in 1754 it was considered that the details were fixed. It appears that during the lengthy design process before the Contract was signed, much of the fine detail was agreed, showing that the Earl had great faith in his young architects to deliver with such accuracy.

The correspondence between the Earls of Dumfries and Loudoun gives us a valuable insight into the difficult final stage of the building project. The scheme may have been brought in almost exactly on the budget as estimated but it was not without its problems. The final payment to the Adam brothers was for the plaster and the wright work. On the completion of the shell and especially the insertion of the sash windows the Earl must have thought he was to get into his new house very soon. He wrote to Lord Loudoun on 25 May 1757,

Fig 3.1 A survey of the Dumfries House plasterwork, including these full details of the Entrance Hall ceiling, was made by the National Art Survey of Scotland in 1900. HES DP074892

Fig 3.2 The Entrance Hall with the 5th Earl's Coat of Arms prominently displayed opposite the front door. HES 2010 DP083217

Fig 3.3 The Drawing Room lies to the east of the Entrance Hall. HES 2007 DP033673

Fig 3.4 *The richly carved interior of the Dining Room marked it out as the principal room of Dumfries House.* HES 2010 DP083181

Fig 3.5 *The North Parlour looking through into the Entrance Hall.* HES 2010 DP083208

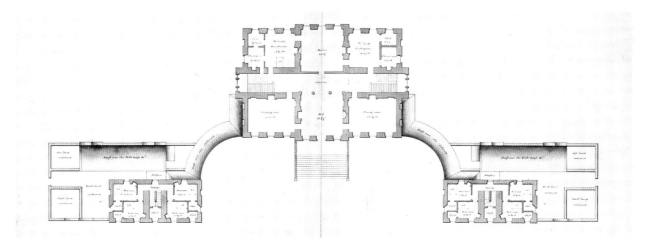

Fig 3.6 The Principal Floor Plan showing the strictly symmetrical layout of the rooms with the principal guest rooms flanking the Hall and the family suite of rooms along the north front. Bute Archives DHP/17

the new house advances very fast 'tis to be roofed in and sashed before the end of summer and they talk of the house warming in August 1758. I should think myself extremely happy to have the honour and pleasure of your lordships company on the occasion.'[5]

It was to be another three years before the House was completed. Responsibility for the fitting out of the interior appears to have rested largely with the Adam brothers whose workmen were responsible for the joinery work and the plasterwork. On 15 October 1758 Lord Dumfries wrote from Leifnorris to Lord Loudoun, 'I have many important things to settle before I set out Mr Robertson & Mr Neilson's accounts and I expect Mr Adams next week to give his final directions for anything within and without the house'.[6] Lord Dumfries was increasingly exasperated by the delays, asking Lord Loudoun to intercede with the Adam brothers on his behalf, on 26 April 1759 he wrote, 'the wrights, plasterers, and painters have been rather delatorie as otherways and Mr Adams was never more needed here than at this present, which I beg your lordship will be so good as to tell him if you chance to meet him.'[7] A month later he complained to his lawyer Andrew Hunter, 'Mr Adam has used me shamefully, as to the stairs, locks and backs of grates that were all broke down or cracked before we came into the house which will I'm afraid never give me real satisfaction and cannot be agreeable to the strangers and others that are soon to see it which … is monstrous.'[8]

John Adam was preoccupied with a number of ongoing projects at this time including Inveraray, Argyll, the Royal Exchange in Edinburgh, Douglas Castle, Lanarkshire, Paxton House, Berwickshire and Ballochmyle, Ayrshire but presumably prompted by the Earl's frustration, he undertook to carry out various works at Dumfries House between 1760 and 1761[9] including, '142 ½ days of a wright putting up pictures & glasses Scribing to the frames of the marble tables in the Dining Room & Drawing Room

putting up blinds in the windows with the upholsters lath … Fitting locks on Clock house, bell house, ice house and to the stair of my Lord's gallery at Cumnock Church.' But despite of his complaints, on 26 May 1760 Lord Dumfries writes from Dumfries House to the 3rd Earl of Bute that, 'I have been in this house some weeks.'[10]

An unusual set of drawings relating to the proposed interior of Dumfries House has survived in the Mount Stuart Archives.[11] This virtually complete set of elevations for the rooms on the principal and upper floors represents a uniquely detailed description of the interior design of a house of this period.[12] In published sources such as *Vitruvius Britannicus*, a number of sections through buildings are shown along with elevations of particularly elaborate rooms. The depiction of the Library at Arniston[13] or the Hall at Hopetoun[14] in *Vitruvius Scoticus* are fine examples of this genre but they were not accompanied by illustrations of the less important spaces. For Dumfries House, however, we have not only the Drawing Room, Dining Room and North Parlour but also the bedrooms, dressing room and closets. These drawings do not appear to have been intended for publication since the decorative plasterwork is omitted apart from the friezes in the Drawing and Dining Rooms and seem instead to have been produced in order to help Lord Dumfries visualise the rooms when choosing furniture and pictures.

There is no documentary evidence to suggest that Robert Adam had a hand in these interior elevations which were most probably prepared in order that John Adam could absent himself from the building phase and travel to Rome, although in the event he was not able to go.[15] There is a marked contrast between the coved ceilings of the North Parlour, bedrooms and Entrance Hall and the newly fashionable flat ceilings of the Drawing and Dining Rooms which emphasises the different character of these rooms for the family as opposed to the grand entertaining spaces.

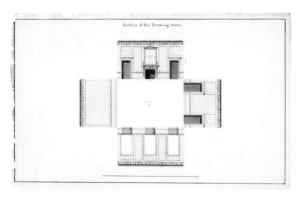

Fig 3.7 Drawing Room elevations showing the original arrangement of the room with doors flanking the chimneypiece. The west end wall is blank to take a tapestry with space for the other between the two doors on the east wall. Bute Archives DHP/3/2

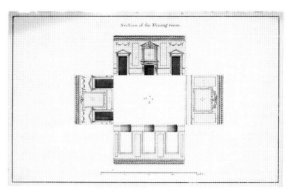

Fig 3.8 The Dining Room elevations show a simplified version of what was executed with further swags being added to the door cases and the frieze being omitted from the overmantle to accommodate the portrait of the 5th Earl. Bute Archives DHP/3/3

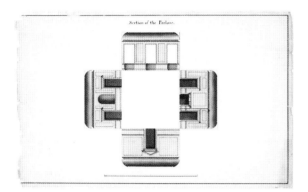

Fig 3.9 The Parlour elevations are much as executed but omit any detail of the cove plasterwork and show the original chimneypiece.
Bute Archives DHP/3/5

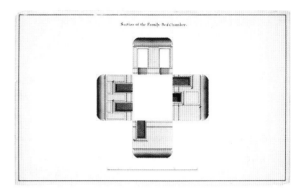

Fig 3.10 The Family Bedroom elevations reflect the simplicity of what was created. In order to accommodate a four poster bed, no panelling was fitted on the south wall. Bute Archives DHP/3/4

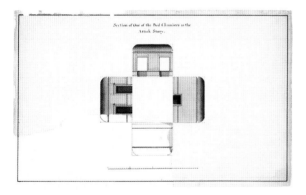

Fig 3.11 The Bedroom elevations repeat the simplicity of those of the Family Bedroom. Bute Archives DHP/3/1

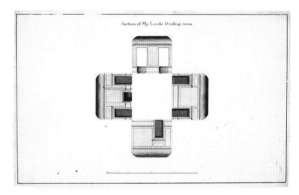

Fig 3.12 The elevations of 'My Lord's Dressing Room' virtually mirror the Family Bedroom arrangement but are fully panelled since there was no requirement for a bed in this room. Bute Archives DHP/3/6

This contrast is not found, for example, in the contemporary reception rooms at Hopetoun or at Arniston where all the ceilings are coved at this time. The fashionable arrangement of Dumfries House in which all the principal rooms are on the same floor means that these variations between flat and coved ceiling form are perhaps more apparent than in earlier buildings such as Yester where the grand reception rooms were arranged on different floors. The elaborate plasterwork at Dumfries House is concentrated in four key areas for maximum impact.

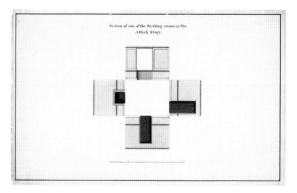

Fig 3.13 The Closet Elevations are equally simple. Bute Archives DHP/3/7

Fig 3.14 The Entrance Hall. HES 2010 DP083218

Entrance Hall

The Entrance Hall appears to have been completely the responsibility of the Adam brothers in that no mention of it is made in the Earl's papers nor was a room elevation produced for it. Originally it was an open, T-shaped space divided by a columned screen to provide an outer hall, lit from the south, and inner transverse gallery lit from the east and west. It is floored throughout with 'clean polished freestone pavement reduced to square with black marble dots at the corners to be furnished and put in by John, Robert and James Adam'.[16] The walls are plainly panelled in wainscot with a simple dado rail, the only decorative flourish being the niche opposite the chimneypiece. Within the head of the niche is an exuberant plasterwork vase of flowers contained by a sinuous naturalistic scroll. Each elevation of the Entrance Hall is symmetrical. The grey free stone pedimented chimneypiece is flanked by door cases and the niche opposite is also flanked by door cases; all the door cases, including those around the two false doors to the north, had their architraves altered by being cut short and having their friezes removed in the late 19th century. Without a room elevation it is difficult to determine the original arrangement but the doors on the west and east walls of the North Parlour are probably the most similar to what originally existed. The doors leading to the Dining and Drawing Rooms are to the south side of the room which means that having come through the front door, it is necessary to double back

in order to enter the principal reception rooms. This seems a rather clumsy arrangement and it is almost certain that the original intention was that one arrived in the Entrance Hall and then passed through the columned screen beneath the heraldic panel, and then turned and entered the Drawing Room or Dining Room through their north doors. To go from the Drawing Room to the Dining Room one would go through the east door, cross the Entrance Hall and enter through the west door, thereby creating an elegant circuit. All the principal rooms open off this inner hall. The door to the North Parlour has scrolled brackets and is taller and wider than the other doors in the Entrance Hall, which emphasises the importance of the room, drawing one beyond the columned screen. In most houses this central door would have led into the principal reception room not, as here, into the family parlour.[17]

The Entrance Hall has an elaborate programme of plasterwork which appears to be all original. The exuberant naturalistic colouring and gilding applied in the 19th century by over emphasising the iconography affects the original balance of the room. The boldly projecting cornice as specified in the Contract is of the Doric order reflecting the transitional nature of the space through which one moves from outside to inside. The four cartouches in the ceiling cove celebrate the lineage and status of the Lord Dumfries, indicating his obvious pride in being awarded the Order of the

Thistle in 1752. The heraldic device is the coat of arms of the 5th Earl with the Crichton lion rampant azure quartered with those of his wife and supported by a coroneted lion azure rampant. This is flanked on the right by the badge of the Order of the Thistle encircled with its motto 'Nemo Me Impune Lacessit'.[18] The badge is heraldically incorrect in that the cross should be a saltire cross set on the diagonal.[19] On the left is

Fig 3.16 The Hall ceiling with its four cartouches. HES 2013 DP155009

Fig 3.15 The Entrance Hall looking towards the front door.
HES 2010 DP083222

the Wyvern, the heraldic beast of the Crichtons, also encircled by the motto of the Order of the Thistle. Each of these elements carries an Earl's coronet. Suspended from the Wyvern and the Thistle badge are pendants depicting St Andrew of Scotland whilst beneath the heraldic shield is a badge of St Andrew with the Thistle motto. All the elements are linked by an elegant naturalistic foliage scroll that incorporates the Crichton Motto 'God Send Grace'. The Wyvern and the 'incorrect' Thistle badge appear again in the metopes of the frieze below. It would have appeared less bombastic originally in that it would not have been painted naturalistically but in white, or a pale stone colour, as would the rest of the room. This followed the fashion that lasted into the 19th century for more austerely treated Entrance Halls that contrasted with the rich decoration of reception rooms beyond.

The cartouche set within the cove above the chimneypiece depicts a stylised view of the old house of Leifnorris looking east across the Lugar Water to Terringzean Castle. It incorporates the two historic seats on the Estate and stresses the ancient lineage of the site even though the Crichtons had only owned it for a little over 120 years. This stylised image of Leifnorris with its high swept roof is the best description of the building that has as yet come to light.[20] The cartouche in the cove above the niche contains a view of Sanquhar

Castle (Crichton Peel) which was the ancient seat of the Lords Crichton of Sanquhar who sold it to the Earl of Queensberry in 1642.[21] These representations of actual rather than imagined landscapes in plasterwork are rare if not unique.[22] The cartouche above the entrance is a hunting trophy with a fox's head at the top which the two supporting hounds are trying to catch, a subject that reflects Lord Dumfries' love of hunting, one of his principal pursuits in later life.

The flat section of the ceiling is richly modelled with foliage; the only direct reference to the Earl is through the use of thistle leaves in the central roundel to symbolise his Order of the Thistle. The fillet below the cartouches and above the cornice appears to make the deeply advanced cornice an alteration, which it is not. The form of the coved ceiling is, for instance, very similar to that designed by John Adam for nearby Ballochmyle in 1760, complete with the cartouches. The Ballochmyle ceiling is, however, simpler perhaps reflecting the more modest aspirations and budget of the Lord Dumfries' friend Alan Whitefoord.

The omission of decorative plasterwork elsewhere in the Hall, beyond a cornice over the staircases, is interesting when compared with the elaborate decoration in, for example, Paxton, also by John Adam and of a similar date. With no evidence to suggest otherwise, the simplicity of the treatment of the staircases at Dumfries House should be seen as representing elegant restraint rather than the need for economy.

Drawing Room

The Drawing Room is one of the most important interiors in Dumfries House and, although it has undergone more change than other rooms within the main block, its function as the principal reception room has remained constant. The elevational drawing (Fig 3.7) shows a markedly different room to the one we see today. Originally there were four doors, two of them false, to create symmetry and balance; the door to the right of the chimneypiece and the right hand door on the east elevation were the working doors. The design of the dado rail and architraves is as shown on the drawings though the position of some of the doors has since changed. The panelled walls were built as shown on the drawing with space being left for tapestries on the whole of the west and part of the east walls. The floorboards of the Drawing Room in the Contract are specified as of wainscot board, described as better quality than the fir deal boards used for the other timber floors.

The plasterwork and the chimneypiece are the most important architectural elements in the room. As stated in the Contract, the Adam brothers were responsible for the former and Lord Dumfries was responsible for the latter. The chimneypieces for both the Drawing Room and the Dining Room were commissioned by Lord Dumfries from George Mercer of London with whom the Adam brothers had dealt on previous occasions.[23]

Fig 3.17 The coved plasterwork ceiling at Ballochmyle House, a simplified version of the Dumfries House Entrance Hall ceiling, complete with the fillet running just above the projecting cornice. HES SC1155122

Their role in the detailed design is unclear but the similarity between the chimneypiece as drawn in the room elevation and the final piece supplied by Mercer suggests that he was at least shown the drawing or that the design was agreed before the elevation was drawn.[24] It is not known if larger scale drawings were produced but the overall dimensions of the chimneypiece are given on the room elevation. The form of the bracket-supported mantelshelf as executed has Burlingtonian-Palladian precedents and is one that the Adam brothers used in almost a hundred designs;[25] a direct source for these can be traced to Isaac Ware's *Designs of Inigo Jones and Others* published in 1731.[26] The Dumfries House chimneypiece cost £130.00,[27] the bill for which was settled by Andrew Hunter in September 1758.[28] The Drawing Room overmantle, which appears to be derived from Plates 34 and 50 of Ware's book, was presumably not made by George Mercer since there is no mention of this in the accounts, neither is it mentioned in the Contract, which implies that it was the responsibility of Lord Dumfries.

The Contract states that the ornamental plasterwork of the ceiling, cornice and frieze was the responsibility of the Adam brothers. The frieze as depicted in the elevational drawing (Fig 3.7) is very ordered with masks centred over the architectural features of the walls below linked by swags and pendants but as executed is very different, being a much less rigid composition of free flowing foliage and flowers which almost explodes out of the frieze in contrast to the

Fig 3.18 *The Drawing Room.* HES 2007 DP033674

restraint and order of the Corinthian cornice with frieze, as specified in the Contract.

The ceiling is composed of naturalistic fronds and leaves which draw in from the cardinal points to a central ceiling rose (Fig 3.20) which is embowered in a writhing mass of naturalistic vegetation and pairs of delicately modelled ho-ho birds. The Order of the Thistle is represented as eight luxuriant thistle plants woven into the design. In the extensive Mount Stuart Archives there is no mention of the plasterer who created the ceilings at Dumfries House but three

Fig 3.19 Detail of the fireplace supplied by George Mercer in 1754.
HES 2007 DP033681

possible candidates have been identified: Thomas Clayton, John Dawson and Philip Robertson. However, the dramatically different character of the four ceilings, especially those in the Drawing and Dining Room, suggests that there may have been more than one craftsman involved.[29] The absence of gilding on both the Drawing Room and Dining Room ceilings at Dumfries House unlike in the Hall and Parlour suggests that the Butes felt they did not need improving and were therefore of great significance.

The ceiling's obvious sophistication suggests the hand of an accomplished designer but, contrary to popular belief, there is no evidence that Robert designed it, neither does he make mention of it in his letters from Italy where he was based when it was executed, although it is possible he may have sketched it out before his departure.[30] The Rococo syle of the ceiling compares with Vassali's work at Hagley Hall, Worcestershire, by Sanderson Miller c1758 with its richly modelled Italianate interiors, and also Newmilns, East Lothian (later called Amisfield), which had been commissioned from Isaac Ware by Francis Charteris, whom Robert had met in August 1754.[31] While he was in Rome, he requested from his sister 'a sett of the Best plans in Scotland such as Braco's house, Yester, Dumfries etc, which with changing and shifting about gives one hints to compose other things' but makes no mention of anything else to do with Dumfries House.[32]

The Drawing Room ceiling as a supreme expression of Rococo design is far removed from Robert's work on his return.

It is possible that Thomas Clayton (fl 1710–60), one of the most celebrated plasterers of the day, executed this ceiling, particularly since he had already worked extensively with the Adam practice. However, a comparison between the ceilings he created for the State rooms of Blair Castle (1755–8) and those at Dumfries House demonstrates that, while some of the modelling of the foliage is comparable, the former is set within a very rigid framework, far removed from the fluidity of the latter. The ceilings would appear to be almost exactly contemporary, which also casts doubt over the involvement of Clayton. John Fleming and Sir John Stirling Maxwell both attribute the plasterwork to Clayton but the plasterwork at Dumfries House is much more free and flowing than other surviving examples of Clayton's work such as at Marchmont, Berwickshire (Fig 3.23), of 1753–7 or St Andrews Parish Church, Glasgow of 1753.[33] Clayton, a craftsman of superlative quality, was a master of 'lavish rococo' foliage which he always appears to have constrained within an architectural framework.[34] In the Drawing Room at Dumfries House this framework is absent and the foliage is set free to create its own patterns. There is nothing in Thomas Clayton's documented works that is in the spirit of the Dumfries House ceiling.

John Dawson, a Scot who had trained with Charles Stanley in London before returning to Scotland c1750 at the behest of the Adam brothers may also have executed the ceilings. He worked at Hopetoun House both as a stone carver and as a plasterer where he created the lavish plasterwork in the principal suite of Dining Room, Drawing Room, State Bedroom and Dressing Room.[35] The cove in the Dining Room has elaborate cartouches at the corners similar to those in the North Parlour and the Entrance Hall at Dumfries House. The form of the cornice and the freedom of the flowing plasterwork of the frieze are similar to the Drawing Room at Dumfries House. The Hopetoun House Drawing Room ceiling (Fig 3.21) is far more elaborate and heavily modelled and, while the modelling is free flowing and Rococo in character, it is held within a boldly outlined framework. The cove is equally richly and freely modelled with corner cartouches that relate most closely to the North Parlour at Dumfries House. It has been suggested that Dawson may be responsible for the plasterwork of the angle-coves in the saloon at Yester (Fig 1.16) which

Fig 3.20 The free flowing plasterwork of the Drawing Room ceiling.
HES 2013 DP155006

Fig 3.21 *The elaborate plasterwork that John Dawson executed in the Red Drawing Room at Hopetoun House is as free as the work at Dumfries House but is constrained within a series of compartments.* HES SC1348381

Fig 3.22 *The Entrance Hall ceiling at Duff House, which is probably by David Crooks, is closest to the style of the Dumfries House ceiling although not as freely expressed.* HES SC1348379

'resembles contemporary work at Dumfries House'.[36] They certainly have a similar form to the angle-coves in the North Parlour.

The Hall at Duff House, Banffshire, has a Rococo ceiling of 1760 (Fig 3.22) which is probably by David Crooks although John Dawson also tendered for the work. This ceiling, with its lack of architectural division and foliate structure, is the closest in overall character to the Drawing Room ceiling at Dumfries House.[37] A comparison between the two reveals similarities in the way that the central design links with the design at the border through the foliage and in the way in which birds are incorporated into the overall design. However, the Dumfries House ceiling is far subtler in the variation of its modelling from shallow to deeply undercut whereas the Duff House ceiling is more evenly undercut and modelled throughout. A further connection between the two is that the Adam brothers were involved with this phase of works at Duff House because they supplied chimneypieces for it in 1757. Despite these parallels

Fig 3.23 *The Drawing Room ceiling at Marchmont House on which Clayton's Rococo plasterwork flows between edged compartments.* HES DP40029

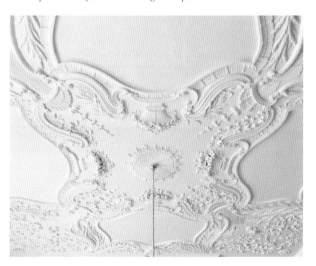

between the work of David Crooks at Duff House and the Drawing Room ceiling at Dumfries house, the ceilings are sufficiently different that an attribution to Crooks would be difficult to support.[38]

Philip Robertson is another possible candidate, being a first cousin of the Adam brothers and a former apprentice of the plasterer Joseph Enzer, who had worked extensively for William Adam.[39] Robertson was working at Buchanan and Inveraray for the Adams whilst work was going on at Dumfries House and went on to work for them at Auchincruive where Adam Smith, who was employed by the Earl of Dumfries as a mason, was the superintendant of works. Philip's brother, David Robertson, supplied most of the new grates, fenders and other metalwork for Dumfries House.[40] Another connection between Dumfries House and the Robertson family is that William Boyd Robertson, a cousin of the Adam brothers, was Lord Dumfries' factor between 1754 and 1756 which coincides with the building of the house.[41] The Auchincruive and Dumfries House ceilings have a similar naturalistic quality; however, Robert Adam designs for the work at Auchincruive, which are dated 1766, are for something far more ordered and regulated having been influenced by his experience abroad.[42]

Dining Room

The Dining Room, complete with carved swags and pedimented door cases, was the most architecturally lavish interior in the House. The room is described as a Dining Room rather than the more common term used at the time – Dining Parlour. Its elaborate decoration reflects the pre-eminence of the Dining Room in 18th century British country houses. Unlike the Drawing Room, the Dining Room as illustrated in the elevational drawing (Fig 3.8) survives much as it was designed, although it was altered somewhat in the execution. It has a very different character to the

Drawing Room with much more elaboration on the door cases, carved decoration on the panelling and a ceiling that looks forward to the elaborate designs that were to become one of the hallmarks of the Adam style after Robert's return from Rome. The arrangement of the doors, chimneypiece and windows is the mirror image of the original arrangement of the Drawing Room, thereby maintaining the overarching symmetry of the original design.

The Contract states that the floor of the Dining Room was to be, as were all wooden floors on the principal and attick floors except for the Drawing Room, of 'first sort of firr deal boards'.[43] This flooring has been replaced with the current oak boards; the junction between the original fir and new oak boards can be clearly seen in the doorway to the Entrance Hall. The Contract also states that the Adams were responsible for lining the walls of the Dining Room 'with firr wood up to the astragall'[44] but the Earl was responsible for 'carvings or enriching of the mouldings that his Lordship, may judge proper in doors windows, bases and surbases'.[45] No bills survive in the Earl's papers for this work but addenda to the room elevations were made in relation to the projected furnishing and picture acquisitions for the room. While it would seem likely that the Adam brothers designed the carved embellishments, since they are included in the room elevations, there is no documentary proof to support this.

A comparison between the drawings and the finished room shows that the pediments on the overdoors shown

Fig 3.24 *The Dining Room was the most elaborate room in the house with its enriched swags and carvings. It was dominated by a portrait of the 5th Earl.* HES 2010 DP083179

Fig 3.25 *Portrait of Anne Countess of Dumfries by Thomas Hudson 1763 which originally hung on the west wall of the Dining Room.* Albert Memorial Art Gallery and Museum, Bridgeman Fine Art RAMM 46/1968

Fig 3.26 *The Dining Room ceiling. HES 2013 DP155007*

Fig 3.27 *Plate XIX from Wood's* Ruins of Palmyra. *This decorative panel design, which became known as the 'Palmyra Ceiling', was widely copied. The central section was one of the sources for the Dumfries House Dining Room ceiling. HES DP149863*

on the elevations were in fact made with shouldered triangular pediments; all the existing evidence clearly suggests that this was an amendment made during the building process. The scrolled brackets on the door cases match the elevational drawing and are enriched with deeply carved frieze panels. The swags above the doors are a simplified version of those drawn, whereas the panel between the doors on the west wall has a more elaborate broken pediment. A correctly orientated badge of the Order of the Thistle replaces the bust shown on the drawing of the west wall while the large panel on the wall opposite is also more elaborately carved with luxuriant grape laden vines flanking the Bacchus head. These decorative elements celebrating plenty were standard elements in fashionable mid 18th century Dining Rooms in Scotland.

The triangular broken pediment with shield on the overmantle (Fig 3.24) is exactly as drawn but the frieze was adapted in order to accommodate the picture which was commissioned in 1757. The State Dining Room at Nostell Priory, Yorkshire, designed by James Paine in 1745–50[46] has a very similar arrangement of broken pedimented overmantle and similar frames at either end of the room in the same form as at Dumfries House. The frieze with its garland of flowers by Joseph Rose the Elder is also similar but the ceiling itself is dramatically different. This suggests that the Adam Brothers were very aware of current fashions and stylistic developments south of the Border.

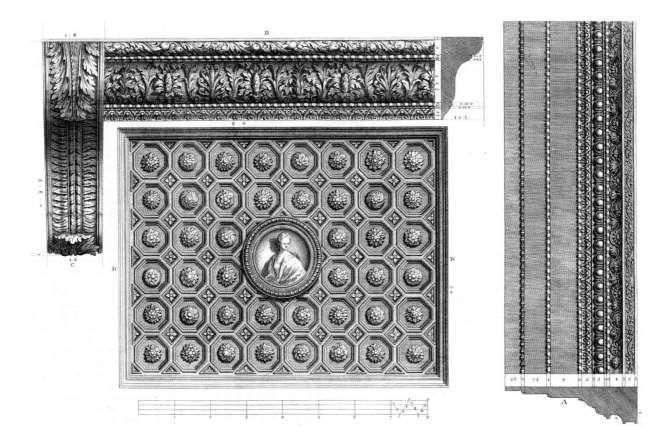

The plaster work and stucco of the ceiling, cornice and frieze were the responsibility of the Adam brothers. The frieze shown on the drawings is a bay leaf garland pattern but as executed it is decorated with linked vines of foliage emanating from a naturalistic palmette at the centre of each wall. The cornice as specified in the Contract is of the Ionic order.

Although there is no documentary evidence for Robert's involvement, the use of the classically inspired pattern of octagons suggests a rudimentary knowledge of classical ideas, probably gathered through engravings. Although the idea of the ceiling being inspired by the Temple of the Sun at Palmyra has been disputed[47] there are elements that suggest an awareness of this ancient site of which engraved views had been published. The ceiling is not a direct copy of the 'Palmyra' design, of which Robert Adam did a more exact version in the Dining Room at Osterley Park 1763–8, but it apparently takes inspiration from the designs as published by Robert Wood in *The Ruins of Palmyra otherwise Tedmor in the Desart* in 1753 (Fig 3.27, Plate XIX 'Soffit' of south recess of the temple). Both have a geometric framework based on a central circle set within a square surrounded by octagons and squared forms. In the Palmyra design, the linked arrangement of the octagons with points touching is the defining element that has come to characterize 'Palmyra ceilings' which are considered as a group, rather than those, such as that at Dumfries House, which are rather different in that the individual

Fig 3.28 Plate VIII from Wood (1753) shows another decorative panel from Palmyra. It was less commonly used as a source for ceiling designs in the 18th century but seems to have inspired the ceiling at Dumfries House.
HES DP149862

elements are isolated from each other.[48] The arrangement of the octagons at Dumfries House is in fact closer to Plate VIII ('Soffit of side door of the temple') in Wood's publication (Fig 3.28). The plasterwork contained within each of the geometric elements is of naturalistic foliage which is the feature that links this design to the adjacent Drawing Room ceiling and especially the vegetation within its central rose.

It seems extremely likely that, since the design of the Dining Room ceiling displays such a contemporary, antiquarian interest, the Adam brothers were involved in its design, most probably John. The Earl's input is likely to have been very minor since he professed to know nothing of these matters.[49] Like the Drawing Room ceiling, it is a beautifully executed virtuoso performance that suggests both an extremely proficient plasterer and a talented designer.

As with the Drawing Room, the Earl was responsible for commissioning the chimneypiece of white marble with its panels of jasper, which also came from George Mercer, at a cost of £95.00.[50] The design in the elevations with its scrolled jambs relates to what was installed but also to Plate 50, a chimneypiece with overmantle, in Isaac Ware's *Designs of Inigo Jones and Others* of 1731 in which the scrolls are repeated in elevation and there is a central rectangular plaque on the frieze.

Isaac Ware was working at Amisfield whilst Dumfries House was being finished and, as we have seen, Robert Adam and the 5th Earl knew the owner Francis Charteris.

Dumfries House was the last commission with which Robert Adam was involved with before leaving for Italy. The interiors of Hatchlands Park, Surrey, and Kedleston, Derbyshire, were among his first commissions on his return.[51] Kedleston was a far larger and grander house than Dumfries House and the great Drawing Room there is far more elaborate and the plasterwork more richly modelled but the cornice is similar to the one in the North Parlour and the plaster ornaments of the cove rest on a fillet or moulding[52] in the same way that they do in the Entrance Hall at Dumfries House. The scale of Hatchlands Park is much more comparable to Dumfries House. The main surviving Adam interior is the Saloon, originally designed as the Dining Room, where the cornice and frieze are very similar to those in the Drawing and Dining Rooms at Dumfries House but the decoration of the ceiling is radically different. It is composed of geometric shapes, a central oval contained within an elongated octagon with the more naturalistic but symmetrically arranged patterns confined within borders. There is no hint of the Rococo subtlety or freedom of the Drawing Room ceiling or the more rigid geometry of the Dining Room.

Fig 3.29 The North Parlour, photographed by RCAHMS in 2010 before the gilding which had been applied to the ceiling's plasterwork was removed. HES 2010 DP083212

North Parlour

The North Parlour was designed as the main family living room conveniently positioned between the Family Bed Chamber, or Lady's Bed Chamber, to the west and the Earl's Dressing Room to the east. The room is entered on axis with the front door and while in larger houses a room on this principal axis would have been another grand reception room (as at Ditchley Park, Oxfordshire, of 1722 or Marchmont House, Berwickshire, of 1750), here this less formal reception room enjoys one of the House's finest views, looking across the Lugar Water to the Gothic Temple Lodge. None of the plasterwork is detailed on the design elevation (Fig 3.9) in the way that it was for the Drawing and Dining Rooms and the walls are simply panelled above the dado rail. As in the Entrance Hall, two of the symmetrically arranged doors on the east and west elevations are false but here the opening doors are at opposite corners, thereby increasing the privacy of the flanking rooms. The doors have simply corniced architraves whereas the door from the Entrance Hall has a pediment supported on scroll brackets. The chimneypiece is on the east wall with a niche (Fig 3.9) opposite, reversing the arrangement of the Entrance Hall (Fig 3.30).

The plasterwork is very elaborate (Figs 3.31–3.32) but has none of the loaded iconographic significance of the Entrance Hall, here it symbolises bucolic plenty with an overflowing basket at each corner of the cove and musical instruments above the chimneypiece whilst opposite is a bow with a quiver of arrows. Above the

Fig 3.30 Detail of the North Parlour niche. HES 2007 DP033661

entrance door is a bottle and a glass whilst over the windows is a jug and a glass. The flat section of the ceiling is centred on an elaborate rose composed of a variety of naturalistic forms enclosed within a circular fillet. These fronds point to further naturalistic swags that relate to the decorations on the cove.[53] It was, like all the other plasterwork, intended to be painted white. The niche is surmounted by the only wall mounted swag outside the Dining Room in the House which, according to the Contract, was also paid for by the Earl as an extra. A Bacchus head lies at the centre of the design set within a grape laden vine linked by a naturalistic scroll which celebrates the welcome and good cheer expected in such a room and sat well with its later use as the main Dining Room. In the Contract it is clearly stated that the Earl will be responsible for any

Fig 3.31 Photographic plan view of the North Parlour ceiling plasterwork, without gilding as originally intended. HES 2013 DP155010

Fig 3.32 A survey of the Dumfries House plasterwork, including these full size details of the North Parlour ceiling, was made by the National Art Survey of Scotland in 1900 when the room was in use as the Dining Room. HES DP074893

marble chimneypieces to be installed[54] but there is no mention of a chimneypiece for this room. The present chimneypiece with its Greek Key dado on either side is a later insertion that replaced the stone, or possibly timber, original.

Bedrooms

The Family Bed Chamber is simply fitted out with wainscoted walls and a firr deal floor with a coved ceiling with dentil cornice. The proposed position of the bed is marked on the principal floor plan against the north wall where there is no raised panelling, a detail common to all the bedrooms here and also, for example, in the State Bedroom at Newhailes, East Lothian, of c1750. The only decoration apart from the cornice is the frieze of the chimneypiece in the form of a bay leaf garland and although this is not detailed on the drawings the overall form of the chimneypiece is very similar to that which survives.

My Lord's Dressing Room is identical to the Family Bed Chamber except for the fact that all the walls are panelled because there is no requirement to provide a large bed for a dressing room, although the positioning of the doors on the east elevation does appear to allow for a large piece of furniture, possibly a bookcase

in the absence of a dedicated Library. These doors lead to a closet and the Charter Room. The design of the chimneypiece is the only variation from the room elevations; its scroll bracketed design is a much simplified version of the Drawing Room chimneypiece in timber.

The lack of a Library is one of the most obvious omissions in the planning of the principal apartments of Dumfries House. However John Adam addressed this in 1763 when he supplied book presses and iron boxes for the Earl's 'Library'.[55] This included 57 yards of shelving and ten white iron boxes at a total cost of £43 8s 5d. The location of these book presses has not been established with certainty but the inclusion of iron boxes for papers and documents suggests that they may relate to the fitting out of the Earl's Charter Room off his Dressing Room, the term Library perhaps referring to the Earl's books rather than to a specific room. A reference in a memorandum from John Adam for 1760–1 refers to fittings for 'my Lord's

Fig 3.34 My Lord's Dressing Room was Lord Dumfries' private business room. HES 2010 DP083226

Fig 3.33 The Family Bedroom is directly accessible from the North Parlour. HES 2007 SC1104268

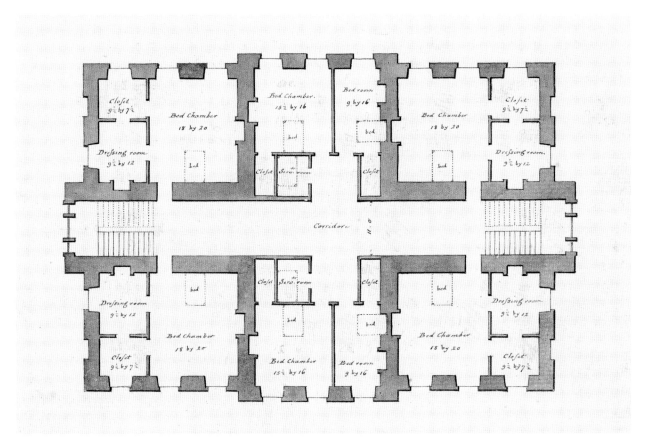

garret.'[56] This room in the garret or the top floor of the house could have been fitted out as a Library although this seems unlikely since there is no mention of it in any of the subsequent inventories.

The four main bedroom suites on the attic floor were finished in the same style as the Family Bed Chamber on the floor below. These four rooms have a plaster badge above their landing doors; above the Blue Bedroom is a crescent moon surrounded by the motto of the Order of the Garter, 'Honi soit qui mal y pense', the same motto repeated around a rose over the door to the north-east bedroom. The two bedrooms in the southern corners have the motto of Order of the Thistle around a thistle above the south-west bedroom door and its badge above the south-east door. Stylistically there is nothing to suggest that these badges are not original. They stress Lord Dumfries' allegiance to the union of Scotland and England by celebrating both chivalric orders. The bedrooms have firr deal floors with wainscot panelling to the cornice and plain coved plaster ceilings. As in the Family Bed Chamber, the panelling is flat where the bed was placed. The only variation between the suites is the form of the chimneypiece. Only 'One of the bed chambers in the Attick Story' is depicted in the room elevations, perhaps unsurprisingly this is the Blue or Best Bedroom, along with one dressing room. The drawing, which has been damaged so that the entrance door from the landing has been lost, illustrates a simple moulded chimneypiece but a far more elaborate one in timber was installed, apparently from the start. The

Fig 3.35 *Contract drawing of the Bedroom Floor, 1754.*
Bute Archives DHP/1/6

Fig 3.36 *The bedrooms are all accessed from a central corridor.*
HES 2007 SC1104215

chimneypieces are similar to those designed by John Adam for Banff Castle (1749–52). The south-west bedroom has a marble chimneypiece which appears to have been inserted later but the other two corner bedrooms have original decorative timber mantles surrounding stone chimneypieces with marble slips. According to the Contract, the Earl was responsible for these decorative items and the marble slips while the Adam brothers were responsible for supplying the freestone chimneypiece to which the marble slips and timber were applied.

One of the few references to the fitting out of these bedrooms is found in a letter from the Earl to Lord Loudoun dated 19 June 1758 in which he

Fig 3.38 The simple architecture of the Southeast Bedroom with its stone fireplace and timber mantlepiece. HES 2007 DP033788

Fig 3.37 The Northwest or Best Bedroom was reserved for important guests and contained the magnificent Bed and tapestry overmantle made by Thomas Chippendale. HES 1956 SC133129]

comments that the damask for the curtains will soon be required because the bed chambers and ceilings are 'far advanced'.[57] He was impatient at the delay in finishing the rooms because, 'all the house has been sashed near a twelve month ago'. There is little documentary evidence about the fitting out of the central four bedrooms which, like the other bedrooms, have wainscoted walls, plain coved ceilings and simple stone chimneypieces with timber mantles. The chimneypieces in these rooms are similar to the one shown in the bedroom elevation. The four bedrooms with adjacent closets in the entresol were fitted out very simply with freestone chimneypieces, firr deal floors and wainscoted walls; they were originally intended as bachelor bedrooms and survive largely unaltered although later used as upper servants' rooms.

Service Accommodation

Despite the fact that it is the ground floor which has been altered the most out of any area of the House, the logic of the original plan form survives. As a working environment, the service areas of country houses underwent dramatic alterations as technology advanced but as a relatively modestly scaled country house, Dumfries House avoided what were often massive 19th century extensions that created numerous extra rooms devoted to particular activities. The service accommodation has been changed and altered gradually and at regular intervals but most of the original service rooms are easily recognisable: although the design set of room elevations does not include any of the service rooms, enough survives to enable a good understanding of these original spaces.

The Contract drawings give us a detailed insight into how this important part of the house worked. The ground floor was planned as the servants' domain (Plan 3) with particular functions grouped in different areas and linked by a vaulted corridor. These functions were divided logically into different departments with the cooking and serving functions to the east and the cleaning and other household duties to the west. At the centre of the north front was the 'Second Table Room' which later became known as the Steward's Room; this was where the senior staff ate their meals. Adjacent to the east is what was called the 'latter meat room' where the lower servants ate. It later became known as the servants' hall and is shown with two fitted beds. At the foot of the east stairs was the vaulted 'My Lords Vally's room' which was directly beneath the stone floored charter room. The valet was positioned with easy access to his master's dressing room and closet on

Fig 3.40 The Wine Cellar. HES 2007 SC1104204

the floor above. The Butler's Room, a Pantry and the Porter's Lodge were located at the south-east corner where the Porters Lodge had a good view of anyone arriving at the front door. The Kitchen is still in its original position in the east pavilion. It was fitted with a large chimneypiece, a three-burner charcoal warming stove[58] and an oven. Next door was a scullery, Cook's Room and Cook's Pantry with a large larder behind. Opening off the passage north of the Kitchen were the Bake House and the Brew House with an ale store adjacent. The east courtyard, named the 'Back Court' on the plan, had an ash yard and a coal yard.

The central part of the main block contained the capacious wine and beer cellars the stone vaults of which support the stone flagged floor of the Entrance Hall above. To the west of the Second Table Room was the Housekeeper's room with a large store room and closet off, which still survives. The Housekeeper was in charge of the female members of staff whilst the Steward looked after the men. At the foot of the west stair was 'My lady's woman's room' with closet. She, like the valet, is located directly below her mistress' dressing room and closet. A nursery with four fitted beds was originally located at the south-west corner of the main block with two closets, but was not occupied during the 5th Earl's time, his only child having died before the house was begun.

The ground floor of the west pavilion contained the Laundry and a 'womans house', a combined work room and bedroom for the women servants complete with two fitted beds. The Laundry was where the smaller and personal items were laundered whilst the bigger items were dealt with in the separate Wash House. To the north was the Milk House and 'scullery for the milk house' where butter and cheese were made from the milk being supplied by the Mains Farm. Off the west courtyard was a poultry house and ash and coal yards. The servants' bedrooms were on the first floors of both pavilions, the plans do not specify the gender

Fig 3.39 The vaulted central corridor links the different functions carried out on the lowest floor. HES 2007 DP033762

separation of the accommodation but this can be inferred from the division of activities between each pavilion, the west for females and the east for males. The segregation of servants' sleeping arrangements was, however, not as strictly observed as in the 19th century with its obsession with propriety.[59] In the small back court of each pavilion was a three-seat 'Necessary House'; there were no similar facilities in the main block.

The fitting out of the servants' accommodation presented an opportunity to reuse materials salvaged from Leifnorris House. These rooms were not for display and would never be seen by most people and so were an obvious area in which to economise in terms of the fittings. In 1762 John Adam presented the account for '281 days of a wright taking down old lyning & fitting it up for surbase lyning in the Housekeepers room, My Ladys womans room, nursery & lyning above the chimneys & mouldings round them'.[60] This makes clear that, although the Earl had moved into his new house in 1760, the fitting out of the interior was still going on. Presumably this work was carried out when the Earl was not in residence, the Housekeeper's Room, for example, being directly below the Family Bed Chamber. Little of the original fitted furniture such as the box beds, deal tables or chairs survives but in the John Adam account for additional wright work 'dealls for tables and shelves in the Milk House' are listed, as is 'fitting up the brewhouse'.[61] In the same account wood from the old house is used make a table in the Second Table Room and to make three presses in the Housekeeper's store room which are still in use.

Paintings and Portraits

Lord Dumfries bought and also commissioned artworks for his new home, some of which contributed to the iconographic programmes created through the interior decoration. The only painting he hung

Fig 3.41 *The Kitchen remains in its original position in the east pavilion. The substantial kitchen range installed in 1923 was still in use in 1993.*
HES 2007 SC1104208

in the Drawing Room was a portrait of Chancellor Hardwicke (Fig 3.42) which was commissioned from Thomas Hudson at a cost £42.00.[62] The choice of subject is perhaps unusual in what is usually regarded as a feminine room but Lord Dumfries was a widower when he decided on the subject, the choice of which made clear his political views.[63] Hardwicke carried out a major reform in 1746 which swept away the feudal power surviving in Scotland in the form of private heritable jurisdictions in the hands of the landed gentry. This was all recent history when Lord Dumfries commissioned the portrait as a demonstration of his allegiance to the Hanoverian Dynasty and his support for a United Kingdom in which Scotland was considered to be North Britain. For the 5th Earl, the Drawing Room was therefore a room of parade where he could show off his political affiliations.

In his Memorandum of November 1755,[64] Lord Dumfries laid down what was required for the completion of the decoration and furnishing of the Dining Room: 'The space between the west doors of the dining room over the sideboard will admit of a Glass anything under 5ft 3in broad by 7ft 6in high including the utmost projection of the frame'; this was eventually the site chosen for the portrait of the Earl's second wife by Thomas Hudson, 1763.[65] Hudson regarded it as one of his best works, writing 'I really think I have never made so good a picture.'[66] At £64 10s 0d, it was the most expensive picture that Lord Dumfries bought for the House. The acquisition of portraits enabled him to celebrate his connections and status. In 1745 he had bought portraits of Lord Stair and Lord Primrose from Alexander Clerk[67] and five years later he bought from Allan Ramsay 'a copy of Lady Loudon's picture by me'.[68] By the time that the new house was being built, more decorative items were being sought such as seven cartoons by Thornhill after Raphael.[69] The commission to John Medina, an Edinburgh painter, in 1758 was perhaps more complex involving new paintings and the alteration of existing works.[70] The first was a portrait of the Admirable James Crichton (1560–82), who was believed by the Earl to be a relative of his mother. The remaining portion of Medina's work appears to have been the aggrandisement of existing portraits; the portrait of the Duke of Bedford receives the Order of the Garter and the Earl of Portmore the Thistle whilst a dress is added to another portrait of him as a boy. This commission reflects Lord Dumfries' desire to be seen as equal to his fellow peers. The portraits he acquired were of living members of the Establishment of North Britain with the honourable exception of the Admirable Crichton. The following year, Medina received another commission for cleaning and varnishing ten pictures, presumably so that they could be hung in the new house.[71] In 1759, Lord Dumfries bought another picture of himself by Thomas Hudson.[72] He also bought pictures from London salerooms; the Jacopo Bassano painting of *Laban and his Flock* in the Dining Room (Fig 4.39) was acquired from the sale of John de Pesters collection on 1 April 1756.[73] The decoration of the east wall of the Dining Room must already have been set, if not completed, by this time since William Mathie had to be employed in 1759 to add an extra frame in order that the space left in the elaborately carved panelling around it was filled.

The Countess of Northumberland Visits

In 1760, the Countess of Northumberland visited the Earl and recorded their convivial evening in her diary, 'Went with Lord Dumfr to see his Paraphenalia. After Dinner we spent the Evening in very agreeable Conversation. Ld Dumfries very drunk, talk'd of being frisky and rummish.' She also wrote on 15 October 1762 that Lord Dumfries had married Anne Duff on 19 June 1762 and that 'Colonel Montgomery expell'd fr. Dumfries House for being behind the window curtain with the Countess.'[74] She also described in detail how the House looked and functioned when newly completed.[75]

> The inside of the House is handsome thoroughly convenient & furnish'd with great Elegance & Expence. By a flight of steps you enter the Hall which is a large handsome room neatly fitted up. On the right is the eating room stucco with pictures himself at whole length over the Chimney a fine Chaillot[76] fire screen [and a] Devonshire Carpet. On the left is a Drawing Room hung with charming Tapestry, Blue Damask Settees & Chairs Ld Hardwick at full length over a very fine Marble Chimney piece a Chaillot & one large Japan Screen a very handsome Devon carpet cost £80. At back of Hall thro Columns runs a long gallery with a Stair case at each end[77] & in front a large eating Room[78] on one side Family Bedchamber furnishd with Work wth a case of fine China [Chippendale's rosewood bookcase], Dressing Room closet, Servts Room in the side a Bedchamber. Lds Dressg Room Closet & up stairs 6 bedchambrs hung and furnish'd with Blue, Green, Crimson & yellow damask & Chintz a worked Bed all rooms have night closets Dressing Rooms to them in the latter of wch all the Bedchambrs & Dressing Rooms are Chaillot Screens & Exeter Carpets there is also in this floor 2 spare Dressing Rooms and 2 Servts Bedchambrs. In the entersole are 4 bedchambrs & Dressing Rooms.

The Countess of Northumberland's description shows how rich and vibrantly coloured the interior furnishings were from the start. The blue, green, crimson, yellow and chintz fabrics used in the different

Fig 3.42 The portrait of Chancellor Hardwicke was commissioned by the 5th Earl from Thomas Hudson in 1757 to hang in pride of place above the Drawing Room chimneypiece. Great Steward of Scotland's Dumfries House Trust

bedrooms must have made a dramatic statement. The contrast between the chaste and austere exterior and the exuberant and luxurious interior was expressed by Lord Dumfries' fellow Scottish peer, the Earl of Marchmont, who when asked why he had chosen a harled exterior for his smart new house quipped that he intended 'to live in the inside of [his] house and not on the outside'.[79] The Countess was well aware of the work of Robert Adam before she arrived at Dumfries House having, with her husband, commissioned him to redesign the interiors of Syon House from 1760. He was also to work for them at both Alnwick Castle, Northumberland, and Northumberland House in London.[80] The Countess, who was clearly highly attuned to current fashions, found Dumfries House 'extreamly handsome'.

Thus an elegant, well equipped house furnished in the latest style was created. Getting it ready for habitation was at times a fraught endeavour and although it was not entirely finished, Lord Dumfries moved in in the spring of 1760. He had created a modern interior with little reference to his personal family history in that the only Crichton family portrait is of the Admirable Crichton, and the Dalrymples were only represented in three portraits. It is the Earl and his second Countess who take pride of place in the Dining Room. Dumfries House was very much of the moment, designed to celebrate Lord Dumfries' own

Fig 3.43 A chair from the Drawing Room suite covered in a recreation of its original blue damask photographed against the tapestry which originally hung in the Drawing Room to illustrate the vibrancy of its original decorative scheme. HES 2013 DP151628

achievements, his close relationship with his peers and his elevation to the Order of the Thistle, rather than his mother's family from whom he inherited both his title and his estates.

The interior of Dumfries House is rightly considered one of the most accomplished of its time in Scotland. The plasterwork in the Drawing Room is justly regarded as one of the high points of Rococo design whereas the Dining Room ceiling shows the tentative steps towards the more neoclassical style championed by Robert Adam on his return from Rome. Whilst the interior was being completed, Lord Dumfries was sourcing the furniture, upholstery, carpets and pictures with which to decorate his new home; it is these acquisitions which have played such an important part in the later history of the house.

1   Quotation from unpublished diary of Countess of Northumberland written about her visit in 1760. Original in Alnwick Castle,Northumberland transcript at Dumfries House.

2   The reference to the tapestries having been gifted to the 2nd Earl of Stair by Louis XVI when Stair was Ambassador in Paris appears to stem from a description of the house in the *New Statistical Account of Scotland* 1845, Vol.5, 482, but no evidence that they were a gift has come to light. The 5th Earl appears to have bought them from his uncle before 1747 but there are no references to them hanging in Leifnorris. The tapestries did not pass to the Earl of Dumfries' younger brother James, who became the 3rd Earl of Stair in 1747.

3   Samuel Smith bill for works May to September 1756, first item on the list 'Mending and cleaning the Tapestry £1.10/-'. Bute Archives DU5/8

4   November Memorandum of 5th Earl of Dumfries. Bute Archives DU 5/20

5   Bute Archives LO/2/102/25

6   Mr Robertson was the estate factor and Mr Neilson was the overseer of the Earl's interests in the building process. Bute Archives LO/2/105/3

7   Bute Archives LO 2/113

8   Bute Archives DU5/33/11

9   'The Rt Hon the Earl of Dumfries and Stair John Adam Architect for additional wright work done in & about Dumfries House in the years 1760 & 1761 not included in former accompts.' Bute Archives DU/5/30/13

10 Bute Archives DU5/30/12

11 Bute Archives DHP3/1–7

12 The closest known parallel to this set of room elevations is a set produced by James Gibbs in the 1720s for Kelmarsh Hall, Northamptonshire. These detail the ceiling plasterwork and are annotated to give information about the proposed construction of the rooms, unlike the Dumfries House set which do not provide this level of detail and which are seemingly intended more for the purpose of assisting with fitting out and furnishing the spaces. RIBA Drawings Collection Catalogue G p44.

13 Adam 1980, plate 41

14 *Ibid*, plate 20

15 Bute Archives GD18/4836

16 Bute Archives DU5/20, 4

17 One of the finest examples of which is Keddleston Hall, Derbyshire, begun in 1759, where the hall leads straight through into the saloon.

18 'No-one attacks me with impunity.'

19 Information from the Ross Herald 'It's one of these interesting anomalies! I suspect that the craftsman may have been confused by the cross (of St George) shown in connection with the Order of the Garter.' Email to the author from Lord Lyon's Office. 23 June 2010

20 There is a schematic image on Smith's estate plan of 1756. Bute Archives DHP 22

21 See Introduction, notes 1 and 2

22 Conversation with A Martindale June 2013

23 'Andrew Hunter remitted to George Mercer by Cavendish Square, the condition of his bill four chimneys marble and four marble tables guilt frames and his receipt in full of all demands.' Lord Dumfries Memorandum Book Accounts in London and Scotland 1756–63, September 1758. Bute Archives DU/5/34/6–7

24 In 1748 John Adam noted, 'Dove, Jaspar, vein'd/ The Jasper to be paid for at the Dimensions Mr Mercer is to produce/ at 50 sh pr ft/5ft 6″ to be discompted for/ prompt payment' John Adam sketchbook, 1748, p.3. RIBA/British Architectural Library Drawings and Manuscripts Collection SE16/3

25 Stillman 1988, 90, 129

26 Although it is not a direct copy the influence of, for example Ware's, plates 2 and 36 can be seen. *Dumfries House Conservation Plan*, Simpson and Brown 2008, 58

27 George Mercer, London, 18 August 1757. 'The Drawing Room chimneypiece agreed at £130;The Dining Room chimneypiece agreed at £95; The four tables with carved frames £88; The packing cases £13.1.3; Total £326.1.3.' Lord Dumfries Memorandum Book Accounts in London and Scotland 1756–63, September 1758. Bute Archives DU/5/20

28 See Note 23 above

29 The Drawing Room created by John Adam at Arniston, Midlothian, where he was completing his father's building to a different design, has a similar, also unattributed, Rococo ceiling to the Dumfries House Drawing Room but lacks its dynamism.

30 'Fortunately Robert [Adam] was allowed more scope for the expression of his talents in the interior where he repeated on a smaller and perhaps more congenial scale the Rococo style of decoration employed at Hopetoun. The ceilings at Dumfries House, especially that of the Drawing Room, are among the finest of their kind in Britain and display the mastery so quickly attained by Robert in this sophisticated style.' Fleming 1962, 96

31 Robert refers to Mr Charteris in a letter to his mother dated 11 August 1754. NRS GD/18/4744

32 Robert Adam writing to his sister Miss Peggy Adam from Rome, 27 March 1756. NRA GD18/4804

33 'He [Lord Dumfries] employed an admirable plasterer, named Clayton' on the similarity with the 'two noble rooms at Blair Atholl'. Stirling Maxwell 1938, 193. Fleming 1962

34 Description of the plasterwork in St Andrews Parish Church. Williamson, Riches and Higgs 1990, 453

35 The Dining and Drawing Rooms are now respectively the Yellow and Red Drawing Rooms.

36 See Fig 1.16 The Saloon at Yester. Dunbar 1972

37 Ian Gow recognises both a Francophile and metropolitan influence but also a certain coarseness in the detail. Gow and Clifford 1995, 47

38 *Ibid*. The Duff House Vestibule ceiling is the only known work by David Crooks.

39 The Simpson and Brown conservation plan suggests Robinson as a contender. Simpson and Brown 2008

40 A remarkable quantity of these survive. Bute Archives DU/5/34/5

41 Information from William Kay and Bute Archives DU/5/61–4

42 Copies of drawings in Sir John Soane's Museum in HES, AYD/71/5–6

43 Dumfries House Contract, 1754, 5 Bute Archives DU 5/20

44 *Ibid*, 7

45 *Ibid*, 17

46 Leach 1988, 147

47 Simpson and Brown, 2008

48 Hewlings 1988, 166–70

49 Letter from John Adam to James Adam; see Chapter 2, 35 NRS GD18/4836

50 George Mercer, London, 18 August 1757. 'The Drawing Room chimneypiece agreed at £130. The Dining Room chimneypiece agreed at £95. The four tables with carved frames £88. The packing cases £13.1.3. Total £326.1.3.' Bute Archives DU/5/34/6–7.

51 Admiral Boscawen had commissioned a new house at Hatchlands from Stiff Leadbetter in 1756 which was roofed in 1757 and commissioned Robert Adam to fit up the interiors soon after his arrival in London in January 1758. Lord Curzon in turn had commissioned a new house at Kedleston from Mathew Brettingham but in December 1758 he met Robert Adam and commissioned him to radically alter the house. Hatchlands and Kedleston Guidebooks, National Trust

52 Harris 2001 plate 27, 26

53 This highly accomplished and broadly symmetrical design was restored in 2011 when the later gilding was painted out and the original balance restored.

54 Dumfries House Contract, 1754, 5 Bute Archives DU 5/20

55 Bute Archives DU/5/30/17

56 '1 iron lock with brass handles for my Lord's garret' and 'levelling standarling and lathing my Lord's garret'. Bute Archives DU/5/30/18

57 Bute Archives LO/2/105/1

58 Argrennan House, Dumfries and Galloway, HES Threatened Buildings Survey photograph shows a charcoal stove of a similar size and form. HES, E54420 CN

59 Girouard 1978, 206

60 'The Rt Hon the Earl of Dumfries and Stair John Adam Architect for additional wright work done in & about Dumfries House in the years 1760 & 1761 not included in former accompts.' Bute Archives DU/5/30/13

61 Bute Archives DU/5/30/13

62 'Thomas Hudson; A whole length portrait of Lord Hardwick £42.00. Ditto Lord Dumfries £42.00, A case to ditto £1.2-, Total 85.2.0.' February 1759. Bute Archives DU/5/33/6

63 After the Battle of Culloden on 16 April 1746, Hardwicke presided at the trial of the Scottish Jacobite peers and although he was judicially impartial he was not generous and has been held partly responsible for the severity of sentencing, and especially for the executions of Charles Radclyffe and Archibald Cameron of Locheil. Lochiel was the last Jacobite to be executed, on 7 June 1753.

64 Bute Archives November Memorandum of 5th Earl of Dumfries

65 Now in the Royal Albert Museum and Gallery, Exeter.

66 Bute Archives DU5/33/8

67 Receipt from Alexander Clerk 30 July 1745 for £18.18.0 for two pictures of Lord Stair and Lord Primrose. Bute Archives DU/5/33/1

68 Discharge note from Allan Ramsay 13 February 1750 for 'a copy of Lady Loudon's picture by me' (Countess of Loudoun) £16.6.0. Bute Archives DU/5/33/2

69 'Copies after Raphael of the seven cartoons by Sir James Thornhill £33.12–' 7 May 1756. Bute Archives DU/5/33/3

70 John Medina, painter Edinburgh 15 May 1758, 'To a ¾ picture of Admirable Creighton; To the painting of the order of the garter on the Duke of Bedfords picture; To painting the order of the Thistle on Earl of Portmore's picture; To painting a dress to the Earl of Portmore when a boy; Total £8.8-' Bute Archives DU/5/33/4

71 Further bill from John Medina for cleaning and varnishing 10 pictures total £7- signed Leifnorris 8 June 1759. Bute Archives DU/5/33/5

72 Thomas Hudson, 13 April 1759 'A ¾ picture of himself and a gold frame £16.11.6'. The picture was later hung in the Business Room. Bute Archives DU5/33/7

73 Catalogue of sale of the pictures of John de Pesters 1 April 1756: 'A Market by G Bassano £63.00; An Agate Marble bust of Bacchus £4.4-.' Bute Archives DU5/33/10a

74 Greig 1926, 25 n.3

75 Extract from unpublished diary of Countess of Northumberland written about her visit in 1760. Original in Alnwick Castle, Northumberland transcript at Dumfries House.

76 Chaillot is a district of Paris where the Gobelin Factory was based until 1826; the term presumably suggests tapestry covered.

77 This is the only known description of the unique principal floor gallery with its staircase at either end.

78 The North Parlour appears to have been used as the family dining room as soon as the House was completed.

79 Macaulay 1987, 166

80 Harris 2001, 65–6

Chapter 4: Furnishing the House 1754–1760
Dr Sebastian Pryke

furnish'd with great elegance and Expence

Countess of Northumberland, 1760[1]

The many remarkable aspects of the history of Dumfries House have undoubtedly been magnified by the prism of privacy which the family has consistently cast over the House. The descendants of the 5th Earl of Dumfries seem always to have appreciated the House's beauty and significance and have immaculately maintained it in a traditional manner. In the 20th century it became a truism that owners of historic country houses invariably believed that their Chippendale-style furniture was actually made by the man himself but the reality was that few were correct in this belief. Dumfries House was an exception. It was furnished by Thomas Chippendale, in his inimitable style, as the family well knew. However, until 1969, when Christopher Gilbert published a comprehensive paper about Chippendale's commission in the *Burlington*, the collection was virtually unknown and unpublished. Intriguingly, after that modest blaze of publicity it then returned to obscurity as the private home of the late Dowager Marchioness of Bute, widow of the 5th Marquess. Christopher Gilbert confidently asserted of Chippendale's commission at Dumfries House that, 'this collection unquestionably forms the outstanding monument to his early Rococo phase,'[2] and in his opinion this was his greatest moment.

An extraordinary quantity of the original furnishings purchased by the Earl of Dumfries for his new house are still *in situ* and can be identified

Fig 4.1 *Detail of the Order of the Thistle cresting on a pier glass for one of the principal Bed Chambers carved by William Mathie in 1759.*
Christie's/Great Steward of Scotland's Dumfries House Trust

Fig 4.2 *Detail of the ho-ho bird on one of the pair of girandoles made by Thomas Chippendale for the Dining Room in 1759.*
Christie's/Great Steward of Scotland's Dumfries House Trust

down to the most humble pieces thanks to the comprehensive accounts which survive for virtually every aspect of this commission.[3] These cover not only the furniture from London made by Thomas Chippendale, but also that from Edinburgh made by Francis Brodie, Alexander Peter and William Mathie, as well as ironmongery, upholstery, carpets, silver and glassware from numerous other London and Edinburgh tradesmen. Whereas Chippendale's furniture is artistically exceptional, these collections of Scottish furnishings are historically exceptional. The accounts are complemented by lively letters to and from Lord Dumfries which shine a unique light on the years during which he furnished his house and the nature of this fascinating patronage.

In Scotland there is nowhere to compare with Dumfries House and indeed there are only a handful of other houses in which documented pieces of Scottish furniture of this period survive. At Blair Castle, Perthshire, there is a considerable quantity of mid 18th century furniture supplied by numerous London craftsmen, as well as pieces by George Sandeman of Perth, but these are individual pieces, and there is no sense of a commissioning process as such.[4] Only at Hopetoun House, West Lothian, is there anything remotely equivalent, but for all its interest the accounts do not give a complete picture, and the surviving identifiable pieces are far fewer, and of lesser quality than at Dumfries House. The 2nd Earl of Hopetoun's interest was building on a magnificent scale[5] and when it came to the furnishings his priority was to create an acceptable effect for the minimum cost. Unlike Lord Hopetoun, Lord Dumfries had rather more sophisticated taste and higher aspirations when it came to furnishing his house, although he still had to be mindful of his expenditure.

As has been discussed in Chapters 1 and 2, Lord Dumfries consulted with various friends and arbiters of taste when it came to the designs of his new house and it is instructive to look at how some of these patrons furnished their own homes. A decade earlier Lord Glenorchy, a diplomat based in England and heir of the Earl of Breadalbane, had felt the need to restore and furnish his apartments at Holyroodhouse in Edinburgh and the family castle (extended by William Adam) at Taymouth, Perthshire. He found the process extremely frustrating and was driven to taking 'a resolution of not laying out a sixpence in the Nation [Scotland] but have all from London',[6] later exclaiming that 'all the Tradesmen are alike in this Countrey, and I'm sure all that I ever had made at Edinr is abominable'

Fig 4.3 Design for the pair of pier glasses in the Parlour, by Thomas Chippendale, published as Plate CLXVIII in his Gentleman and Cabinet Maker's Director *(1762). Christie's/Great Steward of Scotland's Dumfries House Trust*

and repeating his vow to spend what 'little money' he does with 'people who deserve it' in London.[7] In spite of these angry and disillusioned words his personal account books show that he did continually use Edinburgh tradesmen, notably the upholsterers John Schaw and James Caddell, and the cabinet makers Alexander Peter and Francis Brodie both of whom Lord Dumfries turned to when he required furniture.

At Dumfries House the best bed and carved work, particularly pier glasses, were acquired from London, as well as the best quality fabrics and carpets, and this was common at the time. Thus at Hopetoun House the

Fig 4.4 Overmantle mirror made by Francis Brodie, most likely for Lord Dumfries' house in Edinburgh. Christie's/Great Steward of Scotland's Dumfries House Trust

Red Drawing Room pier glasses were made in London by 'a very Eminent Carver and Gilder',[8] and the State Bed was acquired from the London cabinet maker Samuel Norman although, and this is a measure of Lord Hopetoun's parsimony, it was second hand having been purchased from an auction.[9] Unlike Lord Dumfries however, Lord Hopetoun retained James Cullen, an upholsterer and entrepreneur whose eventful career spanned the country from London to Edinburgh, to supervise the entire furnishing of the house over almost two decades. These two collections between them contain virtually all the known documented Scottish furniture of this period.

Fig 4.5 View of the Parlour showing Chippendale's pier glasses and pelmets and one of the pair of card tables and corresponding elbow chairs from the Drawing Room suite he supplied, as well as the chandelier probably bought from Maydwell and Windle in 1759. HES 2010 DP083213

James Cullen was instrumental in coordinating an elite cooperative of cabinet makers and upholsterers in Edinburgh, including Alexander Peter, who was to make so much furniture for Lord Dumfries, into a firm called the Edinburgh Upholstery Company. This company supplied almost four hundred pounds' worth of furniture and upholstery to Hopetoun between 1755 and 1759, exactly the period during which Dumfries House was furnished. The story was similar at Arniston, Midlothian, another William Adam house completed by his sons, where the best pier glasses were made by James Livingston,[10] and at Inveraray, Argyll. The twist at Hopetoun, and at other houses such as Yester, East Lothian, however, was that locally meant not only from Edinburgh but also from the house's estate itself, more of which later.

When buying furniture for his homes Lord Dumfries first turned to Francis Brodie, a cabinet maker William Adam had described as 'the best man in town'.[11] Brodie's first known account for furniture for Lord Dumfries is dated 9 May 1746 and is for two walnut overmantle mirrors and a dressing glass, which can still be identified at Dumfries House and which

Fig 4.6 One of the 22 surviving dining chairs made by Alexander Peter in 1759 for £36; this one showing the original seat covers presumably supplied by Thomas Moore. Christie's/Great Steward of Scotland's Dumfries House Trust

complement the fine, similarly proportioned, giltwood overmantle (Fig 4.4) from 1753, the walnut and parcel gilt mirror, and corner china cabinet and Lady's Closet (Fig 4.12) there.[12] These items were presumably made for Lord Dumfries' Edinburgh house, just yards from Brodie's home and workshops in Cullen's Close (later, and still, known as Brodie's Close) on the Lawnmarket; they may, however, have been made for Leifnorris, which would perhaps better explain their survival at Dumfries House. If so, they would be virtually the only pieces of furniture transferred by Lord Dumfries from his old house to the new one, and must be considered significant on that basis.

Brodie is an exceptional figure in the context of 18th century Scottish tradesmen, not only for the amount of biographical information which it is possible to piece together but also for the details of his life and work. The latter has no doubt contributed to the former, helped by a healthy dose of public interest aroused by the public hanging of his infamous son William Brodie, Deacon of the Wrights at the time of his death and consequently immortalised as Deacon Brodie.

Francis Brodie was born on the 24 June 1708, the eldest son of Ludovick Brodie of Whytfield, a Writer to the Signet, and Hellen Grant. In the words of a contemporary, he:

was a gentleman who was much respected; he was from a branch of a good family in the North of Scotland. He carried on the business of a Wright, Cabinet Maker and Upholsterer, to a very considerable extent, and was employed by some of the best families in this part of the kingdom.[13]

First, however, he had to train, and on 30 June 1725 he was registered as an apprentice with John Antonius. Brodie served a long apprenticeship of ten years, and on 1 November 1735 was appointed to make,

a machogany Desk with drawers below the same, and to draw the draught of a press of the Corinthian order after Palladio.[14]

Within a year he had four journeymen working for him and his first known account is dated March 1737.[15] A measure of his ambition is that over the next four years he employed a further nineteen journeymen.[16] Before Brodie's first child William was born in October of 1741 he had established a new workshop, wareroom and, presumably, home in the 'Second Close above the Old Bank, Lawnmarket'. This close was also known as Cullen's Close, as Lord Cullen (the uncle of both Brodie's wife and his mother) had lived there and this connection presumably facilitated the move. Brodie and his business remained there for the

Fig 4.7 View of the Dining room with Alexander Peter's dining furniture standing on the second of Thomas Whitty's Axminster carpets all supplied in 1759, together with Chippendale's spectacular pair of girandoles (referred to as the 'Grand Girandoles from London' by William Mathie, whose picture frame faces them) flanking the portrait of the 5th Earl of Dumfries. HES DP083179

rest of his life, the whole only being sold after his son's bankruptcy and execution in 1788.

As well as Lord Dumfries, Brodie's known clients included the Dukes of Hamilton, Gordon, Montrose and Argyll, the Earls of Traquair and Stair, Lords Glenorchy, Milton, Arniston and Braco, and the eminent Baronets John and James Clerk.[17] The accounts submitted to Lord Dumfries are on bills which include a remarkable engraving used by Brodie (Fig 4.8). This was certainly unique in a Scottish context; the only known billheads of other cabinet makers and upholsterers are of the fairly standard pattern of a decorative design surrounding a specific piece of furniture, or other emblem, which normally also served as the address and shop sign.[18] The major distinction of Brodie's billhead, especially in the context of its use by a cabinet maker, is the presence of a bust at the centre, inscribed above 'Palladio' and below 'Fras. Brodie'. That the bust represents Palladio and not Brodie becomes clear with the recognition that Brodie's shop was commonly referred to as being at 'Palladio's Head'.

The exact source for this portrait is Sebastiano Ricci's design for the frontispiece of Leoni's 1715 edition of *The Four Books of Palladio*.[19] Did Brodie own a copy of these books, or was he lent

one by a patron? Whatever the circumstances, it was unprecedented at the time for a cabinet maker to associate himself so strongly with the art of architecture. That Brodie chose Palladio as his muse is a good indicator of his knowledge not only of design and fashion but also of the tastes and pretensions of his potential patrons.[20] Thomas Chippendale was content with a chair on his trade card.[21]

Other than the Dumfries House pieces, it has been possible to trace only a very few items of furniture made by Brodie. Two eagle tables can be firmly associated with him, one made for the Duke of Gordon, now at Holyroodhouse,[22] and the one made for Lord Dumfries which shows a distinctly lighter touch (Fig 4.10). He also made one for the Duke of Hamilton,[23] and these three accounts, along with the appearance of such a table on his billhead, clearly mark this type out as something of a speciality.[24] The table at Dumfries House, which has always been in the Entrance Hall, is listed in an account dated 5 August 1753 as 'a Marble Slab supported by an Eagle – guilt in burnished gold'.

This account also lists the 'Corner Cupboard' and 'Chimney Mirror' now at Dumfries House, and especially the 'Lady's Closet'. This is a variant on a bureau writing cabinet and has a lower section in the form of a chest of drawers supported on serpentine bracket feet, surmounted by a cupboard of half the depth with a single door containing a full plate of mirrored glass. The flat section in front folds forward

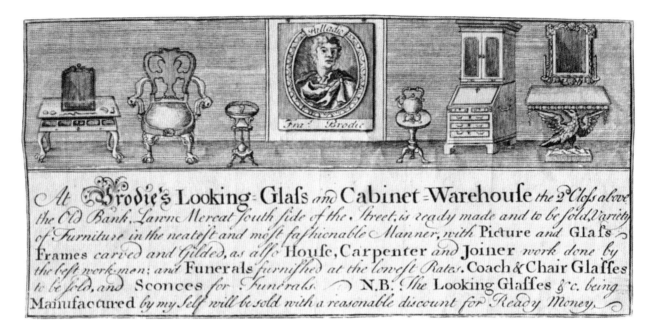

to give a baize lined writing surface. Within, there are two adjustable bookshelves and nine drawers surrounding a small central mirror with a compartment behind it; this was clearly a dressing glass. All the finishes are of very fine padouk and mahogany, and the piece compares favourably with the cabinet depicted on Brodie's billhead. The piece can be identified in the inventory of 1803 residing in the family/Yellow Dressing Room[25] and is a distinctively Scottish form.[26]

Fig 4.9 Insignia of the Knight of the Thistle painted on the hall chairs by John Bonnar at a cost of 3 shillings per chair. Christie's/Great Steward of Scotland's Dumfries House Trust

Fig 4.8 The engraving used by Francis Brodie at the head of his accounts; note the 'Eagle table' similar to the one he made for Lord Dumfries illustrated opposite. Christie's/Great Steward of Scotland's Dumfries House Trust

Although these items predate the building of Dumfries House and must have been made either for Lord Dumfries' Edinburgh house, or his old house of Leifnorris, it is a happy coincidence that they are now in company with Peter's furniture. It is interesting that Lord Dumfries was prepared to buy such fine items from Brodie in the early 1750s, yet does not seem to have purchased any furniture from him for his new house. This does, however, seem to fit a pattern for Brodie's business where, despite having aristocratic patrons, the vast majority of his work appears to have been for their Edinburgh houses.[27]

Brodie was reputed to have had an income of some £900 a year by the time he died,[28] a fairly spectacular sum which speaks for itself, and his status during this period cannot be overestimated. When he died on 1 June 1782, three weeks before his 74th birthday, and mercifully before William's demise, he had been a widower for five years and was survived by only four of his eleven children. His death was reported in the *Edinburgh Advertiser* and the *Caledonian Mercury*, and duly noted in the Brodie Family Bible by his daughter Jean. She included her own epitaph, describing him as 'an honest man, an affectionate husband, an indulgent parent, a faithful friend and a generous master'.[29]

It is a curious coincidence that the cabinet maker Samuel Smith, the first cabinet maker from London to be patronised by Lord Dumfries, had his shop in London at 'The Inigo Jones Head'. His account covers the period between May and September 1756 (Fig 4.13) and in itself this was not a large job,

Fig 4.10 Detail of the Hall with Francis Brodie's 'marble slab supported by an eagle' flanked by two of Alexander Peter's hall chairs HES DP033665

Fig 4.11–12 The 'Lady's Closet' made by Francis Brodie in 1753, with detail showing the distinctive interior. Christie's/Great Steward of Scotland's Dumfries House Trust

although it did involve mending and cleaning Lord Dumfries' Gobelins tapestries, around two of which his Drawing Room was being designed. Smith supplied only one piece of significant furniture, 'a mahogany nettwood Breakfast Table with a draw to ditto £3 3/' (Fig 4.15) which closely resembles a plate in Thomas Chippendale's *Gentleman and Cabinet Maker's Director* pattern book [30] (Fig 4.17). When Chippendale himself came to supply Lord Dumfries with a breakfast table (at a cost of £6 8s) he enclosed the lower shelf 'with Brass Wirework' (Fig 4.38), as he suggests in the notes to the plate, as an alternative to the fretwork panels illustrated, and which Smith used.

A letter from Smith the following year shows that he harboured hopes of a great commission:

Your letter and directions are exceeding plain and shall be particularly observed, there is no explaining things well by small drawings, a sketch for a chair will not be well understood by a small drawing. I presume as your Losp. intends coming to town in the winter it will be time enough to fix on the things you want, and I will take care to be ready with both chairs and Tapestry and drawings for glasses at full size, as I am very desireous of executing your orders in the best manner …

Your furniture, My Lord, must be well considered both as to designe and proportion, that a nobleness and propriety suitable to each appartment may be seen though the whole, in fine I could wish that each piece of furniture may be designed in so proper a manner as to speak the appartment intended for, my idea My Lord is that a drawing room calls for one sort of ornament and a dining room &c for another, and all other rooms suiteable to their use intended, these my Lord are my notions of Finishing and furnishing appartments, which if it should meet with your approbation will be a singular pleasure to My Lord.

Samuel Smith

I herewith send two sketches of Glass frames but to see them at the full size I intend would be the best way of judging of them the expence of such will be about 25 pounds each.[31]

Curiously only one English patron of Smith's is recorded in Beard and Gilbert's *Dictionary of English Furniture Makers* yet five are known in Scotland. For Sir James Dalrymple's new Library at Newhailes he made a 'large mohogoney Library table' for £15 in 1743,[32] and the year before the Duchess of Montrose spent £8 with him.[33] It seems likely that he was also the Smith who sent a great deal of furniture to Scotland for Lord Glenorchy in the 1750s and 1760s,[34] perhaps being one of the 'deserving' English tradesmen who benefited from Lord Glenorchy's disillusionment with Edinburgh. Alas, despite being trusted with the treasured tapestries, and contrary to his expectations, he was not to receive any more work from Lord Dumfries.

In 1755 John Adam was writing to Lord Dumfries regarding the provision of marble tables for Dumfries House, 'Between the windows there should be fine Marble tables with handsome frames … [he then gives the dimensions that they should be] Under these Tables, Jarrs or pieces of China are very proper parts of Ornamental furniture.'[35]

These tables, both the marble tops and the frames, were made in London by George Mercer, a cabinet maker and carver who had worked with the Adams before and who had also supplied the marble chimneypieces for the Drawing and Dining rooms so would have been an obvious choice for this commission. The tables were invoiced on 6 August 1757 as '2 Sienna and 2 Jasper Marble Tables with Carved and Gilt frames, the whole agreed at £88' (Figs 4.14, 4.35). The original estimate allowed only for painting these tables and the subsequent decision to have them gilt cost Lord Dumfries an extra 12

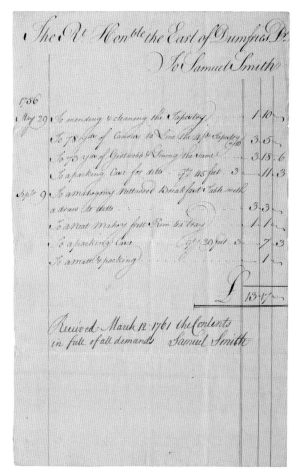

Fig 4.13 Samuel Smith's account of 1756 showing the breakfast table seen in Fig 4.15. Christie's/Great Steward of Scotland's Dumfries House Trust

guineas. This was the sum of Mercer's work at the house.

Meanwhile, the acquisition of suitable furnishing fabric for his Drawing Room appears initially to have exercised the Earl greatly, the damasks of the day being the greatest expression of luxury and taste (as well as wealth, as they were exceptionally expensive) and an elaborate scheme to obtain good quality damask at a reasonable price was outlined to the Earl of Loudoun in letters of June and July 1758.[36] Lord Dumfries desired '500 yards of Genoa damask Crimson, good silk and a good pattern, 300 yards Genoa Damask a good bright green' and hoped that, 'If my lord Loudoun would take the trouble to recommend this commission [the acquisition of the damask] to the Earl of Hume, his lordship will certainly know people in Gibraltar that can faithfully execute the commission at Genoa and the damask could be sent safe to London in some ship of war.' He acknowledges that 'this will be a very great favour,' but this scheme seems never to have come to fruition.

The huge cost of acquiring silk damask for great houses is highlighted in the celebrated correspondence between Lord Dumfries' friend the Earl of Hopetoun and his upholsterer James Cullen

Fig 4.14 The Dining Room with Mathie's pier glass (£28 for the pair of frames – Lord Dumfries supplied the glass) and George Mercer's table (£88 for the pair, including the jasper tops). HES 2010 DP083181

Fig 4.15 Thomas Chippendale's celebrated 'rosewood' (actually padouk) bookcase in the Drawing Room, with Samuel Smith's breakfast table flanked by two of Chippendale's elbow chairs; note also the polescreen made by Chippendale for one of Thomas Moore's 'tapestry' panels, as well as the original Axminster carpet. HES 2010 DP083176

concerning the silk damask for the State Drawing Room at Hopetoun House. Cullen wrote to Lord Hopetoun in 1766 suggesting that 'if you have not furnished yourself with the Crimson silk damask for the grand Appartment I have an Opportunity of getting a quantity for you now much below the market price. there is about 800yds & has been offerd me at 12/6 p. yard. it was brought from abroad by a Nobleman who is going back & at present has not use for it.'[37]

By the summer of 1758, Lord Dumfries' new house was nearing completion, the interior plasterwork had been given time to dry and the pressure was on for the Earl to sort out the furnishings. Dumfries went on to say to Lord Loudon, as if by way of nagging, that the 'damask will be soon needed as the furnishing of the bed chambers and the ceilings are far advanced all the house has been sashed [glazed window sashes installed] near a twelve month ago'.

A month later he is writing to Loudoun again about damask and the problems of getting hold of it, and to emphasise the urgency he writes that 'My Lord Marchmont has a good deal of it at Redbraes,' where his furnishings were described by a contemporary as being in 'high and good taste'. This refers to what is now known as Marchmont, Berwickshire, which was designed for the Earl of Marchmont by Thomas Gibson with advice from Alexander Pope and the Earl of Burlington[38] and therefore could have been regarded as the apogee of contemporary taste. The Earl eventually purchased '366 yards Rich Blue Genoa Damask' £237 18s from Philip Palmer & Son and Robert Fleetwood on Ludgate Hill (total value of invoice £296).[39]

Fig 4.16 Plate CVI of the Director *(1762) with glazing and form closely related to the Dumfries House bookcase.* Christie's/Great Steward of Scotland's Dumfries House Trust

Fig 4.17 Plate LX of the Director *(1762) used by Samuel Smith as the model for his breakfast table (it had originally been published, like all these examples, in 1754).* Christie's/Great Steward of Scotland's Dumfries House Trust

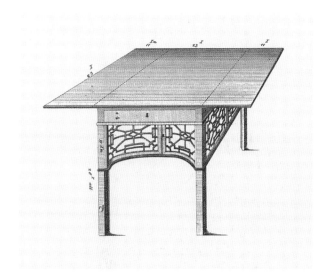

In a subsequent letter to Lord Loudon he further explains his requirements for the house:

> The Drawing room in the new House is to be furnished with tapestrie Hangings which are here. I shall want eighteen Elbow chairs, tapestrie backs and bottoms and two settees to hold three people each, by the two sides of the fire. If Mrs Sinclair would be so good as to see if they can be had at London, I should be greatly obliged to her ladyship; if she finds them to her mind and letes me know the price I shall soon determine myself.

Clearly he eventually decided against tapestry covers for the chairs, the blue being a dramatic choice inspired by his tapestries in the Drawing Room and successfully picking up, as it did, their blue tones. After her visit in 1760 the Countess of Northumberland referred to the Drawing Room being hung with 'charming tapestrie and furnished with blue Damask settees & Chairs'[40] (Fig 3.43).

Eventually Lord Dumfries, no doubt to Lord Loudon's relief, determined to visit London himself and proposed that 'a few weeks should finish my business there, as it is principalie to provide furniture for the new House', confirming that he will 'bring all measures with me for furniture and glasses I may want at London'.[41] It may be that these 'measures' were summarised on the remarkable exploded plans of the House, as discussed in Chapter 3. It was during this historically momentous visit in the spring of 1759 that Lord Dumfries purchased, or commissioned, much of the significant furnishings that remain at Dumfries House. He had had an earlier shopping spree when the House was underway, purchasing heavily via the agent James Crabtree at the auction of the possessions of 'John de Pesters, Esq. of Hanover-Square' on 30 March 1756. These purchases included 'Two fine Dresden swan candlesticks mounted in metal, neatly repaird and gilt £1 19/' and a 'Genuine, Scarce, and Valuable Cabinet of fine China' which contained several fine pieces of Japanese Kakiemon ware, a set of Japanese Imari plates, as well as much Meissen in the Kakiemon style[42] (Fig 4.20). It was also at this sale that Lord Dumfries, clearly not the most selective of collectors, purchased his best decorative picture for the Dining Room, the *Laban and his Flock* by Jacopo Bassano, which still adorns the west wall and whose diminutive scale inspired William Mathie's greatest creation at the House (see below)[43] (Figs 4.38, 4.39).

A group of six bills for fabrics date his stay in London to between February and March 1759; he also purchased a variety of elaborate and beautiful silverware to adorn his new Dining Room from leading London makers. These included four silver gilt figural candlesticks by Paul de Lamerie, salt cellars by David Hemell and a variety of items made by Eliza Godfrey

Fig 4.18 *Lord Dumfries' Grand Orrery which was displayed in the Drawing Room and has been attributed by Christie's to the manufacturer Benjamin Cole and Sons, c1758.* Christie's/Great Steward of Scotland's Dumfries House Trust

including candelabra and salvers. Presumably it was on this trip that Lord Dumfries acquired his spectacular Grand Orrery, which has been attributed to Benjamin Cole & Sons, dated c1758,[44] and which was to be displayed in pride of place in the Drawing Room. (Fig 4.18). It also seems likely that during this time in London he would have visited Crompton & Spinnage, in Charing Cross, from whom he had earlier purchased two Turkey carpets and from whom he commissioned the finest Axminster carpets (to be made by Thomas Whitty) for his two principal reception rooms. Prior to his visit Lord Dumfries had written to Lord Loudon that he wished 'for the drawing room ... the best wilton carpet' adding that 'a good pattern I send you enclosed Mr Adams directions'.[45] These carpets, which survive in the House, are reputed to be the earliest documented Axminster carpets. They were clearly designed by Robert Adam, and their design loosely reflects the pattern of the Drawing Room ceiling. Lord Dumfries did, however, economise, as the carpets are identical (unlike the ceilings in the two rooms), and by copying the same template the weaver was able to save approximately a third of the cost for the second carpet. They were invoiced on 1 September 1759, the first one, a 'Fine Carpet' costing £69 (Fig 4.19). A final shop he may have visited, although the surviving accounts only date from 1763 and 1766 and so do not confirm this, was that of George Maydwell and Richard Windle, Glass Makers to His Majesty, from whom he later bought a pair of crystal chandeliers and candelabra (presumably the '2 chrystal chandeliers on chimneypiece' (Fig 4.22) listed in the Blue Drawing Room in 1803) and a comprehensive set of dining glasses, all still at the House[46] (Fig 4.21).

When he returned from London his agent Andrew Hunter, who seems to have constantly had to worry about his employer's expenditure, wrote to Lord Dumfries, 'I rejoice to see that your Lop has no more sales to attend nor no other things to purchas.'[47]

The other tradesman that Lord Dumfries visited, of course, was Thomas Chippendale. What led him to Chippendale is not known. He was not a subscriber to Chippendale's recently published *Gentleman and Cabinet Maker's Director*, a copy of which has never been recorded in the family's collections,[48] but he would undoubtedly have known of him, or at least of his book. Nevertheless, these were early days in Chippendale's career so the significance of Lord Dumfries' choice should not be underestimated.

Thomas Chippendale needs little introduction. His position as creator and author of the *Gentleman and Cabinet Maker's Director* alone would have guaranteed his place in history, lending his name to a whole era and

Fig 4.19 Axminster carpet made by Thomas Whitty for the Drawing Room to the design of Robert Adam, and supplied to Lord Dumfries by Crompton and Spinnage in 1759 at a cost of £69; it is one of the earliest documented Axminster carpets. Christie's/Great Steward of Scotland's Dumfries House Trust

style of furniture, which travelled across the world and which, many would argue, represented the pinnacle of British cabinet making.[49] However, he is of course also famous for the furniture that he actually made.

Scotland was a place of great importance for Chippendale during the early years of his career. Virtually nothing is known of his earliest work and there is only one tenuous known reference to him carrying out any work prior to publication of the *Director*; it is, however, for the Earl of Burlington, that great arbiter of taste whom Lord Dumfries had naturally consulted regarding the designs of his new house. Chippendale had taken on a Scottish business partner, James Rannie, in 1754, the year the *Director* was published, and there were therefore a disproportionate number of Scottish subscribers for his book. He also had almost exclusively Scottish patrons for the first few years of his career.[50] The *Director* was advertised in the *Caledonian Mercury* in the spring of 1753, at the same time as in papers in London, declaring it would be a

New Book of Designs of Household Furniture in the GOTHIC, CHINESE, and MODERN TASTE.

Publication was announced in May 1754 and advertisements tellingly ended with the note '*N.B. All Sorts of Cabinet and Upholstery Work made by the Author in the neatest and most fashionable Taste, and at the most reasonable Rates.*'

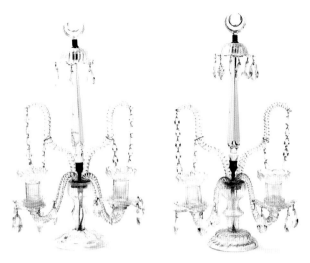

*Fig 4.22 Pair of candelabra probably supplied as part of Lord Dumfries'
purchases from Maydwell and Windle. Visible on the mantlepiece in the
Drawing room (Fig 4.15).* Christie's/Great Steward of Scotland's Dumfries House Trust

The Dumfries House commission, together
with that for much more modest furnishings at
Paxton House, are Chippendale's only substantial
commissions in Scotland but his work can also be
linked to Arniston, Midlothian, and Blair Castle,
Perthshire, for which he supplied minor pieces before
1759, Dalmahoy, West Lothian, for the Earl of Morton
(a subscriber) and for Thomas Mouat in Shetland. He
also, of course, supplied furniture to Scots in London,
notably for Sir William Mansfield, later the Earl of
Mansfield, at Kenwood, and Sir Lawrence Dundas,
who was MP for Edinburgh.

It was not until the 1760s that Chippendale's
career really took off, culminating in the spectacular
sequence of furniture he created for Edwin Lascelles
at Harewood House, so the bulk of the furniture that
we are certain that he made relates to this distinct
second phase of his workshop's output. This furniture
is in the neoclassical taste which had become popular
having been promoted so successfully by Robert
Adam, both architect and cabinet maker moving
on dramatically in stylistic terms from their early
creations at Dumfries House.

The furniture which Lord Dumfries bought from
Chippendale was despatched before the end of May
and so must have been selected in the shop, rather
than being commissioned, with the possible exception
of one or two items. This is the key to the historical
significance of the collection at Dumfries House,
along with the remarkable survival of virtually every
piece insitu and the accounts to accompany them,
because it means that the pieces must be taken to be
representative of Chippendale's stock-in-trade at the
time. Despite the fact that this is the style for which
he is famous, thanks to his published and widely
disseminated designs, furniture from his so called
'Director' period is surprisingly scarce. Of the 50
items Chippendale supplied to Lord Dumfries, three

In the same year, Chippendale moved his family
and workshop to St Martin's Lane, London, joining
the colony of cabinet makers, craftsmen and artists
who lived and worked there in the middle decades
of the 18th century and socialised at the celebrated
Slaughter's Coffee House.

Lord Dumfries' friends the Earl of Hopetoun
and both Francis Charteris of Amisfield and his
wife Mary, were subscribers, as was James Caddell,
an upholsterer in Edinburgh.[51] Robert Dundas of
Arniston and the Scottish carver Thomas Welsh
owned copies (but did not subscribe). There was a
'heavy concentration in the Kingdom of Fife and
counties just south of Edinburgh, with a smaller
contingent from around Aberdeen', in part no doubt
attributable to the local booksellers Hamilton and
Balfour, and perhaps to James Rannie's brother
Thomas, a wine merchant in Edinburgh (and supplier
to Lord Dumfries as well as being his neighbour
on Castlehill). This success is reflected in the fact
that four of Chippendale's first five known patrons
subsequent to the *Director*'s publication lived in
Scotland.

*Fig 4.20 The Parlour with Chippendale's pier glass and window pelmets;
note the Meissen ornaments on the chimneypiece bought in 1756.*
John Batty/NTS 1994

follow plates in the *Director* precisely (Fig 4.28 – 4.29) and a further nine are related to published designs. This correlation is unique amongst his surviving commissions.

Chippendale & Rannie to Ld Dumfries at Liefnorris

London 29 May 1759

My Lord

We wrote to you last Post to inform you that we had ship'd your goods on board the Diligence which saild on Sunday morning early but we have not heard wheither the ship is gone from the Nore yet. As we have pack'd the Damk furniture in glew'd case to prevent any damage by Water we would beg of your Lordship to order the Carriages to have such covering as will turn rain lest they show'd meet it upon the Road. The contents of each case wt proper directions are giv'n to ye Person who goes to put up the furniture. We pay him a Guinea a Week & we make no doubt but he will acquit himself wt your Lordships approbation.

We have insured £700 which we hope is enough as we don't think the Danger is great.[52] (Fig 4.24)

Chippendale supplied the most prominent pieces for the House, including the traditional centrepiece of any grand house, the best guest bed intended for the Blue Bedroom on the first floor, 'To a large mahogany … Bedstead wt a Dome top ornamented in the Inside the feetposts fluted & a Palmbranch twisting round & carv'd Capitals £38'[53] (Fig 4.28).

The bed was included as Plate XXXIX of the third edition of the *Director* which was published in 1762, with the assertion that 'models have been made for the Earls of Dumfries and Morton' (Fig 4.29). Chippendale also supplied six 'large rich carv'd Window Cornices cover'd and laced' (Fig 4.35) for the Drawing and Dining rooms'[54] and, '14 Mahogany Elbowchairs wt. stuffd Backs & Seats Cover'd & brass nailed the Elbows and fronts of the seats richly carv'd and scroll feet & castors' at 90 shilling each (£63 in total)[55] (Figs 4.15, 4.20, 4.38). Lord Dumfries had written to Lord Loudon during their correspondence in 1758 that he 'would only have one patteron Elbow Chair, and the two Settees made at London, and the other I should chose to get made at Edinburgh'.

He subsequently considered buying either eighteen chairs alone, or two settees and twelve chairs but eventually settled on two settees and fourteen chairs, purchasing the entire suite from Chippendale[56] (Fig 4.25) This suite is one of the glories not only of the house but of the period in general and is rightly celebrated. It is complemented by the beautiful 'Pair of mahog. Card tables of fine wood lined wt. superfine green cloth the knees carv'd & scroll toes to match ye Chairs', which cost £11 (Fig 4.5). It seems

Fig 4.23 Set of steel chimney furniture made by David Robertson in 1760 for the Dining room (see fig. 4.6); one of eighteen sets he supplied for the principal rooms of the house for a total of £116, most of which are still in situ. Robertson was a cousin of the Adam brothers. Christie's/Great Steward of Scotland's Dumfries House Trust

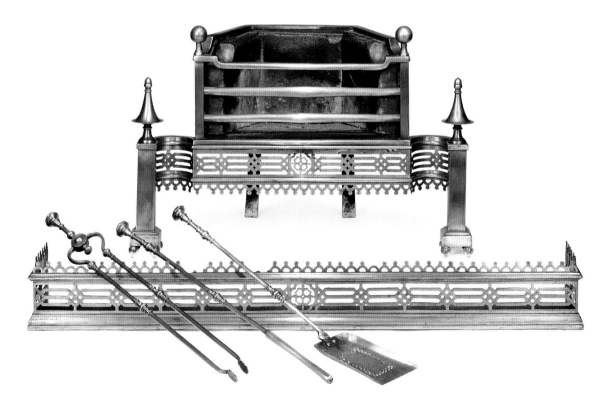

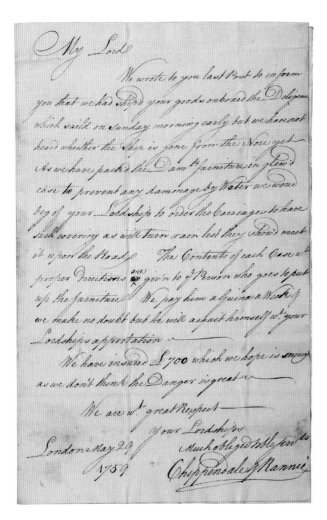

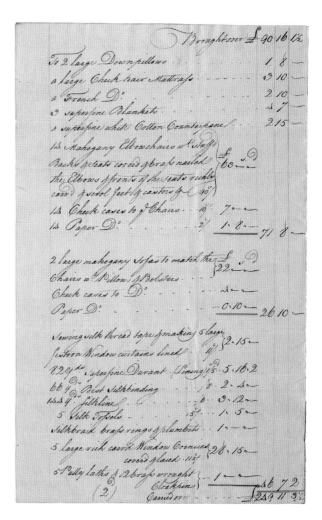

Fig 4.24 Covering letter sent with their account by Chippendale and his partner James Rannie in 1759, addressing details of carriage and insurance for their furniture. Christie's/Great Steward of Scotland's Dumfries House Trust

Fig 4.25 The page of the account with the entry for the Drawing Room suite of fourteen elbow chairs and two sofas. Christie's/Great Steward of Scotland's Dumfries House Trust

hardly surprising that Lord Dumfries could not resist purchasing the entire suite and his Scottish cabinet makers' loss was undoubtedly his gain (if not his pocket's). Many of his peers did not have his conviction and the copying of furniture was rife at the time.

Lord Dumfries' initial desire to 'only have a pattern Elbow Chair' from London and have it copied in Edinburgh was an established economy in Scotland. At Hopetoun the sofa made for the Dining Room by the Edinburgh Upholstery Company was specified by James Cullen to be the model for the sofas made by the estate wright Thomas Welsh (previously mentioned as the owner of a copy of the *Director*) for the Red Drawing Room, and they provided a pattern chair as a model for the chairs. This remains in the House[57] and was listed in the inventory of Hopetoun taken in 1768 as 'one model elbow chair mahogany buffed with crimson morine and check cover'.[58]

It is remarkable that the seat furniture in the Red Drawing Room at Hopetoun, possibly the grandest room in the grandest house in Scotland at the time, was made not in London, or even in Edinburgh, but by the wright employed on the Estate. The quality of furniture

which Welsh made was very high but hardly at the forefront of fashion, despite his posthumous status as a purchaser of the *Director*.

It is possible, given the difficulties of transport in the 18th century, that convenience was as strong a consideration as economy for this practice when it could be allied to fashion in this way. The experience at Dumfries House, where William Mathie had to replace one looking glass at least, bears this out. The furniture from Edinburgh and London sits cheek by jowl, suggesting there was no perceived significantly lower status for the Scottish items.

Lord Marchmont's furniture in 'high and good taste' has already been mentioned and, while it is not known who made it, his neighbour David Gavin of Langton also admired it, sending Robert Young, of the eminent Edinburgh cabinet makers and upholsterers Young and Trotter, to see the House in order that Gavin might have the furniture copied for his own house. Young and Trotter are also part of the story at Dumfries House, but exclusively in their capacity as upholsterers. Thomas Trotter and Robert Young are first recorded in 1747 as providing upholstery for William Hall of Dunglass,[59]

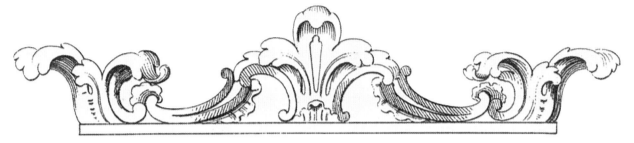

Fig 4.26 Plate XLI of the Director *(1762). Christie's/Great Steward of Scotland's Dumfries House Trust*

and there is a billhead from this time which they used on their earliest accounts.[60] This depicts a pelican feeding its young surrounded by a crude border of acanthus leaves, and their warehouse is declared as being 'at the Pelican within the Head of the Luckenbooths opposite to the Tolbooth'. This was on Edinburgh's High Street and was to remain as their warehouse for the next 36 years.[61] The following year they advertised in the Edinburgh newspapers for the first time, offering a large assortment of upholstery goods.[62] These adverts often carried the pelican engraving as an eye-catcher. The partnership carried out over £700 worth of work for Lord Dumfries, including supplying materials and carpets, between 1760 and 1761, when Lord Dumfries was preparing to move into Dumfries House.[63]

Fig 4.27 A typical 'best' bed chamber with one of Alexander Peter's 'large' beds, this one significantly with cornices derived from a design in the Director *(see above). HES 2010 DP033651*

Robert Young's correspondence with Lord Marchmont's neighbour, David Gavin, illuminates the situation of Lord Dumfries' peers as well as shedding light on Marchmont's furniture 'in high and good taste'.

As I promised after leaving Langtoun I called at Marchmont House & found the drawing Room there had three settees, ... 12 chairs & 2 stools which ... fill the room as it should be. Your drawing Room will not contain so much without crouding it, but 2 sophas & 8 or 9 chairs cannot be too much ... The chairs in Marchmont drawing Room have a fret cut upon the feet whether you would incline yours done so or plain, you will be able to judge from your haveing seen these chairs ...

Young and Trotter eventually made eight chairs, two elbow chairs and two sofas for Gavin, evidently with plain feet.[64] In a similar way, William Shiells made a

large quantity of furniture for the Earl of Lauderdale, submitting an estimate in 1761 for copying furniture at Hatton, the home of Lord Lauderdale's brother, to be used at Thirlestane, his own house. This estimate is worth quoting at length as it reveals some of the complexities which could be involved for a wright working in this capacity, and provides a valuable comparison, being remarkably similar, with the work at Dumfries House.

Estimate of Tables & Chairs proposed to be made by William Shiells for Thirlestane Castle.

He proposes to make side boards like that in the big dining room at Hatton of the same Dimensions Every way, without Fret work and of Elm at 18 shillings he furnishing the Elm or if my Lord furnish it. He will make them for 10 shillings & six pence or for 8 shillings if my Lord pay for planking out the wood

He proposes to make … 18 chairs for the Dining room, and 6 chairs for the bed chamber … of Geen tree[65] or Elm of the same size of those in the big dining room at Hatton & of the same pattern & dimensions every way, with a Notch round the feet of them, My Lord furnishing the wood [&c] … & to furnish oyls for oiling them, but not to furnish or make the seats of them

Fig 4.28 Thomas Chippendale's bed for the Principal Bed Chamber, here shown dressed with its Victorian silk and surrounded by typical examples of Peter's best bedroom furniture. HES 2010 DP083182

Fig 4.29 Plate XXXIX of the Director (1762) showing Lord Dumfries' bed. Christie's/Great Steward of Scotland's Dumfries House Trust

He proposes to make a Settee or Couch of
the same pattern & dimensions of that in the
Drawing Room at Hatton, [&c] … He will also
make 12 armchairs like those in the Drawing
room at Hatton at the same price with the other
chairs.[66]

The principle behind using pattern furniture as a
complement to London furniture was summed up by
the Dowager Marchioness of Lothian in 1776 when
advising her daughter-in-law about redecorating
Newbattle Abbey; she could have been writing to
Lord Dumfries.

*Fig 4.30 Detail of one of the pair of Chippendale's girandoles in the
Dining Room.   Christie's/Great Steward of Scotland's Dumfries House Trust*

*Fig 4.31 The unique overmantle frame made for the Principal Bed Chamber
by Chippendale for £17, enclosing Thomas Moore's 'tapestry picture'.*
Christie's/Great Steward of Scotland's Dumfries House Trust

My humble thought is, that it will be best for you
to get your chairs for the Old Drawing [room],
at London to your taste … as for the other chairs
may be wanted, you had better send pattrons
which you like to Sam: Elliot … and he will
make them.

Elliot was the estate wright at Newbattle, Midlothian,
and apparently a 'most ingenious Creature & complete
workman'.[67]

Returning to Chippendale's commission at
Dumfries House, it is evident that amongst the many
glories of the Rococo age was the freedom the style

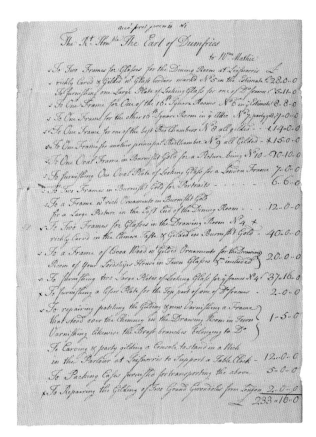

Fig 4.33 William Mathie's account for carving 1760. Christie's/Great Steward of Scotland's Dumfries House Trust

gave to carvers when creating mirror frames, and here Chippendale produced two of the masterpieces of his time. The '2 large Girandoles richly carv'd & gilt in burnish'd gold a Looking glass in each & 2 branches wt. brass leaf Nozles £24 10/' (Figs 4.2, 4.30) which he supplied for the Dining Room can be related to Plate LXXVIII in the third edition of the *Director* but are on a remarkable scale (Fig 4.7). They make an interesting comparison with the '2 large oval Pierglasses wt. rich carv'd frames & painted white £36 15/' which Chippendale made for the family Parlour (and which were subsequently gilded)[68] (Figs 4.3, 4.5).

One of the few pieces to have left Dumfries House is the gilt lantern from the front Hall, which was taken to St John's Lodge, Regent's Park, by the 3rd Marquess; it is now in the Philadelphia Museum of Art. It is related to Plate CLIII in the third edition of the *Director* (1762), and the engraving even shows the wyvern of the Crichton crest. Chippendale states in the *Director* that 'if neatly done in Wood, [as Lord Dumfries' was] and gilt in burnished Gold, would look better, and come much cheaper'. A plainer brass lantern survives on the landing[69] (Fig 4.36). For the Family Bed Chamber on the ground floor, Chippendale provided 'a Jappan'd Cloaths-press' which utilised genuine Oriental lacquer panels (Fig 4.37) and 'a Rosewood Bookcase wt. rich

Fig 4.32 A best bed chamber with one of Mathie's pier glasses flanked by Peter's window pelmets (the bed has matching cornices). HES 2007 SC1104273

carv'd & gilt ornam'ts. on the top & doors a Writing drawer in the underpart & a Cloaths press & drawers at each End' for the grand price of £47 5s (Fig 4.15). This bookcase partly relates to plates in the *Director*, notably the first edition, Plate XVIX, and the third edition, Plate CVI (Fig 4.16), but is especially exceptional for the use of 'rosewood' – actually a stained padouk – and the parquetry hexagonal and inlaid decoration to the doors which stands in great contrast to the fielded panelled doors of most furniture of the time and seems to be a harbinger of the future inlaid glories of Chippendale's neoclassical work. The bookcase was perhaps partly intended to hold the 'Cabinet of fine China' which Lord Dumfries had purchased in 1756.[70]

A further exotic item was the 'French Commode inlaid wt Tortoishell & brass' which cost 15 guineas; this was presumably reconstructed by Chippendale from an older French piece and shows a certain independence of mind on behalf of Lord Dumfries.[71] This independence of Lord Dumfries can again be seen in the 'large Chimney frame richly carv'd & gilt in burnish'd gold for a Tapestry picture & a Glass under it' which Chippendale made for the best bedroom and which uniquely incorporates a carpet pile panel, presumably bought by Lord Dumfries from Thomas Moore (Fig 4.31). Two smaller panels were also used in fire screens supplied by Chippendale.

Chippendale's account was settled on 20 March 1760 and with his partners he reluctantly agreed to reduce it, 'which Abatement we wou'd not submit to if we were not compell'd by necessity and to prevent any longer delay'. This was almost the sum total of Chippendale's known involvement at Dumfries House, but he did supply additional modest items, including a further clothes press, purchased on another visit to London between February and June 1763, presumably in response to a request from the new Lady Dumfries, the Earl having married the year before.[72]

Let us now turn to Chippendale's peer in Edinburgh, Alexander Peter. Peter's first recorded work for Lord Dumfries was in 1744 when he organised the funeral of his father, Col William Dalrymple.[73] The following year he refurbished Lord Dumfries' new house on Castlehill in Edinburgh, for which he supplied a considerable quantity of furniture between 1746 and 1748. This furniture included, amongst many other incidental items, '18 Mahogy. dinning chairs wt black leather and brass Nails @ 16/', together with several other sets of chairs and easy chairs, 'an Eating table of Chouce Mahog. for 12 Covers £4 4/', as well as numerous other tables including 'a large Table & a three Clawed foot', 'two half length frames in Burnished Gold att £2 15/ each', several four poster and other beds and chamber boxes, night tables etc. All in all what must have essentially amounted to the entire furnishing of the house.[74]

Little is known about Alexander Peter and, from this point of view, he is the norm rather than the exception amongst cabinet makers, his significance justifiably resting almost exclusively on the collection of furniture he supplied to Dumfries House.[75] His father was James Peter of Chaple and he was registered as apprentice to James Brownhill on 16 December 1713.[76] Peter only completed his apprenticeship and became a burgess in 1728; this 15 year apprenticeship suggests that he may have joined Brownhill very young.[77] On 4 May 1728 he was appointed to make as his essay piece, 'a Wainscot press pedestall forme lifting off in two parts having ffoure lidds or doors with raised muldings … with Basse & sub basse and an whole intabulator on the head of the Corinthian order after Scamozie'.[78] He was admitted as burgess a month later having completed this task, and over the next year booked three journeymen in his name with the Incorporation of Mary's Chapel.[79]

In 1732 Peter married Isobel, the daughter of Andrew Dunbar of Leneholt, and the first known account in his own name is to the Earl of Islay, later the Duke of Argyll, for the following year.[80] Islay continued to use Peter throughout his life. Among Peter's other patrons can be numbered the Duke of Montrose, the Earls of Hopetoun, Cassillis and Lauderdale, Lords Doune and Carmichall, Lady Hall, Sir John Clerk, and Archibald Grant of Monymusk, as well as, of course, the Earl of Dumfries.[81]

Between the years of 1731 and 1749 Peter registered 37 further journeymen with Mary's Chapel; he took as apprentices William Mathie, son of Captain Thomas Mathie, a merchant in Cockenzie, in 1733; Michael Malcolm, a son of Sir John Malcolm of Lochor in 1737; Daniel Laury, the son of a surgeon, in 1741; and Henry Stuart, son of Robert Stuart of Newmains in 1745.[82] He never held any official posts within the Incorporation, and never did any work for it. He also never worked for the Town Council. Peter rarely placed notices in the papers, and never repeated a notice more than once. He also never used printed billheads, and was clearly a man who simply got on with his job.

Peter lived above his shop in the Horse Wynd from at least 1752[83] until he sold his business in 1772. He also, for a while, maintained a 'large warehouse within Advocate's Close', which he moved to a site in the Cowgate, opposite Old Assembly Close, in 1758. This presumably was his workshop, as well as being his 'Cabinet Warehouse' where he had fitted up 'two large light warehouses … wherein his stock of ready made goods' was shown. It was also conveniently near his house, being almost opposite the Horse Wynd. An advertisement in the *Edinburgh Chronicle* of 23 January 1760 illustrates the range of goods which Peter made, and makes it clear that he was very much a cabinet maker rather than an upholsterer.

He gave notice in 1772 that he was 'intending to give up business' and was 'ready to treat with any person whom it may suit to take his Shop and Yard

Fig 4.34 *Engraving used as a source by Mathie for the Drawing room pier glasses, from Matthias Lock's* New Book of Ornaments for Looking Glass Frames…in the Chinese Taste *of 1752.*
Christie's/Great Steward of Scotland's Dumfries House Trust

and to purchase what quantity of his stock of seasoned wood etc he may have occasion for'. He ends by saying, surely with justification, that, 'as this Shop has been long in repute for Cabinet Work, any person who employs the same hands, and uses proper materials, may expect to meet with proper encouragement'.[84]

The final word came on 20 July 1772, 58 years and six months after he joined James Brownhill, when he announced that he was selling off his last remaining goods 'at least Ten per cent below the usual prices, though they are of equal value with any that ever were made by Mr Peter'.

Peter's first substantial account for furniture for Dumfries House begins in May 1759, just after Lord Dumfries returned from London. It includes furniture for all the bedrooms (except the best one) comprising eight four-poster beds of varying degrees

Fig 4.35 *North wall of the Drawing Room showing the harmony of Mathie's pier glasses ('richly Carv'd in the Chinese Taste'), George Mercer's tables and Chippendale's window pelmets.* HES 2007 SC1104119

of elaborateness and size,[85] the most expensive ones at £5 10s having mahogany 'fluted & carved' foot posts; the 'bed cornishes' were supplied separately and included matching window cornices at £5 a set (Fig 4.32). Although they are all similar, they have variations; one set in particular is significant as the cornices are directly copied from Plate XXVII in the first edition of the *Director* (Figs 4.26–27). The account also includes a dozen 'Mahogany ffrench elbow chairs largest size' at 33s each (compare with Thomas Chippendale's at 90s each), a further three dozen side chairs 'buffd over back and bottom' at 18s or 19s each, a dozen 'Mahogany large sized pillard basson stands' at 15s each, six 'large sized Mahogy. chamber boxes' and 22 'Mahogy. large sized foot stoolls'. Four 'Mahogy night tables [with] cut legings [ledges] on ye top' (Fig 4.28) were sent the following year. Amazingly the bedrooms are still largely furnished with these pieces.

Amongst the finest items Peter supplied were a 'Mahogony fire screen stalk & claw wt Eagles clawd feet' and one 'smaller' as well as a further two with 'a carved pillar, a leaf on ye knee & Lyons claw', and eight 'Mahogy. chairs for the Hall' at 30s each (Fig 4.10). These chairs, whose popular form is of Italian origin, are directly comparable with the set supplied by William Masters to the Duke of Atholl for Blair Castle in 1751.[86] Lord Dumfries had additional armorial crests painted on his by John Bonnar soon after they were delivered[87] (Fig 4.9). The 24 'Mahogy dining room chairs wt carving on ye front & feet' which Peter invoiced in July (on the same date as the Hall chairs) cost 30 shillings each and had 'buff'd over seats [and] osenburgh covers' for which loose covers were undoubtedly intended[88] (Figs 4.6, 4.7, 4.14). At Hopetoun, the Edinburgh Upholstery Company had supplied '20 Mohy fine Carved Eagle Claw foot Chairs' also at a cost of 30 shillings each (and '4 Elbow ditto' for an extra five shillings) for the Dining Room.[89] Although it is accepted that dining chairs made at this time were generally covered with leather[90] or horsehair, these were 'stufft in Canvas with slipping on seats' and supplied with loose 'Crimson all cotton Cheque' cases. These must not be confused with case covers; they were the primary decorative finish. This was something of a trend in Scotland; the Edinburgh Upholstery Company also made dining chairs finished like this for the Earl of Lauderdale in 1762, although only after some discussion with him, their initial suggestion being black figured haircloth, 'which comes full as cheap and lasts as well & is not subjected to throwing the colour nor greasing the cloaths wc is the fault of leather'.[91] The Factor did not think this appropriate, expressing the opinion that 'hair cloth is ye worst of all things and it [is] most unfashionable in a gentleman's house' and requested that the Company 'do them over wt green lining and Baked hair – to be tacked under wt common tacks only & so have covers'.[92] Lord Dumfries seems to have

Fig 4.36 *Chippendale's surviving ormolu lantern, which cost 13 guineas.* John Batty/NTS 1994

solved the problem by purchasing floral tapestry seat covers, possibly from Thomas Moore in London, which still survive in the House (although some of the chairs were reupholstered when they were repolished, the covers were kept).[93]

In the following year Peter also sent a beautiful pair of 'large sqr Mahogany dining tables' en suite with the chairs, for the substantial sum of £20 5s (Fig 4.7, 4.14); these were presumably similar to a pair the Edinburgh Upholstery Company had made for Hopetoun, of the 'finest' mahogany, 'to join' at £4 for a pair,[94] however, the relative costs are telling.

In September 1759 Peter supplied 'a Mahogy side board table for ye dining room … cut wt fret work on ye feet & rails £7' and one 'ditto for ye Parlor £5 10/' (Fig 4.6). The design for the sideboards was taken from Plate XXXVI of the 1754 edition of Chippendale's *Gentleman and Cabinet Maker's Director* but the account makes no specific reference to this, nor indeed to the bed cornices. As such, it is not clear whether Peter possessed his own copy of the *Director* (he was not a subscriber) or was responding to a direct request of Lord Dumfries, who should by this time have received the furniture which he had acquired from Chippendale earlier in the year.[95] Together with the breakfast table made by Samuel Smith these are celebrated examples of furniture copied exactly from the *Director* by other cabinet makers in a house where Thomas Chippendale is known to have worked.

The relationship between Peter and Lord Dumfries was evidently not always easy, which is perhaps only to be expected given the scale of the commission and the extensive quantity of packing, transport and work on site involved; the whole ultimately amounted to some £350. In 1761 Peter had to declare that 'the whole articles of the within Account … are stated att the ordinarie prices for sutch work' and in 1760 Lord Dumfries obliged him to take some mahogany off his hands (presumably surplus after the house was completed). Peter accepted this, deducting £3 2s 6d from his bill, but made a point of commenting that the timber was 'much shaken in ye ends & very badly sawn out'. There is also a lengthy exchange of comments regarding some furniture which Lord Dumfries wished to return, some two years after it was delivered by Peter. As Peter points out,

Therefor it cannot faill of being a considerable loss to have said furniture returnd otherway's than at My Lords risk of sales for ye following reasons. Viz.:

The easy chairs is so much larger than our common demand

The fashion of ye other 15 chairs altering every year, besides that of ye covers being suddled & ye wood darken'd by being so long made, must occasion selling with discount.

And as to ye Bedstead, both in height & Breadth being so much larger than our ordinary demand, might make it ly for years on hand before a Mercht is cast up.

Add to this the risk of breaking in ye carriage as well as ye expence … And at last ye Number of chairs is more than probably what could be sold to one hand, or got matched with ye colour of ye wood of others to be made at such a distance of time.

Both parties were aggrieved but it was Peter who ultimately capitulated. Lord Dumfries did, however, agree to pay for the carriage costs as well as Peter's charges for 'scraping & cleaning up … elbow chairs returnd & helping ye covers'.[96] What is valuable about this exchange is that it confirms that Peter was making furniture for Dumfries House specifically to order and to Lord Dumfries' specifications and of a greater than usual scale and quality. Thus it seems almost certain that the pieces which follow patterns

in the *Director* would have been requested by Lord Dumfries.

In one of his letters to Lord Loudon dated 30 November 1758, Lord Dumfries had asked if his friend 'would be so good as to look out four good glasses for the dining room & the drawing room'[97] while he was in London to go between the windows above George Mercer's marble topped tables. Ultimately, and perhaps surprisingly, he did not purchase these from London, instead commissioning the Edinburgh carver William Mathie to make them to his own particular specifications. The principal account from William Mathie to Lord Dumfries begins in 1759 and totals £325 16s for the complete sequence of mirrors in Dumfries House. This account also details work including the sundry smaller pieces such as dressing glasses and, significantly, repair work to items damaged on their way from London.

It has already been stated that William Mathie was Alexander Peter's apprentice and he waited 27 years before becoming a burgess and Guild Brother in 1760. Such delays were caused by a variety of reasons; in some cases lack of funds may have required it while in others it may not have been deemed necessary by the craftsman in question to pay to acquire his freedom.[98] Mathie was certainly working independently, although probably under the wing of Peter, as early as 1757,

Fig 4.37 The fine 'Jappan'd cloaths-press' with gilt lacquer panels supplied by Chippendale for £17; it was in Lady Dumfries' bedroom in 1795.
HES 2013 DP151638

so it was clearly unnecessary for him to acquire his freedom at that time. It should be acknowledged that this was a considerable break with established tradition and working practices, presumably facilitated by, and in recognition of, his skills as a carver. It has been mentioned that Mathie was the son of Thomas Mathie, a merchant in Cockenzie, and it is notable that Cockenzie was home to the successful cabinet makers Robert Moubray and his son John, and was a well known port through which timber was imported. Charles Douglas, the estate wright employed by the Marquess of Tweeddale at Yester, is known to have purchased mahogany there and it is possible that Mathie's father was involved in this trade and encouraged his precocious son. It is perhaps no coincidence that Lord Dumfries purchased his Edinburgh house on Castlehill from John Moubray in 1745 [99] (however, as we know, he then used Alexander Peter to furnish it).

At Dumfries House Mathie supplied two pairs of pier glasses for the principal reception rooms and four further lesser pier glasses for the bedrooms, including the Principal Bed Chamber; Lord Dumfries clearly supplied most of the plates for the bedroom glasses, their form echoing the early 18th century proportions of the existing glass (Fig 4.32). This was standard practice at the time as glass was so expensive; indeed, it was substantially more expensive than the frames Mathie made, which is hard to comprehend today. [100] The pair for the Drawing Room 'to Two Frames for Glasses in the Drawing Room richly Carv'd in the Chinese Taste & Gilded in Burnisht Gold' cost £40, the principal mirror plates themselves costing a further £37 16s, and a further small upper plate £2, Lord Dumfries suppling the other small plate (Fig 4.35). The design for these frames seems to be have been adapted by Mathie from Plate IV of Matthias Lock's *A New Book of Ornaments for Looking Glass Frames, Chimney Pieces etc. in the Chinese Taste* which had been published c1752. Mathie has simplified the design and importantly replaced the nesting ho-ho bird at the centre of Lock's design with the Crichton family wyvern (the birds survive at the shoulders of the frames) (Fig 4.34). Either Mathie was an exceptionally astute manager of his patron or, more likely, this was Lord Dumfries' suggestion.

In the Dining room, the pair of pier glasses 'richly Carv'd & Gilded wt borders of Glass furnisht' cost £28 and have clearly also been cast around Lord Dumfries' older plates (Fig 4.14). Here Mathie's design effortlessly incorporates the Dumfries and Crichton motifs of the Order of the Thistle and the wyvern (Fig 4.1). However, Mathie's most elegant creation at the House is undoubtedly the elegant scrolling Rococo frame he improvised to make up the space between

Lord Dumfries' painting by Bassano and the frame the Adams had created in the panelling of the Dining Room (Figs 4.38–4.39). While some of his mirror frames are at best charming, this frame more than holds its own with the immediately adjacent pair of girandoles which Christopher Gilbert considered to be the masterpieces of Chippendale's Rococo oeuvre [101] (Fig 4.7). Mathie's frame also bears comparison with the 'Carved & painted Sconce' pier glass frames in the Yellow Drawing Room at Hopetoun House made by the Edinburgh Upholstery Company. [102] They are similarly applied to the wall plane and can be loosely connected to Mathie via Alexander Peter's involvement as a partner of the Edinburgh Upholstery Company.

The repairs Mathie carried out at Dumfries House included furnishing 'one oval plate of Looking Glass for a London frame', presumably one of Chippendale's fine Chinese mirrors in the Saloon, for the sum of £7, and 'repairing the gilding of two Grand Girandoles from London'. It was no doubt inspiring for him to be able to work with such pieces. [103] In May 1760, Lord Dumfries complained to his agent Andrew Hunter that 'Mr Mathie has been extreamly dilatory and neglectfull in the execution of his Commission which in a great measure prevents the furnishing the House completely when the Upholsterers are in the House.' Nevertheless, his contribution to the spectacular interiors at Dumfries House cannot be denied. [104]

From a Scottish perspective there are many significant points to be made about the furnishings of Dumfries House. The inclusion of the Earl of Dumfries' existing historically significant tapestries, the acquisition of the finest items from London, the use of Edinburgh pieces to complement and supplement these, the only documented use of furniture pattern books known in Scotland during this period; the suggestion of the use of pattern furniture which was in essence a judicious blending of status, taste and economy. The only expedient which Lord Dumfries resisted was the use of an estate wright, but the relatively modest scale of his house perhaps did not justify this economy.

This pragmatic attitude is typified by the wealthy Earl of Marchmont, another intimate of Lord Burlington, who justified the economies he took with the exterior of his new house in Berwickshire by famously quipping that he intended 'to live in the inside of [his] house and not on the outside'. [105] A patron such as this must have warmed the hearts of upholsterers and cabinet makers used to playing second fiddle to architects, especially as Lord Marchmont, despite his professed desire to economise, was determined to have, 'the best house in Britain'. Sadly we know little of his furnishings but as already mentioned Marchmont was described soon after completion as finished in 'high and good taste', the writer being disappointed that 'the fine furniture

Fig 4.38 The Dining Room when in use as a second Drawing Room, showing Chippendale's breakfast table with its 'wirework' infills (compare with that in Fig 4.15) as well as Mathie's picture frame and surround in situ (see over). John Batty/NTS 1994

Fig 4.39 William Mathie's remarkable frame for Bassano's painting of Laban and his Flock *bought by Lord Dumfries for the west wall of the Dining Room in 1756; this was his finest picture and one of the few narrative paintings in the house.* Christie's/Great Steward of Scotland's Dumfries House Trust

in Lady Marchmont's room was covered with paper and the library locked up'.[106] All is long dispersed, as has been the case in so many houses of the period in Scotland, which only goes to emphasise how special Dumfries House is. And most fortuitously from a modern perspective, Lord Dumfries not only chose to patronise the most important English cabinet maker of his generation but also the three most important Scottish ones. His collection remains the outstanding monument to their lives. There can be little doubt that Lord Marchmont's friend the Earl of Dumfries intended to have the best house in Scotland of its age and he would surely have been gratified by the Countess of Northumberland's assessment that the house was 'handsome, thoroughly convenient & furnish'd with great elegance and Expence'.[107]

That this major commission should have survived so completely, fully documented, in the house for which it was made is remarkable enough in itself. That the house itself was built entirely from new and furnished over a very short period of time, with a core that has survived almost completely unaltered, provides the exceptional furnishings with an extraordinarily consistent setting which greatly enhances their significance. The House itself of course has an architectural significance of its own but the ensemble is unprecedented, whether seen in a Scottish, British, or international context.

1 Quotation from unpublished diary of Countess of Northumberland written about her visit in 1760. Original in Alnwick Castle, Northumberland transcript at Dumfries House.

2 Gilbert was the doyen of late 20th century furniture historians and Keeper (and cataloguer) of the magnificent collection at Temple Newsam, Leeds. Christopher Gilbert 'Thomas Chippendale at Dumfries House' *Burlington* November 1969. For Dumfries House in the context of Chippendale's career see Gilbert (1978).

3 The accounts and letters for the furnishing of Dumfries House by Chippendale, Brodie, Peter, Mathie and others discussed in this chapter are all held in the Archives at Mount Stuart. However, the Chippendale accounts have been published by Gilbert (1978) and those for the Edinburgh cabinet makers by Bamford (1983). Given these readily available published sources it has been decided not to give references for these accounts in this chapter.

4 See Coleridge 1960

5 The best account of this is Rowan (1984).

6 NRS RH15/10/41/5. 15 June 1743.

7 *Ibid* 29 July 1744. His bile was mostly directed at the wright James Runciman, who had refitted his Holyrood apartments in 1741, and went on to work, unsatisfactorily, at Taymouth. NRS GD112/21/277, 279 & 285

8 Probably in fact Samuel Norman. See Pryke (1992).

9 The furnishing of Hopetoun was first discussed in detail by Anthony Coleridge (1960) and this is still the best published account. It is well illustrated but is too eager in attributing pieces to Cullen for which he was not directly responsible. Coleridge 1966.

10 NRA(S) 3246 vol 63 Household Accounts p398. James Livingston supplied much of the furniture to Arniston, both cabinet and seat, but apart from the above pier glasses, and their corresponding tables, little can now be identified, in part because much of it is not actually itemised in the account books. NRA(S) 3246/vols 51&63. Chippendale is also known to have worked in a minor capacity for Robert Dundas of Arniston. See Gilbert 1978, 128

11 'I sent this day to Mr. Broddie and talked with him about chairs he's the best man in town and I doubt if anybody else would please. I have sent from him a pattern of some chairs he has ready.' William Adam to the Duke of Hamilton 25 November 1740. NRA(S)2177/C3. 1794/1. I am indebted to William Kay for this transcript. Although Adam clearly thought highly of Brodie he also employed Alexander Peter, purchasing in 1736, for instance, a 'mahogany frame' for a marble table which he supplied to Arthur Gordon of Carnoustie RH15/1/18/6.

12 Account dated 12 July 1749, and 1753

13 A Robertson, *Anecdotes and Other Curious Information Concerning William Brodie,* Edinburgh 1788, Vol II, 12. The 'good family', from which Ludovic was descended, were the Brodies of Brodie Castle.

14 City Archives Mary's Chapel Records 1727–40 Bay B Shelf 16.

15 To Sir John Clerk for a 'large Mahogany Standard for a jappaned table 8/'. NRS GD18/1839/1/134

16 Between 1737 and 1769 he took six apprentices, having two at a time. City Archives Mary's Chapel Records 1727–40 Bay B Shelf 16.

17 Bamford 1983 and Pryke 1995.

18 Consider for instance William Lamb's *Gilded Sopha*, William Murray's *Royal Tent*, or James Caddell's *Crown and Cushion*. Brodie used this from at least 1738 to 1758, with only small changes to the text, replacing it with a simpler but more modern Rococo design in 1767, having taken his son William into full partnership. Pryke 1995

19 This was a completely fictional portrait – Palladio was in fact bearded and balding – but was nevertheless the accepted one at the time, even being used by Campbell in his 1728 edition of the *First Book.* For a comprehensive account of the English editions of Palladio see R Wittkower 'English Neoclassicism and the vicissitudes of Palladio's Quattro Libri', *Palladio and English Palladianism,* London 1974, 73–92.

20 For a fuller discussion of the billhead and furniture which can be associated with it see S Pryke 'The Extraordinary Billhead of Francis Brodie', *Regional Furniture 4* 1990, 81–99. Brodie not only used Palladio's head when he placed notices in the newspapers, but also as a book plate, and, significantly, as his seal.

21 Although he did state in the preface to the *Director* that 'Of all the Arts which are either improved or ornamented by Architecture, that of

CABINET-MAKING is not only the most useful and ornamental, but capable of receiving as great Assistance from it as any whatever.'

22 Delivered in 1739, 'To a marble table Suported by ane Eagle guilt in Burnisht gold £16'. NRS GD44/51/465/1/34. This was listed in an inventory of the apartments of Lord Adam Gordon, the Duke's son, in 1796. See Margaret Swain 'Furniture for the French Princes at Holyroodhouse, 1796', *Connoisseur,* January 1978, 27–35

23 In 1738. It was described as a 'sideboard Table supported by an Eagle done in burnisht gold & a Marble Top' and cost 17 guineas. Photographs of the Gallery at Hamilton Palace show a positive flock of them between the windows, and it would be wonderful if Brodie had been responsible for these also. NRS CS238/B/1/79

24 Although this type is associated with William Kent, he is not known to have designed one. There is in the RIBA Drawings collection a design by John Vardy for a pier glass and table which is comparable to Brodie's designs. This is probably of a similar date to the Dumfries House table, although having even more distinct Rococo overtones, with scrolled supports flanking and rather subordinating the position of the eagle, and Rococo foliage playing around the architectural frame for the glass. See Peter Ward-Jackson *English Furniture Designs of the Eighteenth Century* 1958 reprinted 1984 plate 42. Brodie's seem to be the only known accounts for eagle tables. There is also a wonderful architectural case for the clock in the Hall at Arniston which Brodie made in 1739 and which is still in situ. NRS GD18/1839/1/121

25 It was rather clumsily called a 'Mahogany chest drawers cabinet with mirror glass doors'.

26 George Riddell made a walnut 'lady's closet' of identical form for Sir John Clerk in 1722; this still survives at Penicuik House. NRS GD18/1839/1/187

27 Pryke *1995*

28 Robertson, *Anecdotes,* 12

29 The King James Bible at the Huntly House museum in Edinburgh was owned by Francis Brodie and has much biographical information, mostly entered by Francis himself, written on six sheets of paper inserted between the Apocrypha and the New Testament. The entry for William has been excised.

30 Plate XXXIII of 1st edn *Director* 1754. Beard, G and Gilbert, C, *Dictionary of English Furniture Makers 1660–1840* Furniture History Society 1986

31 Dated London 25 August 1757

32 An isolated piece, but the most important in what Samuel Johnson called 'the most learned room in Scotland'. Paul Duncan 'Newhailes, East Lothian II', *Country Life,* 5 February 1987, 58. It still survives in the room for which it was made. NLS MS Acc7228/497.

33 The items are not specified. NRS GD220/6/897/100

34 NRS GD112/21/77–80

35 3 November 1755. Lord Hopetoun meanwhile was commissioning Robert Adam to send him marble tables from Rome for his State Drawing Room and Dining Rooms. Coleridge 1960

36 Bute Archives, Loudon MSS LO/2/105/2

37 Cullen went to great lengths to avoid paying duty on this imported silk, and reported later to Lord Hopetoun that he 'had great Apprehensions of Danger by sending them directed to any House subject to Excise officers as every Grocer is, & therefore have took the Liberty to send them yesterday by the Newcastle Waggon, viz … Messrs B & L H Williamson Lawn Market, Edinburgh. Bertram and Williamson are Linnen Factors & my Friends … I thought of packing in a dry cask but that peice of Cunning might cause it to be searched for Teas, & if in a flatt Case as marble Slabbs or Glasses directed to Miss H … might expose it to the like fate from the curious, this determined me to pack them in Straw in a pack shut corded like Manchester Goods & directed to people who deal in such.' Cullen is best known in England for his involvement in smuggling furniture from France. Geoffrey Wills, 'Furniture smuggling in eighteenth century London', *Apollo* 82 August 1965, 112–17

38 Cruft, Dunbar and Fawcett 2006, 520

39 See C Rostek, 'New light on Thomas Chippendale's Seat Furniture and 'Best' Bed at Dumfries House, Ayrshire', *Furniture History* 68, 2012, 141–54.

40   *Ibid*

41   December 1758. Bute Archives, Loudon MSS LO/2/105/6

42   Christie's 2007 Vol I, 85 Lot 17. He also sold Lord Dumfries a Meissen pair Lot 39; Chinese porcelain tureen and cover Lot 47; pot pourri vases (possibly the 'two china jars with covers' listed in the Blue Drawing room in 1803) Lot 77. The family's magnificent armorial Chinese export dinner service however dates from the 1790s.

43   It was also during this period that Lord Dumfries commissioned the cartoons from Sir James Thornhill, and the portraits from John Medina and Thomas Hudson (see Chapter 3).

44   Christie's 2007 Lot 15

45   Bute Archives, Loudon MSS LO/2/105/6

46   Christie's 2007 Lot 19; Lot 56

47   Bute Archives, DU 5/37/49

48   Although Lord Dumfries was eventually recorded as a patron in the 3rd ed of the *Director* of 1762 (note to Plate XXXIX)

49   As Christopher Gilbert has said, 'It would be difficult to exaggerate the importance of Chippendale's *Director* as a formative influence on mid 18th Century furniture styles.'

50   See Gilbert, 1978

51   Caddell carried out minor upholstery work for Lord Dumfries between 1762 and 1764, mostly relating to curtains at Dumfries House, including sending a journeyman there. Bute Archives DH A719

52   The packing charges were £35 14s 2d.

53   The best guest bedroom was at the north-west corner of the bedroom floor. The bed has recently been restored to its original appearance by the Trust. See Rostek, 'New Light'

54   At a cost of £28 15s. See Chapter 3 for a discussion of the change of plans for these cornices. Chippendale also charged for making 'festoon window curtains'.

55   Check cases 10s each; paper cases 2s each. These chairs have recently been reupholstered.

56   '2 large mahogany sofas to match the Chairs wt. Pillows & Bolster' £22

57   Its origins are obscure, but in 1758 the Edinburgh Upholstery Company had sent a single 'carv'd mohy Elbow Chair' to Hopetoun House. There would perhaps be nothing exceptional about this singularity were it not for the price of the chair: £5. This was more than three times the cost of the 'fine Carved Eagle Claw foot' mahogany dining chairs supplied by the same firm three years earlier and is surely enough to justify an attribution, given the exotic nature of the surviving chair. The price also compares favourably with the £3 5s famously charged by William Hallett for 'a pattern chair for Holkham'. See Coleridge 1968, 42 and Pryke 1995 *Thesis* op.cit.

58   For further discussion of the use of pattern furniture in Scotland see Pryke (1994).

59   NRS GD206/3/2/5/27

60   For instance to the Countess of Cassillis dated 1747. NRS GD25/9/18/23

61   In 1783 it was taken over by Francis Braidwood, another cabinet maker. *Edinburgh Advertiser* 24 June 1783

62   *Caledonian Mercury* 29 February 1748

63   8 February 1760 £613 5s ½d; 12 May 1761 £112 2s 10 ¼d. By comparison at Buchanan, Stirlingshire, the Duke of Montrose had employed John Schaw in 1754 to completely refurnish his old family house. Schaw supplied new suites of furniture for the Drawing Room, Dining Room, Breakfast Room, Staircase lobby, all the bedrooms, and the servants' quarters. As well as this he did all the upholstery and supplied new curtains and carpets throughout, unless he could re-dye and re-make old ones. The total account came to £705 12s 7d, a similar sum to that which Lord Dumfries spent on upholstery alone at Dumfries House. NRS GD220/6/1426/7
The success of the partnership is beyond dispute and it existed in one form or another for over 50 years until William Trotter took over at the beginning of the 19th century. In his hands the firm was to outshine all others in Edinburgh being widely held to have been responsible for the finest furniture created for Edinburgh's Regency New Town. At the risk of overstating the point, accounts survive relating to some 50 patrons, including the Marquesses of Graham and Tweeddale, and the Earls of Cassillis, Dumfries, Hopetoun, Lauderdale and Panmure. Pryke 1995

64   It is noteworthy that the dining chairs Peter made for Dumfries House do have a fret, while the similar ones attributed to him and now at the NTS Georgian House do not. NRS GD282/13/122

65   A type of cherry.

66   NRA(S) 832/14/23. We do not know who made the furniture at Hatton, which belonged to Lauderdale's brother.

67   NRS GD/40/9/177. She may of course be referring to patterns on paper.

68   The difference in cost, which might appear curious today, can partly be explained by the size of the glasses used.

69   This cost £13 13s as opposed to the £34 of the Hall lantern.

70   In Christopher Gilbert's eyes it was 'comparable in importance to the finest pieces at Nostell or Harewood'.

71   David Garrick had a similar commode at his villa on the Thames.

72   Christie's make a well argued case for there being a seam of undocumented furniture at Dumfries House which may be commonplace items from Chippendale's workshop. However, this furniture seems as likely to have been made in Edinburgh, or perhaps even locally. Christie's 2007, 'The Dumfries House Furniture Maker'.

73   The total cost was £33 13s 8d, the coffin alone cost £10, which was a significant amount. A month earlier he had supplied Dalrymple with a Coach Bed (perhaps an invalid bed or chair), an account which was settled by Lord Dumfries after his death. Bute Archives DH A700. In 1755 the funeral of the Countess was carried out by William Baillie at a cost of £20. Bute Archives DH A651.

74   The total account came to just over £159. Bute Archives DH A631. It seems extremely likely that some of this furniture may have subsequently moved to Dumfries House, and possibly accounts for many of the items attributed by Christie's to Alexander Peter. Christie's 2007

75   There are two chairs of identical pattern to the dining chairs at Dumfries House at the Georgian House in Edinburgh, and a set of plain backstools at Gosford House, East Lothian (removed from Amisfield, the home of Lord Dumfries' friend, and subscriber to the *Director*, Francis Charteris) which can confidently be attributed to Peter. No other furniture by him is known.

76   Brownhill was Deacon of the Wrights from 1713 until 1715 and the builder of James Court in the Lawnmarket.

77   Brownhill was undoubtedly essentially a wright rather than a cabinet maker, although he did supply some furniture, notably for Sir John Clerk in 1722. By this time Peter himself may have been responsible for this. NRS GD18/1839/1/100

78   Extracts from V Scamozzi's *L'Idea dell'Architettura Universale* had been widely published by this time.

79   Mary's Chapel Records 1709–20 [includes accounts 1729–48] and 1727–40. Bay B Shelf 16

80   The finest item was a 'walnuttree Desk and Bookcase' which cost £6 10/. NLS MS17643/52

81   Pryke 1995

82   Mary's Chapel Records 1727–40. Bay B Shelf 16.

83   Peter is listed here in Gilhooley's *Directory of Edinburgh* in 1752 and the press notices confirm this from 1759. J Gilhooley, *Directory of Edinburgh in 1752*, Edinburgh 1988.

84   *Edinburgh Evening Courant* 6 May 1772

85   One was later returned; the other seven remarkably all survive in the house.

86   Coleridge 1960 A similar set was also formerly at Rossdhu, Argyll. Masters also supplied the Duke of Atholl with a very large set of upholstered chairs of almost identical form to those Peter supplied for the bed chambers at Dumfries House.

87   'Painted 8 Crests, with the Order of the Garter. on the Back of Hall Chairs 3/ each'. Obviously he meant Order of the Thistle.

88   Osenburgh was a type of heavy linen.

89   NRA(S)631/A720/22

90   As were the ones made for Buchanan. Indeed Peter had made leather covered and brass nailed dining chairs for Lord Dumfries' Edinburgh house in 1746.

91   24 March 1762. NRA(S)832/1/16

92   *Ibid.* The letter is annotated by him.

93   In 1803 they were described as having 'English tapestry bottoms'. Invoice for tapestry chair seats from Thomas Moore. DH34/71

94   They charged an extra shilling for the polished iron 'cleeks' which joined them.

95   It is of note that Lord Dumfries was not a subscriber.

96   Peter advertised second hand furniture at his wareroom, as was common at the time.

97   Bute Archives, Loudon MSS LO/2/105/5

98   For instance Peter Martin was apprenticed to James Tait for six years in 1762, but did not become a burgess until 1797; and John Little, who had been apprenticed to James Brownhill nine years after Peter, waited 50 years before he became registered as a burgess. Martin trained as an upholsterer and his father was a wright in Pathhead, so he may have found it convenient to work for his father without needing to be a burgess.
Register of Edinburgh Apprentices

99   Actually purchased from the 'Children of the deceast Robert Moubray'. Bute Archives DH A719

100 John Schaw provided 'two large glasses' for the State Dining Room (now the Yellow Drawing Room) at Hopetoun House in 1755, at a cost of £102.

101 Gilbert had dismissed Mathie's frames 'although ambitious, [they] appear miserably coarse in design and execution when compared with the sophistication of those supplied by Chippendale [and] are little better than cheerful hack-work' but did accept that this was an object of great beauty, in conversation with the author. He had not been aware that Mathie had made this frame when he published his earlier comments.

102 Frames for the tables and glasses were gilded in 1827. NRA(S)888/87/1

103 Mathie also made various pieces for Lord Dumfries' house in Edinburgh, notably a 'frame of Cocoa Wood wt Gilded Ornaments for the Drawing Room' for £20.

104 Although pieces are known which can be attributed to Mathie the only other identifiable pieces he is known to have carried out are a modest picture frame at Penicuik House, Midlothian, and a serious of simpler mirrors from Amisfield House, East Lothian, which can be firmly attributed to him.

105 Macaulay 1987, 166

106 'Diary of George Ridpath, Minister of Stichel 1755–61'. Quoted by Macaulay.

107 Quoted by Rostek 1987, 'New Light'

I would like to dedicate this chapter to the Very Rev. Allan Maclean of Dochgarroch, to whom I am greatly indebted for many kindnesses.

Sebastian Pryke

Chapter 5: The Estate and its Buildings 1634–1768

Over which the finest prospect of the lawns, plantations, river, bridge and house are got

Quotation from Diary of 1st Duchess of Northumberland August 1760.[1]

The Development of the Estate Buildings

The 5th Earl's aim was to create an efficient, modern estate with Dumfries House at its heart. Throughout the 26 years of his tenure, he devoted a great deal of time and money towards its continual improvement. Ever mindful of his heritage, and to some degree economy, he incorporated existing structures as decorative features in the landscape, such as the deliberately preserved remains of Leifnorris and Terringzean Castle in addition to the Lady's Well and Doocot which had specific practical functions. He invested in agricultural improvements, as to a greater degree did his nephew and heir, and improved the workings of the Estate, constructing an elegant bridge to give easier access to his land on both sides of the river, developing the Mains Farm and rebuilding the walled garden. An earlier building was adapted for stabling, a smart new Coach House was built and a new Wash House established at some distance from the main house. Although somewhat obscured by later planting, it is still possible to get a sense of the mid 18th century landscape in which the setting of each structure was carefully arranged. There was never an intention to create a highly elaborate landscape such as that at Stourhead, Wiltshire, or Pains Hill, Surrey, but simply to provide a suitably varied landscaped setting for a smart new house.

Fig 5.1 A detail of John Home's 1772 plan of the Dumfries House Estate showing the landscape and plantings of the 5th Earl of Dumfries. These included radiating avenues, a bowling green and the circular mounts which are the most distinctive features of the mid 18th century landscape that are still visible. Bute Archives DHP/24

Landscape

Roy's map (Fig 5.7) of 1747–55[2] and 'A plan of the enclosures, Plantations and Policies of Dumfries House, Ayrshire' (Fig 5.8) surveyed by William Smith of 1756[3] provide invaluable information about the Estate and its buildings prior to the completion of the House. An elaborate series of avenues radiated from a point to the east of Leifnorris, a concept ultimately derived from Le Notre's designs for Louis XIV at Versailles, if on a more modest scale. The landscape bears little relation to Leifnorris; instead it represents the initial stage of landscaping around a house on a new site. As a military surveyor, Roy was interested in what existed rather than what might be proposed, which implies that this ambitious scheme of planting must have at least been laid out at this date, if not fully matured. Similarly elaborate French inspired systems of radiating avenues, grand vistas and viewpoints were created at many Scottish country houses including Loudoun Castle, Ayrshire, for the Earl of Loudoun, Taymouth Castle, Perthshire, for the Earls of Breadalbane and Drumlanrig, Dumfriesshire, for the Dukes of Buccleuch.[4]

A few elements from this scheme have survived including the Stair and Dettingen wooded Mounts that commemorated the Earl's military career, the Pennyfadzeoch D's[5] and the avenue through Shaw's Wood (Fig 5.7). One of the most interesting alignments depicted on Roy's map is that which runs through the main block of Dumfries House, between the Pennyfadzeoch D's and Terringzean Castle to the east. Axial arrangements of this sort were very much favoured by Sir William Bruce, most notably at Kinross

Fig 5.2 The Coach House and Stable for Dumfries House lie on the site of Leifnorris House. HES 2008 DP040168

House, Kinross-shire, which is aligned on Lochleven Castle. Although Dumfries House also lies on an axis with Terringzean Castle, none of the principal rooms enjoy the resulting views. This suggests that when the landscape was laid out there may have been alternative sites under consideration for the new house; turning the present house through 90 degrees for example would place the entrance and therefore the principal views on axis with Terringzean Castle, the most ancient monument on the Estate. However, these Baroque landscapes with their formal axial alignments were beginning to seem old fashioned by the mid 18th century and were being swept away to be replaced with more naturalistic landscapes, as was to be the case at Dumfries House in the second half of the 18th century. Fashions in landscape design were changing during this period just as architectural tastes were developing while the house was being designed. A desire to respond to changing fashions is symptomatic of the whole project as undertaken by the Earl and his architects. Vestiges of the scale of the original, formal scheme survive such as the farm steading at Changue, the angled orientation of which appears only to make sense in relation to the south-east radiating avenue which it terminates at almost two kilometres away from the fulcrum at Dumfries House.[6]

The Estate as inherited by the Earl included a number of buildings, some of which he adapted and others of which he demolished. There are records of three houses lying close to the heart of the Estate: Terringzean Castle, Leifnorris and Waterside. In addition, the lands of Mochrum in Dumfriesshire had become part of the Estate in the early 18th century.[7]

Terringzean Castle

Terringzean Castle lies east of the present house, close to Cumnock and now separated from the Estate by the A76. It sits on a steep bank above the Lugar Water and was originally protected by a moat as well as the river. Its prominent location means that it has been an important feature in a designed landscape at least since

Fig 5.3 The fragmentary remains of Terringzean Castle lie to the east of the A76. HES 2013 DP153509

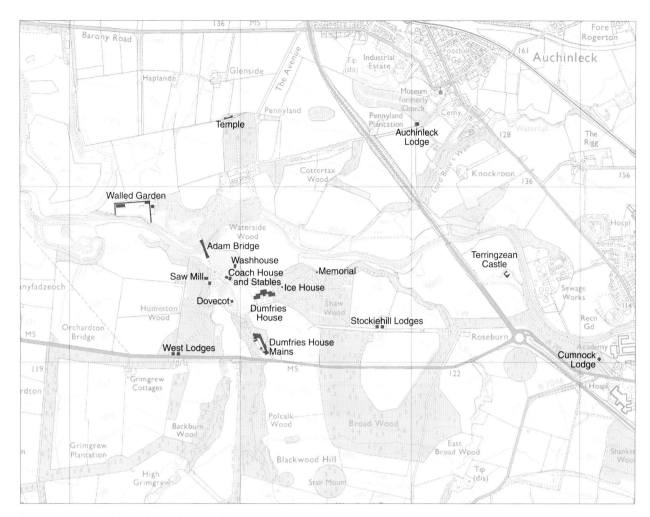

Fig 5.4 *Plan of Estate with Buildings marked.* HES GV005218

becoming part of the Leifnorris estate in 1696.[8] In 1647 it is referred to as 'Craufuirdstone, alias Terringzeane'[9] which suggests that it was the seat of the Craufords before they moved west to Liefnorris.

MacGibbon and Ross[10] illustrate a series of buildings ranged around a courtyard. The oldest part of the structure to survive appears to be the irregularly shaped tower at the south corner which RCAHMS dated to the 14th century.[11] It belonged at one time to the family of Loudoun, holders of the title Baron Terringzean. While the Castle and its surrounding

Fig 5.5 *Terringzean Castle depicted in a cartouche in the Entrance Hall at Dumfries House lying on a hill beyond Leifnorris.* HES 2007 DP033669

lands were retained by the Bute Estates, being excluded from the 2008 sale, it remains a prominent feature in the setting of the House. There are limited historic views of the Castle other than a mid 19th century view of it as a rather romantic ruinous structure.[12] The ruins appear to have been stabilised some time ago and this, along with the fact that the footings of the later buildings are largely exposed within the lines of old excavation trenches, suggests that the 3rd Marquess probably excavated and consolidated the ruins.[13] Terringzean Castle is illustrated in the background of the vignette of Leifnorris in the Entrance Hall at Dumfries House, a composition intended to evoke the ancient history of the Estate (Fig 5.5).

Leifnorris

Nothing survives of this 'Lefnoreys with Tower fortresse, mansion place, orchards, yards and pertinences thereof'[14] which was acquired by the Crichtons in 1635, but a romanticised view of the House appears in the west cartouche in the Entrance Hall of Dumfries House. It is shown as a towerhouse with a steeply pitched roof on a rocky prominence above the Lugar Water with Terringzean Castle in the distance,

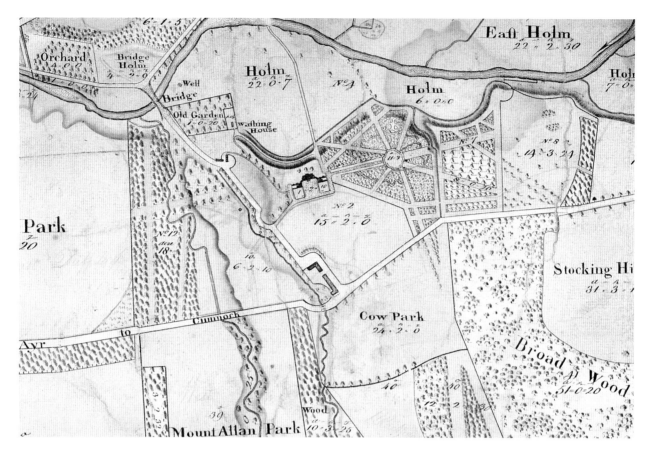

Fig 5.6 John Home's 1772 Plan of the Estate depicts the 5th Earl's landscape with its avenues, ha-ha, mounts and bowling-green. Bute Archives DHP/24

Fig 5.7 The Leifnorris Estate as surveyed by General Roy, 1747–55. Waterside, originally a separate estate, lay to the north of the Lugar where the walled garden now is. Leifnorris is shown as enclosed and arranged in orderly fields with woods and tracks or roads connecting different parts of the Estate which was surrounded on all sides by unimproved landscape. The British Library. Licensor Scran

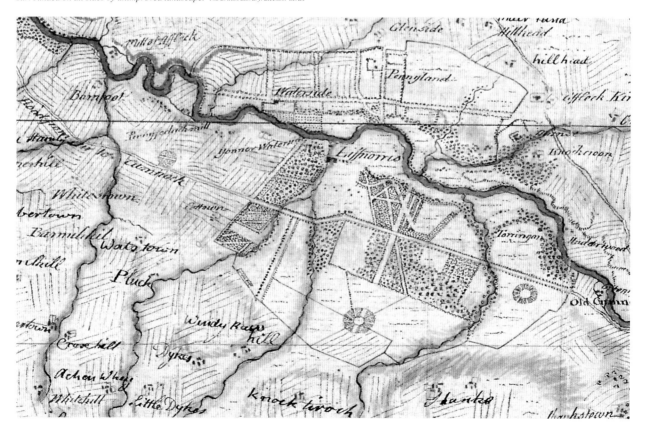

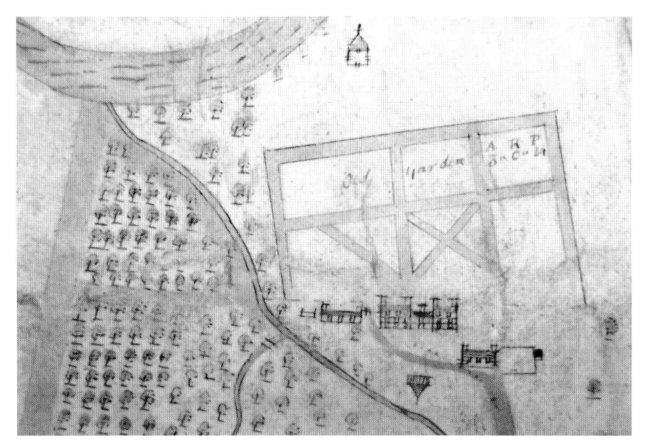

something that is likely to have some basis in reality given that Leifnorris was still extant while Dumfries House was under construction.[15]

It is clear from the rooms listed in a 1662 Inventory[16] that Leifnorris was a substantial dwelling: 'The Matted Roome, the Troung Roume, My Lord's Dressinge Roume, the Droin Roum as folowes outer the Hall, my Ladys Chamber, the mid chamber, the bloue room, the red roum, the Dininie Roum, the mele chamber, the parlour, the wichous, the wine seler and the Kitchen.'

The Crichtons lived at Leifnorris until the completion of the new house. Numerous bills for the house survive including those from June 1735 for new pewter, china, two dozen glasses and a dozen black knives and forks for the second table or steward's room.[17]

During the construction of Dumfries House Leifnorris was partially dismantled and the wood used for various building projects around the Estate, for example on 9 September 1762, John Adam records 'fir timber for the roofs of the Temple & Porters Lodge at the gateway being part of the timber of the old house'.[18] There are also undated estimates from around this time for repairs to the stair of the old house and for paving a room in the low part of the house.[19] Since money continued to be spent on maintaining the building, it must have still been in use despite being partially dismantled. A fine 17th century bolection moulded fireplace which presumably came from Leifnorris represents the single surviving architectural feature

Fig 5.8 Detail from William Smith's Estate Plan of 1756. A single-storey, three-bay block to the south-east is probably intended to show the Stables. A notional representation of Dumfries House, which was under construction at the time, appears at the bottom right corner of the plan. Bute Archives DHP/22

from the house. It was incorporated into the Bothy and Blacksmith's forge range of the Mains Farm (Fig 6.9). Leifnorris was finally demolished in 1771 when Robert Soutar's account of work for the 6th Earl of Dumfries includes 'To throwing down the old house' in January 1771.[20]

The old house of Loch Norris, or Leifnorris, was incorporated into the designed landscape as an eye-catcher, one that was noted by the Countess of

Fig 5.9 An archaeological survey of the site of Leifnorris commissioned by the 3rd Marquess of Bute did not contribute much to a greater understanding of the building. The stable block is shown at the bottom right of the drawing. Bute Archives DHP/ADD/11

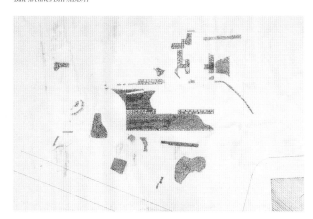

Northumberland on her visit to the Estate in August 1760[21] when describing it as the focal point of one of the radiating avenues, 'They are most of them cut for views & his best objects are the Isle of Arran & the Hills of Cunningham a little ruin'd Octagon Tower [Terringzean Castle] wch stands on a hill with detach'd Trees on it in the Park the Town of Cumnock & the Old House call'd Castle of Loch Norris.'

Leifnorris had already been stripped of materials for use on various new buildings, including the Gothic Temple, so by the time of the Countess visited it had presumably been tidied up as a picturesque ruin to complement the ruin of Terringzean on the other side of the Estate. Leifnorris must have been a prominent element on the approach drive from the north, lying to the front of the Stable and Coach House and clearly visible from the House, although the site is now hidden by Wellingtonias which were planted in the 19th century.

Under the ownership of the Earls of Dumfries the Leifnorris estate became substantial through the acquisition of neighbouring estates and farmland, a tradition that continued up until the end of the 19th century. The family also acquired extensive estates in Clackmannanshire and Wigtonshire during this period.

Waterside

A building titled Waterside is shown on Roy's map[22] (Fig 5.7) on the northern side of the Dumfries House walled garden. All that is known about this building is that it was taken down in the spring of 1763. Bills presented by John Thomson, quarrier, include 'for taking off the roof and throwing down the old house at Wattersyde and carrying out the buildable stones' and 'to throwing down the old vault and other stone walls at Waterside'.[23] The only remnant of Waterside is a substantial sycamore in the walled garden which was described in 1899 as being at least 300 years old and 'by far the oldest living thing in the parish of Old Cumnock'.[24] A doocot that must have served the house is shown to the west on the 1772 estate map, but no trace of it survives.

Lord Dumfries inherited a working estate and incorporated various buildings and structures into the setting of his new home, both functional, such as the ha-ha and the Doocot and ornamentals such as the early 18th century sundial[25] and the Lady's Well. The Stable adjacent to the site of Leifnorris is the largest building that predates the mid 18th century redevelopment of the Estate.

The Ha-Has

The eastern ha-ha, or boundary wall and ditch, runs north from the Stockiehill Lodges and appears not to relate to any aspect of the 18th century landscape.[26] It is built of large blocks of masonry which are far larger than the blocks that make up the western ha-ha which

Fig 5.10 *The substantial western ha-ha, or boundary wall and ditch, survives largely intact and now forms a pathway. In the foreground is a later passage which was cut through to provide access to a new garden.* HES 2010 DP083867

suggests that it is of an earlier date. Its course stretching from the old Ayr–Cumnock road to the bank just south of where the Rose Burn joins the Lugar Water is clearly shown on Roy's map (Fig 5.7) as the eastern boundary of a plantation which may represent either a deer park or the division between the earlier, separate estates of Leifnorris and Terringzean.[27] The western ha-ha runs north from the West Gate lodges, also on the Ayr–Cumnock road, to the Waterloo Bridge over the Polcalk Burn just before it enters the Lugar Water. It probably marked another boundary since Roy's map marks the area west of it as 'Yonner Waterside'. These boundaries show that the original estate of Leifnorris was relatively modest.

The Doocot

The Doocot is the oldest surviving structure on the Dumfries House Estate. It lies just west of the House and has the date of 1671 carved in a panel above the door and on the south-east skew putt.[28] The latter is also dated 1851 with the same incised numerals, presumably to record the date of its restoration or repair although no record of this has as yet come to light. Its simple, crow-stepped gabled rectangular form is a good example of this building type.[29] Doocots were not only historically an important source of winter food and manure but also a status symbol.

Although doocots were sometimes extremely elaborate, the Dumfries House example is quite restrained except for its fine moulded door case and heraldic panel. It is unusual that the string course stops short of, rather than going around, the heraldic panel and the consequent dis-junction of the two elements is not very satisfactory. The door case and panel do not appear to have been designed as complementary elements. Heraldic display on a doocot is not unusual, for example the doocot dated 1647 at Westquarter,

Fig 5.11 *A c1900 National Art Survey of Scotland survey of the 1671 Doocot.* HES DP142874

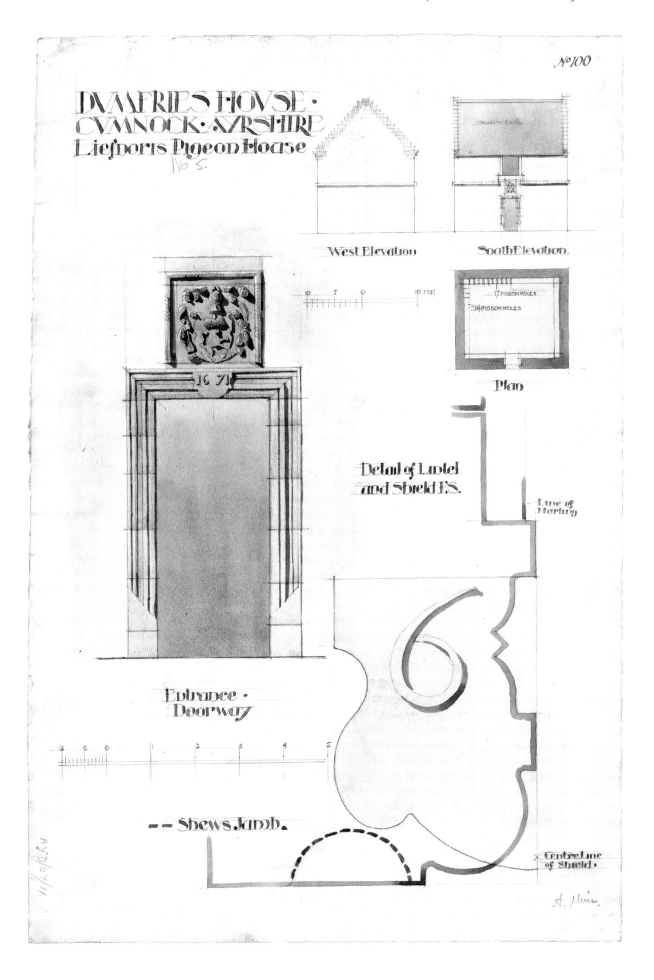

N°100

DVMFRIES HOVSE·
CVMNOCK·AYRSHIRE
Liefnoris Pigeon House
No 5.

West Elevation   South Elevation.

10 5 0 10 FEET

17 PIGEON HOLES
14 PIGEON HOLES

Plan

Detail of Lintel
and Shield F.S.

Line of
Harling

16 71

Entrance·
Doorway

12 6 0 1 2 3 4 5

-- Shews Jamb.

Centre Line
of Shield·

A. Muir.

Fig 5.12 The Doocot retains its original stone nesting boxes.
HES 2010 DP083650

Fig 5.13 The Doocot is the most complete surviving building that pre-dates the 5th Earl of Dumfries' transformation of the Estate. HES 2010 DP083655

Falkirk, bears the coat of arms of the Livingston family. However, the fine moulded dressed yellow and red stonework of the door case with associated dated panel on the Dumfries House Doocot is unusually elaborate for what is essentially a service door. It is of much higher quality than the other dressed openings of the Doocot which would suggest that the doorway and its heraldic panel were re-used from different parts of Leifnorris during the restoration of 1851[30] were it not for the fact that the heraldic panel is not of the Earls of Dumfries who owned Leifnorris in 1671 but that of the McDoualls of Freugh. In 1720 Lady Elizabeth Crichton-Dalrymple, sister of the future 5th Earl of Dumfries, married John McDouall of Freugh; their son became the 6th Earl and lived at Dumfries House from 1768 until 1803. The 6th Earl sold his father's estate at Freugh and dropped the name whilst retaining his uncle's name and estates in Ayrshire and at Mochrum. This suggests that it was the 6th Earl who re-sited the heraldic panel and door case from Freugh when he sold that estate and installed them in the Doocot. A less likely alternative is that the heraldic panel might have been stored on the Estate and inserted here during the work that prompted the insertion of the 1851 date. This was during the minority of the 3rd Marquess and would have been at the behest of Sir Charles Fergusson, who was resident at Dumfries House at the time in his role as one of Lord Bute's trustees.

The original location of the door case itself is also problematic though it seems possible that it came from Leifnorris. The significance of the 1671 date has yet to be determined: was this date repeated on the skew putt in incised numerals during the restoration in 1851 or was it a more unlikely coincidence that the doocot and the door case were of the same date?

The Stable

The Stable as we see it today dates from the early 18th century, though it may contain earlier fabric. It lies to the north of the Coach House and to the south-east of the site of Leifnorris. This large, rectangular building which pre-dates the nearby Coach House and Wash House has smooth ashlar dressings that are unlike the diagonally droved dressings that characterise all the other buildings by the Adam brothers on the Estate. Its relatively small windows do not relate to any of the other windows in post-1754 subsidiary structures on the Estate, such as those in the service courtyards of the main house. They do not adequately light the interior, in contrast to, for example, those in the stables provided by the Adam office at Hopetoun House. The sundial on the west elevation is oddly located as opposed to being an integral part of the design of the building. The large

Fig 5.14 The harled walls, proportions and small windows of the stable building suggest that it was built before Dumfries House as part of the Leifnorris Estate. HES 2010 DP083698

hipped roof, the stone cornice and the harled walls are also unlike any others on the Estate except for the Doocot.

The 'Abstract of the accounts betwixt The Rt Hon The Earl of Dumfries & Stair and John Adam Architect in Edinburgh' dated 9 September 1762 relates to the building of the House, the Coach House, the Wash House, the wall and gate at the Mains Farm, the erection of two obelisks and the building of the bridge over the Lugar, the Adam Bridge.[31] The fact that the Stables are not mentioned in any of the Adam accounts suggests that they were built at a different time. This building seems to be the Leifnorris Estate building referred to as the 'present barn' in the Adam contact which is shown on Smith's map of 1756 (Fig 5.8) as

Fig 5.15 The magnificent north wing of Hopetoun House houses the stables. HES 1995 SC767093

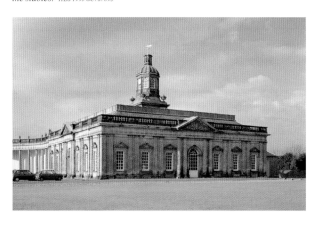

a single-storey block of three bays to the south-east of Leifnorris.[32] On 11 February 1760 John Adam presented an 'Estimate of Stable and Coach House for the Rt Hon Earl of Dumfries proposed to be built at the West end of the present barn'.[33] He also quoted the same price in the same document for an additional Stable and Coach House to built upon the north side of the barn bringing the total cost to £1358 17s 8d.[34] The estimate is clearly marked 'not carried out' but it demonstrates the extensive scale of the proposals for retaining the existing barn as part of a much larger scheme with a series of buildings ranged around a courtyard where the day to day workings of the stable yard would be contained. There is no other mention of stables in the Adam accounts, which tends to suggest that they were accommodated in an existing building, probably the barn mentioned above.

The original, possibly 17th century, building has been altered and adapted. Only through removing the harl would it be possible to establish with more certainty the building's history. The unusual form of the existing Stables with their very deep plan and stalls on either side of a central passage is unlike contemporary designs illustrated in, for example, *Vitruvius Scoticus* but is closer to designs by James Gibbs such as the stable at Kelmarsh, Oxfordshire.[35] This supports the theory that the building that now houses the Stable

pre-dated Dumfries House and formed part of the ancillary buildings of Leifnorris.

Early 18th century stables and coach houses tended to be located in the wings of the main house, as at Paxton House, Berwickshire, and Hopetoun, West Lothian (Fig 5.15). The stables were one of the series of buildings that could be grouped together to enhance the grandeur of the main house with a *cour d'honneur*, as created by Sir John Vanburgh at Seaton Delaval, Tyne and Wear. The design of the Stable and Coach

Fig 5.17 Arniston House, Midlothian, is comparable in size to Dumfries House but its stables are more luxuriously appointed with ornamental stalls and dressed stone arcades. They were incorporated into the plan of the house rather than being located in a separate structure. HES 1995 SC767044

Fig 5.16 Although the stalls in the Stable date from the 1930s, there is no evidence of earlier feed shoots or feeding troughs built into the walls. HES 2010 DP083692

House at Dumfries House illustrates a move away from this concept towards a separation of functions, not only for the purpose of removing the smells and noise of the stables from the immediate environs of the house but also to create a new type of status building.[36] This trend is also seen in the arrangement of the House, where the kitchens are located in a wing rather than in the main block. John Adam designed a detached stable court at Cherry Park for Inveraray Castle in 1759–61.[37] Sir James Clerk of Penicuik erected a fine, detached Stable court with Coach House and Doocot at Penicuik in 1760 which is exactly contemporary with the Coach House at Dumfries House although on a completely different scale. The Stable block and the Coach House at Dumfries House are rather hidden from view in a dip which greatly reduces their architectural presence The financial necessity to adapt an existing building as the stable fixed the location and precluded the creation of an enclosed stable courtyard as at Penicuik.

The Stable is a large rectangular piend-roofed building which provides stabling and a tack room on the ground floor with hayloft above. The exterior does not reflect the function of the interior with walls cutting across windows and a lack of ancillary spaces that necessitated the addition of a number of rooms (since removed). The first floor hay loft is not readily accessible and seems to have been built without a first floor hay door through which hay could have been transferred directly from a cart to the loft rather than being carried up the steps. Although the interior has been refitted on a number of occasions, there is no evidence of built-in feed shutes or even hay hecks,[38] which would have been a prerequisite of a well designed stable.

The Lady's Well

The scattered remains of what was once a charming eye-catcher lie on the south bank of the Lugar Water to the east of the Adam Bridge. It is not shown on Roy's map[39] but is on Smith's Estate plan of 1756.[40] It is on axis with Leifnorris and the Doocot to the south of the House. The Lady's Well was a square structure of four rusticated, belted Doric columns linked by key-stoned, semi-circular arches supporting a frieze and cornice. It had a stone clad pyramidal roof capped with a belted ball finial with ball finials at the corners and appears to date from the early 18th century. A c1940 photograph shows the building set close to a metal railed paddock next to the site of Leifnorris' walled garden. It has precedents in the designs of James Gibbs as illustrated in his *Book of Architecture* of 1728.[41] A scheme by Robert Adam for 'A Rusticated Temple Designed for Mount Stair at Leifnorris' is for a much larger monument than the Lady's Well but depicts a very similar square structure complete with pyramidal roof, rusticated columns, ball finials and key-stoned arches

Fig 5.18 The early 18th century Lady's Well was an ornamental feature of the gardens north of Leifnorris. HES 1950 SC1331281

with a spiral stair in one of the corners to access a viewing platform. The use of 'Leifnorris' in the title of the drawing implies that the design precedes the laying of the foundation stone in July 1754 at which the name Dumfries House was adopted.[42]

In the Estate papers there is a claim for compensation from the Army for the destruction of the Lady's Well, 'reported as partly destroyed on 10 April 1944'.[43] £1,077 was offered in compensation but since this was not calculated against a realistic estimate the Well was not repaired and the remaining structure was finally dismantled in 1963.

Fig 5.19 Robert Adam designed this undated 'rusticated temple', which was never built, to crown the Stair Mount. Bute Archives

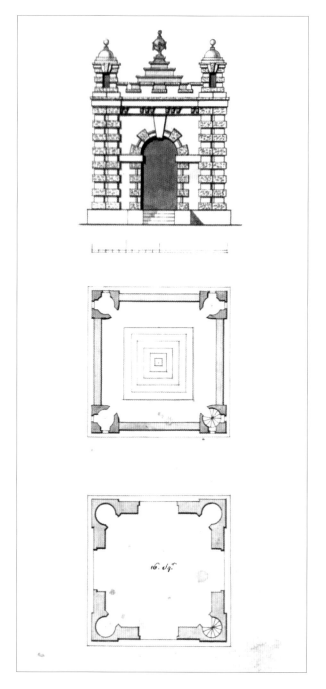

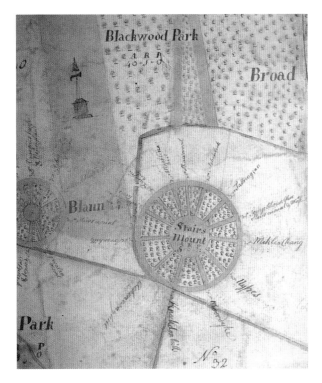

Fig 5.20 The 1756 Dumfries House Estate Plan marks not only the Mounts but also the views from each of them. Bute Archives DHP/22

Fig 5.21 A c1750 plan and specification for the construction of the Mounts. Bute Archives, uncatalogued

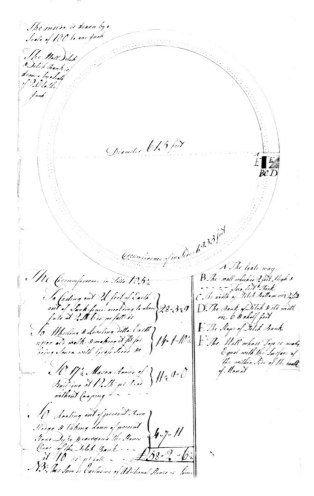

Roy's map[44] depicts the extensive formal landscape that had been planted around the proposed site for Dumfries House by the mid 18th century. Only vestigial elements of this extensive landscape survive, the most prominent being the circular wooded mounts. A mains farm was another essential element of a working estate and this, along with the walled garden, seems to have been developed before work on the new house began.

The Mounts

A series of circular mounts were planted with trees to provide focal points in the landscape and were cut through with radiating paths that in turn afforded views across the Estate to other points of interest. This arrangement is clearly shown on the Smith plan (Fig 5.20).[45] In the Mount Stuart Archives is an undated construction drawing that shows the plan and estimate of a circular mount surrounded by a ditch (Fig 5.21).[46] The dimensions of '615 feet' in diameter relate almost exactly to the existing Stair Mount. This is shown on both Roy and Smith's maps which implies that this drawing is dated prior to the building of Dumfries House. The style of the script suggests an 18th century date in which case this is the only design for the formal landscape created before the building of Dumfries House to have survived.

Mains Farm

The Estate was largely agrarian and so the Mains Farm was an important element, especially as a means of achieving agricultural improvements across the Estate. A programme of field drainage to improve the productivity of the land was a high priority from the start, with a brick and tile works being established on the estate at Sandend to provide clay drainage pipes. The Mains Farm had to provide not only accommodation to store crops and house animals but also stabling for the farm horses that provided the principal means of transport and power. The farm workers from the farmer down to the labourers and boys also needed accommodation. An 18th century farm was quite a substantial employer and formed a community within itself.

Roy's map[47] shows a group of four buildings at a pronounced corner of the Ayr–Cumnock road, to the east of the Polcalk Burn; the present complex appears to be somewhat to the west of this site. There is no visible evidence of the earlier buildings. Dumfries House Mains Farm has had a variety of names; on the First Edition Ordnance Survey Map surveyed in 1857, it is recorded as Causeyhead but by the time gas lighting was installed in 1867, the house at the Mains is described as 'Woodburn Cottage' and is the residence of the factor.[48]

The Mains Farm is clearly shown on Smith's Estate Plan of 1756 which, combined with the absence of any mention in the exhaustive John Adam accounts for the

Fig 5.22 Dumfries House with, in the foreground, the large Stair Mount and the smaller Bland Mount. HES 2013 DP153678

Fig 5.23 The Mains Farmhouse with its later extensions is attached to white-harled ranges of single-storey farm buildings which are arranged around a west-facing courtyard. The adjacent metal Dutch barns and north-east range have been taken down since the photograph was taken. HES 2008 DP040179

Fig 5.24 The only contemporary depiction of the Mains Farm complex appears on John Home's Estate Plan of 1772 where it is shown to the left of the newly completed Dumfries House. Bute Archives DHP/24

construction of any buildings at the Mains, suggests that it was already constructed when the map was in preparation.[49] Adam's only involvement appears to have been 'for building the gate & wall at the Mains'.[50]

Stylistically, the earliest parts of the Mains Farm house and steading date from the 1740s and so may have been constructed by Lord Dumfries soon after his accession to the title and estates in 1742 but no records relating to its initial construction survive. Arranging the farm buildings around a courtyard open to the west provided an enclosed service yard hidden from the drive with the farm house acting as the first gate lodge. The organisation of the farm buildings around a courtyard rather than in a looser association relates to the agricultural improvements that were spreading across Scotland in the early 18th century.[51] It is not an expression of architectural display, as seen in the semi-circular Maam Steading on the Inveraray Estate designed by Robert Mylne 1787–90; instead, this is a practical farm, built without architectural pretensions, which has grown and been altered as and when required. The Mains Farm sits at an entrance to the Estate, which must have acted as the principal approach to Leifnorris but which subsequently became the service entrance to the new Dumfries House estate. The road was not adopted as a Turnpike road until 1767.[52]

The Mains Farm seems initially to have consisted of three buildings. A two-storey, three-bay house to the south with a piend roof which forms the core of the present building with a single-storey wing at the rear; further north a detached block formed part of the east side of the open courtyard and an L-plan single-storey range completed the steading. A gateway is marked on the plan between the central and northern ranges. By 1772 the house and the adjacent building were joined (Fig 5.1).[53] The original ranges are discernible within the current complex which was developed piecemeal rather than redeveloped as part of a scheme of agricultural improvements as, for example, at Rosebery Steading, Midlothian, or the Home Farm at Culzean, Ayrshire. A fine 17th century bolection moulded fireplace which probably came from Leifnorris has been incorporated into the Bothy and Blacksmith's forge range but it is not known when this surviving feature from the old house was inserted.

Walled Garden

The walled garden lies on the north bank of the Lugar Water (Fig 5.4) on the site of what was once a separate estate known as Waterside. That house, of which there is now no trace, lay on the northern side of the existing garden and is shown on Roy's map (Fig 5.7) as set within an enclosure that appears to reflect the extent of the current walled garden.

The date of the present walled garden is uncertain but it is first mentioned in the Lord Dumfries' correspondence when Thomas Harrison was employed to repair the garden walls in 1764[54] and Andrew Morton to rebuild some of them two years later.[55] The earliest detailed drawing we have of the walled gardens is c1818[56] and shows a group of service buildings built against the outer face of the north garden wall with glass houses on the south side.[57] During the 19th century, the gardens were further developed with defined areas for kitchen gardens, fruit trees,

Fig 5.25 The walled garden has undergone many changes; this painting by Jacob Thomson of the garden in 1830 shows Dumfries House in the background beyond the Adam Bridge and gives an impression of what was at the time a very productive garden. The Bute Collection

orchard and a flower garden. The walled garden was an important source of food for the house and required a skilled workforce to manage it. In the later 19th century, balustrades and terraces were introduced as recorded in a painted view of the upper terrace of the walled garden with the Adam Bridge in the middle distance and Dumfries House, without its late 19th century additions, beyond.

None of the existing garden buildings are easily identifiable as 18th century, having undergone a number of later alterations, but a plan of the area to the north of the Adam Bridge c1760[58] includes two parallel walls for fruit trees which are completely separate from the walled garden.[59]

Lord Dumfries maintained his interest in planting trees at Dumfries House which had begun with the creation of wooded avenues and mounts.[60] There seems to have been little interest in creating a flower garden although part of the walled garden almost certainly would have provided flowers for the house. A hot-house for peaches was built much closer to the House on the east bank of the Polcalk burn to the north of the Mains, the platform for which survives. This is one of the few garden buildings that appears regularly in both John Adam's and the Earl's accounts.[61] The foundations were dug in February 1763 and the interior was decorated a

year later.[62] No images survive for this building which was a modest, rectangular structure, presumably similar to an orangery, with large glazed windows on its south elevation and access stairs.[63] The garden buildings at Culzean Castle, such as the Camellia House, are the geographically closest examples of this type of building if more elaborate. Thomas Waitt painted an 'alcove' for a small pavilion beside the bowling green to the east of the House but this is the only reference to that structure.[64]

With his new house reaching completion, the 5th Earl, with John Adam, turned his attention to the provision of ancillary estate buildings. A Coach House was built close to the old building that he had adapted as a Stable as well as a Wash House and Ice House. In addition, the new approach to the house from the north required both a new bridge and a grand new entrance gateway.

The Coach House

The Coach House is a modest five-bay building of diagonally droved ashlar which closely matches that used on the pavilions of the main house, smartly detailed with a pediment and '*oeil de boeuf*' window.[65] It sits in a hollow to the north-west of the house and is aligned so as to be perpendicular to the ridge line of the Stable block behind. The estimates refer to an old Coach House nearby and since the present building is close to the site of Leifnorris it is possible that it was developed on an existing site. The building originally

provided space for five carriages, each with separate arched doors. Thomas Waitt[66] was employed to paint the woodwork in the Coach House in 1761, as well as some blind windows which are probably the windows on the west elevation that have since been opened up; his bill also includes fitting old doors into the groom's room and fitting hinges on the round window. In John Adam's account for 1760–1, he mentions 'taking up old floors for sarking to the Coach House', one of several examples of materials being reclaimed from the old house.[67] The Coach House was an important but subsidiary building to the Stable: the horses rather than

the carriages they pulled were the focus of the attention of most 18th century gentlemen. In the 19th century, chimney stacks were added to match those added to the original Wash House and, in the late 19th century, a rear wing and further first floor accommodation was created to house two families. In the 1950s these were combined to create a larger flat for a chauffeur.

Wash House

The Wash House lies to the north of the Coach House on the northern side of the bank which was planted with sequoia by the 3rd Marquess and at the south-eastern corner of the original walled garden of Leifnorris.[68] The building originally consisted of a three-bay, two-storey structure in a walled bleaching green where washing was spread out to dry and bleach in the sun.[69] The location of the Wash House some distance from the main house, while at a convenient distance, was preferable in terms of visibility and fumes but also in terms of space since there was a periodic need to launder a large volume of household linen.[70] The building originally had a piend roof, while a stepped chimney stack on the east elevation, since removed, was added later, matching those added to the Coach House in the 19th century.

The building was constructed of diagonally droved, rubble stonework. John Adam refers in the 1761 account

Fig 5.28 The combined coach house and stables block at Penicuik House, Midlothian of 1766 are in marked contrast to those at Dumfries House. HES DP041597

Fig 5.26 The Coach House, Stable and Adam Bridge. HES 2008 DP040192

Fig 5.29 The Wash House before conversion. The original three-bay building, to the left, was extended in the late-19th century. HES 2010 DP083841

Fig 5.30 The arched doorway of the Ice House is original but the upper walls and slated roof date from when it was converted into a game-larder for the 4th Marquess. HES 2010 DP083664

Fig 5.31 A detail of John Home's 1772 Estate Pan showing the Wash House and bleaching green in the corner of the old walled garden.
Bute Archives DHP/24

to 'making a horse for drying the linen', '44 days of wright taking off old doors & fitting them on the Grooms rooms & washing house' and 'To painting 8 old windows in Coach House and washing house.'[71] In 1761 Thomas Waitt[72] was paid for painting doors, window shutters, blind windows and a closet in the Wash House. Here again needless expense was avoided in the creation of modern convenience.[73]

The Laundry in the west pavilion of the main house was where personal items would have been laundered by the laundry maid or personal servants whereas the household washing was carried out by the lower ranks in the Wash House. This room was incorporated into a new suite of rooms that provided access to the Turkish Bath when it was installed in 1867. The Wash House was extended by two bays in the later 19th century which suggests that the functions of the Laundry were then transferred there as part of accommodating the Turkish Bath. This does not appear to have been the work of Robert Weir Schultz because it bears none of his distinctive detailing, such as his use of diagonally droved ashlar. The upper floor appears to have provided accommodation for the laundry maids. When surveyed by RCAHMS in 2010 the remains of the original stair were visible in the north-east corner along with a good 18th century chimneypiece on the first floor.[74]

Ice House
The Ice House, which lies to the north-east of the main house, was essential to the running of the kitchens in providing a plentiful supply of ice for food storage.[75] It was built to the designs of John Adam[76] and although now it seems isolated from the House, this was not unusual at the time because the location of an ice house was determined more on geographical reasons, the preference being for a cool, north facing site where it was possible to dig a large hole to and from which it was easy to transport large blocks of ice.[77] Originally, an arched doorway would have led via a passageway to a, probably egg-shaped, chamber in which the ice was packed. The domed chamber, quite possibly covered over with soil for added insulation, had a drain at the bottom. Although the lower portion of the Ice House has been filled in,

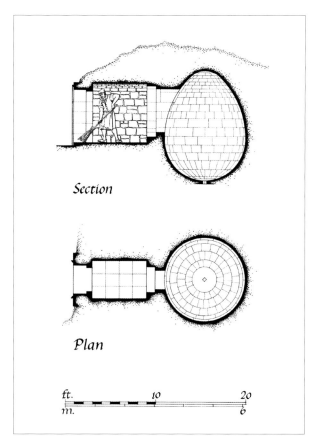

Fig 5.32 Section and plan of the mid-18th century ice house at the Whim, Borders, is similar in form to the original Ice House at Dumfries House.
HES SC714584

probably using the masonry from the dome, the central drain survives.

The Ice House at Dumfries House may have been intended as an incident on a walk leading to the bowling green but as such, it was a much less elaborate feature than, for example, the grotto fronted ice house at Gosford, East Lothian. It was converted into a game larder once technology had made the ice house a redundant concept, most probably during the time of the 4th Marquess, who was a keen sportsman.

The Adam Bridge
The magnificent Adam Bridge was designed by John Adam in 1760[78] to carry the main drive over the Lugar Water from the entrance to the Estate just south of Auchinleck Church. Inspired by his father William's Aberfeldy Bridge,[79] which has the same arrangement of solid and balustraded parapet with four tall obelisks at the ends,[80] it takes the form of a triple arched bridge, the central arch spanning 50 ft over the river with flanking arches to allow access along either riverbank. A balustraded parapet originally rose to the central horizontal section; this was replaced with an open timber parapet in the mid 20th century. It is almost contemporary with the Garden Bridge at Inveraray which John Adam designed using the same elliptical archway, an unusual feature at this time (Fig 5.34).[81]

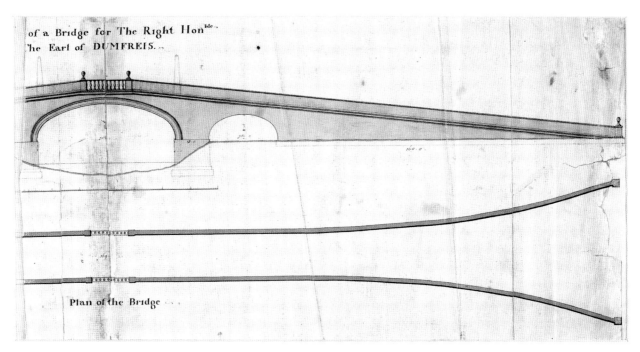

Fig 5.33 The first design for the Adam Bridge shows it without obelisks, which were later pencilled in as the design was developed, and a higher central span. Bute Archives DHP/23

At Dumfries House he adopted a similar steep rise to gain the view as he had when building the Garron Bridge, Inverarary, to Roger Morris' design in 1748.[82]

The development of the design for the Adam Bridge is illustrated by a design drawing of c1760 (Fig 5.33) which comprises three elliptical arches with long swept parapets and a short stretch of balustrade at the apex with ball finials and which has been annotated with the addition of obelisks and an extended balustrade.[83] This change to the design is corroborated by a bill from John Adam dated 1762[84] which states that 'the expense of the additional balustrades and obelisks on the bridge not included'. The Bridge became more of a garden feature giving access to the smaller, northern part of the Estate when the new drives and lodges were constructed to the south off the Ochiltree to Cumnock turn-pike in the early 19th century. It appears in a series of romantic paintings of the Estate commissioned by the Bute

Fig 5.34 John Adam's Garden Bridge at Inveraray, 1759–61, has a similar elliptical arch to the bridge he designed for Dumfries House. HES SC458255

family in the 19th century[85] and on a plan entitled 'A plan of Piercy Bridge and Wood with Northumberland Mount'[86] which, although undated, is dedicated to the Earl of Dumfries and Stair, which dates it between 1760 and 1768. This is the only document that refers to the Adam-designed bridge as Piercy Bridge. To the north the circular Northumberland Mount is marked which, unlike the other Mounts, was not planted with trees and of which nothing survives. To the south is an area highlighted as 'a bank of flowering shrubs and evergreens over which the finest prospect of the lawns, plantations, river, bridge & house are got'. Despite the fact that Lord Dumfries concentrated most of his time and money on the completion of his new house, the way in which structures, old and new, were used within the landscape to picturesque effect makes clear that he was also concerned with providing it with an appropriate setting.

Gothic Temple Lodge

An estimate for building a 'Gateway, Porter's Lodge, Temple and Walls adjoining being an Entrance propos'd for the Right Hon the Earl of Dumfries' Park at Leifnorris' was provided by John Adam in 1760.[87] A site was chosen on axis with the centre of the new house on the skyline to the north. It appears to have been initially intended as the main approach, being the only lodge included in the John Adam estimates. However, Lord Dumfries did not own the land north of the lodge which would have connected it to the road running between Auchinleck and Ochiltree. The 6th Earl negotiated again unsuccessfully with his neighbour, Lord Auchinleck, for a right of access in 1773. The Lodge appears to have been designed with its principal elevation facing south overlooking the House rather than facing the approach as would usually

Fig 5.35 The Adam Bridge has a distinctive elliptical arch; its timber balustrade replaced the original stone one in the 20th century. HES 2010 DP083247

Fig 5.36 John Adam designed this bridge with its obelisks and swept balustrades as a fittingly grand means of approaching Dumfries House across the Lugar.
HES 2013 DP153493

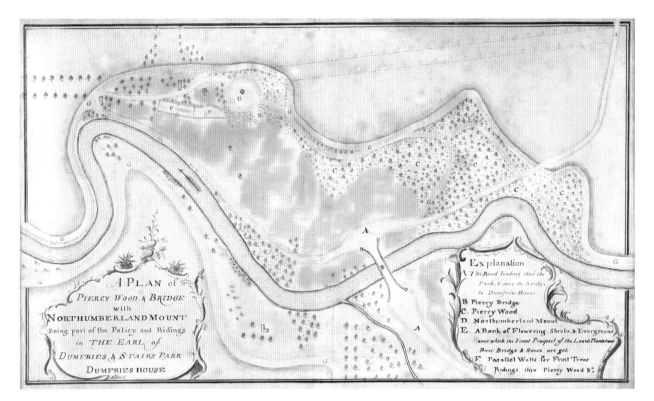

be the case. This suggests that it was designed as an eye-catcher on the skyline which could also have functioned as an entrance. As with the design for the wings of the main house, a desire to create a strong silhouette is apparent here and, once again, William Adam's Chatelherault can be seen as an influence. As late as 1857 there was still no driveway to the building, the principal driveway being from Auchinleck until this was in turn superseded by the new drives with their paired gate lodges created in the early 19th century south of the Lugar Water.

The Gothic Temple Lodge (Figs 5.38–5.39) originally consisted of a large central ogee arch flanked by clustered columns, topped by a pierced parapet terminated with paired obelisks and linked by castellated screen walls on either side to a pair of two-storey castellated towers set on angle with further castellated screen walls on their other flank. The west tower contained the Temple and the east one the Porters Lodge with worker accommodation behind the screen wall. It was built with 'firr timber for the roofs of the Temple & Porters Lodge at the gateway being part of the timber of the old house'.[88] The sandstone has the same characteristic red colouration as that from the Pennyland Quarry, a little way to the east, which was used for the inner walls of Dumfries House.

This use of what appears to be a folly for an essentially functional purpose can be seen in many other buildings of the time; for example, the Castle on the Sledmere Estate in Yorkshire designed by John Carr of York c1790 for Sir Tatton Sykes served as the Kennels for the House. At Dumfries House, the Temple Lodge is a skyline feature visible from the

Fig 5.37 A plan of part of the Dumfries House Estate c1765 shows that 'Parallel Walls for Fruit Trees' were a feature of the walled garden. It also shows the Adam Bridge and various rides and walks along with a Mount which was presumably named in honour of the Countess of Northumberland. Bute Archives DHP/ADD/1

House but with no obvious drive leading to it. Although no drawings survive for this Lodge, it is likely that it was designed by John Adam. He was aware of contemporary examples of the Gothic style having visited Whitton Place, Middlesex, one of the homes of The Duke of Argyll, on his trip to London in 1748[89] where he sketched the ornamental c1730 Gothic tower and other examples of Gothic design. The Shobdon Arches, Herefordshire, are another example of this Gothic taste where genuine medieval and Norman arches were re-erected as an eye-catcher with additional Gothic ornaments in 1751. The Lodge at Dumfries House was altered in 1818 and made into two houses with the insertion of hearths and the linking of the different rooms. The discussions with the Boswalls of Auchinleck about gaining access across their land to the Lodge continued without resolution into the next generation.[90]

On completing the House and Estate buildings, Lord Dumfries turned his attention to the development of the mineral reserves on his estate. His father had developed the coal mines on his Clackmannanshire estates but his son had to sell these in 1762 in order to realise some capital, presumably to help fund the building of Dumfries House.[91]

Lord Dumfries began exploiting the mineral potential of the Dumfries House Estate in the later 1760s. He opened the coal working at Garlaff, near Skares, due south of the house on 4 April 1767.[92] In 1768, Garlaff Coal works and Benston Lime Quarry on the Estate were

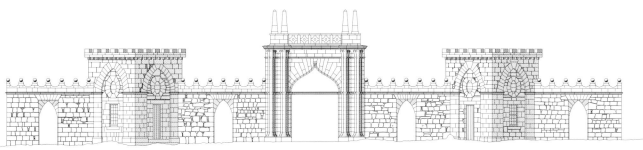

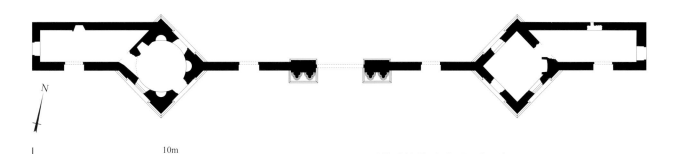

Figs 5.38–5.39 The Gothic Temple Lodge. HES 2010 GV005217, DP083816

leased to William Moore. Agricultural improvement increased the demand for coal, which was used as part of the process of creating lime for the fields, and in 1770 the 6th Earl opened another pit at Coalburn, New Cumnock, to meet the demand. In 1771 he installed a steam engine for pumping water at Garlaff to deepen the workings. Lord Dumfries leased his Ayrshire coal workings to James Taylor in the 1790s. The sale of coal outwith the immediate area was not profitable until the arrival of the railway in 1850.[93] The coal workings on the Estate were let during the 19th century and,

during the 20th century, the large Barony Colliery and Highhead Colliery at Auchinleck continued the extraction of the Estate's coal in the immediate vicinity of the House and policies. Great care was taken not to undermine any of the estate buildings, especially the House, even during the increased demand created by the Second World War.[94] The dramatic A-frame of the Barony Pit is a fitting memorial to this extensive, now largely vanished, industry. In the latter part of the 20th century, the landscape surrounding Dumfries House gradually returned to a more peaceful, agrarian state.

1   Unpublished manuscript held at Alnwick Castle, Northumberland.

2   Roy's Military Survey of Scotland 1747–1755 British Library Maps C.9.b

3   Bute Archives DHP/22 in fragmentary condition

4   Roy's Military Survey of Scotland 1747–1755 British Library Maps C.9.b

5   A circular plantation lying to the west of the present house, dissected by drive, created two D shaped woods.

6   Changue Farm steading is shown on Roy's map and on the First Edition Ordnance Survey Map surveyed in 1857.

7   The estate of Mochrum, Wigtonshire, complete with its ruinous castle, Old Place of Mochrum, was acquired by Colonel William Dalrymple c1737. (Undated letter c1737 concerning the purchase of the Mochrum Estate in Wigtonshire. Bute Archives DU/4/55/7.) However, Groome's Gazetteer records that 'Since the close of the 17th century the Old Place and estate of Mochrum have been held by the Earls of Dumfries and Marquises of Bute (F H Groome *Ordnance Gazetteer of Scotland: A Survey of Scottish Topography, Statistical, Biographical and Historical*, 1884, Vol. V.37) which suggests that they may have leased part of the estate up until that point. From the time of the 5th Earl, the Mochrum Estate was managed as part of the Dumfries House Estate. It was bequeathed by the 4th Marquess of Bute to his daughter and remains in that branch of the family.

8   Stevens 1899, 83

9   Warrick 1899, 154

10 MacGibbon and Ross, 1887–1892, Vol III, 352

11 HES Canmore Site NS52SE 2

12 Paterson 1863, 307

13 Measured Survey Drawing of Terringzean Castle, c1880 HES A 27108

14 Charter dated 17 January 1635 'That she (Anne Kennedye spouse to Mr Mathew Crawford) was in noe waies compelled nor coached by the said Mathew Crawfurd her husband to the making and subscrybeinge of ane disposition made by her sayd spouse and certayne other persons and her (self) to ane noble& potent William Earle of Dumfries of all & whole the foure markeland of Lefnoreys aith Tower fortresse mansion place orchards yards and pertinences thereof.' Bute Archives DU/2/31/1

15 The cartouche of Sanquhar Castle also in the Entrance Hall appears to be reasonably architecturally accurate which suggests that the depiction of Leifnorris is also accurate.

16 Bute Archives DU/3/13 Inventory dated 12 December

17 Bute Archives D/5/30/21

18 Bute Archives DU/5/9/38

19 '16ft by 18ft, to twelve steps of a stair at 4¼ feet long, for leading of pavement and stair, for loading of sand for the pavement at a total £8.4.1 ½' Bute Archives DU/5/30/21

20 Bute Archives DU/6/34

21 Diary of 1st Duchess of Northumberland August 1760. Unpublished manuscript held at Alnwick Castle, Northumberland.

22 Roy Military Survey of Scotland 1747–1755. British Library Maps, C.9.b

23 Bute Archives DU/6/23

24 Warrick 1899, 155

25 The sundial is now located on the lawn west of the house. W B Stevenson 'Sundials of Six Counties near Glasgow' offprint of *Transactions of the Glasgow Archaeological Society* 9(4), 265

26 Dumfries House & Landscape Ayrshire, Working Draft Conservation Plan, Simpson and Brown 2008, 21

27 Roy Military Survey of Scotland, 1747–1755. British Library Maps C.9.b

28 HES Photograph A 78772/CN

29 In 1617 the right of owning or maintaining a pigeon house was limited by statute to Lairds whose lands produced each year 'ten chalders of victual' or grain within two miles of the cote; one chalder equalled 16 bolls of 1¼ hundredweight therefore 10 chalders is approximately 10 tons. They were sometimes the vehicle for architectural display such as the circular tower at Daldowie, Lanarkshire, the picturesque beehive at Phantassie, East Lothian, or the symmetrical doocots that flank Ackergill Tower in Caithness but the Dumfries House Doocot is relatively modest. Buxbaum 1987, 7

30 An idea suggested by Michael Davis

31 Bute Archives DU/5/30/16

32 Bute Archives DHP/22

33 The estimated cost of construction was £679 8s 10d Bute Archives DU/5/30/1

34 Estimates by John Adam 11 February 1760 'Estimate of Stable and Coach House for the Rt Hon Earl of Dumfries proposed to be built at the West end of the present barn. Total cost £679.8.10; Same price for another stable and Coach House to built upon the north side of the barn' Bute Archives DU/5/30/1

35 Gibbs 1728, pl.38

36 Giles Worsley suggests that Houghton Hall, Norfolk, has the first example of a detached quadrangle of stables designed by William Kent in c1732. Worsley 2005, 124

37 Cherry Park was completed by William Mylne in 1772. Walker 2000, 321

38 The original stables at Penicuik House, for example, have elaborately dressed stone niches for the hecks (mangers or feed troughs) but there is no evidence of such a feature at Dumfries House.

39 Roy Military Survey of Scotland 1747–1755. British Library Maps C.9.b

40 Bute Archives DHP/22

41 Plate 77 shows 'Eight Square Pavilions for my lord Cobham' one of which has a ball finialed, pyramidal roof, and Plate 87 shows '3 designs for columns for Publick places or private grounds' which includes a rustic column very similar to those of the Lady's Well. Gibbs 1728, pl 77

42 Bute Archives uncatalogued photograph. HES AY1003

43 Bute Archives Dumfries Estate Papers Box 156, 1947–55

44 Roy Military Survey of Scotland 1747–1755. British Library Maps C.9.b

45 Bute Archives DHP/22

46 The estimate for construction was for £58 2s 6d, the drawings comprise a scaled plan and section. Bute Archives uncatalogued drawing. HES photograph A 27035

47 Roy Military Survey of Scotland 1747–1755. British Library Maps C.9.b

48 Bute Archives Report by Messers Lindsay Jamieson & Haldane on the Accounts of the Cashiers & Factors for the Most Noble The Marquess of Bute from 12 September 1867–12 September 1868 p.66.

49 Bute Archives DHP/22

50 'The Rt Hon the Earl of Dumfries and Stair to John Adam Architect for building the gate & wall at the mains in 1760 & 1761.' Bute Archives DU/5/30/11

51 Glendinning and Wade Martins *Buildings of the Land* 2008, Introduction

52 The Ayr Road Act of 1767 which was defined as 'An Act for repairing and widening several roads leading from the town of Ayr, and other roads therin mentioned in the County of Ayr.' McClure 1994, 49

53 On the 1772 Home Estate Plan, the vignette of the mains shows a three-bay house with the single-storey range of buildings behind. Bute Archives DHP/24

54 Thomas Harrison bricklayer for building a garden wall and a wall about the hothouse at Dumfries House 8–11 October 1764. Bute Archives DU/5/67

55 Account to Rt Hon to Andrew Morton, 24 December 1766, settled 4 December 1767. Building of garden walls and repairs to a house for the new estate factor Mr Paterson. Total £119.0. Bute Archives D/5/30/28

56 Bute Archives DHP/26

57 An 1873 drawing shows the bothy range before an extra storey was added to the house. Bute Archives DHP/ADD/6

58 'A plan of Percy Wood & Bridge with Northumberland Mount being part of the policy and ridings in the Earl of Dumfries & Stair's Park Dumfries House' c1760 (after Lord Dumfries became the Earl of Stair in 1760 and before he died in 1768). Bute Archives DHP/ADD/1

59 The 1772 Estate Plan shows this area as an orchard. Bute Archives DHP/24

60 3 January Lord Dumfries to Lord Loudoun writing from Leifnorris. 1754/1. Discussion on the planting of tree seeds and the celebration of Lady Eglinton's birthday. Bute Archives LO/2/86

61 'Account The Right Hon The Earl of Dumfries & Stair to John Adam architect for day work perform'd to his Lop from 17th September 1762 to 1st November 1763. Includes laying foundations of the hothouse. 2000

slates delivered to Mr Colly for covering the hothouse.' Bute Archives D/5/30/18

62 Statement by Alexander Collie gardener at Dumfries House including reference to digging foundations for a hothouse, February 1763. James Waitt painter account for decorator work inside house, lamp posts of the bridge and new hothouse in the grounds discharged 2 February 1764. John Harrison bricklayer for building a garden wall and a wall about the hothouse at Dumfries House 8–11 October 1764. Bute Archives DU/5/67

63 Andrew Morton's account dated 29 October 1766. Includes building of stairs at east and west ends of hothouse. Bute Archives DU/5/30/32

64 Receipt of Thomas Waitt painter 1761. Total £14 5s 6d 'To the Alcove shade inside Green, the outside white four times over and laid over with sand.' Bute Archives DU/5/30/10

65 The Coach House was built in 1762 for £558 6s 7½d, this also included the cost of building the Wash House. Bute Archives DU/5/30/11

66 Receipt of Thomas Waitt painter 1761 total £14.5.6 'Coach House painting the doors, window shutters, 4 blind windows in Coach House and wash house. Washing house doors, window shutters, Whiting the East Office house, Closet in washing house. To the Alcove shade inside Green, the outside white four times over and laid over with sand.' Bute Archives DU/5/30/10

67 'The Rt Hon the Earl of Dumfries and Stair John Adam Architect for additional wright work done in & about Dumfries House in the years 1760 & 1761 not included in former accompts. 281 days of a wright taking down old lyning & fitting it up for surbase lyning in the Housekeepers room, My Ladys womans room, nursery & lyning above the chimneys & mouldings round them, taking up old floors for sarking to the Coach House (the rest) was afterwards used by Mr Neilson for other purposes.' Bute Archives DU/5/30/13

68 Described on the 1772 Home Plan as the 'Old Garden'. Bute Archives DHP/24

69 Washing took the form of large-scale intermittent cleaning of household textiles such as bed, table and kitchen linen, together with larger and simpler items of personal 'body linen such as shifts, shirts and underskirts'. Sambrook 2003, 44

70 The location of the laundry in Kilmory Bay on Rum removed all aspects of the laundry from the Kinloch Castle on the other side of the island. Robert Lorimer at Hill of Tarvit, Fife, built a new laundry in 1907 close to the stables, at a suitable distance from the house. The laundry at Cullen House, Banffshire, by William Robertson of the 1820s is apart from the house and is now a separate dwelling.

71 'The Rt Hon the Earl of Dumfries and Stair John Adam Architect for building the Coach House & Washing Hose etc at Dumfries House £558.6.67/12' Bute Archives DU/5/30/1

'John Adam Architect for building the Coach-house & washing house all Dumfries House & the gate & wall at the mains & two obelisks in 1760 & 1761 35ft of architraves round two of the doors, 44 days of wright taking off old doors & fitting them on the Grooms rooms & washing house, supporting the roof of the old coach house, making a horse for drying the linen, cutting a hatchway in the floor and ceiling above the well for the pump rod.'

'To painting 8 old windows in coach house and washing house, 3 pairs of edge hinges for the round window on the front of the coach house, 112½ days of a mason at Kitchen stoves Setting grates etc, External stair at coach house mentioned also setting up of the two obelisks.' Bute Archives DU/5/30/11

72 See footnote 66

73 'The Edinburgh plumber Robert Selby completed the laying on of the water supply to the Wash House on 19 September 1761 at a cost of £18.16/6.' Bute Archives DU/5/30/1

74 The Wash House was converted into artists' studios; these were opened by HRH Duke of Rothesay on 22 October 2012.

75 An ice house stored meat carcasses, barrels of fish, beer and wine, confectionary and spring water. Bottles were generally wrapped in chaff and set into the ice itself, whereas other produce was placed in matting on top. Fruit, vegetables and dairy products were more likely to be suspended on wooden trays in the cool air above, or placed on stone shelves. Buxbaum 1989, 106

76 1762 John Adam 'cutting the Ice-house door and fixing the arch'd part of it' Bute Archives DU5/30/13

77 The Ice House at Duff House is similarly located on a bluff above a river.

78 Estimates by John Adam; 11 February 1760 'Estimate of a bridge for Rt Hon Earl of Dumfries, £430.16.2 carried out'. Bute Archives DU/5/30/1

79 Ruddock 1979, 118

80 The estimate was presented 11 February 1760. The eventual bill for the bridge came to £543.0.10

'The Extras

Cost of the Accessories of Dumfries House		TOTAL
1760 laying on water to house £90.18.9		
1760	£19.3.6	
1761 laying on water to wash house	£18.16.6	£128.18.9
Coach House, Wash house etc	£558.6.7	
1760–1 Coach House, Wash house etc painting	£14.5.6	£572.12.1
Bridge	£430.16.2	
1760–2 Bridge Balustrades and obelisks	£112.4.8	£543.0.10
1760–2 Gateway or Temple	£279.17.7'	

Bute Archives DU/5/30/1

81 Ted Ruddock regards these as 'the two best bridges built in the early years of the (Adam) brothers' practice. Ruddock 1979, 118

82 Walker 2000, 322

83 Design 'for a Bridge for Right Hon The Earl of Dumfries' c1760. Bute Archives DHP/23

84 9 Sept 1762 'Account relates to the building of the house, the Coach House, washing house, wall and gate at the mains and erecting 2 obelisks, building the bridge, the expense of the additional balustrades and obelisks on the bridge not included. Total owed by Dumfries to John Adam £1237.17.1 ⅓. Abstract of the accounts betwixt The Rt Hon The Earl of Dumfries & Stair and John Adam, Architect, in Edinburgh £1239.5.7 ⅓.' Bute Archives D/5/30/16

85 The picture by Jacob Thomson, 1830, hangs in the gallery of the main hall at Mount Stuart.

86 Bute Archives DHP/ADD/1 c1760

87 At an estimated cost of £279.17.7 ½. Bute Archives DU/5/30/1

88 Bute Archives D/5/30/21

89 RIBA/British Architectural Library Drawings and Archives Collection. John Adam Sketchbook SE 16/3

90 See Chapter 6, 85

91 30 October 1762. Letter from Andrew Hunter re purchase of the Clackmannan Estate by Sir Lawrence Dundas Bute Archives DU/5/36/23. Sale of Clackmannan agreed for £22,000, 11 November 1762. Bute Archives DU/5/36/24

92 Estimate of a water engine for the coal work of Rt Hon 5th Earl by Edward Ker in Kilmarnock 28 February 1767. Total cost £140.11.4. Bute Archives DU/5/9/24

93 Strawhorn 1966, 41–3

94 Uncatalogued plans of the WWII coal workings held in the 6th Earl's papers. Bute Archives

Chapter 6: The 6th Earl of Dumfries 1768–1803

*best assistant that ever delighted a man who
delights in improvements*

Andrew Wight, 1778[1]

The 6th Earl and his Countess

On the death of the 5th Earl in 1768, his 42 year old nephew, Colonel Patrick McDouall of Freugh, son of his sister Elizabeth, succeeded him. Once it had become evident that the 5th Earl's second marriage was not to produce an heir, a Deed of Entail was drawn up on 14 December 1765 which listed the Earl's various lands in order to keep the Estate together by passing it on to a single heir rather than dispersing it through the wider family. This was especially important because of the indirect line of descent of the estate and the titles through his sister.[2] The entailed lands included the estates in Ayrshire and at Mochrum in Galloway all of which were to pass to the 6th Earl.[3]

During the stewardship of the 6th Earl and his Countess, Dumfries House became a family home for the first time, but the way in which the house functioned was only subtly changed so that minor alterations were all that were made to the building. The exquisite furnishings installed by the 5th Earl were augmented, rather than swept away, as fashions changed; this restrained approach may have been in part necessitated by the considerable gambling debts that the 6th Earl had incurred in London.[4] The most dramatic alterations and improvements were made to the running of the Estate. Under the guidance of the Countess, the agricultural land was drained, tenanted farms improved and various industrial and commercial schemes promoted. The biggest changes occurred in the immediate policies as the 5th Earl's formal landscape with its avenues and viewpoints was adapted to produce

a more 'natural' landscape of the kind made fashionable throughout Britain by Lancelot 'Capability' Brown. The picturesque remains of the old house of Leifnorris were removed and the Gothic Temple Lodge and Castle of Terringzean were hidden from view from the house, no longer functioning as eye-catchers although still delightful prospects to be discovered whilst walking or riding around the Estate. During this period, the principal entrance to the Estate was shifted to the south and Robert Adam was commissioned to design a new set of gates on the Ayr to Cumnock turnpike road. Whilst these were never built, two pairs of gatehouses were erected on this road to mark the main entrances to the Estate just before the death of the 6th Earl in 1803.

Patrick McDouall was, like his uncle, a professional soldier. He also played an active role in public life, sitting for thirteen years in the House of Lords as one of sixteen elected Scottish Representative Peers[5] and serving as Grandmaster of the Grand Lodge of Scotland from 1771 until 1773. On succeeding to the Estate and titles he added Crichton to his name. His marriage to Margaret Crauford, the daughter of Ronald Crauford of Restalrig, in 1761[6] produced a single child, Lady Elizabeth Penelope, who was born on 25 November 1772. Dumfries House was the principal seat of the 6th Earl for over 35 years, throughout which time the Estate, rather than the House, was his main focus. A description of Dumfries House and its Estate at this time is provided by Andrew Wight's report on the *Present State of Husbandry in Scotland* of 1778:[7]

> Dumfries-house was built by the late Earl, who at the same time inclosed and planted much, in particular, 35 acres, not far from the house, where planted with oaks, which are

Fig 6.1 Sir Henry Raeburn painted a pair of companion portraits of Patrick McDouall Crichton, 6th Earl of Dumfries, and his family in 1793. Lord Dumfries was pictured with his ward, Lady Flora Mure-Campbell.
The Bute Collection

now beautiful and grow luxuriously. This has encouraged the present Earl to continue the plantations in belts round his inclosures, and clumps on every height, which embellish the country at present, and in time will be very profitable. The land which the Earl has in his own hand extends to 1,200 acres, including pleasure ground.

Extensive tribute is paid to the role played by Lady Dumfries in running the Estate while her husband was away on military service or in the House of Lords, 'relieving her Lord almost wholly of the trouble of attendance':

Lady Dumfries is the best assistant that ever blessed a man who delights in improvements. She is the very soul of husbandry and manufacturers in that part of the country. She zealously patronizes the woollen manufacture at Cumnock, and the linen manufacture all around, giving premiums to promote each. In that view, her Ladyship has excellent crops of Flax on her Lord's farm, so extensive, as more than once to have gained premiums given by the trustees for manufactures.[8] She is a substitute that leaves nothing undone. A field of level ground, frequently under water by the over flowing of the river Lugar, was rendered no better than a bog. Much draining was necessary, and parallel drains were opened; the distance more or less, according to the degree of wetness, and all filled with brushwood. The ground being made now dry, a

Fig 6.2 Portrait of Lady Margaret, Countess of Dumfries, and her daughter Lady Elizabeth, by Sir Henry Raeburn, 1793. The Bute Collection

Fig 6.3 The Home Estate plan of 1772 indicates the extent of the 5th Earl's formal scheme of tree planting and the size of the Dumfries House Estate four years after the 6th Earl had inherited. Leifnorris had been demolished by this time and the landscape was centred on Dumfries House. Bute Archives DHP/24

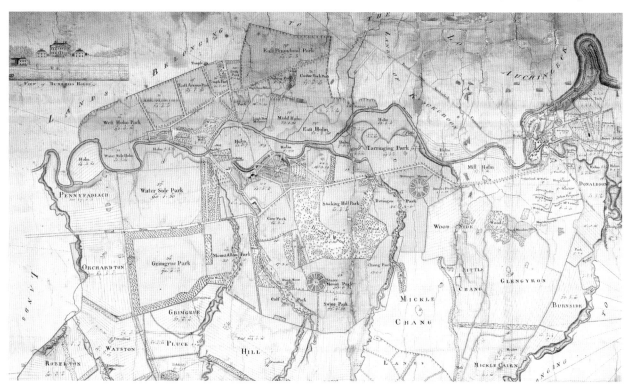

Fig 6.4 An aerial view showing Dumfries House in relation to the Mains Farm to the left, the walled garden beside the river to the right and the village of Ochiltree beyond. The row of light green trees to the bottom left follows the line of the old road. HES 2013 DP153624

part proper for turnip was dunged in the rows, well hoed, and a very good crop raised. The rest was fallowed for corn, straight ridges made 10 feet broad and 50 bolls shell lime given to each acre. One half was sown with wheat: I saw the crop, which was uncommonly good. The barley on the remaining part was good. The whole was sown with grass-seeds, never to be opened again … Turnip, cabbage, potatoes, pease and beans are raised on the light soils, all in drills, which make a fine preparation for barley and grass-seeds. The clay land is summer fallowed for wheat. On land opened from ley, oats is the first crop. If it be very stiff, a second crop of oats is taken, in order that the sward may be thoroughly rotted. The next crop is drilled beans with dung.[9]

Her husband's contribution is largely confined to his engineering operations in relation to the Lugar Water, 'The Earl, by a laborious work, has widened its bed, raised banks with an easy slope, and sowed natural grass to bring a sward on the bank, that may preserve it from being pitted by the water in a flood.'

As the 18th century progressed, developments in agricultural methods from improved drainage to the application of fertilisers and animal husbandry meant that landed estates, if well managed and maintained, could produce a healthy income. In 1772, the Earl commissioned a *Plan for the Improvement of Ground Adjacent to Dumfries House*.[10] The plan is not signed

but a document outlining the improvements carried out to the Estate[11] states that the Earl 'Had a plan of the demesne also drawn by Mr (Capability) Robertson on a scale for an intended deer park.' This was James Robertson, whose career was based on his association, albeit tenuous, with Capability Brown.[12] Robertson had worked on various Scottish estates including Livingstone, Hopetoun, Dalkeith, Dalhousie, Niddry, The Whim and Moredun.[13] The Dumfries House plan, which is in the style of Capability Brown, sought to remove the formality of earlier generations and sweep parkland, set with naturalistically planted clumps of trees, up to the walls of a house.[14]

The area included in the Plan lay immediately around the House, stretching south to the (old) line of the Ayr–Cumnock road, north to the Gothic Temple Lodge, east to the line of the Stockiehill Ha-ha and west to include the walled garden. The Plan proposes creating a new entrance to the Estate off the Ayr–Cumnock Road to the west of the Nest Burn to be set in a relatively dense plantation leading to a short drive skirting the edge of the Shaw Wood to the east of the House. This wood was to be thinned out into clumps and the bowling green was to be removed. The drive would have passed through clumps of trees and provided periodic glimpses of the House but the Mains

Farm, along with the Stables and Coach House, were to be shielded from view within plantations. A picturesque walk through a plantation with a series of sheltered clearings along the west side of the Polcalk Burn was also proposed. Although this area was developed by succeeding generations with elements such as the bowling green and avenues being overplanted, there is no surviving evidence to suggest that this particular plan was carried out.

The main intervention planned was to be a new drive running from the north to the Gothic Temple Lodge and then down to the Adam Bridge through the parkland (Fig 5.4). Discussions about a new road leading from the Barony Road to the Gothic Temple Lodge continued unsuccessfully with the Boswells of Auchinleck. James Boswell wrote in his journal of 2 November 1778, that at a dinner in Rosemount:

> [The Earl of Dumfries] was exceedingly attentive to me [...] I was upon my guard, as I well knew that he and his Countess flattered themselves that they would get from me that road through our Estate which my father had refused, and which in truth I was still more positive for refusing [etc.][15]

Boswell repeated in a later entry that the families were not on visiting terms, on account of the dispute about the road. The Gothic Temple Lodge was to be surrounded with a large plantation so as to completely obscure its main south facing front which had originally been designed as an eye-catcher on axis with the House. Once again, there is no evidence that any part of this landscaping plan was carried out.

In 1784, the Earl commissioned Robert Adam to design a new gateway and lodges but there is no indication on the surviving design drawings as to which entrance this relates to. John Adam's entrance to the Mains Farm is too constricted to have accommodated these structures which would have interfered with the existing farmhouse which was at this time acting as a gate lodge. The main approach from the north at Auchinleck is rather hidden from public view and it seems unlikely that a smart new entrance would have been designed for such a site. The obvious location is that identified on the 1772 Improvement Plan as the new entrance to the Estate from the Ayr–Cumnock turnpike road. However, this is located on a bend in the road whereas the Adam drawing appears to show a site parallel to the road.[16] Adam produced two variant designs. The first shows a central carriage gateway

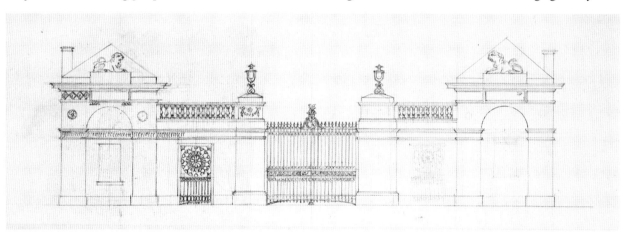

Fig 6.5 Robert Adam's alternative design for a gateway at Dumfries House, c1784. *Sir John Soane's Museum, Adam 51 058*

Fig 6.6 Robert Adam's design for a substantial gateway with lodges, 17 February 1784. *Sir John Soane's Museum, Adam 51 059*

Fig 6.7 The Countess seems to have been largely responsible for the continuing development of the Mains Farm including the addition of a doocot. HES 2010 DP083574

Fig 6.8 The drying kiln represented a technological innovation which improved the productivity of the Estate. HES 2010 DP083589

Fig 6.9 A bolection moulded stone fireplace removed from Leifnorris and adapted for use in the Mains Farm bothy. HES 2010 DP083592

with wrought iron gates, complete with the Earl's crest and Wyvern, with gate piers topped with lamps linked by balustraded walls with pedestrian gates to square pavilions, each of which has a recumbent lion on the blocking course of each parapet (Fig 6.5). The drawing for the alternative scheme, which is not fully worked up, proposes the same plan but with far more elaborate gate piers with belted columns and urns in niches topped with larger lamps linked to simpler pavilions (Fig 6.6).

The first scheme is similar to other lodges designed by Robert Adam including the Stag Lodges at Saltram House, Devon, c1773 and the Wyke Green entrance at Osterley Park, Middlesex, of 1777, while the urns in niches and lions are found on the entrance screen

of Syon House, London, 1769. The alternative design includes rusticated columns which are only found in two works by Robert and James Adam: the garden door at Blair Adam of 1755–61 and the Osterley Park Bridge of 1768.[17]

Although Wight describes the improvements made to the Estate by the Earl and his Countess in general terms, we have very little documentary evidence as to the precise nature of these improvements other than an itemised listing of over a hundred different works carried out under the direction of the Earl.[18] Item 41, for example, refers to the Mains Farm being further developed with 'farm stables & coach house' built 'at great expense' c1776.[19] This refers to buildings in the

Fig 6.10 The 6th Earl built two pairs of lodges to mark the approach to the Estate from the south via the Ayr–Cumnock road. The West Gate Lodges flank what was to become the main entrance to Dumfries House. HES 2010 DP152940

Mains Farm steading and not to the John Adam Coach House which had been completed and paid for in 1761.[20] Further additions were made to the Mains Farm, 'built very considerable additions to the farmyard in Barns, sheds, Granaries, smith & wright shops, hen house etc etc.'[21] These works include the substantial Doocot at the north-east corner of the complex adjacent to the Blacksmith's forge. The 6th Earl, 'finished [the] Garden Wall begun by the Late Earl', which refers either to the continued development of the walled garden or the fruit walls shown on the Piercy Bridge plan.[22] This work on the walled garden is corroborated by a bill from Thomas Morton[23] for making bricks, including 8,000 for the hot-wall in the Kitchen Garden. A new ha-ha was also created in front of the main house.[24] The most dramatic 'improvement', however, was that 'The old house of Leifnorris and old garden wall [were] taken down and the stones removed'[25] by David Soutar in 1771.[26] This suggests that the 17th century window surround and bolection moulded fireplace (Fig 6.9) incorporated into the steading, which was built at this time, came from Leifnorris. This final eradication of the ancient seat of Leifnorris emphasises how tastes in landscape design had changed through the course of the 18th century. The 5th Earl had preserved the old house as a romantic ruin, even recording it in his Entrance Hall, but his nephew swept it away and turned the focus of the House away from the picturesque drive that crossed the Lugar Water by John Adam's elegant bridge and instead towards a general view of the landscape south of the river. The 'Old house of Pennyland', which had housed construction workers during the building of Dumfries House,[27] appears to have also been demolished to enhance the landscape setting of the main house. It lay to the north of the Lugar Water to the east of the Gothic Temple Lodge.

The main contribution that the 6th Earl made to the Estate was to create two new access drives with associated gate lodges. The drives follow picturesque routes through the Estate and maintain the original Adam intention that the principal, south front of the house should be viewed on the oblique in order to fully appreciate the design. Little is known about this phase of work but the date of construction of the lodges is recorded in a Memorandum following the death of the Earl which refers to the 'five porters lodges built immediately before the death of the late earl'.[28]

As yet there is no evidence to suggest that the associated drives were laid down any earlier than the lodges. The pairs of lodges at Stockiehill and at the West Entrance show a refined architectural knowledge that is inspired by fashionable publications of the day such as John Plaw's *Rural Architecture from The Simple Cottage to the Decorated Villa* of 1802 and *Ferme Ornée or Rural Improvements* of 1795. As originally built, each lodge was a hip-roofed and white harled rectangular building with a Palladian window facing the road (Fig 6.10).[29] The paired lodges are linked by low walls and a representative set of their original distinctive wrought iron gates survives at the West Entrance and Stockiehill. The two pairs of lodges have been sensitively extended. The fifth lodge was at the Auchinleck entrance, the main North Entrance to the Estate at the time, and has been more extensively altered. The architect may well have been James Neilson of Kilmarnock, who worked on the Estate for the Earl's grandson, the 2nd Marquess of Bute, in the early 19th century. A set of the gates from the Auchinleck drive was gifted by the 6th Marquess to Hill of Tarvit, Fife, a property of the National Trust for Scotland.[30]

Lady Dumfries did not confine her attention to agricultural matters but also invested in a range of local

Fig 6.11 The Stockiehill Lodges, built by the 6th Earl, were marooned when the road was realigned in the 19th century. HES 2013 DP153500

industries. In 1770 graphite was discovered at Craigman near Cumnock and since blending graphite with fireclay enabled the construction of high quality kilns that could withstand very high temperatures, it was possible to establish a pottery.[31] Although this pottery failed in the 1780s, Lady Dumfries saw the potential benefits of this type of manufacture for the local community and in 1792 commissioned James Taylor to establish a new pottery with a loan of £500 which enabled three potters to be brought over from Glasgow. All the raw materials could be supplied locally: fireclay for the kilns, coal to heat them, clay suitable for brown glazed domestic ware and, from the Dumfries Estate, porcellaneous clay for more expensive wares, examples of which survive at Dumfries House. Taylor went on to use the graphite in pencils which were produced in Cumnock until the 1840s. The Countess also invested in the weaving industry, constructing the 'Jeannie House' on Lugar Street, Cumnock which housed a number of looms.[32]

Sixteen years after inheriting Dumfries House, the Earl and Countess decided that repair and redecoration was required and commenced with the two rooms most heavily used for entertaining. In January 1784 James Waitt[33] was paid for redecorating the Dining Room, which included repairing the ornaments and revarnishing the pictures. In March he had moved on to the Entrance Hall, carrying out both repairs and redecoration; both rooms were painted white.[34] The Dining Room referred to was probably the original North Parlour which had become the main Dining Room, the original Dining Room becoming the second Drawing Room.

The only architectural drawing that survives for alterations to the House from the time of the 6th Earl is a 'Plan of part of the Pavilions of Dumfries House with a new addition intended for a hot bath or cold bath' (Fig 6.12).[35] The development of bathrooms in the 18th century was gradual, uncoordinated and ad hoc, their design dependent on a variety of medical opinions because they were built primarily for their health promoting properties rather than cleanliness per se.[36] Although doctors recognised that some people bathed for pleasure, the health giving aspect was paramount and so initially it was cold baths that were recommended. As the century progressed, however, many doctors conceded that it was the general principle of bathing, as opposed to the specific temperature, that was beneficial, and cold baths were relegated to the realm of 'desperate remedies'.[37]

At Dumfries House, the decision was made to have a bathhouse in the service court, rather than in the grounds. A number of examples survive of bathhouses built some distance from the house designed as eye-catchers with a functional purpose as at Stourhead, 1758, and Corsham Court, 1761, both in Wiltshire. The location of the Dumfries House example in the west courtyard, conveniently close to the coal shed and ash yard, suggests that it was constructed for health, as opposed to fashionable, reasons. This may appear at odds with modern perceptions of bathing but here it seems to have been a practical solution to providing a health enhancing apparatus rather than a private luxury. Although we know that water was piped into the house in 1760,[38] we don't know where it arrived but presumably it was piped to both pavilions where the 'wet' activities of the household took place, namely the kitchens and laundry.

The access to the Bathhouse through the Laundry may appear curious but this room would have been clean and dry and the most 'polite' of the spaces in the west pavilion. It also was probably not in constant use given that it was only used for the personal laundry, the more arduous business of the household linens being dealt with in the Wash House in the grounds. The absence of a dressing room further suggests that this was a functional room. In 1779 Robert Adam designed a bathhouse for the Earl of Cassillis at Culzean Castle which was accommodated in a new west wing that also housed a large brew house and a bake house. Here the bath is approached via a large dressing room and, although located in a service wing, could be approached either from the outside or from the bedroom floor above. Although the Bathhouse itself is architecturally much grander and larger than that at Dumfries House, the bath itself is of a similar form and approached by a similar set of five steps. Cassillis was obviously interested in bathing having also constructed facilities for sea bathing at Culzean. That the Earl of Dumfries most probably had direct knowledge of the bath at Culzean is supported by the fact that, although

John Macilwraith is documented as installing the boiler for the Dumfries House Bathhouse,[39] the paper is actually signed by Hugh Cairncross, Master of Works at Culzean Castle. Although Robert Adam designed baths at Mellerstain, Berwickshire, and at Alva, Clackmannanshire, there is no evidence that he was involved in creating the Bathhouse at Dumfries House. The fact that all the tradesmen's bills survive in the Mount Stuart Archive without reference to an architect suggests that this simple building was designed by the factor, possibly with an input from the Countess with her close involvement in the management of the Estate.

Although the drawing for the Bathhouse is unsigned and undated, it is competently executed which suggests at least a semi-professional hand and relates to the series of bills dating from May 1782 to October 1784. A building of 13 ft by 20 ft was attached to the west gable of the west pavilion, set within the courtyard and hidden behind the south wall of the courtyard. The new room was accessed from the Laundry via a staircase which rose 4 ft 9 in to accommodate the depth of the bath. The bath itself was entered via a staircase at its north end and was 9 ft long by 4 ft 6 in wide; it was lit by windows overlooking the courtyard. The water was heated by a boiler located in the 'scullery for the milk house' with the water pipe laid beneath the external passage. The drawing shows that the bath drained into the existing Great Drain which ran beneath the courtyard and the new bath.[40]

Fig 6.12 A plan and section of the hot bath built in the courtyard of the west pavilion in 1783 that illustrates the drainage and the way in which the hot water was to be supplied. Bute Archives DHP/8

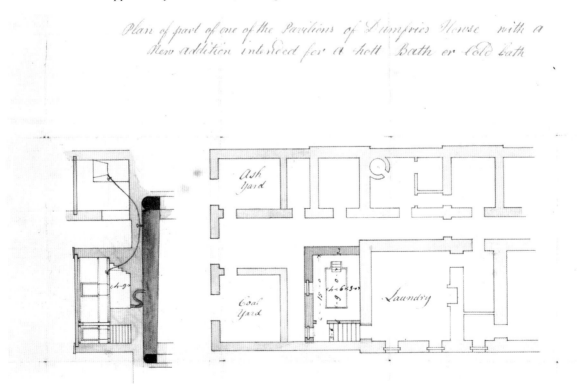

Plan of part of one of the Pavilions of Dumfries House with a New addition intended for a hott Bath or Cold Bath

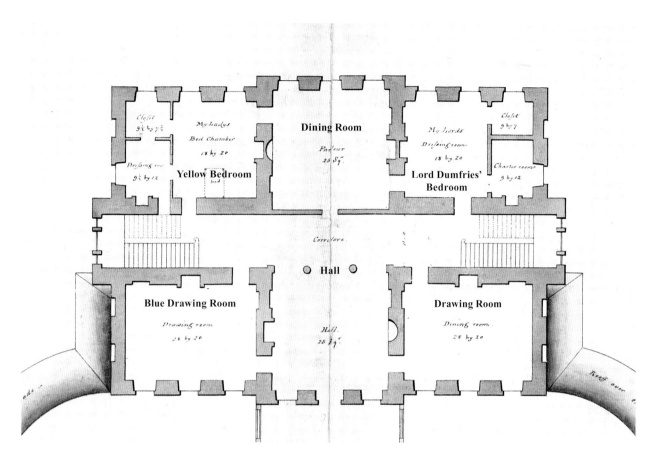

Fig 6.13 The 1754 plan of the principal floor with the rooms named according to the 1803 Inventory. Lord Dumfries used his Dressing Room as his bedroom after the death of his wife in 1799. Bute Archives DHP/I/5

In December 1782 Lord Dumfries purchased a water closet, something that was considered at the time to be a luxurious item.[41] In the drawing for the new plumbing system to be installed in 1818[42] it refers to 'old water closet' on the 'sunk floor' which was to be attached to the new main water supply serving the west end of the House. This suggests that the water closet was perhaps near the foot of the west staircase in order to be reasonably accessible from the Family Bed Chamber and close to the Great Drain. A water closet is shown on the 1894 survey by Robert Weir Schultz[43] in the block to the north of the west pavilion (now demolished) which is probably the 1782 Bramah water closet. In 1784 John Maclure[44] was paid £1.0.8 ½ for plastering the water closet as part of a programme of repairs that included work in the House and on the Dairy, Bake House, Servants' Hall and passages, as well as repairs to the ceiling of one of the dressing rooms. Repair work was also carried out on some of the Estate buildings including the Gardener's House, the Coach House and the Wash House. The House now bears little evidence of the occupation of the 6th Earl and his family except for the magnificent Raeburn portraits and some satinwood furniture.[45]

In May 1795, an 'Inventory of the Household Furniture in Dumfries House' was carried out which gives an impression of how the House was used, having been the principal residence of the 6th Earl and his Countess for 27 years. The precise reason for making it is uncertain; inventories were carried out for a variety of purposes, most commonly at a death but also for insurance purposes and occasionally as good housekeeping. A more detailed inventory was taken on the death of the 6th Earl in 1803 and these examined together give us an insight into the arrangement of the principal rooms and how they had changed since the completion of the house 40 years previously. The Entrance Hall was furnished with '8 mahogany hall chairs', a 'marble slab table and gilt frame' and 'large round table'. The 'centre lamp brass' probably refers to the Chippendale lantern, which is possibly the one now in Philadelphia Museum of Art. A painting of a Hermit is recorded along with a pair of 'french elbow chairs hair cloth' and a pair of tables. The floor was covered with '43 yards' of 'Spanish Matting'.

To the west, the original Drawing Room is described as the 'Drawing Room' in 1795 and the 'Blue Drawing Room' in 1803. It is furnished with the Chippendale suite of '12 mahogany chairs armed blue satin covers' and '2 sofas' and the windows are hung with curtains of 'blue silk damask'.[46] '3 pieces French Tapestry large' are hung on the walls, the two hung by the 5th Earl on the east and west walls and the additional third tapestry hung to the left of the fireplace.[47] The floor was covered with the 'Axminster carpet', the '2 large mirrors' with 'gilt frames very rich' hang above the '2 jasper tables with gilt frames and leather covers'. There is also a 'Broadwood piano' in the room in both inventories. The room is lit by '2 crystal chandeliers on chimneypiece' but no mention is made of a central chandelier.

The original Dining Room east of the Entrance Hall is called the 'Principal Dining Room' in 1795 but becomes the 'Drawing Room' in 1803. In both inventories it is furnished as a Drawing Room and is more heavily furnished than the Blue Drawing Room but it also has blue damask curtains. Its furnishings include '17 mahogany chairs with 2 sets of slips black ground English tapestry bottoms, 4 cane bottomed bamboo chairs, a settee, 2 work foot stools, and 2 red leather ditto, 1 small beautiful square tea table, 2 mahogany card tables, a satin wood work table'. The gilt pier glasses and their tables are mentioned along with 'a Wilton carpet red and white ground, as well as '3 new window curtains fringed festooned and lined'. The portrait of the 5th Earl by Thomas Hudson over the fireplace is included as is the portrait of his second wife, which is now in the Royal Albert Museum and Gallery in Exeter.[48] The room is lit by '2 crystal chandeliers' and furnished with a variety of game tables, music stands and tea chests. In 1795 it contained both a 'piano forte and harpsichord'. By 1803 the 'harpsichord by Kirckman London 1771' was in the Blue Drawing Room but a piano forte remained in this room. The furnishings described suggest that this was the most frequently used reception room.

In the 1795 Inventory, the room between the Family Bed Chamber and the Business Room retains its original name 'Parlour' but is furnished as the Dining Room. The retention of the original name despite its change of function suggests that this was a recent change of use. It is furnished with '2 French elbow chairs, 6 mahogany chairs large seats, 10 mahogany chairs smaller seats, 2 dumb waiters, a mahogany side table, a mahogany round dining table' and 'ditto joining table 3 pieces' and a 'mahogany book stand'. At this stage the '2 large oval mirrors' on the north wall were in their original, ungilded 'white frames'. The relocation of the Dining Room to the North Parlour meant that all the food and labour-intensive serving and clearing still had to be carried out without a pantry and with everything passing through the Entrance Hall. In the original design, the Dining Room could be serviced through the north door which was at least partly hidden from view at the foot of the east stair.[49]

The Family Bed Chamber is described as the 'Yellow Bedroom' and was comfortably furnished with a '4 posted mahogany bed' with 'yellow silk and worsted curtains, 2 French elbow chairs, 4 chairs with English tapestry covers and foot stools'. The celebrated Chippendale 'mahogany china and book press with ornamented and gilded glass doors and drawers' was also in this room, most probably on the north wall between the windows.[50] The room also contained

Fig 6.14 The South Middle Bedroom with the suite of bedroom furniture that was acquired for Lady Elizabeth Crichton McDouall c1792.
HES 2007 SC1104269

'a large japanned India clothes press, a mahogany Escretoire and bookcases, a small mahogany table, a mahogany night table, Dressing glas' and seven paintings'. The furnishings of the 'Yellow Dressing Room' off the bedroom with connecting doors to both the Stair Hall and the closet included a 'Mahogany chest drawers, cabinet with mirror glass doors 38 by 23 inches, mahogany book stand, and a mahogany writing table', whilst the closet contained more furniture for the storage of clothes. On the other side of the Dining Room was 'Lord Dumfries' Bedroom.'[51] The Earl may have moved into this room permanently following the death of his wife on 5 May 1799. It clearly served a dual function with both a '4 posted mahogany bed' and 'large mahogany writing table' along with an 'easy chair and 3 stuffed chairs.' The Dressing Room adjacent was equipped with a bidet. The Charter Room and its contents are not included in this inventory.

The bedrooms on the floor above are all comfortably furnished with the north-west or 'Blue Bedroom' as principal guest room containing the 'best' Chippendale bed and the Chippendale 'tapestry' overmantle. A few choice pieces were added to the original complement of furniture, including a satinwood dressing table and a satin-birch display cabinet which were both probably made for Lady Penelope in the 1780s.[52]

The servants' quarters were also included in the inventory with the status of the different members of staff being reflected in their beds: a '4 posted bed and green cloth embroidered curtains old' for the butler and 'a tent bed with red stripped curtains' for the housekeeper, whereas other staff were accommodated on box beds and 'fir bed bottoms'. The Factor's Room, which may have originally been the Nursery, contained 'a mahogany desk, a round table and 4 chairs', whilst the 'second table room' included '2 square tables a round one 10 small and two arm chairs leather bottomed'.[53] The rooms in the pavilions were dealt with separately. The west pavilion courtyard contained the Dairy and Cheese Room with the Laundry and Women's Room occupying the ground floor of the pavilion, thereby maintaining the logical functional arrangement of the original Adam plan. Neither the Bramah water closet nor the hot bath is mentioned, presumably because these were not movable items.[54]

While Lord Dumfries and his Countess were leading an active life, managing their extensive estates in Ayrshire and Dumfriesshire and fulfilling their public duties, another Scottish family, the Stuarts of Bute, were in the ascendant. John Stuart, 3rd Earl of Bute, had a well documented political career, culminating in his appointment as Prime Minister and was a great favourite of both George III and the Prince of Wales.[55] In 1761, his wife became Baroness Mountstuart of Wortley, an honour partly bestowed in recognition of her husband's political career.[56] With the marriage came property in Yorkshire and Cornwall valued at between £500,000 and £1,340,000 which enabled Lord Bute to buy an English estate closer

Fig 6.15 Lord Dumfries' Dressing Room was also the room from which the Estate business was run. HES 2010 DP083226

to London. In 1763 he purchased the Luton Park Estate and employed Lancelot 'Capability' Brown to landscape the 1,200 acre park and Robert Adam to remodel, enlarge and decorate the house.[57]

The 3rd Earl of Bute's eldest son, John, Lord Mountstuart, was born on 30 June 1744. His marriage to Hon. Charlotte Hickman-Windsor on 12 November 1766 brought with it extensive estates in South Wales, the revenue from which was eventually to transform the fortunes of the Bute family. On 25 September 1767 they had a son, also John, and nine years later, on the death of Charlotte's mother Lady Windsor, they inherited the Glamorgan Estates consisting of 11,211 acres[58] and the Clavering properties in County Durham including Axwell Park. Within three years, Baron and Baroness Cardiff of Cardiff Castle, as they were also titled by then, were in financial difficulties due to their extravagant lifestyle and Lord Mountstuart had no choice but to take up a salaried diplomatic post as envoy at Turin. In 1783 he was appointed ambassador at Madrid.

On 10 March 1792, the 3rd Earl died and the title passed to his eldest son who inherited the life tenancy of family estates in Scotland and Bedfordshire. Highcliffe, the house in Hampshire, and almost all the 3rd Earl's personal estate went to one of his younger sons, Sir Charles Stuart,[59] while the 4th Earl was bequeathed a mortgage of £43,500, raised upon the Luton estates, to provide support for his siblings. Under his mother's will, the 4th Earl received £4,000, the majority of her personal property being bequeathed to her son William and daughter Louisa. The vast Wortley possessions went to another brother, James.[60] The 4th Earl felt he had been cheated and, unsuccessfully, contested the fact that the Wortley lands had been given to his brother. In 1794 he, like his father, accepted the Spanish ambassadorship for financial reasons.

The 4th Earl resigned his Spanish ambassadorship in 1796 when he became Viscount Mountjoy, Earl of Windsor and Marquess of Bute. The King had been anxious to raise his friend to the British peerage but couldn't before 1782 when a law was passed to enable Scottish peers to receive British titles, at which point he honoured his son whose measured thanks to the King included the words 'at least it secures the name and dignity of my family from being totally obliterated'.[61] Charlotte, Marchioness of Bute, died aged 54 in January 1800 and was buried in London but in September of the same year was re-interred in the church at Roath now in Cardiff. The 1st Marquess then married Frances Coutts of the banking family who received £100,000 on the morning of her wedding, £20,000 on her father's death and further money from her stepmother. After their marriage the couple appear not to have settled in any of their various homes and lived largely on the Continent.

In October 1792, Lord Mountstuart, the 4th Earl's eldest son, married Lady Elizabeth McDouall-Crichton, sole heir of the Crichton estates in Ayrshire and Galloway, including Dumfries House, which were larger and potentially more productive than those on the Isle of Bute.[62] The alliance between the Stewarts and the Crichtons was the cause of long negotiations which were not resolved before the marriage, culminating in a case being brought before the Lord Chancellor in August 1793.[63] In February 1794, before a decision had been reached, Lord Mountstuart died after a fall from his horse aged 25 leaving a one year old son, John Patrick Herbert, and a pregnant wife who gave birth to her second son, James, six months later. Lady Mountstuart and her young family chose to live with her parents at Dumfries House with both of his grandfathers acting as guardians but only three years later she too died, aged 24. Her sons remained in the care of their maternal grandparents at Dumfries House. Two years after her death, her eldest son, John, Earl of Windsor, was placed in the sole care of his paternal grandfather, the 1st Marquess of Bute, moving with him around the Bute properties and travelling on the Continent.[64] On the death of the 6th Earl of Dumfries in 1803, the Dumfries estates and titles passed to the nine year old John, who became the 7th Earl of Dumfries; two years later he changed his name to Crichton-Stuart which remains the family name of the Marquess of Bute. In 1809 he went up to Christ's College Cambridge, combining his studies with extensive travels on the Continent until 1814 when his grandfather died in Geneva and he became the 2nd Marquess of Bute.[65] Henceforth Dumfries House was no longer the principal residence of a Scottish Earl but one of the residences of a British Marquess.

The future of Dumfries House could have been in jeopardy as one of the family's smaller houses and of no particular importance to the 1st Marquess but for fact that the 2nd Marquess had spent his early childhood there. The 6th Earl of Dumfries and his Countess had maintained and developed the Estate whilst preserving the House and the lavishly furnished interiors created by his uncle, and their apparent lack of interest in

Fig 6.17 Lady Elizabeth, sole heiress of the Dumfries title and estates, who through her marriage united the Crichtons of Dumfries with the Stuarts of Bute, 1793. Detail of a portrait by Sir Henry Raeburn, 1793.
The Bute Collection

either contemporary architecture or fashions in interior decoration meant that Dumfries House entered the 19th century much as it had been created almost half a century earlier. The respect of succeeding generations for the integrity of the mid-Georgian house can be seen as having begun with this laissez-faire approach. The improvements made to the Dumfries House Estate rendered it a much more valuable commodity which must also have played a part in the brokering of the marriage between the Crichtons and the Stuarts, thus securing the long term future of the family name, the title and the House.

Fig 6.16 Mather Brown's 1793 portrait of Lord Mountstuart, the eldest son of John 1st Marquess of Bute who predeceased his father.
The Bute Collection

1 Quotation from report by Andrew Wight 1778; see note 5.

2 The ability of titles to pass through the female line is enshrined in Scots law whereas it is not in English law.

3 Lands mentioned in deed of entail 14 December 1765: 'Barony of Cumnock, Dalhanny, Nether Garrieve, Garclaugh, Templelands with Burgh of Barony and regality of Cumnock, Leiffnorris, Waird, Blackwoodhill,Templelands & Clachan of Cumnock, Lowes, Over Sherrington & Blackhall, Crocklar, Boylston and Grierston, Blacklands, Broad meadow of Logan Clockloghair and Cubbs Cloon,Auchencross, Barony of Glenmuir, Glenmuir, Pepperthill, Schaw, Castle Coole, Dornall,Little Chang, Over Glaisnock, Shiell and Powhapple, Mossmark, Brunston, Craigman, Knockdons, Waterside, Pennyland, Kirkland, Glasshead, Glenside, Hapland, Old Byre, Ballanceholm, Fauld and Bank, Writing Acre, Hundred Merkland, Waterside, Pennyfadzeoch Easter, Barony of Mochrum, May Brae, Upper and Nether Gleulings, Airilick, Corval, Shallochglass, Drumdrew, Drummatt, Gargarries-Hither and Nether, Craigach, Craiglary, Half Merk, Kirriehallock, Parkhill, Lochronald, Mains of Lochronald, Ballineinoch, Drummalloch, Merks, Airieligg, Arriesses, Sleudonnan, Craigarrie, Derries, Monandorie-Over &Nether, Alterkinross, Craigenadie, Kilgallick, Dennycarsh, Eldrack, Lewisland, Kilglassoch, Inshank, Erriolglassals, Deroachline and Drummaine' Bute Archives DU/5/2

4 'March 12 1771. About this time Lord Dumfries it was reported lost £20,000 at Almacks' (a club in St James', London). Greig 1926, 144

5 The 3rd and 4th Earls of Bute were also Scottish Representative peers the latter being a contemporary of the 6th Earl of Dumfries. *Burkes Peerage and Baronetage* 1925, 407

6 Margaret had inherited c1755 at least part of her father's estates which included Restalrig House, now in Edinburgh. The estates of Hay of Restalrig were forfeited after the 1745 Rebellion. Hay's estate of Restalrig, on which his mansion has given place to the present Restalrig House (later St Mary's Catholic Home) became the property of Mr Ronald Crauford. No mention of this estate has been found in the papers relating to the 6th Earl so presumably it was sold. Margaret's sister Jane married William Fergusson of Raith.

7 Post Culloden there was a move by the government to improve the lot of the Highlanders to prevent further uprisings. The Commissioners for the Annexed Estates administered the estates confiscated after the 1745 rebellion from the supporters of the Jacobite cause. The commissioners eventually resolved to instruct Andrew Wight, an East Lothian Tenant farmer, to tour Scotland and report on the best farming practices that could then be applied to improving the annexed estates. Wight surveyed all the mainland counties except Argyll. Report on the Present state of Husbandry in Scotland. The Earl of Hopetoun was one of the commissioners of the annexed estates, the sort of lucrative post that the 5th Earl of Dumfries would have relished. Extracted from *Reports made to the Commissioners of the Annexed Estates*, and published in their authority in two volumes Edinburgh 1778. By Andrew Wight. Glendining and Wade Martins 2008, 48, 78

8 The 'Commissioners and Trustees for Improveing Fisherys and Manufactures in Scotland' were established 1727

9 *Ibid*

10 Bute Archives DHP 25

11 Bute Archives DU/6/23

12 Tait 1980, 2

13 Loudoun 1822, 82

14 *Ibid*, 72–3

15 James Boswell's diaries, September 1780

16 Later, the 6th Earl was to construct two pairs of gate lodges on this road which confirmed the Ayr–Cumnock road as the main approach to the Estate.

17 King 2001, 325

18 Improvements by Patrick Earl of Dumfries 1768–1803. Bute Archives DU/6/23

19 *Ibid* item 41

20 The itemised list of works of the 6th Earl includes extensive draining and enclosing of lands and improving farm buildings across the estate. Bute Archives DU/6/23

21 *Ibid* item 49

22 Bute Archives DHP/ADD/1

23 18 December 1783. 'To Thomas Morton for making bricks £17.2/1; 2,250 bricks for the hot house; 1,000 bricks sent for Mrs Mackay's sample; 8,000 yet in the kiln to used for the hot wall in the kitchen garden.' Bute Archives DU/6/45/6

24 *Ibid* item 85

25 *Ibid* item 95

26 Robert Soutar's account of work for the Earl of Dumfries including, 'To throwing down the old house' in January 1771. Bute Archives DU/6/34

27 *Ibid* item 96

28 'William Brown the Carter lives in one of the East lodges but will be moved into one of the dwelling houses at the farm offices. The other lodge on the East approach and the two on the west approach have not yet been occupied.' Bute Archives DU/6/23, 19. Report on Estate Improvements of the 6th Earl.

29 This was a design that was fashionable at the time eg Samuel Wyatt's Milford Lodges, Shugborough, Staffordshire, 1803–6

30 The 6th Marquess was Chairman of the National Trust For Scotland and President 1991–3

31 Strawhorn 1966, 45

32 Torrie & Coleman 1988, 18

33 January 1784. 'To James Waitt painter 17 Days from this date 13 January 1784 cleaning, mending, and whitening the Dining Room ceiling, cleaning, puttying and mending the broken ornaments of said room and cleaning and varnishing the pictures there in £3.16/9.' Bute Archives DU/6/34

34 March 1784 'To James Waitt painter for 11 days from this date to 20 March 1784 cleaning, mending and whitening the lobby ceiling and walls etc @ 3/- a day.' The Dining Room was mentioned in relation to the carriage of whitening for both lobby and Dining Room. Bute Archives DU/6/45/79.
The south wall of North Parlour, which was used as the Dining Room at this time, before redecoration in 2011 clearly showed the 1820s oak grained paint scheme and beneath that a thick layer of white paint was clearly visible. Notes taken by RCAHMS survey in 2007.

35 Bute Archives DHP/8

36 Graham 2010

37 'Baths were taken on medical instruction, often under medical supervision, because the process itself was considered to be dangerous. The trick was to walk down the steps and then suddenly plunge the whole body under the water hence the 19th century term "plunge bath" although in the 18th century doctors and architects called them baths. The sudden shock drove the blood away from the extremities to the inmost parts. This caused the fibres (of which the body was composed) to contract sharply. When one got out of the water, the renewed rush of blood to the fibres found them more elastic because they'd contracted. Likewise the heart was reinvigorated by having had to cope with the extra blood flow. This is why most baths are deep, because you are going to have to immerse yourself in it completely and suddenly–hence the steps. The sudden shock of bathing–"taking a dip"–might be repeated many times in a day. One woman is recorded as having taken 22 dips in a morning, so we are to understand that taking a bath was not necessarily a long process.' *Ibid*

38 Bute Archives DU/5/30/1

39 Relates to hot bath, water closet, etc. Thomas Macilwrath for supplying a copper boiler 1 March 1783 (attested at Culzean Castle by Hugh Cairncross). Bute Archives DU/6/44 09 November 1782 – 28 November 1783

40 2 July 1783 'To Robert Buchan for building the bath house £22.10/1' which includes 'to finishing the inside of the bath', 'for finishing the bath and setting up the copper'. Bute Archives DU/6/44/83. 8 October 1784 to John McClure 'to plastering the bath house £1.18/8' Bute Archives DU/6/45/128. Alex White supplied the tiles for 'tyles and terras for bason to a bath' £9.11.5 ½. ('9th May 1782 to 84 Dozen of best white tyles at 2/9 per dozen £8.8/-, to 12 ½ packs of terras at 1/3 £0.5/7 ¼, to half a hogshead and 2 packing cases for the tyles £0.6/6, to cash paid beading and cooperage of cask 0/10, to bill paid carting, shipping and shore duties at Leith 0/6) Bute Archives DU/6/44/8. Thomas Macilwraith supplied 'the copper boiler for the hot bath' £19.3/10. Bute Archives DU/6/44/36.

Messrs Bogle & Scott supplied the furnace door for the boiler £3.7/1 ½. Bute Archives DU/6/44/9

41 Joseph Bramah was paid for a patent apparatus and other furnishings for a water closet at a cost of £14.9.7. Bramah had patented his invention in 1778, which was an improvement on earlier water closets because his had a valve at the bottom of the bowl that worked on a hinge, a precursor of the modern ballcock. Sir John Harington had invented the first water closet in 1596 for his godmother Queen Elizabeth I. It was not however until 1775 that the design was improved upon and the first flushing water closet was invented by Alexander Cummings. 'The Earl of Dumfries to Joseph Bramah for a patent apparatus and other furnishings for a water closet paid 14 December 1782; £14.7.9.' Bute Archives DU/6/44/7

42 Plan showing the manner in which water is conducted into Dumfries House. Signed James Nielson 1818. Bute Archives DHP10

43 Survey plan of ground floor dated January 1894. Bute Archives DHP 11/1

44 'To plastering the bath house (£1.18/8); water closet (£1.0/8 ½); Gardeners House (£3.15/2); Hot House (£2.1/11 ½); a dressing room roof (£0.12/3)' Bute Archives DU/6/45/128. 8 October 1784 to John McClure 'To mending plaster in Garden's lads room, coach house, dairy, bakehouse, servants hall and passages, washing house etc. (£2.1/11 ½) Total £10.7/-8' Bute Archives DU/6/45/128

45 Satinwood furniture was acquired c1780 probably for Lady Elizabeth Crichton's rooms. Christie's 2007, items 198 & 199.

46 The blue damask was rewoven in 2011 and the room is now known as the Blue Drawing Room.

47 Moxon & Carfrae (painters) Bill, HES MS/23/300

48 Royal Albert Memorial Museum and Art Gallery object number 46/1968

49 The distinctive grey marble chimneypiece with its inverted scroll jambs and white marble panels is a later insertion. Information from a conversation, February 2013, with Ian Gow who supported conclusions drawn at a Society of Architectural Historians of Great Britain Study Day 2008.

50 Charlotte Rostek suggests alternatively that the Chippendale bookcase might have stood in the dressing room opposite the chimneypiece. Email correspondence 27 May 2013

51 Later known as the Business Room.

52 Christie's 2007 Vol. II, 70–1

53 This room below the North Parlour was later known as the Steward's Room.

54 John Caird Auctioneer of Edinburgh valued the household furniture, bed and table linen at £3,612 1/7 on 13 August 1803. Bute Archives, Sederunt Book Report of Crawford Tait factor to Earl of Dumfries for Marquess of Bute. 1802–3

55 Russell 2004

56 Until 1782 this was the only method available to the Crown for giving British titles to Scottish peers. Turberville, A 1958, 103–4

57 He also commissioned a house in Berkeley Square from Robert Adam in addition to his other London properties; a villa at Brompton, now part of Kensington and Chelsea, and a house in South Audley Street. In 1773 he began building a very large house on the Hampshire coast for his retirement. This building has been attributed to Robert Adam although this is disputed. King 2001, 404

58 Davies 1981, 31

59 Charles was the 8th of 11 children and the 4th son.

60 James Stuart was created Lord Wharncliffe in 1820. Davies, J 1981, 7

61 *Ibid*, 10 and note 24

62 McKerlie, P 1906 I, 343–351

63 Davies 1981, 13 (Sandon Hall Archive XX & XX1)

64 *Ibid*, 14

65 In 1809 on a cruise in the Mediterranean he met and befriended the Duke of Orleans, who was later to become Louis Phillipe I King of France, from 1830 until his abdication in 1848. In 1812 the Earl of Dumfries wintered in Stockholm where he became acquainted with Mme de Stael. The following year he travelled to Moscow, St Petersburg and Vienna and in 1814 visited Napoleon on Elba. *Ibid*

Chapter 7: The 2nd Marquess of Bute 1803–1848

completely in order for the reception of Lord and Lady Bute

Arthur Moore to Adam Crichton[1]

With the death of Patrick the 6th Earl, ownership of Dumfries House and its estates passed from the Crichtons to the Stuarts, and the House thereby became an integral part of the extensive Bute estates. Although it was largely closed up for a decade with only a skeleton staff to oversee its maintenance, as soon as the 2nd Marquess came of age Dumfries House became a home once more and he visited regularly making alterations and redecorating the interior.

During the minority of John Stuart, 7th Earl of Dumfries, his estates had been managed by a board of factors and administrators which had been created on 3 July 1803 after the death of his maternal grandfather.[2] The Board's management of the estates was prudently guided by the Estate Factor Mr Crawford Tate who recorded the details of the improvements undertaken at Dumfries House in his Sederunt Book.[3] External advice was also sought, for example, Dr Coventry of Edinburgh University was commissioned to advise on how to increase the productivity and rents of the Galloway Estate.[4] During the eleven years of the 7th Earl of Dumfries' minority his Trustees spent £65,542.16/- on land acquisitions, thereby substantially enlarging what were already extensive land holdings.[5]

For the first time the House and contents were insured.[6] In October 1803 John McDouall, Trustee and brother of the 6th Earl, agreed to live at Dumfries House on the condition that a small staff was engaged to look after the House. Mrs Cairns, a Housekeeper, two chambermaids and a house porter, William Ballantyne, were appointed. The former Coachman, John Murray, was appointed as Gamekeeper along

with a gardener, Gilbert Ross, an under-gardener and a labourer. The annual expense of running the house was £282 4s while the cost of managing the gardens, woods and plantations was a further £142 13s. McDouall died only five months after moving in, and despite offers to replace him, the Trustees decided not to seek another tenant. By the following year the house staff was reduced to two, Mrs Cairns and a maid, and the building remained little used for a decade until the accession of the 2nd Marquess in 1814.[7] The first recorded work undertaken at Dumfries House by the 2nd Marquess was to commission William Simson of Cumnock to produce a plan of proposed works[8] which included a new entrance and drive off the Cumnock to Kilmarnock road, although there is no evidence that this was ever carried out. The earliest surviving structure built under his auspices is the Waterloo Bridge of 1816, constructed over the Polcalk Burn as a practical celebration of the famous victory.

The interior of the House underwent two main phases of refurbishment, 1818–20 and 1845–8, each prompted by marriage and the arrival of a new marchioness. In 1817 James Neilson was commissioned to prepare a report for Lord Bute regarding repair work needed at Dumfries House.[9] Neilson was a partner in J & J Neilson of Glasgow, a firm of 'architects & measurers' as well as 'lead merchants & plumbers' who were ideally suited for the work they were to carry out at Dumfries House.[10] Work began in May 1818 to make the House more comfortable prior to the Marquess' marriage to Lady Maria North on 29 July that year.[11] The marriage of a Bute to a North formed an alliance between the descendants of two of George III's prime ministers, the 3rd Earl of Bute and Lord North. Lady North brought £4,000 to her marriage and in 1827

Fig 7.1 John, 2nd Marquess of Bute, swathed in his ancestral tartan portrayed against a romantically Scottish landscape by Sir Henry Raeburn. The Bute Collection

inherited the Kirtling Estate, Cambridgeshire, and the Harlow Estate, Essex, from her uncle Frederick, 5th Earl of Guilford (1766–1827).[12] Despite having inherited substantial wealth and property, the 2nd Marquess and his wife shunned social life and retreated to Mount Stuart on Bute where, because of his failing eyesight and her chronic ill health, they remained in quiet seclusion until 1820 when his health improved.[13]

The 1818 works at Dumfries House were largely concerned with plumbing and draft proofing. A new water supply to the House was created in order to service the provision of two new water closets on the principal floor and a further two on the bedroom floor along with connections to the existing hot bath, old water closet and various cisterns.[14] The closet under the west stair survives although the water closet itself does not. Dumfries House is relatively unusual in that the insertion of water closets into earlier houses was usually achieved through the addition of a dedicated wing or tower, often with a cistern on the top floor, as at Balavil, Grampian, or in the Wardrop and Reid wing at Culzean.[15] The plan for this work (Fig 7.7) shows that two buildings to house cisterns were to be built south of the House, the most northerly with its castellated parapet on what became known as 'Cistern Mount'. The second lay further south, beyond the Stair and Bland Mounts and close to the spring.[16] Water was piped under

Fig 7.2 *This profile portrait of Maria North, first wife of the 2nd Marquess, is located in the closet off the Family Bedroom in Dumfries House. The original is in the church at Kirtling, Cambridgeshire, where she is buried with her husband.* HES 2013 DP151637

the High Road and entered the house beneath the front steps over the Great Drain.[17]

A set of four unsigned and undated drawings (Figs 7.3–7.6), probably by James Neilson, propose an alternative scheme for the installation of water closets into Dumfries House which would have involved rebuilding the entrance stair as a perron incorporating

Fig 7.3 *An unexecuted design by James Neilson, c1818, for a perron staircase to replace the existing straight flight at Dumfries House and the addition of a ground floor entrance.* Bute Archives

Fig 7.4 James Neilson's unexecuted design for the addition of water closets flanking a new entrance passage in the lower ground floor of Dumfries House c1818.
Bute Archives

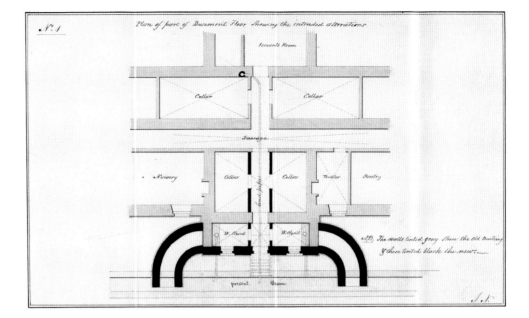

Fig 7.5 Annotations to James Neilson's Principal Floor Plan show that the drawing predates the insertion of the stair lobby doors in 1818. It also shows the sole alteration to the interior at this level, a pipe serving the bedroom floor water closets which is shown in the south wall of the North Parlour.
Bute Archives

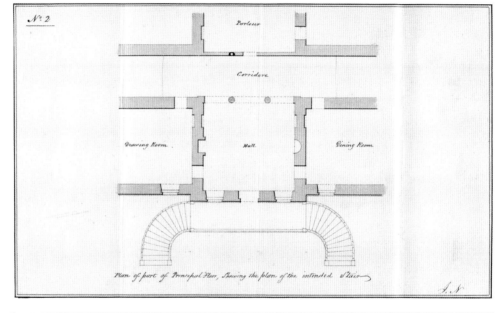

Fig 7.6 James Neilson's plan of the Bedroom Floor shows the location of proposed water closets either side of the central corridor and their adjoining plumbing, c1818.
Bute Archives

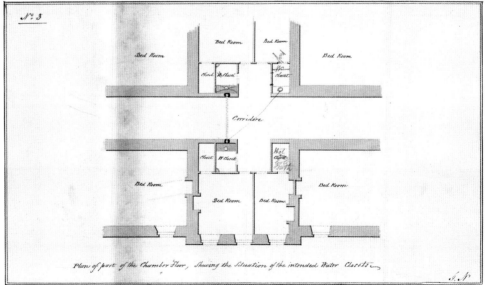

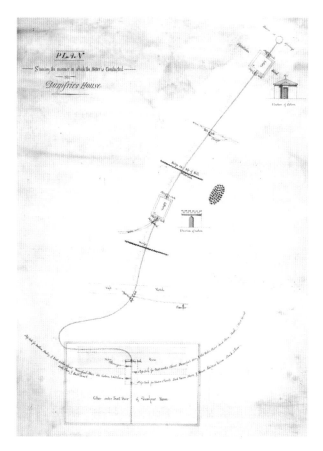

Fig 7.7 *A design for a new water system for Dumfries House by James Neilson showing how the water was to be piped into and distributed around the House, 1818.* Bute Archives DHP/10

Fig 7.8 *The new screen walls in the Entrance Hall were constructed to the highest quality with their cornices and skirting boards being run to match the existing ones. Only the reeding of the door cases betrays the fact that they are an insertion.* HES 2007 SC1104113

Fig 7.9 *This decorative cistern house was positioned to serve as an eye-catcher from Dumfries House.* Bute Archives

a pair of water closets flanking a central entrance passage on the ground floor.[18] This new entrance would have provided an everyday way into the House at ground floor level in addition to a formal entrance on the floor above as at Nostell Priory, Yorkshire, and Kedleston Hall, Derbyshire. The plans have been annotated in pencil to show a possible location of the screens between the Entrance Hall and staircases which Neilson added in 1818.[19] The choice of the simpler scheme could have been made on the grounds of cost but may also be seen as the earliest example of the family's desire to retain the external integrity of Dumfries House, thereby preserving the Palladian character of the original design.

The Entrance Hall screens added by Neilson affected the flow of air through the house and reduced the drafts as did the provision of inner storm doors at the main entrance which were also installed at this date to a similar design.[20] His concern to integrate the new work is demonstrated by the way in which the partitions are set back and the detailing of the new work in which the 'cornice [is] to be the same as the one at present round the corridor'.[21] The doors themselves were made by Matthew Morison.[22] The insertion of the new doors led to other alterations including the removal of the outer green baize Dining Room door, 'the place where the hinges are to be neatly filled so as they may be painted',[23] and 'the doors at the top of the stairs to the basement floor are also to be done with a row of panes in place of the upper panels'. These alterations sought to make the House more practical by enabling the servants to move around with minimal disturbance to the family. The absence of a service stair must have always been problematic but the installation of the lobby doors meant that the staircases could at least be isolated from the principal suite of rooms. It would have been relatively easy to enclose one stair to create a pantry in the stair lobby, probably the east one, so that food

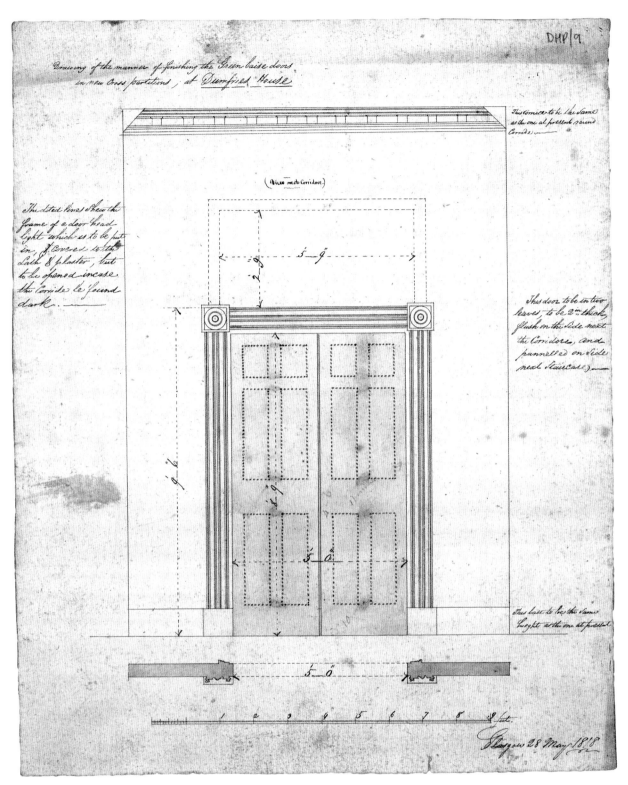

Drawing of the manner of finishing the Green baise doors in new Cross partitions, at Dumfries House

DHP/9

This cornice to be the same as the one at present round Corridor

(View into Corridore)

The dotted lines shew the frame of a door head light which is to be put in, & covered with Lath & plaster, but to be opened incase the Corridor be found dark.

This door to be in two leaves, to be 2in thick, flush on the side next the Corridore, and pannelled on side next Staircase.

This base to be the same height as the one at present

Glasgow 28 May 1818

Fig 7.10 James Neilson also provided a design for creating stair lobbies through the introduction of screens and new doors into the Entrance Hall. This drawing dated 27 May 1818 is extensively annotated to provide information about the alterations necessary for the insertion of the doors.
Bute Archives DHP/9

could arrive more easily in the Dining Room, but in rejecting this option, the architectural integrity of the twin staircases was maintained. The Dining Room appears to have remained in the North Parlour which meant, even with the alterations, all the food and crockery still had to pass through the Entrance Hall, there being no service pantry adjacent to the room in which food was being served. Works were still ongoing when Lord James, Lord Bute's younger brother, visited the house in September.[24] The following month, Neilson writes to Adam Crichton instructing that the doors be painted and not covered in baize. He also mentions that Robertson Reid and Bother, who were carrying out upholstery work at Mount Stuart, were to be at Dumfries House soon to do some work, the detail of which is unknown.[25]

On 11 November 1818, Arthur Moore, the Mount Stuart Factor, wrote from Rothesay to Adam Crichton, the Dumfries House Factor: 'write me if the house is completely in order for the reception of Lord and Lady Bute and how everything looks, particularly the Dining Room, Hall of Entrance, Inner Front Door, partitions which divide the hall from the staircases, Doors, water closets etc and of the machinery of the closets as well also of the supply of water appears good.'[26] The reference to the Dining Room suggests that it has undergone a noticeable transformation. The chimneypiece in the original North Parlour (by this time the Dining Room) has for some time been puzzling. In the original Contract for the House, the Earl was to supply any marble chimneypieces that he required and while we have clear documentary evidence that George Mercer designed and supplied chimneypieces in the original Drawing and Dining Rooms, there is no mention of one for this room. The chimneypiece shown on the original room elevations is of a similar form to the present one with its central rectangular tablet but has scrolled brackets supporting the mantle-shelf. The present chimneypiece with its inverted scroll jambs and mixture of white and grey

figured marbles is very different from the other examples at Dumfries House, which suggests that it was inserted later. It relates perfectly to the panelling above and to the flanking skirting boards, which implies that it was made specifically for this location and not brought in from another property and may perhaps have been installed when this room became the formal Dining Room in the 1790s, hence the tablet's depiction of a basket of grapes.[27] However, the Greek Key pattern moulding on the flanking stretch of dado suggests a slightly later date of the early 19th century. The 1818 architrave joinery in the Entrance Hall follows contemporary fashion with its reeded panels and rosettes and it would follow logically that the new dado required to flank a new chimneypiece in the former North Parlour would be designed to be equally fashionable, in this case adopting a more elaborate Greek Key pattern suitable for the room that was now the Dining Room (Fig 7.12).

In November 1820, the fashionable Edinburgh firm of Moxon & Carfae were employed to completely redecorate the house.[28] The work was carried out over the winter and assessed on 14 April 1821.[29] The Specification details that the woodwork in the Entrance Hall was painted 'fawn colour dead' and that everything else was painted 'best French white' including the 'frieze over the columns', the cornice, the 'enriched ceiling', the glass entrance door and all the doors except that to the Dining Room which was to be grained as oak. This refers to the door to the original North Parlour. The stone chimneypiece received three coats of varnish. In the Specification, the 'Eagle supporting marble slab' and the 'lamp' are 'to be gilded with oil gold', items which are not included in the final account.

The walls and ceiling of the original Drawing Room, which was now called the West Drawing Room, were painted 'dead French white'. It is clear that a third tapestry has been hung because the 'door under arras' was to be painted with four coats of paint. This most probably refers to the false door to the left of the chimneypiece rather than the useable one to its right. Although there are various examples of tapestries being hung over doors that are in use, it is never a very satisfactory solution, especially in a room that would only have had one other door at that time. In 1824 Moxon & Carfae were called back to do further work in this room including, '2 rich stands for marble tables done oak where white before say 10/6 each' which demonstrates that by this time the elaborate Drawing Room pier tables, unlike those in the Dining Room, had not been gilded.[30]

Fig 7.11 Moxon & Carfrae redecorated the North Parlour, Family Bedroom and My Lord's Dressing Room at Dumfries House in 1820 using the newly fashionable technique of wood graining as popularised by Sir Walter Scott, who had used it extensively at Abbotsford, his home in the Scottish Borders. Abbotsford Entrance Hall. HES SC887583

Fig 7.12 The chimneypiece in the North Parlour appears to have been inserted in 1820. Its pale grey marble sets off the white marble panels carved with grapes to reflect the use of the room at this time as the main Dining Room. The dado rail either side of the chimneypiece was also replaced with a fashionable Greek Key pattern. HES 2010 DP083216

The original Dining Room, which was now called 'Drawing' room 'to Southeast', was also painted entirely in 'dead French white' including all the wall and ceiling enrichments. The south facing window shutters received eight coats of paint to counteract the harmful effect of the sun. The Specification states that 'standards supporting marble slabs to be gilded oil gold as at present'. The gilding of the pier tables from the beginning reflects the high status of the mid 18th century Dining Room.

The suite of rooms along the north front, which had originally been designed as the private apartments of the 5th Earl (Plan 4), underwent the most radical re-decoration with a scheme of 'best imitation oak' applied to all the panelled walls, windows, shutters, architraves and doors. This was a very fashionable scheme of decoration, Sir Walter Scott having recently made similarly extensive use of graining at Abbotsford, his home in the Scottish Borders (Fig 7.11). The coved ceilings were painted cream; the plaster niche opposite the fireplace in the new Dining Room with its elaborate swag was also oak grained.[31] The omission of any mention in the painting specification or the bill for the varnishing or painting of the chimneypiece suggests that it was marble at this time since all the stone chimneypieces were varnished and wooden ones painted.

The two rooms off the Family Bed Chamber, originally described as a dressing room and closet, were described as 'Lord Bute's Dressing Room', to the south with direct access to the Stair Hall, and 'Lady Bute's Dressing Room' in the north-west corner. The former has a charming profile plaque of the 2nd Marquess' first wife, Maria North (Fig 7.2).[32] In an alteration to the 1818 plan, a further water closet had been installed in a room off Lady Bute's Dressing Room.[33] The west facing window, originally a blind window, was opened up at this time into what is a disproportionally large window for such a modest space. There is a curious note in the Specification, 'NB The door from dressing closet which contains the black lead writing is now to be put on ingo from this room to Dining Room that side on which the writing is to remain untouched either with washing or painting' but there is no record as to the detail of this inscription.

Lord Bute's Business Room lay to the east of the Dining Room and was decorated in 'best imitation oak'. The fact that the stone chimneypiece required varnishing highlights the fact that this room was of higher status than the bedrooms, which had timber chimneypieces, but not as important as the Drawing and Dining Rooms with their marble ones. It puts this room on a par with the Entrance Hall in the elaborate hierarchy of materials which informs the status of each room. The Specification includes a 'mirror glass frame to be gilded with oil gold' which is not included in the account. The original Charter Room is called the 'Safe',

reflecting the importance of its contents. The absence of any account for gilding in the Moxon & Carfrae accounts suggests that this may have been carried out by different craftsmen.

All the rooms on the bedroom floor (Plan 5), including the Blue Bedroom, had walls and woodwork painted 'fawn colour dead' with size white ceilings. Despite the importance of the Blue Bedroom as principal guest room it received no special attention, perhaps because as such it had suffered less wear. The smallest bedroom on the south front was not painted because it was 'locked up' and 'full of books', as a storeroom rather than a library. The Gallery on the bedroom floor was painted 'best French white' as were the walls and ceilings of both staircases.

The Moxon & Carfrae scheme extended to the servants' quarters on the ground floor of the main block but the pavilions, including the Kitchen, were not included in the work. The account gives the names of the rooms, which conform to the original room use except that Mr Crichton the Factor is using the original Nursery, at the south-west corner of the main block, as his office. A serviceable stone colour was chosen for the walls, with white ceilings and chocolate brown on a number of the doors. The fitted furniture, for example the Housekeeper's cupboards, was all painted, along with the servants' hall table. There is no mention of the panelling in the Steward's Room which must have been inserted later.

All the external windows were painted '2 coats of stone colour' which would have given the House a very different look, affording greater prominence to the architectural features such as the pediments rather than providing the crisp contrast of white woodwork and stone now more commonly associated with Georgian architecture. The painter work extended to gilding the external clock and painting the bell housing, the garden gates and even the garden roller. The total cost of this extensive programme of work was £729 0s 10½d.

After 1820 Lord Bute was in better health and was able to devote more time to estate administration and improvement. He had an extensive portfolio of properties spread across the country, the management of which became his life work. He travelled continually between his estates including Mount Stuart; Dumfries House; Axwell Park, County Durham; Kirtling Tower, Cambridgeshire; Wroxton Abbey, Oxfordshire; Luton Park, Bedfordshire; his London houses at Camden Hill and 80 Piccadilly; and Cardiff Castle, Glamorganshire. All of the houses were staffed and maintained along with their respective estates.

In 1826 Lady Bute commissioned John Gandy to design a new gate lodge for Dumfries House. At this time he was working on the designs for the County Gaol in Cardiff and so was probably known to the Butes through proximity to their Welsh seat.[34] The lodge was to be sited on the 'High Road', the Cumnock

Fig 7.13 In 1826 London architect John Gandy was commissioned by Lady Bute to provide designs for a new gate lodge at Dumfries House. Bute Archives

Fig 7.14 Alternative design for a gate lodge for Dumfries House, John Gandy, 1826. Bute Archives

to Ayr turnpike road that ran south of the House, the old road having been realigned further away from the House, thereby isolating the Stockiehill Lodges to the south-east (Fig 6.11). The design, although for a modest building, had architectural pretensions and was clearly intended to lie at the principal entrance to the Estate (Fig 7.13). A classical temple as herald of the entrance to an estate was a popular device in early 19th century Britain, as with the Doric Lodge at the entrance to Earl Fitzwilliam's estate at Wentworth Woodhouse, Yorkshire, of c1818.[35] The lodge was not built but the design was exhibited at the Royal Academy in 1827.[36]

After many unrealised schemes, a new entrance drive was created in 1840. Adam French provided a 'Plan of the entrance to the new approach to Dumfries House'.[37] This created a new eastern approach,

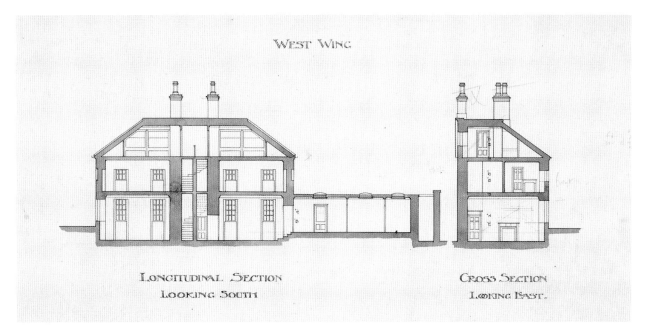

WEST WING

LONGITUDINAL SECTION
LOOKING SOUTH

CROSS SECTION
LOOKING EAST.

Fig 7.15 The attic servants' bedrooms created by the 2nd Marquess retained the profile of the roofs on the south front but altered the cross section. The new rooms contained box beds which were not removed until the late 1890s and are therefore shown on Robert Weir Schultz's survey of 1894. Bute Archives DHP/11/8

replacing the earlier drive from the Stockiehill Lodges which led from Bridgend on the western outskirts of Cumnock. The elaborate gate lodge which marks this new entrance was not built until the 1870s. This entrance to the estate was rendered obsolete by the building of a new stretch of the A76 in 1992.

In the original design for Dumfries House, service accommodation was limited to the lower floor and the first floor of each of the pavilions. In order to increase this accommodation, new bedrooms were created in the attics of both pavilions but the Marquess, in adapting the House to make it more practical, appears to have gone to considerable trouble to preserve its visual integrity. A report by Alexander Goodall and William Black[38] refers to arbitration over this work which was carried out by Alex Davidson, Joiner of Ayr.[39] This report in turn refers to an undated document[40] which describes alterations to both pavilions to alter the roof and provide two new servants' bedrooms within the extended roof space complete with fitted box beds (Fig 7.15). The creation of these rooms involved keeping the original pitch and hips of the roofline at the front and building a raised north wall that accommodated windows for the new rooms topped with a flat leaded roof.[41] This scheme is visible on pre-1897 photographs and on the 1894 Robert Weir Schultz survey drawings.[42] The newly created north wall was to provide a starting point for later extensions.

In the account for the work to the pavilions is a separate section that details proposed alterations to a library that appears to have been housed in the attic. This may be 'My Lord's Garret' which is referred to in the John Adam bills of 1760.[43] The specification, which refers to plans that have subsequently been lost, suggests that this library was situated at the head of the east, stone staircase on the garret floor, 'The present partition and door at landing of stone stair at entrance

to library to be removed and the stair railing returned round to the wall' and 'New doors to be made at Entrance to library and Lumber rooms of a proper size'. The room was to be lit from above and finished with pilasters and wainscot panelling at a total cost of £202. There is no evidence that this was carried out and no other references to this room have as yet been found. However, in 1829 John Smith of Glasgow was employed to write a catalogue of 760 books at Dumfries House, a volume that suggests that they would most likely have been accommodated in a designated space.[44]

Lord Bute played a prominent part in public and religious life and, although an active Presbyterian, he actively promoted Catholic emancipation.[45] Through his entrepreneurial activities he considerably extended and consolidated the family's fortune, part of which was re-invested in the Dumfries House Estate. On his death he was described as 'A product of his age, a mixture of evangelical earnestness, aristocratic arrogance and the confident ruthlessness of an early 19th century industrialist.'[46] The work for which he is principally remembered is the creation of Cardiff Docks, which transformed the economy of South Wales and generated spectacular wealth for the family. The Marquess' carefully integrated management of all his agricultural estates, including that of Dumfries House, provided the capital for embarking on this ambitious scheme to create a 'Second Liverpool', with staff and produce being moved between each estate to maximise efficiency. Industrialists moved from Newcastle to Glamorgan, colliers and mineral surveyors moved from Ayrshire to South Wales, servants from Luton were sent to Cardiff, Galloway cattle and tree seedlings were sent from Ayrshire to Glamorgan, and Luton Park was heated by County Durham coal. The pigs at Dumfries House were fed with acorns collected at Llanishen, Glamorgan, and the trees that were to stand over the Marquess' grave at Kirtling were raised at Cardiff. The Marquess' success was all the more remarkable in view of the severe eye disease which afflicted him; it made reading and writing difficult and meant that he had to be led when walking or riding. The magnificent Raeburn portrait of him which hangs in the Dining Room at Mount Stuart gives no hint of these afflictions; instead it celebrates a great man whose achievements were recognised in 1843 when he was created a Knight of the Thistle.

In order to manage his extensive estates, the Marquess spent his life in continual progress between them.[47] However, at an early stage, he recognised that his holdings should be to some degree consolidated so that Cardiff could be his principal focus, and in 1821 he attempted to sell his Luton Estate to support the venture: 'If I sell the (Luton) estate within £20,000 of the value (£200,000) I should after establishing my library and pictures at Mount Stuart or Cardiff and after relieving myself of every encumbrance, have so large a landed income as at this moment, if the residue money were laid out,' to enable the acquisition of more property and mineral rights 'in Glamorgan'.[48] Some five years later,

Fig 7.16 The ancestral seat of the Bute family was and remains Mount Stuart on the Isle of Bute. The new house begun by the 2nd Earl of Bute began in 1718 was engraved for Vitruvius Scoticus. *HES DP144157*

after no suitable offer had been made, he commissioned Sir Robert Smirke, who had already been employed to remodel parts of Cardiff Castle, to recast the existing Robert Adam house into a more fashionable residence.[49] In the 1840s Luton Park was put up for sale once again, partly as the result of a devastating fire of 1843 in which many of the contents were lost. By 1846 most of the Bedfordshire estates were sold and the Luton Park Estate renamed Luton Hoo by its next owner, John Shaw Leigh, who rebuilt the house.

In 1841, Maria, Marchioness of Bute, died childless at the age of 48. Under their marriage settlement the Marquess had the use of the income of his wife's share of the North estates until his death when the properties passed to Lady Susan North, Maria's only surviving sister. He appears to have mourned her deeply and had a row of almshouses built in her memory at Kirtling, Cambridgeshire. In 1845 he fell off his horse and splinters from his spectacles pierced his eye, the effect of which can be seen in the correspondence he wrote after this in which his handwriting becomes almost wholly illegible. In the same year at the age of 52 he married 36 year old Lady Sophia Frederica Christina Rawdon-Hastings, the daughter of the 1st Marquess of Hastings and Flora Countess of Loudoun, at Loudoun Castle, Ayrshire. Sophia's mother had spent part of her childhood at Dumfries House with the 6th Earl and his Countess and is depicted in one of the Raeburn portraits that hangs in the Drawing Room (Fig 6.1). The marriage appears to have been a love match since she did not have a substantial dowry, although she did of course possess the invaluable potential to bear

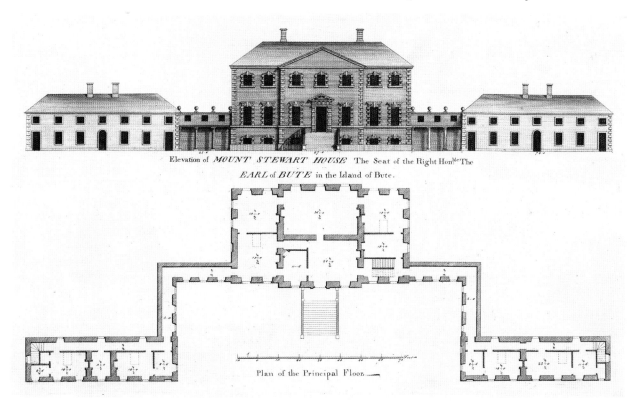

Elevation of *MOUNT STEWART HOUSE* The Seat of the Right Honble The *EARL of BUTE* in the Island of Bute.

Plan of the Principal Floor.

him an heir. The couple spent the first part of their honeymoon at Dumfries House.[50]

In 1845 proposals were drawn up for further minor improvements and alterations to the pavilions.[51] The scheme, which was not carried out, proposed the enlargement of the Kitchen within the existing east pavilion and the insertion of extra servants' bedrooms between the toofalls on the north side of each courtyard.[52] Throughout the Marquess' time, a continuous stream of estate improvements were made including the addition of new farm buildings[53] and cottages[54] and extensive improvements and drainage of estate farm land.[55] His second marriage necessitated a smartening up of the interior of Dumfries House, in particular its soft furnishings, and so furniture was re-upholstered and curtains and carpets replaced.[56] In 1846 John Wilson & Co Cabinetmakers & Upholsterers of 13 Sandgate Street, Ayr, were called in for various jobs including providing '89 ½ yards of rich brocade blue silk damask for covering Drawing Room furniture' and 'repairing and double gilding 3 Drawing Room window cornices'. The final bill came to the substantial sum of £530, which was paid in 1848.[57]

In addition to smartening up the interior, the workings of the House were modernised. The rooms at the south-west corner of the main block on the ground floor, which in the original design had been conceived (Plan 3) as nurseries and which had subsequently housed Mr Crichton the Factor, were converted into a Still Room with Pantry.[58] Traditionally, the Still Room was where the lady of the house prepared home remedies such as ointments and salves but by the mid 19th century it had become the preserve of the Housekeeper as a place to prepare afternoon tea so as not to disturb the preparation of dinner in the main Kitchen. The Still Room's location at the south-west corner of the ground floor is within the area controlled by the Housekeeper and therefore conforms to Adam's original division of the functions of the house.

Fig 7.17 The medieval west range at Cardiff Castle was remodelled by Henry Holland to provide the 1st Marquess of Bute and his descendants with a suitable residence when visiting Wales. Cardiff City Council, Cardiff Museum

Almost two and a half years after their marriage, Sophia gave birth to a son, John Patrick, on 12 September 1847 at Mount Stuart, only to be widowed six months later when the 2nd Marquess died in Cardiff on 18 March 1848.[59] Lady Charlotte Guest wrote:

> He was just at the height of his glory. He had brought his long wished for little heir to Cardiff for the first time he had received deputations of congratulations from the authorities on the event … he was in the highest apparent health and spirits, visiting day by day his docks and the institutions of the Second Liverpool[60]

Attended by 31 carriages, his funeral was reported to have drawn larger crowds than those of George IV and William IV. By the end of his life, he was managing a vast series of estates including a number of major country houses: Mount Stuart, Dumfries House, Axwell Park, Kirtling Tower, Luton Park and Cardiff Castle. Once again, the Dumfries House estates came under the control of a group of Trustees but this time the problems were greatly magnified by the addition of the extensive Bute properties. Throughout his life, Lord Bute had made a series of very complicated financial arrangements which were to stand the succeeding generations of his family in very good stead. In 1818 he had restricted his own funds by granting all his estates in Wales and England to Sir Charles Stuart and the Bishop of Lincoln to hold in Trust for the eldest son of his marriage to Lady Maria North and to raise portions for any other children and a jointure for the Marchioness. By the late 1820s, with various purchases of land, only three-quarters of the Glamorgan properties were in Trust. In 1825 the Marquess began planning the removal of the lands around Cardiff from the settlement, achieving this through acts of Parliament in 1827 and 1837. The 1827 act vested the entailed parts of the Dumfries Estate to Lord Bute in fee simple, giving him the freehold, while the 1837 act granted the Dumfries Estate to the Trustees in lieu of the docks and urban lands of Cardiff.[61]

On his second marriage, a new settlement was arranged that excluded the Glamorgan estates which became a trust subservient to the settlement vested in his brother Lord James Stuart. This was to be partially responsible for the eventual breakdown of the relationship between Lord James and Lady Sophia since he had expected to inherit the entire family fortune but was now supplanted by his infant nephew. The Marquess nominated two people, his 'dearest and most intimate friend', Onesiphorous Tyndall Bruce, and his wife's relation J M M McNabb, not 'with the intention of divesting myself of absolute control … but only providing for management in

Fig 7.18 The carriage which carried the 2nd Marquess and his 2nd wife, Lady Sophia Hastings, from their wedding at Loudoun Castle to their honeymoon at Dumfries House was decorated with their family crests to celebrate their union. HES 2010 DP083440

the event of his being prevented by illness or absence from attending thereto'.[62] Tyndall Bruce held a very favoured position and Lord Bute instructed that Estate officials were authorised to talk with him 'without reserve on any point of my affairs'.[63] With the birth of his long awaited heir, the Marquess constructed an elaborate will, leaving everything to him and awarding full power to Bruce and MacNabb to act as trustees. His extensive entreprencurial activities had come close to bankrupting the family, especially the financing, construction and the maintenance of the docks in Cardiff, but his gambles eventually paid off handsomely.[64] By the time he died, he had rationalised and concentrated his various estates into four principal and dynastic family parts: the Bute estates of the Stuarts, the Ayrshire Estates of the Crichtons, the Durham Estates of the Claverings and the Glamorgan Estates of the Windsors. With the North Estates of Wroxton and Kirtling returning to the North family on his death and the sale of Luton Park and the Bedfordshire Estates, the administrative duties of his son's Trustees were greatly simplified.

1 Quotation from a letter dated 11 November 1818 from Arthur Moore to Adam Crichton Bute Archives A/1158

2 The Board consisted of the Marquess of Bute, Earl of Dalkeith, Reverend William McDouall, Robert Fergusson of Raith, Brigadier General Ronald Crawfurd Fergusson, Alexander Buchanan of Cambusmore, Mr McDouall of the East India Company, Mr Edmonstone and Mr Tait. Reverend William McDouall and John McDouall were both brothers of the late 6th Earl of Dumfries. Bute Archives, Mr Tate's Sederunt Book

3 Item 20 Plans and elevations of houses (and steadings) built on the Dumfries Estate 1809. Bute Archives A/1273

4 The total annual rents from the Ayrshire and Galloway estates amounted to £6,038 19s 7½d at Martinmass 1803; by 1814 they had risen to £9,702.

5 On 4 July 1809 the neighbouring Ochiltree Estate lying to the west of Dumfries House was acquired at a cost of £27,892 16s.

6 Mr Tate arranged for the house to be insured for £5,000 and the furniture for £3,000. Bute Archives, Mr Tate's Sederunt Book.

7 Maclean 2007, 5

8 2nd Marquess letters 1814. Bute Archives Bundle A 1468

9 Papers of 2nd Marquess 1817. Bute Archives Bundle 557

10 84 Clyde Street, Glasgow; *Glasgow Post Office Directory* 1818, 131

11 'Plan shewing the manner in which water is conducted into Dumfries House 1818'. As part of the improvements on the estate in 1818 Neilson also designed a kitchen extension for the Mains Farmhouse, then the factor's house at a cost of £44 9s 6d. '1818 Estimate of proposed addition to Mr Crighton's House'; Bute Archives DHP10. Bute Archives 2nd Marquess letter bundle 622a

12 The Kirling Estate was of 2,945 acres and the Harlow Estate was of 350 acres. Lady Bute's uncle Frederick, Earl of Guildford, had joined the Greek Orthodox Church and was chancellor of his own university on Corfu. Davies 1918, 15

13 'they did not gamble, breed racehorses, flirt, hunt or shoot, he was not a collector' *Ibid*, 245

14 Bute Archives A/1158 and DE/1/15

15 The water supply and drainage for the two water closets off the gallery on the bedroom floor were threaded through the north wall of the Entrance Hall. Bute Archives Uncatalogued drawing HES DP106898

16 Neilson's drawing notes where the water was being directed to with separate water cocks for the 'Butler's Pantry & East water closet principal floor', 'old cistern & kitchen Sunk floor and East court', the 'West Water closet principal floor & old water closet sunk floor, bath & West court' and 'Water closets bedroom floor & housekeepers Room sunk floor'. Bute Archives DHP/10

17 Letter signed James Neilson, Glasgow Bute Archives A/1158

18 2nd Marquess letter bundle. Bute Archives Letter 623

19 The line pencilled on the drawings shows an alternative location of the screens sitting beyond the doors to the south facing rooms therefore closer to the staircases; see note 15.

20 This refers to the inner storm door as well as the staircase lobby doors 2nd Marquess Letter Bundle 623 The drawings for the stair lobby doors are dated 28 May 1818 and signed by James Neilson. Bute Archives DHP/9

21 Description written on the drawing. Bute Archives DHP/10

22 2nd Marquess Letter. Bute Archives Bundle 623

23 Description written on the drawing. Bute Archives DHP/10

24 *Ibid*

25 2nd Marquess Letter bundle. Bute Archives A/1158 (DE/1/15)

26 *Ibid*

27 In the later wings of Dumfries House chimneypieces were brought in from other Bute properties.

28 'Specification of Painting for the Most Noble the Marquis of Bute at Dumfries House', May 1820. Bute Archives Bundle A/1233; Moxon & Carfrae document of works carried out at Dumfries House HES Moxon & Carfrae Account Book 247, 1820

29 Moxon & Carfrae was an Edinburgh firm of painters and decorators established in 1774 and finally closed in 1946. Their extensive client list included the Dukes of Buccleuch and the Society of Advocates. NRS GD1/548/2

30 Moxon & Carfrae Account Book 247, 1820 HES

31 A fragment of this graining could be seen on the north wall prior to its redecoration in winter 2011.

32 An identical plaque was used on Maria North's memorial in Kirtling Parish Church, Cambridgeshire, identified by Matthew Williams, Curator of Cardiff Castle.

33 Bute Archives DHP/10

34 Colvin 1995, 386

35 Design attributed to J P Pritchet and Charles Watson. Mowl 1985, 111

36 The uncatalogued alternative designs are held in the Mount Stuart Archives, one inscribed 'for the Marchioness of Bute' and dated 1826. Colvin 1995, 386

37 Bute Archives DHP/ADD/3

38 The report is dated 3 January 1833. Bute Archives 2nd Marquess letter Bundle A 1542

39 The work was estimated to cost £213 but the final bill came to £352 13s, hence the need for arbitration.

40 2nd Marquess Letters Bundle. Bute Archives A/1226

41 The pavilion attic rooms without their box beds and windows remain, now top lit following the late 19th century extensions.

42 Bute Archives DHP11/8 and DHP11/11

43 'The Rt Hon the Earl of Dumfries and Stair John Adam Architect for additional wright work done in & about Dumfries House in the years 1760 & 1761 not included in former accompts'; 'Work on My Lord's garret and pavilion garrets.' Bute Archives DU/5/30/13

44 The only architectural books included were: *Vitruvius Britannicus* Colen Campbell 1731; *Essay on the origin and principles of Gothic Architecture* by Sir James Hall Edin 1797; *The Designs of Inigo Jones consisting of plans and elevations for public and private buildings* W Kent 2 vols in 1 folio 1727; *The architecture of Palladio containing a short treatise of the five orders and the most necessary observations concerning all sorts of building* revised and published by Giacomo Leoni translated from the Italian 2 vols 1742; *Discorsi sopra L'Artichita di Roma de Vicena Scamozzi* 1582. The 5th Earl of Dumfries' subscribers' copy of *The Ruins of Spalatro* by Robert and James Adam is now also in the library at Mount Stuart. Bute Archives Catalogue of the Library at Dumfries House created by John Smith & Sons Glasgow in 1829. Held in the library at Mount Stuart

45 The Marquess addressed the House of Lords on 57 separate occasions and was an early champion of Catholic emancipation having made a speech on the subject in 1828. From 1842 to 1846 he was Her Majesty's Commissioner to the General Assembly of the Church of Scotland where he was involved in aftermath of the disruption when Church of Scotland was rent asunder largely over the role of the Heritors and the Free Church was created. He resigned in 1846 over misgivings about the Queen's oath to the Church of Scotland. Davies 1981, 17–20

46 *Ibid*, 13

47 One of the last families to continue such a progress between family estates were the Buccleuchs, who moved between Boughton, Northamptonshire, Drumlanrig, Dumfriesshire and Bowhill, Scottish Borders. *Ibid*, 17

48 CCL B IX 19 1815–17 National Library of Wales B 140

49 Colvin 1995, 880

50 The coach in which they were brought to Dumfries House after their wedding (Fig 7.18) was recorded by RCAHMS, on 9 July 2010 in the Dumfries House Coach House and is now at Mount Stuart. DP083440

51 James Paton 'forwarding pencil sketches of alterations he would propose in the East or Kitchen wing of Dumfries House sending plan of alterations on west wing; no change in outside appearance of house'. Bute Archives Papers of 2nd Marquess of Bute 7 October 1845, letter 534.

52 Four sheets showing proposed alterations to the East and west pavilions uncatalogued stored with the Dumfries House drawings. Bute Archives *Ibid*

53 Bute Archives Bundle A/1275 Sheet 14 1842

54 A simple row of two roomed cottages. Bute Archives Bundle A/1275 Sheet 70 & Bundle A/1275

55 Bute Archives Bundle A/1275 Sheet 87

56 In 1844 over 288 yards of Brussels carpeting was ordered from Gregory Thomsons & Co of Kilmarnock at a cost of £65 6s 4d including the 'expenses of a man with patterns at Dumfries House'. Bute Archives Bundle A/1226

57 John Wilson & Co Cabinet makers & Upholsterers, 13 Sandgate Street, Ayr. Extensive works include: New hangings for Chintz room 23 October 1846; 89 ½ yards of rich brocade blue silk damask for covering drawing room furniture; repairing and double gilding three Drawing Room window cornices; new blue hangings for family bedroom, new silk hangings for blue bed etc 4 February 1847 £450; 6 March 1848 £80; Bill paid in full £530 on 6 March 1848; outer paper has black edge and black seal. Bute Archives Bundle A/1226

58 On 23 February 1846 Lord Bute wrote a note concerning moving the office of the factor, Mr Crichton, to his house at the Mains Farm. Bute Archives Bundle A/1275 1846 Sheet 69

59 Lord Bute chose to be buried at Kirtling alongside his first wife rather than at Mount Stuart, his ancestral seat.

60 Bessborough 1950, 33

61 Decree of Court of Session 1838. National Library of Wales B 26

62 Trust Deed 1845 CCL B IX 15 indenture 1845. National Library of Wales B 140

63 NRS HB MSS 198

64 Davies 1981, 251

Chapter 8: The 3rd Marquess of Bute 1848–1896

I should like Lord Bute's ideas to be carried out

William Frame, 1884[1]

John Patrick Crichton-Stuart, 3rd Marquess of Bute, was passionate about buildings. He altered and embellished all the houses he inherited, bought and leased throughout his short life. His alterations to Dumfries House began before he reached his majority with the installation of a Turkish Bath and continued with extensive redecoration. There were continual projects ongoing at Dumfries House prompted by advances in modern technology as well as stylistic embellishments but all these are tempered with a desire to preserve the 18th century interiors with their exquisite plasterwork. His main architectural projects concerned Cardiff Castle and his ancestral seat of Mount Stuart but Dumfries House was never forgotten and he conceived a scheme to recreate one of England's greatest 18th century pleasure gardens beside the House. Lord Bute was also greatly concerned to provide a chapel for Dumfries House and commissioned a complete survey of the House as it existed from his friend, the architect Robert Weir Schultz, as the basis for altering one of his favourite homes.

In 1848, when just six months old, John Patrick Crichton-Stuart had become the 3rd Marquess of Bute, inheriting four estates: Mount Stuart on Isle of Bute, the Glamorgan estates including Cardiff Castle, the Clavering Estate in County Durham and the Ayrshire and Wigtonshire estate of Dumfries House.[2] He also inherited debts of £493,887.[3] Lady Bute and her young son continued to live between their various houses much as they had prior to the death of the 2nd Marquess. One of the few references to Dumfries House in the family papers at this period is in a letter addressed to Lady Bute from David Shaw, the Estate

Fig 8.1 Photograph of John Patrick, 3rd Marquess of Bute, and his mother Sophia Dowager Marchioness c1858.   The Bute Collection

Factor, describing a drive in a carriage from Dumfries House to New Cumnock via the new south-east drive.[4] The absence of further references to the Estate suggests that it was being run effectively by the Factor. Under the will of the 2nd Marquess, the estates were to be managed by Trustees until the 3rd Marquess came of age. Onesiphorous Tyndall Bruce, a close friend of the 2nd Marquess and J M M MacNabb were appointed the Trustees of the estates.[5] After the death of O T Bruce in 1855, new Trustees were appointed: John Boyle of Calder Hall, Glasgow, a friend of Lady Bute's family, and Charles Stuart and William Stuart, both of whom were relations of the 2nd Marquess. The Trustees were exemplary in their financial management and cleared all the charges against the Estate during John Patrick's minority including all loans, debts and mortgages whilst expanding the landholdings and continuing the development of Cardiff. Acts of Parliament were obtained in 1848 and 1853 that gave the Trustees the authority to lease mineral land, appoint a dock manager and postpone the sale of the family art collection until John Patrick came of age. The latter is perhaps symptomatic of an almost perilous financial situation, The 2nd Marquess had invested virtually everything in the development of Cardiff but this gamble, which almost fatally compromised the Bute family fortunes, ultimately paid off handsomely.[6]

Lady Bute died in Edinburgh on 28 December 1859 and was buried at Mount Stuart. She had nominated her distant cousin Lady Elizabeth Moore (Fig 8.2) and General Charles Stuart, a second cousin once removed of the 2nd Marquess, as joint guardians of her twelve year old son. The arrangement did not always run smoothly; at an early stage the guardians quarrelled over John Patrick's education with the result that he,

163

siding with Lady Elizabeth, was smuggled to Scotland to live with her at Dumfries House in 1860. The House was smartened up on their arrival with Wylie and Lochhead of Glasgow supplying furnishings and some additional furniture being bought from Col J H D C Stuart.[7] Litigation followed, prompted by General Stuart,[8] over the nationality of Lord Bute on the grounds that the courts would not give up a domiciled Scot to a guardian appointed by an English court.[9] General Stuart's claim was upheld by the House of Lords, he was appointed sole guardian and Lady Elizabeth Moore was paid off by the Trustees.[10] General Stuart arranged for John Patrick to attend Mary Place, a preparatory school in Malvern, Worcestershire, and to live at Galloway House, Wigtonshire (Fig 8.3),[11] in the holidays with Randolph Stewart, 9th Earl of Galloway, his wife Lady Harriet Somerset and their eleven children.[12] John Patrick fitted into this large family between the eighth and ninth daughters Lady Emily and Lady Henrietta. He was a shy boy, brought up as an only child surrounded by adults, but he seems to have been happy with this arrangement. He kept in touch with Lady Elizabeth Moore writing to her soon after his arrival at Galloway House in December 1860, 'This house is like Dumfries House but much prettier. I have a charming room, not at all lonely. Lord and Lady G are so kind to me, and the little girls treat me like a brother.'[13]

In 1861 when the young Marquess turned fourteen, General Stuart arranged for the Trustees to go to the Court of Session in Edinburgh to formally appoint curators of the properties in Scotland.[14] Sir James Fergusson, Sir Hastings Guthrie, Lt Col William Stuart, Mr David Mure, Mr Archibald Boyle and General Stuart were appointed, with Sir James Fergusson chosen as personal guardian. Fergusson was certainly in residence at Dumfries House from October 1862 when he had a stable fitted up.[15] The maintenance of all the Estates was among the Trustees highest priorities.[16] Dumfries House underwent a series of running repairs including the repair of the Doocot in 1851,[17] the re-slating of the wings and of the Factor's house in 1853, as well as the regular renewal of the interior furnishings. In the same period, £2,377 5s 10½d was spent on new buildings and repairs to the Estate buildings.[18]

Between 1862 and 1865 Lord Bute attended Harrow School before going up to Christ Church College, Oxford. On leaving Harrow at eighteen, rather than going back to Galloway House in the holidays, he chose to return to Dumfries House to stay with Sir James and Lady Edith Fergusson. The Reverend David Hunter Blair writes affectionately on Christmas Day 1865, 'I saw a good deal of him when he was living at Dumfries House under the tutelage of Sir James Fergusson. He used to come down to the smoking-room at night arrayed in a gorgeous garment of pale blue and gold.'[19] The location of this smoking room is uncertain. It was most probably one of the two ground floor rooms in the

Fig 8.2 Lady Elizabeth Moore, Lord Bute's guardian until 1861.
The Bute Collection

west pavilion, most probably the western room which, by 1894, had become a billiard room.[20] It would have had a much lower floor level, at the level of the ground floor of the main block and east wing. It has since been raised. The room's original proportions would have been similar to that of the Kitchen in the east pavilion.

Now that he was spending more time at Dumfries House, Lord Bute began in a modest way to make his mark on the interior. He employed Wylie and Lochhead to fit out his bedroom with a brass French bedstead and crimson furnishings.[21] He also chose metal bedsteads for his bachelor bedrooms at Cardiff Castle and Castell Coch, possibly for hygenic as well as aesthetic reasons since they were regarded at the time as being more resistant to pests than wooden bedsteads.[22] Mindful of his ancestry, he also requested that 'the two full length portraits of Lord and Lady Dumfries by Raeburn' (Figs 6.1–6.2) be repaired and the frames regilded.[23] It is not clear where these large paintings were hung, though certainly not in the Drawing Room which was hung with the tapestries at this time. In 1848 they were hanging in the North Parlour and in the later 19th century they were displayed in the Entrance Hall, either side of the door into the North Parlour.[24]

General Stuart had encouraged his charge to travel abroad from the age of seventeen if accompanied by suitable adults.[25] In 1866 Lord Bute travelled to the Mediterranean with Reverend Charles Williams, an expert on the Orthodox Church. His first visit to Constantinople was an experience that was to have a profound effect on the rest of his life, influencing his approach to religion, the visual arts and especially architecture.[26] It is not recorded whether they visited a Hammam but they may well have done, the first mention of the installation of a Turkish Bath at Dumfries House being a year later in a letter from Sir James Fergusson dated 10 July 1867:[27] 'I hope you will put in hand as soon as possible the various work at Dumfries House agreed upon with Lord Bute and to check the Curators have specified they are the Turkish Bath, the gas and a new kitchen range.'

This was clearly a specific request by the young Lord Bute as part of a major scheme of modernisation.[28] William Railton of Kilmarnock[29] was the architect for the work in 1868, adapting and extending the existing 18th century hot bath attached to the west pavilion.[30] The building occupied by the 1783 hot bath appears to have been subdivided, a smaller plunge bath being constructed in the southern half and a bathroom in the northern part (Fig 8.4).[31] The Turkish Bath consisted of three rooms. From the existing bathroom, a door led into a new room added to the west called 'Turkish Bath', subdivided by a partition. A furnace was installed between this room and the original outer wall of the courtyard and all the spaces connected,

Fig 8.3 Galloway House, Wigtonshire, where Lord Bute lodged with the 9th Earl of Galloway and his family during the school holidays. HES SC1138112

with the baths lit by circular roof lights. The suite of rooms was only accessible from the west room of the west pavilion, called the Billiard Room in 1894 and the Smoking Room in 1897, which indicates that the Turkish Bath was considered to be a male preserve. No visible evidence of the Turkish Bath survives but it is shown on the Robert Weir Schultz survey of 1894.[32]

The unusual proposal to install a private Turkish Bath prompted concerns from both the insurance company, 'Herewith I send a memorandum on the construction of the baths to satisfy the Insurance Co and also a tracing of the plan to show the flues',[33] and from a health and safety point of view:

I now send you a short description of the baths with a plan to enable anyone to take charge of the furnaces and apparatus … some instructions from a competent party for the proper mode of using the Turkish Baths as I believe if in judicial use is taken they may be injurious and caution is required to avoid too hasty an exposure to the cold air after being subjected to a very high temperature. In public baths the attendants give the necessary advice – but in a private one like this there may be no one to do so.[34]

Sir James Fergusson, in his capacity as both the 3rd Marquess' guardian and resident at Dumfries House, was involved in the detail. Railton wrote, 'I was at Dumfries House on Saturday Sir James Fergusson

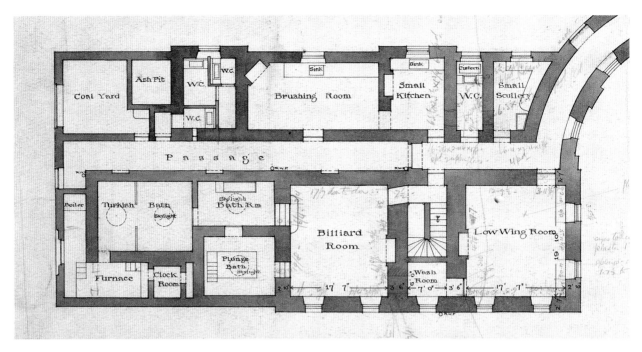

was in the bathrooms when I arrived and he seems well pleased with the arrangements and style of the baths.' He suggested 'covering the passage with glass the whole length – this done in a simple way would cost from £10–£15.[35] This passage ran along the north side of the Turkish Baths and was decorated with three blind Moorish arches. Galbraith and Winton of 129 St Vincent Street, Glasgow, supplied and laid the mosaic floors, the white glazed tiles and the majolica tiles at a cost of £32 5s[36] There are no drawings or photographs of 'the ornamental tile floor'[37] but a roughly contemporary example survives at Cragside, Northumberland.[38] The Turkish Bath at Dumfries House, which was installed five years earlier, is the earliest known 19th century example in Scotland.[39] It was in use until the death of Lord Bute in 1900, only removed when the new Billiard Room Library was created by Robert Weir Schultz for the 4th Marquess.[40]

The installation of a system of piped gas for lighting and cooking was the other major project undertaken by William Railton at this time. By the mid 19th century gas lighting had become an efficient, if expensive, method of improving the illumination of domestic interiors. James Hislop produced a report in April 1867 on how a gas supply could be installed at the house.[41] It is implicit from the specification just how disruptive the work to install the gas lighting must have been.[42] In the main block a ¾ inch pipe was to be run along each side of the ground floor vaulted corridor at the springing of the arch. On the principal floor an inch pipe was to be carried up through the wall by the door of the Charter Room through to floor above, 'and pipes shall be laid in floors to centre of each public room below for pendants'. This would have involved taking up the floors on the bedroom floor and the drilling of holes through the elaborate plasterwork ceilings of the three

Fig 8.4 The suite of rooms that made up the Turkish Bath was entered through the Billiard Room, the western room in the west pavilion. The Bath, which consisted of a shampooing room, a plunge bath and a Turkish Bath, was lit by skylights and concealed behind the original courtyard wall. Bute Archives DHP/11/1

principal reception rooms and the Entrance Hall.[43] At the same time gas lighting was installed in the Stables, Wash House, Stockiehill Lodges and in Woodburn Cottage, the Factor's house at the Mains. External lighting was also considered. On 5 September 1867, William Railton wrote to Charles Shaw:

> William Kay was asking about lights at the main door. I think these would be best managed by handsome lamps two at the foot of the flight of stairs to the front door and two behind the house at the corners of the main building. I have given a sketch and instructions about the pantry but the particulars of the cupboards would require to be put to the butler himself. The range is in hand… the plumber commences to his department Monday first.[44]

Fig 8.5 The central stove in the Kitchen was installed in the 1880s leaving the early 19th century range in the fireplace. HES 1956 SC1135283

Fig 8.6 The Chippendale, or 'best' bed, shown here in the south-west bedroom, was re-upholstered in a blue cretonne in 1868. HES 2007 SC1104217

This is the only reference to the creation of the Butler's Pantry by knocking through an opening between the vaulted Porter's Lodge and vaulted Pantry at the south-east corner of the main block as seen on the 1894 survey plan.[45] The existing lamps on the front stairs were installed in the mid 20th century.[46]

A gas fired range was also installed in the Kitchen (Fig 8.5), something that was relatively unusual at the time; despite the fact that cooking by gas had been promoted at the Great Exhibition of 1851, it did not become widespread until the 1880s.[47] On the 1894 survey plan (Plan 9), the gas range appears to be marked on the west wall opposite the original range but it is not shown on the 1905 plan (Plan 11).[48]

The earliest reference to the redecoration of Dumfries House under the guidance of the 3rd Marquess is to a decorative scheme that Railton devised for the Entrance Hall, the details of which are not recorded.[49] The gilding and naturalistic painting of the plasterwork may have begun at this period but it appears to relate more closely to the work of Campbell and Smith ten years later. One of the most important pieces of Chippendale furniture, the four poster 'best' bed, was restored and recovered with a 'blue cretonne chintz' in February 1868 (Fig 8.6) by John Reid & Co Upholsterers of Ayr.[50]

On 12 September 1868 the Marquess came of age, an event marked with various lavish celebrations, the one at Cardiff being attended by Benjamin Disraeli. Through the good management of his Trustees and the business acumen of his father, he now benefited from an enormous income of £300,000 per annum which ensured lifelong freedom from financial worries, if also a continual stream of begging letters.[51] He inherited three principal seats; Cardiff Castle in Glamorganshire, Mount Stuart on Bute, and Dumfries House in Ayrshire, all of which he was to transform to varying degrees during his lifetime.

At Oxford his fascination with the medieval world was nurtured and he began to question his religious beliefs. His mother had been a Protestant and his father an Anglican when in England but a Presbyterian in Scotland where he held a senior position in the Church of Scotland hierarchy. Lord Bute came under the influence of Monsignor Capel in Oxford who introduced him to the Roman Catholic liturgy and he appears to have seen conversion to Catholicism as a logical extension of his interest in medievalism. This eventually led to his entry into the Catholic Church on 8 December 1868 when he was received by Monsignor

Capel at The Notre Dame Convent in Southwark, subsequently being confirmed by Pius IX in his private chapel in Rome the following year. After his conversion Lord Bute set out for a trip to the Holy Land with Lady Loudoun and, resolving that his heart was to be buried in Jerusalem, he set out to achieve this by, in the first instance, acquiring property in Jerusalem.[52] The Protestant Scottish press was less than kind about Bute's conversion: *The Glasgow Herald*, for example, reported 'If, as is most likely, this perversion is the result of priestly influences acting upon a weak, ductile, and naturally superstitious mind, we may expect a continual eclipse of all intellectual vigour.'[53]

Becoming a Catholic dramatically altered his marriage prospects because he now wished to marry someone of the same faith.[54] The Honorable Gwendolen Fitzalan-Howard, eldest daughter of 1st Lord Howard of Glossop and granddaughter of the Duke of Norfolk was the eventual and happy choice (Fig 8.7).[55] During this period, 'Having at this time, no London residence Lord and Lady Bute spent their year chiefly between Cardiff and Mount Stuart with occasional visits to Dumfries House for which Bute had always a particular affection.'[56]

One of Lord Bute's greatest pleasures was the process of researching, designing and building, and the family archives preserved at Mount Stuart record the myriad schemes with which he was involved. Many more projects were proposed than were realised, every scheme being revised and altered to the extent that none of his personal projects were complete by the time of his death. The three family seats that he inherited were obvious candidates for transformation. Cardiff Castle, the most ancient and his only inhabitable castle, was his first major project and an ideal focus for his youthful exuberance. Mount Stuart was the principal project of his thirties. The dynastic family seat had to be re-created after a fire in 1877 and he took the opportunity to build on a scale that reflected the status of the family and which provided a suitable setting for the Bute collections. In his forties, amongst many other projects, he turned to his third seat, Dumfries House, where a much subtler, sympathetic approach was taken as he worked with the existing building rather than seeking to radically transform it into something else.

The 15th century mansion block at Cardiff Castle (Fig 7.17) had been modernised for the 1st Marquess by Henry Holland in the 1770s. However after the eighteen year old Lord Bute met architect and medievalist William Burges, a scheme was developed to transform the Castle into something worthy of its medieval past. The foundation stone of the first phase, the magnificent Clock Tower, was laid on 12 March 1869. The elaborate recreation of Cardiff Castle into something it never was is regarded as one of the greatest expressions of both the High Victorian medieval revival and of William Burges' architectural skill (Figs 8.8–8.9). This fashion

Fig 8.7 *Lady Gwendolen Fitzalan-Howard on her marriage to the 3rd Marquess of Bute, 26 April 1872. The Bute Collection*

for the embellishment of existing castles is reflected in the works of his fellow aristocrats the Duke of Northumberland at Alnwick Castle, Northumberland, and the Duke of Norfolk at Arundel Castle, Sussex. The grandiose scheme at Cardiff was barely begun in 1872 and so the newly married couple would have been accommodated in something very different to the splendour we see today. Bute wrote to prepare his fiancée for the work in progress, 'Pray don't imagine, my dear, that the house is all done up as if we were living in the reign of Henry III. There is only my sitting room, the oratory and the new tower. The rest is by no means satisfactory and has been the victim of every barbarism since the Renaissance.'[57]

The ancestral home of the Bute Family, Mount Stuart on the island of Bute, had been built by the 2nd Earl of Bute to designs by Alexander MacGill (Fig 7.16) between 1718 and 1722. William Adam had rebuilt the central block in the 1740s for the 3rd Earl but it had been little changed since. Lord Bute began a series of major alterations (Figs 8.10–8.11), acutely aware that Mount Stuart was the Bute family's ancestral seat; 'Bute is my real home' he proclaimed and 'Mount Stuart, as you know, is the house of our predilection.'[58] The importance of Mount Stuart to Lord Bute is also underlined by the fact that both he and his beloved mother are buried there.[59]

Fig 8.8 William Burges and Lord Bute transformed the relatively modest west range of Cardiff Castle into an amazing Gothic Revival fantasy. The earlier Gothick house is still visible amidst the later towers. The project, which was begun in 1869, was incomplete on Lord Bute's death in 1900.
Cardiff City Council, Cardiff Museum

Fig 8.9 The Winter Smoking Room in Cardiff Castle, which was completed by 1873, was a richly decorated expression of Lord Bute's and Burges' Gothic ideal, far removed from the Georgian restraint of Dumfries House.
Cardiff City Council, Cardiff Museum

The third of his seats was Dumfries House. Previous minor alterations had maintained it as a very comfortable home. He now undertook a series of improvements, writing to his new wife that Dumfries House, 'has been a good deal turned topsy turvy and must be turned back'.[60] Following his marriage, the first alteration carried out at Dumfries House was the installation of a new bathroom in the closet off his dressing room at the north-east corner of the House. The fittings that remain, including a shower over the bath, appear to date from this period.[61]

The firm of C Campbell and Smith were employed to redecorate the Entrance Hall and North Parlour which was still being used as the main Dining Room. No drawings or detailed specification for the paint scheme survive but the treatment of the plasterwork with partial gilding and naturalistic colouring appears to have been the focus of the work. The firm's account includes painting the panelled walls, 'gilding the mouldings of panels and cornice' and 'decorating the niche'.[62] The ceiling was to be painted, the 'raised ornaments' gilded and the foliage 'coloured naturally.' The scheme was similar for the Entrance Hall with additional instructions for 'emblazoning arms' and 'gilding and colouring fascia as instructed by His Lordship'. There is no evidence that the plasterwork in either the Tapestry Drawing Room or the Morning Drawing Room (the original Dining Room) was repainted at this time.[63]

It has been suggested that Lady Bute was responsible for this work, which may explain its relative restraint,

but there is no documentary evidence to this effect.[64]
However Lord Bute would almost certainly have had
a hand in the heraldry, one of his many passions. In
1875 he had been made a Knight of the Thistle, an
honour which had also been bestowed on his ancestor,
the 5th Earl of Dumfries, who had included its emblem
in the plasterwork, something that Lord Bute ensured
was picked out in the redecoration. As with all his
architectural projects, there were different phases of
redecoration and he employed the same tradesmen to
work at each of his various properties. In his accounts
for Dumfries House, the architect Robert Weir Schultz
records '1896/7 Decoration in hall by Cardiff men' and
'Designs etc for long frieze, coat of arms and of flowers
etc'[65] when referring to the colouring and gilding of the
plasterwork in the Entrance Hall and the North Parlour.
The earliest record of this scheme is that made by the
surveyors of the National Art Survey of Scotland who
drew and photographed the Entrance Hall and North
Parlour ceilings between April and November 1900.
One of the photographs (Fig 9.30) shows what appears
to be either embossed leather or tapestry on the wall of
the Entrance Hall above the fireplace[66] as well as a large
painting above the door to the Drawing Room which
fits snugly between the frieze and the doorframe which
appears to have been altered with the removal of its
frieze to accommodate the picture.[67] A photograph of
c1927 (Fig 8.13) shows that this large picture was part
of a set of four positioned above each of the four side
doors in the Entrance Hall.[68] Although these paintings

Fig 8.10 Robert Rowand Anderson's magnificent new Mount Stuart, begun in 1879, retained the wings of the earlier house; the original harled north wing can be seen to the left. HES 1904 SC695853

Fig 8.11 The main staircase at Mount Stuart. HES 1904 SC695859

had been removed by the 1960s, the doorframe friezes were not reinstated.

No structural alterations were carried out during this phase of work, something that was in stark contrast to the work that was being undertaken at Mount Stuart prior to the fire where for example the redecoration of the Drawing Room necessitated the insertion of a new ceiling. Although the work at Dumfries House completely altered the visual balance of the largely unaltered 18th century rooms, it rendered them more fashionable without the necessity for physical intervention. In the North Parlour, the gilding and naturalistically painted foliage might have overwhelmed the room in decorative terms, save for the fact that the walls were hung with a large number of paintings and so the relationship between the treatment of the walls and ceiling was sufficiently balanced. The niche opposite the chimneypiece was also painted a rich dark colour. An elaborate what-not for displaying china was designed to fit into this niche and is shown in-situ in a photograph c1926 (Fig 10.18).[69]

Under the careful stewardship of the Trustees, the Estate and its buildings had been well maintained with tenant farmers being encouraged to continue the improvement of their farms. Annual accounts include regular payments for minor improvements across the Estate, for example, in 1858 William Railton of Kilmarnock supplied a design for a new Gardener's

Fig 8.12 A new bathroom, complete with shower, was installed at Dumfries House for Lord Bute in 1872 in the original closet off 'My Lord's Dressing Room'. HES 2007 DP033653

House which may relate to the addition of an upper storey to the house which is attached to the north wall of the walled garden.[70] Further alterations and improvements were carried out to the Gardener's House, the Peach House and the walled garden in 1868.[71] The existing Gardener's House appears to have been constructed in 1870 according to the accounts[72] and may also have been designed by William Railton who, it appears, had become the Estate architect.[73] A painting at Mount Stuart (Fig 5.25) gives an impression of the elaborate form of the walled garden in the 19th century with its balustraded terraces stepping down towards the Lugar Water. The Mains Farm continued to be developed and improved as agricultural technology advanced.[74] In 1868 Railton supplied the designs for a new two-storey block (Fig 8.16) in the centre of the west range of the Mains combining an entrance pend, barn, stables and harness room on the ground floor with a hayloft and bothy, or grooms accommodation, above.[75] As part of the 19th century improvements to the estate a saw mill was built north of the Mains. The machinery was powered by a waterwheel fed from a millpond on the Back Burn and processed the estate timber.[76]

Between 1874 and 1875 a new gate lodge[77] was built on the drive from Cumnock (Fig 8.15), which had been constructed in the 1850s and described in a letter to Sophia Marchioness of Bute as 'the new drive'.[78] This lodge with its classical details and the use of the round arch affording it an element of grandeur was probably designed by William Railton, not least because he was carrying out various other works on the Estate at the time but also because of its similarity to some of his work in Kilmarnock such as the Sheriff Court buildings on St Marnock Street. This lodge was built at what was at the time the principal entrance into the Estate from which the drive passed through the well wooded policies over the Ladies Bridge to approach the house from the south-east. In addition to these practical improvements, Lord Bute created a series of walks around the Estate in the 1870s.[79]

On 3 December 1877 a devastating fire ravaged Mount Stuart, and Dumfries House was pressed into service as the main family seat in Scotland while Mount Stuart was being rebuilt.[80] The family also rented Balmory House at Ascog[81] on Bute, presumably so that Lord Bute had influence over building work on what was to be his largest and probably most complex building project.[82]

Throughout his life Lord Bute took what he perceived as his civic responsibilities very seriously, commissioning or supporting the building of a wide variety of public buildings including several in the vicinity of the Dumfries House Estate. The accounts for 1884 alone include payments for the 'Cottage Hospital, Cumnock, Sister's House at Birnieknowe, Muirkirk Presbytery, St John's Church, Cumnock, Priests House, Cumnock, Cumnock School Chapel, School

erected by LB at Galston'.[83] Lord Bute's commitment to the Catholic faith spread further than his personal requirements through the commissioning of new churches to serve local communities. In Ayrshire, for example, his commissions included St John the Baptist in Cumnock (Fig 8.19), designed by Lord Bute's great friend and collaborator William Burges in 1878–80 and completed by J F Bentley. The Byzantine inspired St Sophia, Galston (Fig 8.22), by Robert Rowand Anderson, 1884–6, was perhaps the most distinctive parish church he commissioned. He also supported the building funds of numerous other Catholic parishes beyond the confines of his extensive estates.

Lord Bute also sponsored research at home and abroad into a wide variety of subjects paying for archaeological digs and architectural surveys of a variety of sites including the Abbeys of Paisley[84] and Crossraguel (Fig 8.24). Closer to home, he commissioned archaeological excavations of Leifnorris (Fig 5.9), Terringzean Castle and Sanquhar Castle (Fig 8.27),[85] the last two projects leading to partial restorations. He also appears to have been a sponsor of the National Art Survey of Scotland,[86] which was a project masterminded by one of his architects, Robert Rowand Anderson, to record Scotland's historic architecture.

Although Lord Bute had resisted buying a property in London, from the mid 1870s leased several houses

Fig 8.13 The Entrance Hall at Dumfries House c1926, which retained its naturalistically painted plasterwork, was heavily furnished compared with its original arrangement. Note that the door case to the right of the chimneypiece has been cut down to accommodate the large canvas above. Bute Archives

there, his earliest residence in the capital being a house in Eccleston Square, Pimlico. He went on to exercise considerable taste and discernment in his choices, renting a series of neoclassical buildings of great architectural importance. In 1879 he took Sudbrook Park (Fig 8.17) at Richmond, Surrey,[87] an elegant villa which was designed for the 2nd Duke of Argyll and

Fig 8.14 A similar example of the richly coloured painting of the plasterwork commissioned by Lord Bute for Dumfries House can be seen at House of Falkland, which he decorated during the 1890s in a similar style.
Falkland Centre for Stewardship

Fig 8.15 *The Cumnock Lodge of 1875, which was probably designed by William Railton of Kilmarnock, became the principal entrance to the Dumfries House Estate from the east.* HES 2013 DP152924

Fig 8.16 *In 1868 William Railton designed a two-storey building for the Mains which combined a barn, hayloft, stable and first floor bothy.* HES 2010 DP083576

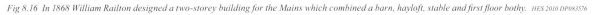

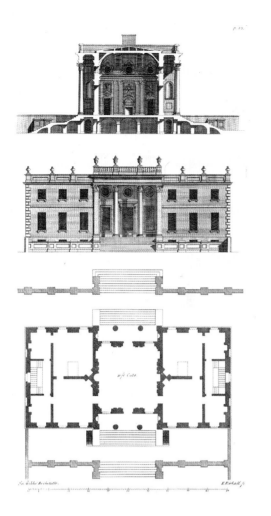

Fig 8.17 In 1879 Lord Bute leased Sudbrook Park, Surrey, both for its architectural interest and its proximity to London. Plate 40, James Gibbs' Book of Architecture. HES SC1152383

Greenwich by James Gibbs in 1715. Aside from its inherent architectural influence, it may be that Gibbs' influence on the design of Dumfries House contributed to Lord Bute's decision to lease the building.[88]

In 1881, while still renting Sudbrook Park, Lord Bute took a lease on Chiswick House (Fig 8.18),[89] now in the London Borough of Hounslow; it is one of the

most architecturally important early 18th century houses in England.[90] With his passion for historical research Lord Bute may well have been aware of Lord Burlington's approbation for the design of Dumfries House,[91] a factor which perhaps influenced his choice. The villa, which was designed by the Earl of Burlington c1726 for himself, is regarded as one of the greatest expressions of the Palladian revival in Britain.[92] In 1892, Lord Bute acquired the spectacular pair of tables[93] designed by William Kent for Chiswick Villa c1730 with the intention of installing them in the casino in the New Chiswick Garden he was creating at Dumfries House.[94]

St John's Lodge, possibly the grandest house in London, set in extensive gardens within Regents Park was the next house leased by Lord Bute. It was designed by John Raffield in 1817 and subsequently enlarged by Decimus Burton and Sir Charles Barry.[95] Almost immediately Lord Bute employed George Trollope and Sons builders to carry out an extensive programme of redecoration and alteration. From 1891 Robert Weir Schultz and W H Lonsdale continued to transform the house, creating lavish interiors and adding a new theological library and a chapel. In the gardens which Weir Schultz remodelled he also created a further subterranean chapel.[96]

With the rebuilding of Mount Stuart firmly underway, Lord Bute set about acquiring, altering, conserving and restoring a wide variety of buildings; during the course of his life he was responsible for over 60 building projects and was patron to a dozen architects.[97] In the mid 1870s he commissioned Richard Park to begin the restoration of Old Place of Mochrum which had been part of the Scottish estates since the 18th century[98] and which had only been completed in the early 20th century by the 4th Marquess.

In 1886 he bought The Garrison (Fig 8.25), a large marine villa at Millport on Great Cumbrae, from the Earl of Glasgow to add to the other Bute properties

Fig 8.19 The interior of the Roman Catholic church of St John, Cumnock, was designed by Lord Bute's great friend William Burges, 1878–80, and was completed by J F Bentley and N J Westlake. Lord Bute not only paid for the building but also subsidised the parish. HES SC1127122

Fig 8.18 Lord Burlington's Chiswick House formed the central section of one of the London houses leased by Lord Bute. English Heritage BB85-00249

Fig 8.20 St John's Lodge Regents Park as seen through the archway designed by Robert Weir Schultz. This house was rented as the principal London home of Lord Bute. English Heritage CC53-00433

on Great Cumbrae.[99] It was to become one of the favourite homes of Lady Bute in her widowhood. In 1887 he purchased the Falkland Estate (Fig 8.26) from the son of his father's great friend Onesiphorous Tyndall Bruce, who had been one of his Trustees in his minority. He had visited House of Falkland,

Fig 8.21 Old Place of Mochrum, Dumfriesshire, was acquired by the father of the 5th Earl of Dumfries in the mid 18th century. In the 1870s Lord Bute employed Richard Park to begin its restoration. HES SC1220462

a large Jacobean mansion built in 1839 by William Burn, with his mother and later during his sojurn to Scotland with Lady Elizabeth Moore.[100] The real prize of this new estate and the focus of Bute's attention was the former Royal Hunting Lodge of Falkland Palace (Fig 8.23) which came with the title of hereditary Keeper.[101] Dumfries House remained a constant within the maelstrom of acquisition and building projects and he wrote that, 'Falkland is probably the most luxurious of my houses but I think Dumfries House is, perhaps, the homeliest of them all.'[102] In 1894 he bought Sanquhar Castle, the ancient seat of the Crichtons, from the Duke of Queensberry to whose ancestor it had been sold in the 17th century.[103] Lord Bute and Weir Schultz set about recording and then restoring the castle but this was one of the projects that was to be halted on Lord Bute's death.

The friendship that developed between Lord Bute and Robert Weir Schultz (1860–1951)[104] mirrored his earlier relationship with William Burges. It is uncertain when they first met. Weir Schultz had been an assistant of Robert Rowand Anderson and may have been involved with both Mount Stuart and St Sophia at Galston. He had then moved to London in 1884 and worked in the offices of both Richard Norman Shaw and Sir Ernest George & Peto, two of the most

Fig 8.22 Lord Bute commissioned Robert Rowand Anderson to design St Sophia Roman Catholic Church in Galston, 1884–6, having been greatly influenced by Byzantine architecture during his travels in the Mediterranean. Its dedication not only recalls Hagia Sophia in Istanbul but also the fact that his mother was born at nearby Loudoun Castle. HES DP041013

Fig 8.23 The 16th century Palace of Falkland, created by James IV and James V, was the antiquarian prize won by Lord Bute on the acquisition of the House of Falkland Estate. Its restoration was halted at his death with only the Chapel and Gatehouse range having been completed. HES SC397095

Fig 8.24 Crossraguel Abbey, a Cluniac foundation near Maybole. Lord Bute sponsored an archaeological investigation of the Abbey and its repair by James A Morris, 1897–9. HES SC1202625

Fig 8.25 The Garrison, Millport, was a marine villa built for the Earl of Glasgow, 1819–20, which Lord Bute bought in 1886. HES SC574062

Fig 8.26 House of Falkland, 1839–44, was designed by William Burn for Onesiphorous Tyndall-Bruce, a close friend of the 2nd Marquess. Lord Bute bought the estate in 1887. HES SC395531

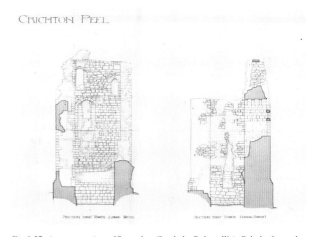

Fig 8.27 A cross-section of Sanquhar Castle by Robert Weir Schultz formed part of a measured survey commissioned by Lord Bute on buying back the ancient seat of the Crichtons in 1894, the family having sold it in 1638. HES DP142819

influential and fashionable offices of the period.[105] His
first recorded meeting with Lord Bute was on 4 January
1889 where they discussed Greek Medieval churches
and the design of the Zodiac Hall windows at Mount
Stuart, as well as meeting with the artist Horatio W
Lonsdale.[106] In May that year he met with Weir Schultz
at St John's Lodge, London, to consider the new Chapel
at House of Falkland where Weir Schultz was to replace
William Frame as the architect.[107] As William Burges
had been Lord Bute's friend and mentor as well as
architect on the restoration of Cardiff Castle and Castell
Coch, so Weir Schultz was to fulfil that role from the
early 1890s onwards. The architectural projects were
too numerous for a single architect but Weir Schultz
shared many interests with his patron and was involved
in a wide variety of other activities including several
archaeological investigations, furniture designs and
antique collecting in addition to architectural projects
such as the remodelling of the wings at Dumfries
House. On relinquishing the lease on Chiswick Villa in
1891, Lord Bute and Weir Schultz immediately began
to develop the idea of creating a new garden to the west
of Dumfries House, a scheme that was clearly inspired
by the gardens at Chiswick which had been designed
around a casino.[108]

The new garden was referred to as 'New Chiswick'
(Fig 8.29) in the Estate accounts, although on the plans
it is referred to as 'Proposed plantings on the site of
the Casino'.[109] The proposed site for the garden, which
measured approximately 1,200 ft east–west by 700 ft
north-south, lay at some distance from the House
beyond the western ha-ha and therefore would not have
been visible from any of the principal rooms. Although

*Fig 8.28 Lord Bute commissioned this Corpus Christi frieze from William
Lonsdale in 1892 for the family bedroom at House of Falkland.*
Falkland Centre for Stewardship

little evidence of it survives apart from an oak gate cut
into the western ha-ha, there are numerous payments
for planting from 1893 to 1900.[110] Three schemes were
prepared by Weir Schultz: the first in April 1892;[111]
the second, which is for a larger scheme is, dated 10
January 1893; and the third, dated October 1893, which
has simpler but no less extensive planting. On the death
of Lord Bute the whole project was abandoned.

All the designs are centred on a square casino
which is shown as having a hexastyle portico on its
east elevation. This appears to have been intended as
a recreation of Chiswick Villa since the dimensions
match the original building at 70 ft square.[112] The
simple block plan shows exactly the same arrangement
of external staircases and portico as was designed
by Burlington at Chiswick. However, the Chiswick
House which Bute rented was the much larger
building described above; what he proposed to erect
at Dumfries House was a recreation of Burlington's
original Chiswick Villa, complete with the garden
staircase which had been removed in 1778, and to set
it in a landscape that reflected what Burlington had
laid out at Chiswick. Burlington's original Villa[113] was
designed not as a house but as a retreat which combined
the display of his treasures on the upper floor and his
library on the lower one, an arrangement which made
it a particularly suitable model for Lord Bute who was
a passionate antiquarian and bibliophile. In May 1897,
the form of the proposed buildings was still being
discussed, as recorded by Weir Schultz in his Contract

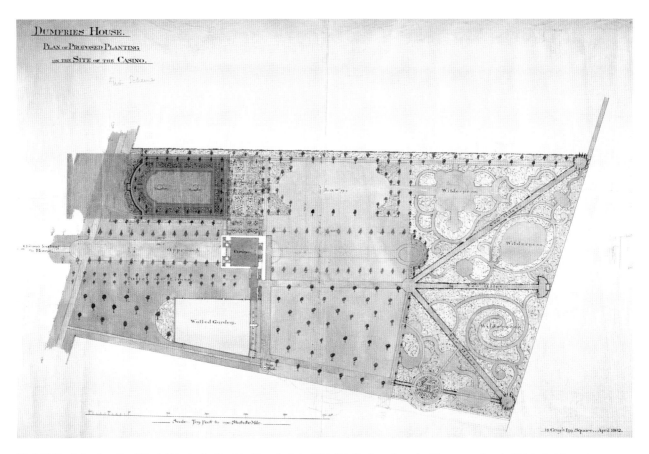

Fig 8.29 *The design for a New Chiswick Garden for Dumfries House by Robert Weir Schultz shows the scale of the proposed work which had, at its centre, a recreation of Lord Burlington's Chiswick Villa, or 'Casino'.* Bute Archives DHP/27/1

Fig 8.30 *This 1896 plan by Robert Weir Schultz shows the sunken garden in front of Dumfries House.* Bute Archives DHP/ADD/8

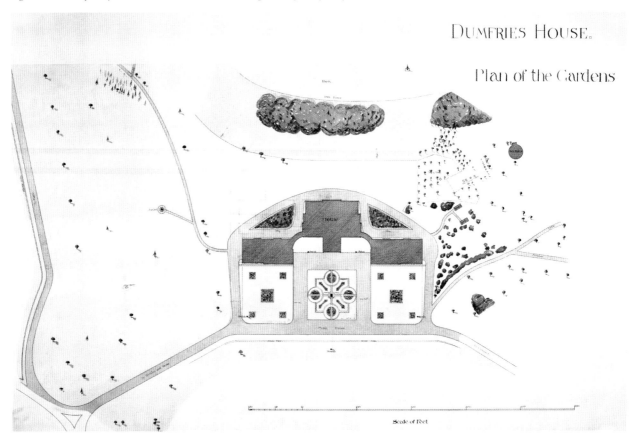

Journal, 'Time of self and assistant in preparing two sketch designs of proposed orangery & portico at New Chiswick'.[114]

The first scheme[115] was the most elaborate and conforms most closely to the plan of Chiswick as engraved. It includes a fountain garden and flower gardens to the south of the casino, mirroring a similar arrangement at Chiswick, and a walled garden to the north. The second scheme[116] expanded the design to the south-west, and the third rationalised the details while maintaining much of the original concept. A pencil addition to the third scheme[117] introduced another idea from Chiswick, an amphitheatre to be located to the south-west of the casino, a version of the famous orange tree garden but without a temple.

At the north-west corner of the casino, a small, narrow building was to be attached which conforms exactly to the Burlington link building. At Chiswick this building linked the new Villa to the existing manor house via the summer parlour. From the central axis of the link building another axis parallel to the entrance axis was created. To the west of the casino at Dumfries House a yew exedra was planned with eight niches, each with a plinth for a sculpture and beyond that a wilderness cut by curving walks linking a circular rose garden and other features. This was intended to be a recreation of the Chiswick garden with the important omission of the water. John Roque's plan of Chiswick,[118] published in 1736, shows the same relationship between the villa, the link building, the various allee, the yew exedra with sculpture, a wilderness with serpentine walks and a '*patte d'oie*', or goose foot arrangement, of radiating walks.

If this design had been fully realised it would have been a great monument to the partnership of Lord Bute and Weir Schultz, a demonstration of their ability to embrace and embellish the setting of the 18th century Dumfries House with an evocation of one of the 18th century's greatest landscape gardens. None of the buildings proposed as part of this designed landscape appear to have got off the drawing board but the associated planting was begun. The scheme appears to be the creation of Lord Bute and Weir Schultz alone because there is no record of a garden designer's involvement. Lord Bute employed Thomas Mawson, one of the most eminent of late 19th century garden designers, to design areas of garden at Mount Stuart in 1896 including the Via Dolorosa and the Calvary Pond but there is no reference to him having had any input into the New Chiswick gardens.[119]

A more modest garden was realised at this time when a sunken garden was created in the forecourt of the house. Lord Bute had sketched a design inspired by the plan of Byzantine churches when staying at Dumfries House following the Mount Stuart fire.[120] It is unclear whether it was this design that was executed or whether it was passed to Robert Weir Schultz to

Fig 8.31 *Portrait of Robert Weir Schultz when he was Master of the Art Workers Guild by G. Clausen 1920. Schultz reversed his surname due to anti-German sentiments in the First World War.* Master of the Art Workers Guild

realise. The only surviving design for this garden, dated April 1896 (Fig 8.30), is marked with Weir Schultz' London office address.[121] The sunken garden provided a more interesting foreground prospect to the south front of the House than the earlier gravel square shown in an undated watercolour in the Mount Stuart Archives. The garden had four circular beds at the cardinal points, originally with a statue on the central plinth.[122] The lawns to either side had a central square bed and a small bed at each corner laid around the obelisks designed by John Adam which remained in their original positions. Triangular beds were shown to the north of both of the pavilion wings but there is no evidence that these were dug since their sites are now under the later additions.

The 3rd Marquess made his first alterations at Dumfries House before he came of age by installing the first private Turkish Bath in Scotland. In his twenties Cardiff Castle became the focus of his attention where he embarked on the exuberant medieval inspired rebuilding with his architect and friend William Burges. The reconstruction of Mount Stuart following the fire of 1878 then became the major project though all the time he was busy undertaking various other research and building projects. Although he stayed at Dumfries House regularly he did not feel it necessary to alter and extend it until the 1890s. At

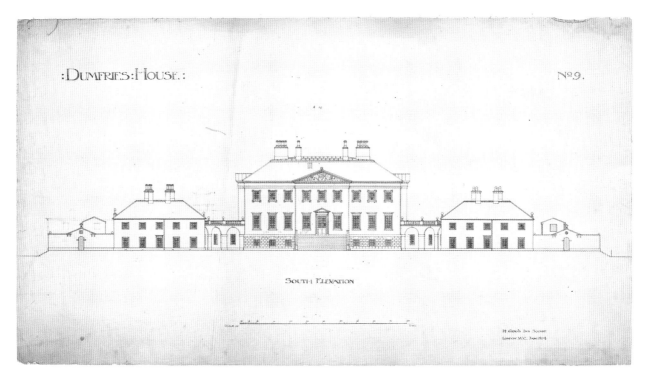

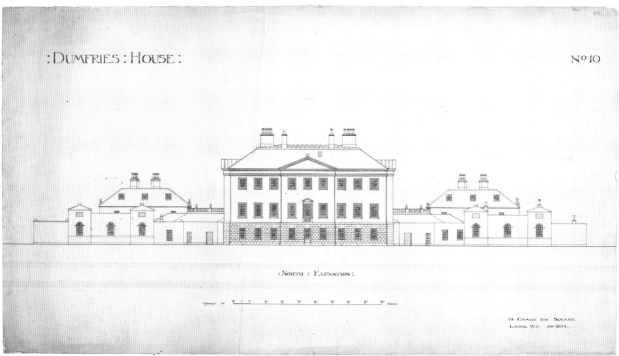

Figs 8.32–8.33 Robert Weir Schultz's 1894 survey of the North and South Elevations of Dumfries House carefully documented every aspect of the building as it then was. They show how little had been altered since the House was completed almost 140 years before. Bute Archives DHP 11/9 & 10

Cardiff Castle all had been about display whereas at Dumfries House the new work is hidden from view. Thus from the very start of his architectural patronage, Lord Bute's particular attitude to the 18th century character and importance of Dumfries House was

evident. He restricted himself to painting and gilding some of the plasterwork but preserved untouched the ceilings in the Drawing Room and Dining Room whereas at old Mount Stuart he had, for example, inserted an elaborate heraldic ceiling in the Drawing Room. The devastating fire at Mount Stuart in the late 1870s necessitated its rebuilding but, rather than using a Georgian style to reflect the original 18th century house, the Gothic style was chosen for the ancestral seat.

1   William Frame to Estate Factor. Bute Archives, Frame Letter Book, 12 February 1884

2   Two months after his father's death John Patrick was constituted as a ward in chancery with his mother being nominated his guardian. The court directed that the estate should pay £5,000 per annum for his maintenance. Davies 1981, 22

3   These debts were accrued largely due to the acquisition of land in and around Cardiff in order to consolidate that estate and fund the development of Cardiff and its docks. Cardiff County Library, BXi

4   Bute Archives, Hastings Papers dated 21 March 1859

5   The 3rd Marquess was later to buy the Bruce estates at Falkland including both Falkland Palace and the House of Falkland.

6   Davies 1981, 71–2

7   Wylie and Lochhead of Glasgow were paid £117 12s and Col Stuart was paid £60 17s 8d for furniture. Bute Archives, Report by Messers Lindsay Jamieson & Haldane on the Accounts of the Curators of the Most Noble Marquess of Bute 12 September 1861–12 September 1862

8   General Stuart also served as a JP for Bute and as Vice Lord Lieutenant of Bute.

9   The appellate jurisdiction of the House of Lords in Scots cases illustrated by the litigation relating to the custody of the Marquess of Bute. Macpherson 1861

10   'To Lady Elizabeth Moore paid per balance of her account £517.1/8.' Bute Archives, Report by Messers Lindsay Jamieson & Haldane on the Accounts of the Curators of the Most Noble Marquess of Bute 30 September 1860–12 September 1861

11   Galloway House was designed by John Douglas in the early 18th century and had been enlarged and modernised for the 9th Earl by William Burn in 1841. Gifford 1996, 309

12   This arrangement was supported by financial remuneration the Earl being paid £850 for half a year in 1861 for 'his residence with him'. Bute Archives, Report by Messers Lindsay Jamieson & Haldane on the Accounts of the Curators of the Most Noble Marquess of Bute 30 September 1860–12 September 1861

13   Hunter Blair 1921, 43

14   Under the Scots law, derived from Roman law, a child to the age of fourteen if male, had legal status of 'pupil' and was under legal control of an adult deemed 'tutor'. From that age until aged 21 the child had legal status of a 'minor', and might have a responsible adult deemed 'curator' or have no responsible adult (being referred to as 'fors familiated').

15   8 October 1862. McDowall Stevens & Co Ironworkers Estimate for fitting up stable for Sir James Fergusson. Bute Archives A/2084

16   Abstract of the accounts between the executors of the deceased Most Noble John Marquess of Bute and Mr Muir the factor on the Buteshire estate from 31 July 1852–31 July 1853. Bute Archives

17   'William Gibson for mason work on houses, Offices etc at Mains £32.2/7.' Bute Archives, Abstract of the accounts between the executors of the deceased Most Noble John Marquess of Bute and Mr Muir the factor on the Buteshire estate from 31 July 1851–31 July 1852, 13

18   'Expenditure on Repairs and Improvements; Connected with Dumfries House and Offices; James Meikle for painting in Dumfries House £11.6/-. Reid & Co Upholsters for renewing Venetian Blinds £4.4/10. Wright & Sons for re-slating roofs of wings at DH and roof of Causeyhead House and for sundry repairs at DH £57.5/10. W Gibson Mason for sundry repairs and jobbings £23.18/7. J Whitefield for lime repairs £7.11/-.' Bute Archives, Abstract of the accounts between the executors of the deceased Most Noble John Marquess of Bute and Mr Muir the factor on the Buteshire estate from 31 July 1852–31 July 1853, 18

19   Hunter Blair 1921, 33

20   Survey of the house carried out by Robert Weir Schultz in 1894. Bute Archives DHP 11/1–11

21   21 January 1869 John Reid & Co Upholsterers Ayr, bill of £274 4s including a carpet for blue bedroom and a brass French bedstead for Lord Bute's Room. 28 February 1868 Wylie and Lochhead Cabinetmakers Glasgow. 'Articles got for Lord Bute's Rooms. 1 mahogany elliptic front washstand with marble top, 1 large basin & ewer, 1 mahogany circular centre table, 1 crimson thread rug, 1 crimson embroidered table cover, total £21.6/8.' Bute Archives, Bundle A/2078 1865–8

22   The improved hygiene of metal bedsteads was promoted at the Great Exhibition. Joy 1977, 201–3

23   'Repairs to Dumfries House & Offices £69.0/9 6. Account for furnishings £12.17/11 6, Sum paid to James Douglas Edinburgh for lining repairing and regilding two full length portraits of Lord and Lady Dumfries by "Raeburn" £28.5/-.' Bute Archives, Abstract of the accounts between the executors of the deceased Most Noble John Marquess of Bute and Mr Muir the factor on the Buteshire estate from 12 September 1865–12 September 1866, 10

24   The only other possible location within the principal rooms large enough to take the portraits was the south wall of the North Parlour flanking the door to the Entrance Hall. Conversation with Charlotte Rostek and Andrew Maclean July 2011.

25   In 1868 he and his friend Lord Rosebery made a tour of the North Sea including visiting Russia. He also made extensive trips around Scotland and the Baltic Sea as well as journeys to France, Germany, Italy and Greece. Hannah 2012, 170

26   Ibid, 256

27   Letter from Sir James Fergusson 3 Park Street Westminster to Charles Shaw. Bute Archives, bundle A 1574 10 July 1867

28   The concept of the Turkish Bath or Hammam had been promoted in Britain by David Urquhart in 'Pillars of Hercules' published in 1850. He had worked with Dr Richard Barter to build the first modern Turkish Bath at St Ann's Hydropathic Establishment outside Cork in 1856 and a year later one was set up in Manchester and by 1860 the first had been opened in London. Shifrin 2011. Until 2011 a 'moorish' archway was visible in the corridor running to the north of the Billiard Room, the location of the former bath.

29   William Railton (1820–1902) may have come to the attention of the young Marquess through his antiquarian interests having worked with MacGibbon and Ross providing measured surveys and sketches of a series of castles in Ayrshire and surveying Kildonan Castle on Bute for their seminal work *The Castellated and Domestic Architecture of Scotland*. Dictionary of Scottish Architects.

30   'Expenditure on Dumfries House, Repairs on House offices etc £73.2/4. Conveying Gas to houses & Offices £496.18/-; Expense of kitchen range & hot water pipes £306.2/6; Restoration of garden wall £491.5/6; Sundries £89.7/-; Restoration of Old mansion house of Ochiltree £887.' Bute Archives, Abstract of the accounts between the executors of the deceased Most Noble John Marquess of Bute and Mr Muir the factor on the Buteshire estate from 12 September 1867–12 September 1868

31   Ibid bundle A/1574

32   A letter dated 29 November 1867 from William Railton writing to Charles G Shaw shows that work was well underway and explains that 'something should now be arranged about furniture for the bath'. A further letter on 3 December 1867 describes some of the detail discussions; 'I send by book post Plan of the proposed closets which I think be arranged very conveniently and at the least possible cost being quite close both to a water supply and a drain – I propose a urinal basin in the corner of the larger closet if it should be considered advisable to put it in. I will get an estimate from plumber and joiner – I think £25 should cover both – the mason work is jobbing and might be done on time'. Ibid Bundle A/1575

33   Letter from William Railton St Marnock Place, Kilmarnock to Charles G Shaw 12 December 1867 . Bute Archives, A/1575

34   Letter from William Railton St Marnock Place, Kilmarnock to Charles G Shaw 16 December 1867. Bute Archives, A/1575

35   Ibid

36   Bute Archives, bundle A/2077

37   Bute Archives, bundle A/1574

38   George Crawshay also had one built at Tynemouth House, Tynemouth, in 1857 which is recorded as the earliest in England. Shifrin 2011

39   11 October 1867 William Railton to Charles Shaw 'work reaching completion on bath square lamp chosen for outside basement doors'. Bute Archives, bundle A/1574

40   Bute Archives, DHP/18/1

41   Bute Archives, bundle A/2077

42   Bute Archives, bundle A/2077

43 The Cumnock Gas Co was paid £115 16s for laying the gas pipes to the House on 16 October and on 28 October Miller & Sons of 178 Piccadilly, London supplied '4 polished & lacquered 2 light gas brackets at £17.14/6' which were presumably to light the four main rooms on the principal floor. Bute Archives, bundle A/2077

44 Bute Archives, bundle A/1574

45 Bute Archives DHP/11/1

46 Watson Salmond and Gray archive at Mitchell Library Special Collections, Glasgow.

47 On 28 December 1867 William Railton wrote to Charles G Shaw saying that I 'have seen the oven & hot plate at Messers Stewarts' and that 'they will be ready on Monday' and that 'The gas stove has been fitted and was left to be connected.' Bute Archives, bundle A/1575

48 The total cost of all these improvements completed in 1867 and overseen by Railton was £1,820 15s 11d. Bute Archives, Abstract of the accounts between the executors of the deceased Most Noble John Marquess of Bute and Mr Muir the factor on the Buteshire estate from 12 September 1867 – 12 September 1868

49 Bute Archives, 6 May 1867 Bute Papers A/1573

50 Charlotte Rostek 'Chippendale's bed at Dumfries House' unpublished paper given at the State Bed Conference, Hopetoun House October 2010 and Bute Archives, Estate Box 169 bundle A/2078

51 Hunter Blair 1921, 72

52 Lord Bute bought property in Jerusalem in 1892 partly with the idea that it would become part of his daughter's inheritance and would also enable his heart to be buried there. Hannah 2012, 292

53 *Glasgow Herald* 7 January 1869

54 Hannah 2012, 77

55 They were married at the Oratory Church London on 26 April 1872 by Archbishop Manning with Monsignor Capel assisting. Lord Mauchlen, Bute's cousin and later Earl of Loudoun, was best man and Gwendolen was escorted by seven bridesmaids. *Ibid*, 94

56 Hunter Blair 1921, 109

57 Mordaunt Crook 1981 Bute letters quoted on page 267

58 Hunter Blair 1921, 94

59 His heart was buried on the Mount of Olives in the Holy Land in a plot that he had acquired. Information from a conversation between the author and Peregrine Bertie, 13 November 2012.

60 Maclean 2007, 26

61 'Dumfries House Erection of New Bathroom and other furnishings £479.8/6; Home Farm New Dairy £68.5/9; Account for repairing clocks at DH £20. /6.' Bute Archives, Report by Messers Lindsay Jamieson & Haldane on the accounts of the cashiers & factors for the most noble the Marquess of Bute from 31 July 1872 – 31 July 1873, 38

62 C Campbell and Smith were also working at Cardiff Castle and Mount Stuart at this time. Their account for £419 8s 10d was presented on 14 June 1877. Bute Archives, Account for works by Messrs C Campbell & Smith 14 June 1877

63 Paint Analysis Report by University of Lincoln held at Dumfries House

64 Dr Rosemary Hannah, transcript of a lecture given at Dumfries House 2010, 5 – 6

65 Contract Journal 1903 – 33. HES. Robert Weir Schultz Journals NMRS Survey of Private Collections P109, 37 – 49

66 HES National Art Survey Photograph board DP089191

67 *Ibid* National Art Survey Photograph board DP089191

68 Bute Archives, Photograph Album dated c1926

69 The what-not survives in storage at Dumfries House.

70 Simpson and Brown 2008, 107

71 'Restoration of garden wall addition to gardeners house, repair of peach house and general improvement of garden £491.5/6.' Bute Archives, Report by Messers Lindsay Jamieson & Haldane on the accounts of the cashiers & factors for the most noble the Marquess of Bute from 12 September 1867 – 12 September 1868, 66

72 'Alterations and repairs on DH and stables etc at Dalblair £211.14/10. New House for Gardener at DH £430.13.6.' Bute Archives, Report by Messers Lindsay Jamieson & Haldane on the accounts of the cashiers & factors for the most noble the Marquess of Bute from 31 July 1869 – 31 July 1870

73 The unsigned design for the decorative barge boarding and other details dated 1869 survives in the archives Bute Archives, DHP/ADD/4

74 2 July 1869 John MacIlwraith received £34 10s 10d for plumber work at Dumfries House. Rebuilding work at estate farms and many additions and alterations at mains farm including ceramic troughs and feeders and varnishing of the stables at the Mains. Bute Archives, Bundle A/2075 1865 – 8

75 Bute Archives, A/2086

76 The saw mill and pond are shown on the First Edition Ordnance Survey Map sheet XXXV surveyed in 1857. HES MS749/335 3-5.

77 The lodge was relatively modest in size but it had high quality architectural detail and elaborate cast iron gates and flanking railings. 'New Lodge Dumfries House £766.10/9 of which £300 was paid last year. Dumfries House and Domain repairs and improvements £238.6/6.' Bute Archives, Report by Messers Lindsay Jamieson & Haldane on the accounts of the cashiers & factors for the most noble the Marquess of Bute from 31 July 1874 – 31 July 1875

78 Lady Bute to Bruce Scot PRO HB MSS 198 undated pre 1859

79 'Expense of laying out new walks in the policies £247.5/8.' Bute Archives, Report by Messers Lindsay Jamieson & Haldane on the accounts of the cashiers & factors for the most noble the Marquess of Bute from 31 July 1876 – 31 July 1877

80 Dr Rosemary Hannah, transcript of a lecture given at Dumfries House 2010

81 Kingarth Parish HBNUM 44984 Historic Scotland Statutory List

82 Robert Rowand Anderson was chosen as architect for the rebuilding of Mount Stuart. After numerous discussions and various proposals it was decided to preserve the 18th century wings, one of which contained a small chapel designed by William Burges, and slot a completely new building between them.

83 Total cost £3,733 18s 9d. Bute Archives, Report by Messers Lindsay Jamieson & Haldane on the accounts of the cashiers & factors for the most noble the Marquess of Bute from 31 July 1883 – 31 July 1884.

84 '3rd Marquess' Miscellaneous expenditure 25 February 1875 paid Anderson architect his fee for visiting and examining Paisley Abbey £5.14/6.' Bute Archives, Report by Messers Lindsay Jamieson & Haldane on the accounts of the cashiers & factors for the most noble the Marquess of Bute from 31 July 1874 – 31 July 1875.

85 'Expenses connected with the excavations at Sanquhar Castle £146.17/6.' Bute Archives, Report by Messers Lindsay Jamieson & Haldane on the accounts of the cashiers & factors for the most noble the Marquess of Bute from 31 July 1876 – 31 July 1877.

86 Gow 1984, 543 – 554

87 '3rd Marquess' expenses rent of Sudbrook Park £391/19/7' Bute Archives, Report by Messers Lindsay Jamieson & Haldane on the accounts of the cashiers & factors for the most noble the Marquess of Bute from 31 July1879 – 31 July 1880.

88 Sudbrook Park has been described by Terry Freidman as 'a small compactly planned suburban seat used as a convenient place of temporary retirement'. Friedman 1984, 133

89 He took the lease from the Devonshire Estate which included some of the original contents.

90 Charlton 1984, 3

91 See Chapter 1 p.6

92 John Harris described Chiswick as 'the most strictly disciplined of all Palladian houses, perhaps even more than Palladio's own, and the way in which in almost every single detail can be found in Palladio'. Harris 1981 75

93 Which had been at Chiswick when he rented the house; see the photograph in Christie's Catalogue 1996, 86

94 These tables are still regarded as a key feature of the interior and were bought by English Heritage from the Bute Christie's sale in 1996. They are now back in their original positions at Chiswick. *Ibid*, 80

95 J Mordaunt Crook 'The Villas of Regent's Park II' *Country Life* 11 July 1968, 85

96 Stamp 1981, 19

97 A Maclean, *Mount Stuart Guidebook*, 7

98 'Restoration of Mochrum Castle £690.3/-.' Bute Archives, Report by Messers Lindsay Jamieson & Haldane on the accounts of the cashiers & factors for the most noble the Marquess of Bute from 31 July 1874–31 July 1875

99 Michael Moss, 'George Boyle 6th Earl of Glasgow – the Dangerous Price of Heaven' paper to the 'Sermons in Stone' Conference 16 October 2010

100 Falkland Estate cost £192,000 paid for by dividend on 17,000 Bute Docks Company Shares until full amount paid (£68,000 paid in first year). Bute Archives, Report by Messers Lindsay Jamieson & Haldane on the accounts of the cashiers & factors for the most noble the Marquess of Bute from 31 July 1887–31 July 1888

101 The architect John Kinross was employed for the archaeological investigation into and the careful restoration of the Palace. Only the south or chapel range, the gatehouse and the royal tennis court were restored before the death of Lord Bute. He also had the interior of House of Falkland transformed initially using the architect William Frame and then later Robert Weir Schultz. Gifford 1988, 214 & 223

102 Lord Bute's fondness for Dumfries House probably stems from the happy times he spent there in his childhood. Hannah 2012, 35

103 Sanquhar Castle lies in northern Dumfries-shire 27 kilometres south-east of Dumfries House. It was the seat of the Crichton Lords of Sanquhar from the 15th century. It occupies a high bank sloping steeply to the north and west commanding the narrow upper valley of the upper Nith. The castle was originally also protected by ditches to the south and east. In the 14th century the barony passed by marriage to the Crichtons who began building the castle in the late 14th century. The roughly rectangular castle containing an inner and outer court was enlarged and remodelled in the early and mid 15th century including rebuilding the curtain wall and the erection of new ranges in the inner courtyard. There were further additions and alterations in the 16th and 17th centuries. The range of buildings marking the boundary between the inner and outer courts is the best preserved and includes the most distinctive feature, the Drum Tower. The 14th century keep to the south-west was the part most heavily restored by Weir Schultz and Bute. The Drum Tower, which is the most prominent feature in a survey drawing of 1786 in the HES collections, relates closely to the stylised depiction in the Entrance Hall at Dumfries House. HES DFD 94/24–36 & DFD 94/3. Gifford 1996, 514–7

104 Hannah 2012, 293

105 In 1887 he won an RA Gold Medal for his design of a railway terminus and also won the RA Travelling Scholarship which was worth £200. This enabled him to travel in Greece, Turkey and Italy in 1887 and 1888 with one of his friends from Shaw's, office Sidney Barnsley. Weir Schultz and

Barnsley were also the recipients of a grant from the Palestine Research Fund to which Lord Bute was a substantial donor. In 1888–1891 he was in Greece with the British Archaeological School in Athens. Stamp 1981, 8

106 Stamp 1981, 12

107 On his return from Greece Weir Schultz went straight into private practice opening an office at 9 Hart Street then moving to 14 Grays Inn Square on a stair opposite his fellow Scot Francis Troup. The patronage of the Bute family was to be one of the mainstays of Weir Schultz' busy architectural practice up until the First World War. The work at House of Falkland involved remodelling the interior including inserting a dome into the Entrance Hall, installing a new Byzantine chapel replacing the incomplete chapel by William Frame, panelling the Dining Room and boudoir along with the creation of the dramatic vine corridor on the first floor and the bedrooms it serves. He made no additions to the exterior, the work all being concentrated on remodelling the interior.

108 Charlton 1984, 5

109 'Expenses connected with policies and gardens Sundry work about policies in connection with planting at New Chiswick £320.11/2.' Bute Archives, Report by Messers Lindsay Jamieson & Haldane on the accounts of the cashiers & factors for the most noble the Marquess of Bute from 31 July 1893–31 July 1894

110 £2,010 0s 8d was spent on the planting of the New Chiswick Garden. An aerial photograph taken in 1948 shows some of the planting. Bute Archives, Report by Messers Lindsay Jamieson & Haldane on the accounts of the cashiers & factors for the most noble the Marquess of Bute from 31 July 1893–31 July 1900

111 Marked in pencil 'first scheme'.

112 Flitcroft Drawing of Lord Burlington's villa with scale. Harris 1994, 117

113 Charlton 1984, 4

114 Robert Weir Schultz Contract Journal 1903–33. HES transcript in NMRS Survey of Private Collections P109, 37–49

115 Bute Archives, DHP 27/1

116 Bute Archives, DHP 27/2

117 Bute Archives, DHP 27/3

118 Harris 1994, 219

119 A Maclean, *Mount Stuart Guidebook*, 40

120 Taylor and Peel 2012, 149

121 Bute Archives DHP/27/3

122 HES photograph SC1241529

Chapter 9: Adapting the House 1894–1900

Care about the smallest detail is a hallmark of fine architecture in any age

R W Schultz, 1909[1]

In his late forties, Lord Bute turned his attention to how best to incorporate additional elements, such as a chapel and study, into the well preserved Georgian splendour of Dumfries House. Having collaborated on Cardiff Castle with William Burges, he worked with another friend and architect, Robert Weir Schultz, at Dumfries House to create something very different but which was nonetheless representative of his approach to the adaptation of historic buildings.

Having converted to Roman Catholicism, Lord Bute was determined that there should be a chapel in each of his residences. An oratory was added to Cardiff Castle in the late 1870s.[2] At Mount Stuart, William Burges designed an exquisite chapel in the north wing in 1873 while Rowand Anderson designed a much larger chapel in 1896. Initially at Dumfries House, one of the Drawing Rooms was used for worship[3] which may explain the reference to hiring of a Harmonium in the accounts for 1874.[4] However, Lord Bute needed a more suitable chapel, an issue that he raised in a letter to his new wife in 1872, 'My greatest crux is that I cannot find a room that will do for a chapel – of course for the present it do'n't matter – but it is very awkward, and I think we shall come to building one before very long.'[5] In fact, although a small chapel was created in the 1890s, the larger chapel was still incomplete at his death. As a studious antiquarian, he also needed a library or, as he referred to it, a book room, in order to distinguish it as a place of study as opposed to an informal socialising space. In preparation for these alterations, he commissioned Robert Weir Schultz to produce a complete survey of the entire building in 1894. These sections, elevations and plans (Plans 7 – 10)

Fig 9.1 John Patrick, 3rd Marquess of Bute, c1890. Bute Archives

allowed Lord Bute to fully understand the complexities and subtleties of the existing house and informed his planned interventions. This degree of interest in understanding the building as it existed was relatively rare in a client and demonstrated Lord Bute's concern to deal sympathetically with Dumfries House.

The plans illustrate the way in which Lord and Lady Bute were using the House at the time. On the principal floor (Plan 10, Fig 9.2), the Entrance Hall is flanked by the 'Tapestried Drawing Rm.' to the west and the 'Morning Drawing Rm.' to the east with, straight ahead, the 'Dining Room' which has Lady Bute's bedroom to the west, a dressing room to the south-west and a water closet cubicle in the north-west room. 'Lord Bute's Dressing Room' lies to the east of the Dining Room with a bathroom and water closet to the north-east and the strong room to the south-east. The original blind window at the north end of the east elevation had been opened to light Lord Bute's water closet while further water closets are located underneath each staircase. The 'Cross Section Looking East' shows that the architraves of the doors in the Entrance Hall and Dining Room have no friezes so that the cornices rest on the architraves. On the floor above, little appears to have changed in terms of the original room arrangement except that two water closets have been inserted in top-lit closets off the lobbies to north and south of the Gallery. The entresol bedrooms are shown as originally designed and the attic rooms as storage except for the north-west one, which is described as 'Lady Bute's Workroom'.

On the ground floor of the main block (Plan 9), the principal changes from the original plan are that the Nursery and its adjacent closets at the south-west corner have become the Still Room with associated pantry

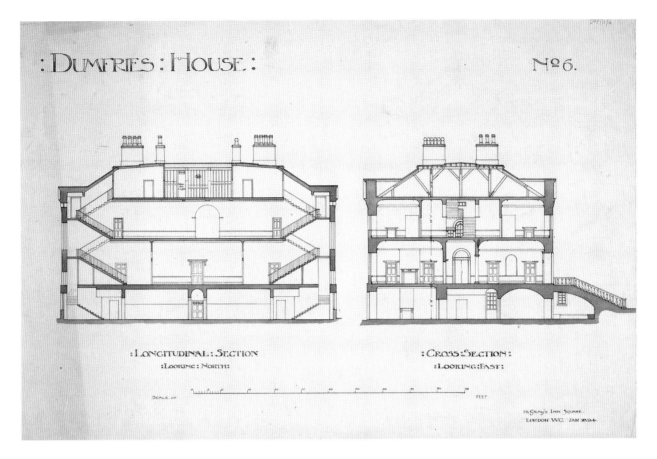

Fig 9.2 Before embarking on the alteration of Dumfries House, Lord Bute commissioned a complete survey of the building that included these cross-sections by Robert Weir Schultz, 1894. Bute Archives DHP/11/6

Fig 9.3 Robert Weir Schultz's survey of the existing principal floor plan of 1894 shows how little Dumfries House had changed since the 5th Earl had commissioned the House in 1754. Bute Archives DHP/11/2

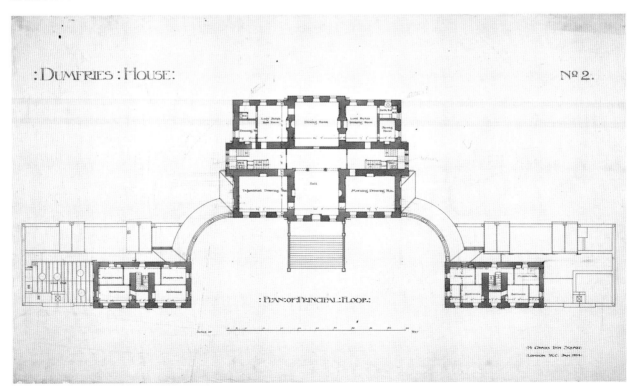

Fig 9.4 Duntreath Castle, Stirlingshire, a modest courtyard house, was transformed into a Baronial Palace by A G Sydney Mitchell, 1889–93. HES SC694747

Fig 9.5 This photograph of the Butler and footmen was taken at Dumfries House in the late 19th century when liveried staff moved with the family between houses with a more modest staff being maintained at each property. Great Steward of Scotland's Dumfries House Trust

and storeroom. A Butler's Pantry has been created out of the two vaulted room at the south-east corner with a silver pantry in the adjacent vaulted room. The Second Table Room has become the Steward's Room and a water closet has been installed under the east staircase. The east pavilion still contained the Kitchen, with a meat larder and cook's baking rooms to the east. In the toofall to the north is a Scullery and the Bake House. In the courtyard beyond the Kitchen there is a Brew House, a joiner's shop, an ash yard, a coal yard and an 'empties shed'. In the west pavilion, 'the low wing room' occupies the east side and the Billiard Room the west off which is the Turkish Bath. This toofall contained a large brushing room flanked by a small kitchen and water closets. The service quarters appear surprisingly modest but during this time it was never intended that Dumfries House should be a place for large scale entertaining. Most of Lord and Lady Bute's socialising beyond family and immediate friends was confined to occasions when they were in London.[6]

In 1895 Weir Schultz made a visit to Dumfries House specifically to discuss the proposed alterations[7] having prepared 'Complete sketch plans of three alternative designs for adds to house in shape of new wings & alts to present wings.'[8] By February 1897 he was preparing what was presumably the final scheme.[9] The work was carried out in three distinct phases: the west wing containing the Book Room and Tapestry Room; the east wing containing the Chapel; and the

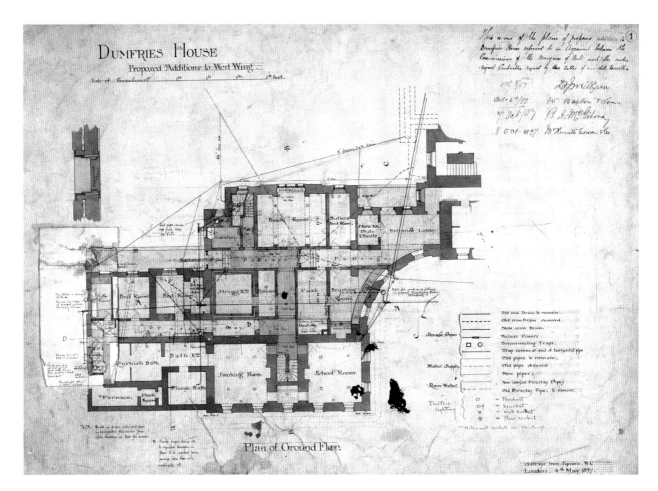

Fig 9.6 Contract drawing for the ground floor of the additions to the west wing on which the existing walls are coloured brown and the new work is coloured blue to indicate masonry and red for the brick work. The drawing, which is dated May 1897, was signed by the tradesmen in October that year. Bute Archives DHP/12/1

central block. Records survive for the first and second elements, including the contract drawings, but there are none relating to the extensive work carried out on the main block. The overall scheme must have been more or less finalised before work began on the first phase since the design as a whole is consistently worked out. The transformation of Dumfries House from a modestly proportioned 18th century house into one suitable for a Marquess could have involved wholesale rebuilding, as seen for example at Duntreath Castle, Stirlingshire (Fig 9.4), where a small towerhouse was transformed into a vast French Baronial palace by A G Sydney Mitchell for the Edmonstones, as well as Lord Bute's other homes, Cardiff Castle and Mount Stuart. At Dumfries House, a subtler approach was taken that stitched in the additions in order that the original 18th century house remained the dominant element.

The west wing contained functions that could be suspended without significant disruption to life in the House whilst the work was going on.[10] The existing pavilion block was retained and the new work slotted in behind it, in deference to the original Adam design. Externally the additions were clothed in sandstone, carefully chosen and diagonally droved to match the existing stonework. Each elevation was designed so

that stringcourses and other details would run between the old and new work. The balustraded quadrant link was retained, along with the walls of the courtyard, the pavilion and the western toofall. Two modest, if distinctive, flourishes were made in the domed pepperpot turrets (Fig 9.10) which add an element of verticality to the composition and, more importantly, disguise the bulk of the roof of the extension, and in the exquisite lead rainwater goods (Figs 9.11–9.13),

Fig 9.7 The diagonally droved stonework of the west wing demonstrates the superlative quality of the work of Robert Weir Schultz's craftsmen. HES 2013 DP151648

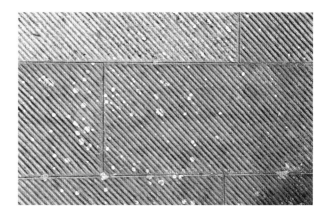

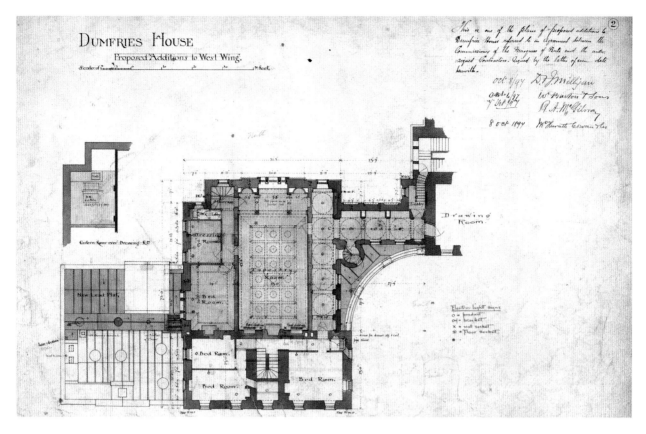

Fig 9.8 *The contract drawings for the first floor of the alterations to the west wing show that the Tapestry Room and domed corridor were the principal additions proposed in 1897.* Bute Archives DHP/12/2

Fig 9.9 *The designs for additions to the west wing show the care taken to ensure the alterations were sympathetic to the original building. This drawing illlustrates the new domed pepperpot turret rising above the roofline and shows that the original west toofall was to be retained at this stage, although it was to be demolished less than ten years later.* Bute Archives DHP/12/4

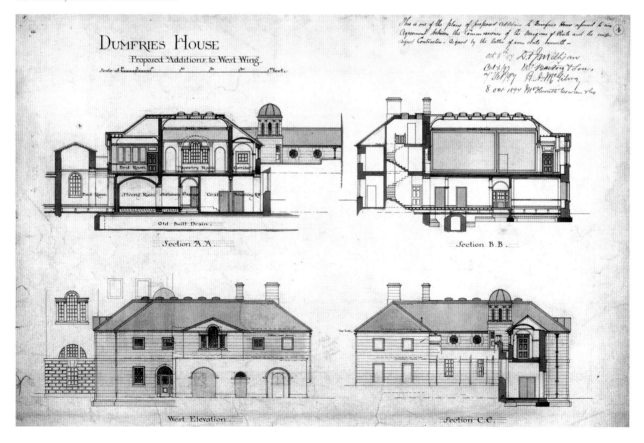

Figs 9.11 – 13 The lead work by W Dodds of London is the most overt Arts and Crafts statement at Dumfries House. It bears the Crichton Wyvern, Lady Bute's initials and the date of the additions. HES 2007 DP033623, DP033624 & DP033626

one of the few overtly Arts and Crafts elements to be introduced by Weir Schultz.

The single-storey buildings in the courtyard, including the Turkish Bath, were retained as was the toofall on its north side. The ground floor level of the west pavilion was raised, thereby improving the proportions of the rooms and rendering them more domestic in scale.[11] The Low Wing Room became the School Room, which was linked behind the original stair to the Smoking Room that had replaced the earlier Billiard Room, which in turn opened into the Turkish Bath. The original passage leading to two new servants' bedrooms and a bathroom with its Moorish arches was retained. The change of floor level meant that both the Smoking Room and the School Room had to be completely refitted; Weir Schultz's scheme for the School Room (Fig 9.14) with its restrained panelled walls, 18th century inspired chimneypiece and delicate plasterwork survives.

The 'Bachelors Entrance', which was created to the side of the new wing (Fig 9.6), led into an L-plan corridor off which was a lavatory and water closet, a private stair and the new Book Room, a relatively modest sized room with no fitted bookshelves and a heating 'coil' beneath the window instead of a fireplace. It was lit by a tripartite window and divided into three sections with columned screens. A detailed drawing[12] omits the columns but retains the tripartite arrangement with pilasters and beams, the vine scroll plasterwork on which appears to be part of the original scheme.

Fig 9.10 Robert Weir Schultz's new turret rises up behind the 18th century curved linking wall. This is one of the few flourishes on the south front of Dumfries House which otherwise does not betray the scale of the late 19th century alterations and additions. HES 2007 DP033631

Opposite the new entrance was a door to the servants' quarters, a notional green baize door opening onto a short flight of stairs down to the level of the original ground floor. Here the new wing provided a large service entrance lobby with a store for 'plate chests', a brushing room with a coal store and a bedroom for the butler. A large strong room and stationery store was slotted in between the new entrance corridor and the old Turkish Bath passage. The second half of the entrance corridor led to the original pavilion with its central staircase.

This staircase led up to the first floor of the pavilion and via a corridor to the main architectural focus of this part of the alterations, which was a new reception room, at 45 ft long the largest in the house and specifically designed to display the four tapestries that had been acquired by the 5th Earl of Dumfries.[13] In the 18th century house as originally designed, two of the tapestries had hung in the Drawing Room and these had been joined by a third in the early 19th century. This scheme united the four tapestries for the first time since the mid 18th century in a room lit by eighteen circular roof lights and a Venetian window. Weir Schultz masked the scale of this Tapestry Room by projecting the volume into the roof space whilst having windows only in the short north wall. Externally the mass of the room is disguised on the long west elevation by being placed behind the projecting bedroom suite. The tapestries hang on the long walls, the north end of the room has a columned screen with niches flanking the Venetian window, the south wall has a fireplace flanked by presses and the woodwork is of cedar, chosen to deter moths, which might have damaged the tapestries.

Fig 9.14 The School Room in the south-east corner of the west pavilion. Robert Weir Schultz installed panelling and a chimneypiece in a suitably restrained 18th century style whereas his plasterwork, while equally sophisticated, is in a more contemporary style. HES 2013 DP083164

Fig 9.15 The Dining Room at Mount Stuart, the chimneypiece is the pair to the one in the Tapestry Room at Dumfries House.
The Bute Collection

Various alternative schemes survive for the carved decoration, which was carried out by the Cardiff Workshops.[14] Although the plasterwork is dated 1898, the room was not completed until 1908 under the direction of the 4th Marquess and Weir Schultz.[15] The 3rd Marquess may well have proposed that the plaster decoration be naturalistically decorated as in the adjacent corridor but no evidence of this has survived.[16] At the north end beyond the screen the decorative plaster central vault is flanked by smaller square vaults with foliated ribs.[17] With Lord Bute's failing health, Lady Bute became more involved with the works, writing to Mr Turner at the Cardiff Workshops in 1899 to encourage him to speed up the completion of the Gallery.[18] Glazed fitted cabinets with panels above were chosen to flank the fireplace rather than the more elaborate pedimented cabinets suggested in the 1897 drawings.[19] A number of alternative schemes were devised for the treatment of the north end of the room that suggest the use of different materials, including marble, but which adhere to the same plan. One undated drawing shows an Adamesque scheme for the frieze which was later to be filled with putti cavorting within a luxuriant vine.

The white marble chimneypiece which is prominently positioned at the south end of the Tapestry Room is (Fig 9.17) of extremely high quality and is one

Fig 9.16 *The new, top-lit, Tapestry Room enabled all four of the tapestries acquired by the 5th Earl from his uncle the 2nd Earl of Stair to be hung in the same room in Dumfries House. The portrait of the 2nd Earl of Stair, above the chimneypiece, was moved here at a later date.* HES 2010 DP083170

of several commissioned by the 3rd Earl of Bute for Luton Park in Bedfordshire, a house designed for him by Robert Adam in 1771.[20] Although Adam supplied various chimneypieces for Luton Park, James Byres also sent five from Rome in 1771 and 1772.[21] A pair of these were described by Byres as 'The chimney with

trufses mark'd E for the E and W parts of the centre room of the library to have an elegant frize of ornament those for it from the Herculaneum 2 of these to be done … In the chimney marked D for the library there is a tablet containing a bas-relief of various figures which is valued at £30.00 – a drawing of which is sent full size, in case the same should be got done abroad at a much cheaper rate. There is two wanted of this size. But the

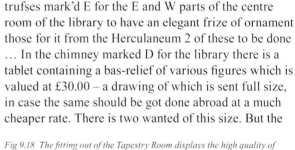

Fig 9.17 *The Tapestry Room chimneypiece, designed by James Byres of Tonley in Rome, is one of a pair installed by Robert Adam in the 3rd Earl of Bute's house, Luton Park, Bedfordshire. After a fire in the mid 19th century they were moved to Mount Stuart; one was subsequently installed at Dumfries House. The mantle-shelf still carries the scars of its complicated history.* HES 2007 DP033699

Fig 9.18 *The fitting out of the Tapestry Room displays the high quality of craftsmanship demanded by Lord Bute and Robert Weir Schultz.* HES 2010 DP033695

subject of one is only fixt on. The subject of the other may be chosen abroad.'[22] Lady Coke noted that 'a great many of the Chimney pieces were done in Italy: the designs very pretty, but … they don't polish the Marble so highly as they do here.'[23]

The shallow relief and matt finish of the Tapestry Room chimneypiece appears to relate closely to the frieze which Byres describes, 'As the Bas reliefs it is thought may be executed as well if not better abroad than in England and certainly much cheaper the separate valuation of them is mentioned. But particular directions should be given to the statuary not to raise the figures too high as they are apt to give too much relief to them at Rome.'[24]

A chimneypiece in the Dining Room at Mount Stuart (Fig 9.15) and that in Tapestry Room at Dumfries House[25] appear to be the pair ordered for the central room of the Library at Luton Park.[26] While Adam-designed chimneypieces are characteristically crisply detailed and symmetrically organised, such as those in the ante-room at Luton, 1769,[27] and the Dining Room at Newby Hall, Yorkshire, c1769[28], the Luton Park chimneypieces are very different in character.[29]

The first floor of the 18th century west pavilion originally contained four servants' bedrooms served by the central staircase that then rose to the two attic

Fig 9.19 Early 20th century view of the Pewter Corridor.
The Bute Collection

Fig 9.20 The original decoration of one dome in the Pewter Corridor was conserved while the rest of the scheme was repainted to restore the original effect. HES 2013 DP155008

Fig 9.21 The vaulted corridors that surround the central hall at Mount Stuart are similar in form to the Pewter and East Corridors at Dumfries House though in a Gothic manner. HES SC695862

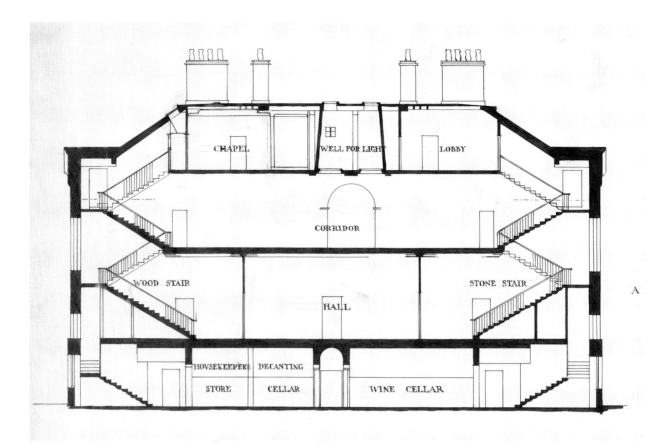

Fig 9.22 The temporary chapel in the attic at Dumfries House is shown on this Robert Weir Schultz's drawing of 1905 as are the roof lights he introduced to illuminate the first floor corridor. Bute Archives DHP/8/14

bedrooms added by the 2nd Marquess. The first floor bedrooms were reduced to three with a corridor linking to the new wing. The new T-plan corridor linked the new Tapestry Room to the original Drawing Room and the west pavilion staircase, via a small stair, to the main west staircase. This greatly improved the circulation at the west end of the house. This corridor is a very elaborate architectural and decorative tour-de-force consisting of eight square compartments each with a circular dome connected by semi-circular arches (Fig 9.19). While its form is inspired by Byzantine architecture, the Adamesque decoration applied transforms it into an Adam Revival interior worthy of comparison with, for example, the exceptional work carried out by Wright and Mansfield at Haddo House, Aberdeenshire, in the 1880s.[30] Although various drawings for alternative schemes survive there are none for the complex scheme that was executed but it has been suggested that W H Lonsdale,[31] who worked extensively for Lord Bute, may have been responsible. The details of the intricate design were probably finalised on site through discussion between Bute, Weir Schultz and the craftsmen.[32] Weir Schultz took numerous photographs and always carried a sketch book[33] so that these deliberations could have taken place wherever was convenient. A suite consisting of a bedroom, dressing room and water closet (Plan 12) was created to the west of the Tapestry Room. These

comfortable, panelled rooms provided accomodation at one remove from the rest of the house. They were at one time known as Lord James' Rooms and could easily have been used for short visits without the need to open up the entire House. The west wing as a whole would have provided convenient, relatively informal living with its Book Room, School Room, Smoking Room and bedroom on the first floor of the pavilion.[34] The two-storey 18th century toofall on this wing was at first retained, despite the fact that it almost entirely blocked the view from the new bedroom's Venetian window, but was removed c1900.

In order to carry out this phase of work, William Swanston, Clerk of Works, assembled a team of craftsmen, mostly from Kilmarnock and Cumnock but with some specialists from Edinburgh and Glasgow. The principal contractors were D & J Milligan of Ayr who carried out the high quality mason work, R A McGilvray, the plasterer, and D White, the painter. The Albert Works Company supplied the oak parquetry floor in the corridor at a cost of £100[35] and Galbraith and Winton of Glasgow supplied the marble work. While most of those employed were from Scotland, Lawrence A Turner from England was employed for carving and modelling, most probably for the Tapestry Room.[36] He also appears to have been involved with the putti and vine frieze in this room which was not produced until a decade later.[37] Another firm employed from outwith Scotland was M & M Corbett, seemingly from Cardiff, who were paid 'for work done by Bute Shops'.[38]

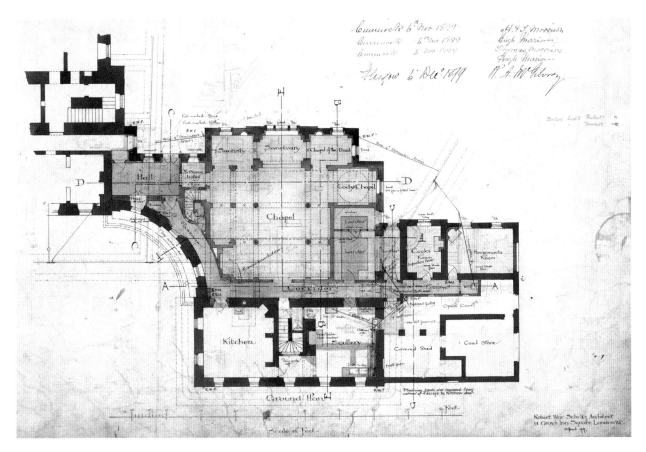

Fig 9.23 The east wing was altered by Robert Weir Schultz to accommodate a magnificent three-storey chapel, 1899. Bute Archives DHP/14/1

Fig 9.24 This contract drawing by Robert Weir Schultz of 1899 shows the upper gallery level of the new Chapel and is detailed to show the intermediate family gallery which was approached by its own corridor. Bute Archives DHP/14/2

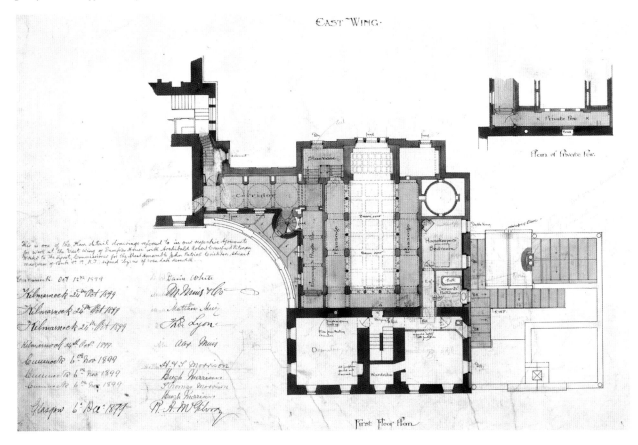

DUMFRIES·HOUSE· · CHAPEL· INTERIOR· VIEW II

While additions were being made to the west wing, the need for a dedicated chapel became paramount. It appears that using one of the Drawing Rooms as an occasional chapel had become an increasingly unsatisfactory interim arrangement and so, while the large chapel proposed for the new wing was already under discussion, a temporary chapel was created at the head of the west staircase in the attic. Robert Weir Schultz was 'Preparing working drawings for chapel' in his accounts for 1897 and his accounts also list 'arrange painting of new chapel in roof of old house' and 'designing new altar'.[39] This chapel appears on the 1905 plan and sections as a modest room without any of the exuberance of the Burges chapel at Mount Stuart or his oratory at Cardiff Castle; nothing of it survived the reconstruction of the roof and attic in the early 20th century.

The planning of alterations to the east wing was already underway before the west wing was completed, the drawings being dated April 1899. Externally, the building mirrored the form of the west wing extensions to the extent of preserving the 18th century toofall, thereby maintaining the symmetry of both north and south elevations which was deemed of paramount importance. The new Chapel was to occupy most of the building with two levels of galleries. The original east pavilion was retained and the Kitchen remained where it always had been. While the floor level had been altered in the west pavilion, it was maintained at the lower 18th century level in the east pavilion, the eastern part of which became a large Scullery. The original buildings on the north side of the courtyard beyond the extension, including the toofall, were converted to accommodate a new larder, the Cook's Room and the Housemaids' Room. The original covered shed and coal shed were retained and two new larders created to the north of the Kitchen on the eastern side of the Chapel.

The Chapel was orientated north to south with only the domed Lady Chapel traditionally orientated to the east. The stained glass window[40] in the Lady Chapel, which was brought from St John's Lodge,[41] Regents Park, London, is the only surviving fixture from the original Chapel. A series of piers divided the space (Figs 9.23–9.24) into a central nave with flanking aisles, to the east of the altar was the Sacristy and to the west the Chapel of the Dead, adjacent to the Lady Chapel. On the ground floor, the Chapel was entered either from the south via a passage running parallel to the pavilion or from the west through a new west hall. A staircase adjacent to this entrance rose to the first floor contained within the eastern pepperpot turret. The upper floor levels of the Chapel were rather complicated. On the principal floor, a domed corridor led from the 18th century Dining Room to the Chapel via a jib door.

Fig 9.25 This perspective view of the proposed chapel indicates its scale and importance as well as the continuing influence of Byzantine architecture on both Lord Bute and Robert Weir Schultz. Bute Archives DHP/17/6

Fig 9.26 A stained glass window from St John's Lodge, the London home of Lord Bute, was installed in the new Lady Chapel at Dumfries House in 1899. It is the most prominent survival from the Chapel which is no longer extant. HES 2007 DP033777

This corridor is of a similar form to the western one but is of only five bays, three of which are domed, and originally ended in a blank wall. Although various schemes for decoration survive, it appears never to have been completed, has no applied decorative plasterwork and always appears to have been painted white. The door to the Dining Room from the corridor is disguised as a double door of which only the left half opens. A staircase on the left above the Sacristy led to the upper gallery where a corridor ran parallel to the Chapel providing access to the family pew which was located above the service passage and below the upper gallery at the southern end of the Chapel.

Sleeping accommodation for the maids was located on the first floor and in the attic of the east pavilion while a new Housekeeper's Room and a bathroom were

Fig 9.27 This early 20th century view of the Drawing Room shows the pair of doors recently inserted in the west wall. Of the doors which originally flanked the chimneypiece, the one to the west has been removed and that on the right has been converted into a jib door. The Bute Collection

Fig 9.28 The two light-wells inserted by Robert Weir Schultz into the first floor corridor which must originally have been rather dark, being lit only from either end. The Bute Collection

located above the new larders adjacent to the Chapel. The structure of the new east wing seems to have been largely completed before the death of Lord Bute in October 1900 but the elaborate interior decorative scheme had hardly been started beyond the treatment of the structural piers. The Chapel was to be mainly lit from above with only the stained glass window on the east elevation giving any hint of the exuberant ecclesiastical interior within. William Swanston remained as Clerk of Works but M Muir & Co replaced Milligan's of Ayr as the masons.[42]

The drawings dated May 1897[43] show only those parts of the main central block of the house where the works on the west pavilion were to touch it. The door from the domed west corridor into the Drawing Room is presented as the only intervention; the dummy door to its north, being a less structural alteration, is not shown. The alterations to the main block carried out during this period are relatively extensive. In March 1905, Robert Weir Schultz produced another complete set of survey plans (Plans 11–14) of the House which illustrate the alterations that had been carried out but which do not show any further proposed work.[44] A photograph (Fig 9.29) taken prior to November 1900[45] reveals that a blind window shown on the 1894 plans had already been opened up to light the water closet cubicle in the south-east bedroom. It also shows that a large ramp had been constructed up the front steps, presumably to allow the easy access of building materials into the main block.

Fig 9.29 Dumfries House was photographed by National Art Survey of Scotland draughtsmen in 1900 when building work on the alterations was underway. This view of the ramp built to facilitate access to the main block is the only record of work being carried out within the main block of the house. HES SC1241529

A comparison between the 1894 and 1905 survey plans, combined with the drawings for the alterations to the east and west wings in 1897 and 1899 respectively, reveals the extent of the unrecorded phase of works, the majority of which must have been commissioned by the 3rd Marquess. The form of the principal floor was maintained but a number of alterations took place such as the installation of a new bathroom in the north-west closet off Lady Bute's Bedroom which involved the opening of a blind window on the west elevation to light the separate water closet cubicle. The two water closets under the stairs were removed and a small flight of stairs linking the main east staircase to the east wing corridor was inserted, mirroring the arrangement at the west end.[46] The Dining Room, which was once again in its original position to the east of the Entrance Hall, was little altered save for the introduction of a jib door to access the east corridor leading to the Chapel. However, it appears that at this time a new oak floor was installed in this room which matches the wood, if not the elaborate parquetry design, found in the east and west corridors. The 1905 survey plans also show that at this time the intention was to finish the Chapel in the east wing as originally proposed.

Fig 9.30 This National Art Survey photograph of the Entrance Hall in 1900 provides the only record of the embossed leather which was hung on the wall below the naturalistically painted ceiling by the 3rd Marquess. HES DP089191

Fig 9.31 J Gillespie and A Muir of the National Art Survey arriving to survey Dumfries House c1900. HES DP089191

The most dramatic alteration was occasioned by the removal of the tapestries from the Drawing Room, enabling the hanging of the two magnificent double portraits by Sir Henry Raeburn either side of the chimneypiece. These portraits depict both of the 3rd Marquess' grandmothers as children and two of his great grandparents. They were painted specifically to hang at Dumfries House and represent the most obvious contribution made to the interior by the 6th Earl and Countess of Dumfries. The room as originally designed was a mirror image of the Dining Room (Figs 3.7–3.8) on the other side of the Entrance Hall but whereas a jib door was seen as a satisfactory solution by which the Dining Room could gain access to the east corridor, it appears that a more elaborate solution was deemed necessary for the Drawing Room. This involved the removal of the door cases on the north wall, turning the east door into a jib door and removing any sign of the west dummy door (Fig 9.27). These two door cases were relocated onto the west wall, one accessing the new corridor to the Tapestry Room and the other being a dummy door which involved not only moving the architraves but also adapting the dado and panelling of the west wall. This sophisticated solution maintained the symmetry of each elevation of the room, if not of the plan in that the doors on the west wall are closer together than those on the east wall.

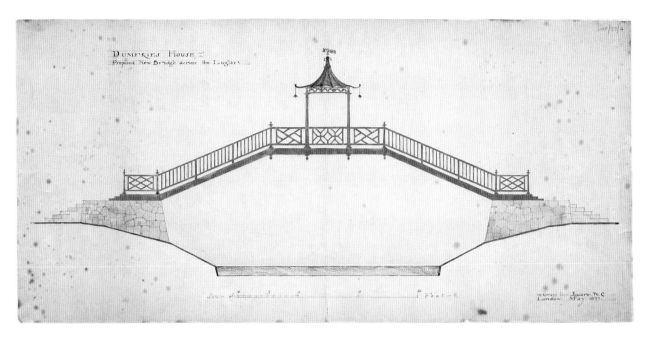

Fig 9.32 While building work on Dumfries House was underway and the planting of his New Chiswick Garden was ongoing, Lord Bute commissioned Robert Weir Schultz to design a Chinese Bridge, to span the Lugar Water. The bridge was never built. Bute Archives DHP/27/4

The bedroom floor also underwent a series of alterations. The most dramatic intervention was the opening of the blind windows in the four corner closets off the bedrooms. These were to light the four new cubicles each containing a water closet. The existing water closet to the north of the corridor was enlarged into the adjacent closet and a bath installed, the one to the south of the corridor was removed and, in conjunction with the adjacent closet, was opened up into the south-west central bedroom. A columned screen divided the recess from the bedroom creating an alcove for the bed very much in the style of early 18th century bed recesses, a deliberately antiquarian, if historically inaccurate, approach since bed recesses had gone out of fashion by the time that Dumfries House was built. In the main corridor, two lay lights were introduced with decorative glazed screens, transforming what must have quite a dark space but retaining the original plasterwork (Fig 9.28). The attics remained very much the same apart from the insertion of the Chapel and the introduction of new light wells to light the corridor (Fig 9.22). It appears that by this time Lady Bute no longer had a work room in the attic. The late 19th century plans of the house do not show any designated nurseries but four children were accommodated comfortably somewhere close to their parents on the principal floor.[47] A series of minor alterations occurred on the ground floor of the main block: a 'Hot Water Furnace Room' was created off the Lamp Room under the Entrance Hall, the west Wine or 'Stock' Cellar was subdivided to form a new Housekeeper's Store and a Decanting Cellar, and the two north-west corner rooms were joined to create a lady's maid's room. The north blind window on the west elevation was opened up which, although it

created a balanced facade with no blind windows, means that the relatively small room at the north-west corner has three disproportionately large windows. The north-east corner room was subdivided to form a Boys' Room and a Valet's Room.

At Dumfries House, the 3rd Marquess and Weir Schultz embraced the restrictions of its 18th century form and celebrated it with a restraint that he did not always display at his other properties. In a period in which many country houses were radically altered to accommodate new technologies and meet aspirations of increased comfort, these necessities were woven into the existing fabric at Dumfries House. Although Lord Bute built extensions to accommodate a grand Chapel and installed the earliest private Turkish Bath in Scotland, he maintained the 18th century form of the House, despite the fact that he had ample funds with which to carry out a radical rebuilding.[48] His redecoration, with its naturalistically coloured plasterwork and gilding, was not in the spirit of the 18th century but he did not alter or augment the original plasterwork and respectfully preserved untouched the two most important plaster ceilings of the original Drawing and Dining Rooms. He did, however, use the House rather differently to his predecessor, moving the everyday entrance to the west and using the Entrance Hall as both reception space and sitting room. His last commission for Weir Schultz at Dumfries House was an unrealised scheme for an exquisite Chinese bridge to be built over the Lugar Water (Fig 9.30).[49]

1   Schultz 1909

2   He went on to embellish the existing domestic Chapel in the Castle and was in his later years proposing the complete remodelling of the keep as a much larger chapel. Mordaunt Crook 1981 268

3   Maclean 2007, 26

4   'Brown and Wardrop's account for repairs and improvements Dumfries House and domain £317.11/17 ½. Hire of a Harmonium £5.15/6.' Bute Archives, Report by Messers Lindsay Jamieson & Haldane on the accounts of the cashiers & factors for the most noble the Marquess of Bute from 31 July 1873–31 July 1874

5   Maclean 2007, 26

6   St John's Lodge in Regent's Park, London with its magnificent ballroom appears to have been the property at which Lord and Lady Bute entertained most frequently. Lord Bute described its convenience, 'there is a certain piquancy about a place which almost simulates to be a country house and yet is only a shilling cab from Piccadilly'. Stamp 1981, 22

7   None of these drawings have survived. HES Robert Weir Schultz Contract Journal 1903–33 transcript in NMRS Survey of Private Collections P109, 37–49

8   Ibid

9   Ibid

10   The drawings for the alterations to the west wing are dated 4 May 1897 and were signed by the contractors between 6 and 8 October. Bute Archives DHP 12/ 1–6

11   The Kitchen in the east wing gives some idea of the original, taller, proportions.

12   Dated May 1897 'No 16' Bute Archives DHP 13/5

13   Contrary to the established understanding the four tapestries acquired by the 5th Earl of Dumfries from the 2nd Earl of Stair are not from the Gobelins factory but were made at the workshop of Leyniers-Reyndams in Brussels after 1717 and therefore would have been bought by the 2nd Earl after his time in Paris. Information from Charlotte Rostek in email of 27 May 2013

14   Letter from Mr Turner at the Cardiff Workshops to Weir Schultz about the Tapestry Room woodwork. RIBA/British Architectural Library Drawings and Archives PB 394

15   '9 March 1908 Paid R W Schultz architect balance of his fees in connection with alterations on Dumfries House £105.17/-.' Bute Archives, Report by Lindsay Jamieson & Haldane on accounts of cashiers and factors for Most Hon John Crichton-Stuart Fourth Marquis of Bute 1905–1909 Accounts for 1908

16   The current decorative paint scheme appears to date from the mid 20th century.

17   These square vaults flanking the central one were uncovered in 2013.

18   Letter from Mr Turner at the Cardiff Workshops to Weir Schultz 'I received a letter from Lady Bute this morning [and] her ladyship is anxious to have as much work as possible sent on for Tapestry Room. I have informed her ladyship that we will send on all the work we have ready for this room…Please hurry up'. RIBA Archives PB 394

19   Bute Archives DHP 13/1 No 11

20   The chimneypiece is shown in outline on the May 1897 drawing. HES 'Dumfries House West Wing Detail of Ends of Tapestry Room' photograph of drawing in NMRS not listed in the Dumfries House Drawings Collection HES A 27085

21   Harris 2001, 252

22   Notes on James Byers of Tonley uncatalogued typescript at Mount Stuart

23   Coke 1970, 390

24   Notes on James Byers of Tonley uncatalogued typescript at Mount Stuart

25   Mount Stuart Guidebook 2001, 22

26   The pair of chimneypieces were installed in 1772 in Luton Park at a cost respectively of £131.16/- and £154.7/-. Notes on James Byers of Tonley uncatalogued typescript at Mount Stuart

27   Sir John Soane's Museum: Adam drawings, vol 22:251. Harris 2001, figure 370

28   Harris 2001, 222

29   They were sent from Luton Park to Mount Stuart along with the chimneypiece fitted into the New Dining Room at Dumfries House after the fire of 1845 during which the damage to the mantle-shelves occurred.

30   Information from Weir Schultz Sketchbook, then at The Barn, Schultz's former home now lost. Stamp 1981 76 n.86

31   Discussion with Andrew Mclean, Archivist at Mount Stuart

32   'Pemberry' is recorded as the decorator of the west corridor in Weir Schultz's Contract Journal and in the Weir Schultz album. He and his other works have yet to be identified. HES Robert Weir Schultz Contract Journal 1903–33. Transcript in NMRS Survey of Private Collections P109, 40. Stamp 1981, 76 n.86

33   Robert Weir Schultz's sketchbooks are held in the RIBA Drawings Collection at the V&A.

34   Bute Archives DHP/12/1

35   This was probably the Edinburgh joinery firm of Scott Morton & Co who were based at the Albert Works in Edinburgh. Scott Morton Collection held at HES. SA Lammie, unpublished thesis: 'Scott Morton & Co, The Survival of a Small Family Business in the Luxury Furniture Trade 1880–1960', University of Edinburgh 2012, 34

36   Turner went onto work with G F Bodley at Holy Trinity Church, South Kensington, and was a secretary of Society for the Protection of Ancient Buildings.

37   June 1908 recorded in RWS Fee book noted in Stamp 1981, 76 n.87

38   The accounts show that the building of the west wing cost a total of £3,893 17s which included itemised accounts of each of the trades including Shultz's fees. 'Paid M&M Corbett for work done by Bute Shops for Dumfries House £61.10/3. Paid M&M Corbett for work done by Bute Shops for Church at Cumnock £161.18/2.' It is not known if they were related to E W M Corbett who was the Bute Estate Architect in Cardiff. Bute Archives, Report by Messers Lindsay Jamieson & Haldane on the accounts of the cashiers & factors for the most noble the Marquess of Bute from 31 July 1896 – 31 July 1898

39   HES Robert Weir Schultz Contract Journal 1903–33. Transcript in NMRS Survey of Private Collections P109, 37–49.

40   Annotated drawing 'window from St John's Lodge 20 April 1899'. Bute Archives, DHP 16/1

41   Lord Bute took a 27 year lease of St John's Lodge in Regent's Park in September 1888 which gave him the seclusion he desired combined with a city location. Hannah 2012, 263. St John's Lodge had been designed by John Raffield in 1818–19 and much extended by Decimus Burton and Charles Barry and was considerably larger than Chiswick. Lord Bute commissioned various alterations including a new staircase and two chapels. He did not move in until January 1891 remaining at Chiswick until then. Cherry and Pevsner 1991, 624

42   The eventual cost of the east wing with the incomplete Chapel came to £3,958 6s 4d including Weir Schultz's fees. Dumfries House Estate Accounts for work carried out, 1900–1902

'Paid H & T Morrison on account of plumber work at east wing £250; Paid R A McGilvray Plasterwork west wing £200; Shirley & Co for supplying fittings for Lord Dumfries' Room £82.14/-; Paid Mr D White for painter & joiner work executed at DH £450; Paid Wm Swanston Clerk of Works Salary & expenses £25.2/10; P.9 Debts due by the deceased.

Payments to contractors in connection with houses

16 Oct 1900 paid Wm Swanston Clerk of Works £25./6; 18 Oct 1900 paid M Muir & Co mason work £500; 5 Dec 1900 paid Wm Swanston Clerk of Works £24.14/-; 24 Dec 1900 paid M Muir & Co mason work £500; 31 Dec 1900 D White joiner to account £250;

28 Jan 1901 R W Schultz architect to account; 1899 £45.3/-; 1898 £46.4; 1897–1900 £124.2/-

13 Feb 1901 Wm Swanston Clerk of Works £38.16/-; 21 Feb 1901 M Muir & Co Masons balance of account £371.7/6; 4 Mar 1901 D White Joiner £100 & £77.10/11; H & T Morrison slaters balance of account £230.1/1; Boyd & Sons heating works £183.14/6; J Finlay & Co Ltd

alterations on kitchen range; G Jack for sketch of frieze for gun room £4; 11 Mar 1901 R A McGilvray balance of account for plasterwork £177.14/5; 29 Mar 1901 W Dodds London balance of account for leadwork 51.13/9; 30 Mar 1901 Galbraith & Winton balance on account for marble work £230.18/6; 30 Mar 1901 Galbraith & Winton balance on account for tiling £98.11/3; 2 Apr 1901 Reid & Co for bells & alterations £37.9/5; 7 Jun 1901 D White joiner balance of account £64.16/8; 7 Jun 1901 D White painter balance of account £62.6/4

21 Jun 1901 R W Schultz architect further to account of fees £200 Total £3,958.6/4'

Bute Archives, Marquess of Bute's Executry Accounts of the executors with reports by Messrs Lindsay, Jamieson, & Haldane, CA thereon from 9 October 1900 (the date of his lordship's death) to 31 July 1902, 6

43   Bute Archives, DHP 12

44   The accounts for this phase of alteration are presumably embedded in those for the works to the wings.

45   HES National Art Survey Photographic board DP089191

46   This arrangement is clearly shown on the 1905 survey drawings. It has since been skilfully altered to eliminate the stairs creating a level access from the main house to the east corridor. See Plan 16.

47   Conversation between the author and Peregrine Bertie 13 November 2012

48   In his account's for 1897–1900 Weir Schultz recorded some of the care that he expended on the work. The 'alterations to old portion of wing and joining on new work, involving considerably more trouble than the new work … ornamented finishings of interior, plaster modelling, wood panelling & carving, etc., etc.,involving special designing of a variety of elaborate and varied detail & special attention & trouble over the execution of same by workmen.' Stamp 1981, 33

49   'New Bridge in grounds preparing drawing of proposed new wooden Chinese bridge over the Lugar where iron bridge formerly stood £2.2/-' Drawing dated May 1899 by Robert Weir Schultz. Bute Archives DHP/27/4

Chapter 10: The House Preserved 1900–1993

now the house is being regularly occupied, I feel it should be finished

Lord Bute to Henry Heaton[1]

The 3rd Marquess died in the family bedroom at Dumfries House on 9 October 1900;[2] the 4th Marquess therefore came into his extensive inheritance at the age of nineteen when still legally a minor, a shy and retiring young man who, like his father, was a passionate collector of buildings and objects, including an important collection of Toby jugs as well glass and fine art.[3] He was also an adventurous traveller and acquired extensive properties in North Africa.[4]

At this time Dumfries House was a building site, as were all the major properties the 3rd Marquess passed onto his eldest son.[5] It appears that the 3rd Marquess' widow had a say in the completion of these building projects, some being rationalised, such as the grand staircase at Cardiff Castle, and some abandoned, such as the rebuilding of Rothesay Castle. Rowand Anderson, architect of the new Mount Stuart, recorded that the 3rd Marquess preferred the process of designing and building to completing a project.[6]

Despite this quantity of ongoing work, the young Marquess was not afraid to embark on new projects of his own. Although he never attempted to compete with the building mania of his father, he too was fascinated with historic buildings. He bought 5 Charlotte Square (Fig 10.2) in Edinburgh, restoring it to use as his Edinburgh townhouse and going on to acquire numbers 6 and 7, the three principal houses designed by Robert Adam on the north side of Scotland's most important Georgian square. He also restored two of the finest 17th century houses in Edinburgh, Acheson House on the Canongate and Lamb's House (Fig 10.3) in Leith. In 1912 he founded the Dovecot Studio,

Fig 10.1 John Crichton Stuart, 4th Marquess of Bute, inherited a wealth of unfinished projects but this did not deter him from embarking on those of his own. The Bute Collection

a tapestry workshop which created the magnificent tapestries 'The Lord of the Hunt' and 'The Time of the Meeting' that adorn the Hall at Mount Stuart.

At Dumfries House, building work on the west wing was largely complete but it is unclear how much of the interior was fitted out; certainly the Tapestry Room was not finished until 1908, the cherub frieze which was carved by the Cardiff Workshops (Fig 10.6) being the last element to be installed.[7] The 1900 Inventory refers to the fact that the Chapel, which had been created in the attic as a temporary solution by Schultz, was still operational.[8] Otherwise, the House was functioning much as it had when the 3rd Marquess was alive, with Drawing Rooms flanking the Entrance Hall and the Dining Room in the original North Parlour. Schultz continued to carry out various minor works such as the installation of glazed screens in the Servants' Bathroom and the Lamp Room as well as installing a new bathroom for the upper servants in 1905–6.[9] Lord Bute, like his father, worked closely with Schultz but although he adapted and altered the plans, for example replacing his father's Turkish Bath with a Billiard Room, it is difficult to determine the precise chronology of the works because of the superlative quality of the craftsmanship and the experienced professional hand of Schultz which is evident in all the works. The most dramatic deviations from the contract plans as agreed by the 3rd Marquess and Schultz are in the west pavilion, although further alterations were carried out throughout the House. A few mentions in the accounts of Lord Bute and Schultz are the only other record we have of the building works carried out in the first decade of the 20th century.

The creation of the Billiard Room and Smoking Room (Plan 11) represents one of the most sophisticated

interventions of this period. The Dumfries House accounts give an impression of the scale of the work, which was begun in 1904 and completed in 1905 and involved the demolition of the west wall of the pavilion, the removal of the Turkish Bath and the creation of a new split-level room lit by a large skylight. The Billiard Room (Fig 10.7) at the level of the original courtyard is completely hidden behind the 18th century courtyard walls, the only external intervention being the replacement of a doorway with a window in the west elevation. The room is lined with bookcases which were designed to accommodate a collection of books acquired from Loudoun Castle.[10] The west wall of the pavilion has been replaced with two pairs of columns, and three steps lead up to the Smoking Room area, organised around a large marble chimneypiece and also lined with bookcases. The change in level allowed observers to watch the game of billiards whilst not disrupting the game. Robert Lorimer was to use a very similar design at Ardkinglas for Sir Andrew Noble in 1908.[11] One of the master strokes at Dumfries House was to insert such a practical, modern arrangement into an existing building without disturbing the exterior elevations. The style of the interior is 18th century classical and reflects the sensibilities of the 4th Marquess but also respects the original house. The new room must have been barely completed when a survey plan was made in 1905 since the magnificent 'Smoking Room chimneypiece' is listed as being installed by 1905.[12]

Fig 10.2 Lord Bute bought 5 Charlotte Square, Edinburgh, to use as his townhouse. This view taken c1940 shows the ceiling he commissioned, a re-working of a Robert Adam design for Luton Park, which had once been owned by the Butes. HES SC1342636

Fig 10.3 Lamb's House, Edinburgh, is a 17th century merchant's house in the heart of Leith which was acquired and restored by Lord Bute and later gifted to the National Trust for Scotland. HES SC621188

Fig 10.4 Crucifixes were erected at Mount Stuart and Dumfries House in memory of the 3rd Marquess; only the one at Dumfries House remains. HES 2010 DP083501

A number of the same tradesmen and craftsmen employed for this job had worked at Dumfries House before including two well regarded artist craftsmen of the age, Lawrence Turner and William Dodds.[13] Turner was paid 'for ceiling cornice, frieze etc & for wood carving to bookcases' at a cost of £206.[14] William Dodds taught the art of metalwork at the Central School of Arts and Crafts, London, under its founding principal William Lethaby and was probably known to Schultz through the architect's close friendship with Lethaby, which had begun when they met in Norman Shaw's office in the 1880s. Dodds had executed the exquisite exterior leadwork downpipes and hoppers on the pavilions and was commissioned to make the 'lead clock dial' (Fig 10.5).[15] Other specialists were employed including 'Stuarts Granolithic Co. for suspended roof and floor to Billiard Room', 'Henry Nelmes & Co for billiard table' and 'P & W MacLellan for Steel joists'.[16] The placement of this suite of rooms on the ground level of the extended pavilion shows that they were public spaces. The Bachelors' Entrance with its cloakroom conveniently nearby became the everyday entrance to the House, a change that transformed the original Entrance Hall into a lounge hall (Fig 10.15) as part of a suite of reception rooms running along the south front of the House that afforded the family some privacy from visitors and staff.

The remaining courtyard was redeveloped with the removal of the 18th century toofall and the insertion of three bedrooms for male servants, and a bathroom. These rooms were placed at the higher level of the Smoking Room rather than the lower level of the original courtyard in order to accommodate a short tunnel that linked these rooms with the main service corridor. The surviving 18th century Great Drain (Plan 13) facilitated the construction of the tunnel. The absence of a service stair continued to be a problem and so the creation of a tunnel linking the staff bedrooms with the main service corridor helped segregate the staff from the family so that they could go about their jobs without having to interrupt them and vice-versa.

The south-east pavilion room, previously the School Room, became a Business Room which, with its pleasant aspect to both south and west, became one of the Lord Bute's favourite rooms. The adjacent 18th century staircase was removed and a larger oak one installed (Fig 10.9). Unlike its predecessor it stretched to the outside wall and was well lit by the existing south facing window thereby providing a more pleasant approach to the principal floor. The other alteration was transformation of the 3rd Marquess' Book Room (Fig 10.10), created only a few years previously, into a Gun Room, which involved the insertion of a chimney flue and fireplace, a challenge where no easily accessible chimney flue existed.[16] The room was also lined with shelves and cupboards, and gun cabinets created in the deeper recesses either side of the fireplace through the addition of secure steel doors.[17] In 1901, George Jack, a friend of Schultz and disciple and assistant of Philip Webb, designed a frieze for the Gun Room.[18] While there is no evidence that it was actually installed, the panelling has been

Fig 10.5 The clock face in the West Courtyard, which was designed and made by William Dodds, incorporates the Irish Shamrock, for Lady Bute, in addition to the Scottish Thistle and the English Rose. HES 2007 DP033616

Fig 10.6 The Tapestry Room frieze carved by the Cardiff Workshops was the final element to be installed in 1908. HES 2010 DP083174

designed to accommodate such a frieze. Jack was also responsible for the magnificent, if somewhat eccentric, decoration in the 'seagull' sitting room at House of Falkland which was created in 1895 for Lady Margaret, elder sister of the 4th Marquess.

The Tapestry Room is shown on the 1905 survey plan as if complete although it was not finished until three years later. In the original west pavilion, the new staircase only rises to this level and the thick flue bearing wall to its west has been cut back to accommodate a small separate stair to the servants' bedrooms in the attic which had been created by the 2nd Marquess. This created a more spacious landing which, with its plain plastered walls and oak floor, gives no hint of the exuberant corridor beyond that leads to the reception rooms. The relative austerity of the hall and stairs leading from the Bachelors' Entrance up to the principal floor must have been a deliberate design choice in order to create a contrast with the richness of the decoration in the domed west corridor.

The east wing, although unfinished at the time of the death of the 3rd Marquess, was also altered between 1899, when the plans (Fig 9.23, Plan 11) for the proposed works were drawn up, and the 1905 Survey. The 18th century toofall was removed and a scheme prepared for building three larders along the north side of the courtyard but this was re-thought so that, by 1905, the space was occupied by a Maids' Sitting Room with adjacent water closet and lavatory, the main structural intervention being the insertion of a corner

fireplace. The 1905 survey plans show that it was still intended to complete the Chapel in the form envisaged by the 3rd Marquess. In 1906 Schultz was supervising the 'fitting up of Private Pew, Chapel, Ceiling, Marble lining etc' (Fig 10.11). Marble samples were still being sought for its decoration as late as 1907.[19] However, in a 1920 Inventory,[20] the 'proposed chapel' is listed as containing a wide variety of odds and ends including 'four carved mahogany panelled Adam design doors … and three similar doors valued at £140.00'.[21] This room was known as the Chapel Library or the Chapel Book Store but the next room mentioned in the Inventory is the 'Chapel Over' which must refer to the space subsequently occupied by the New Dining Room. This substantial space appears to have been in use as a Roman Catholic chapel since its furnishings include a 'five ft 2in Oak Altar Table with arched front and linen and laced edged altar cloth … Lime Tree wood framed rush seated 22 chairs, four richly carved red pine prie-dieu chairs upholstered in silk … and Missal Romanism and sundries'.[22] A new floor had been inserted between 1908, when the building of the original double galleried Chapel was still under discussion, and the 1920 Inventory. Very little information is known about this work other than the fact that an attic Chapel is shown on a drawing of 1913[23] which suggests that this predates the insertion of the floor. The room is also

referred to in a letter from Lady Bute's Secretary as having been in use as a chapel at some point prior to 1927.[24] It is unclear how the interior was decorated but some elements of this scheme may survive above the coffered ceiling in the window bay which was inserted in the 1960s.

An examination of the sash and case windows throughout the house has revealed that they all date

Fig 10.8 Robert Weir Schultz, Ernest Gimson and the Barnsley brothers were responsible for completing the restoration of Old Place of Mochrum, Dumfries-shire. Lord Bute was very attached to this isolated house where he had spent his honeymoon. HES SC1220461

from c1900, apparently being replaced at the same time that the bathroom windows were being inserted into the original blind windows. In the Steward's Room there is a pane of glass in the door which bears the diamond cut inscription, 'Charming Montgomerie, Montgomerie Charming', which may relate to the gentleman of the same name who was caught in compromising circumstances with Lady Dumfries soon after her marriage to the 5th Earl.[25] Presumably the pane of glass was preserved because of its romantic associations and inserted in the Steward's Room door during these alterations.

While work was underway at Dumfries House, Lord Bute began acquiring buildings and commissioning building projects of his own. One of his earliest purchases was 5 Charlotte Square (Fig 10.2), Edinburgh.[26] While his father had been content to rent a townhouse in Edinburgh, Lord Bute bought one of the best houses in the city's finest square. He, like his father, enjoyed the building process and worked closely with Balfour Paul on an extensive restoration that aimed to re-Georganise the interior by adapting Robert Adam's design for the ceiling of Lady Bute's dressing room[27] at Luton Park for the first floor Drawing Room.[28] He worked with Schultz on Old Place of Mochrum, transforming it from what had been in effect his

Fig 10.9 A new oak staircase was installed in the west pavilion once it had become one of the principal routes from the family rooms on the ground floor to the more formal rooms above. IIES 2007 SC1104143

father's holiday home, 'a queer two-storied tower set in the middle of a wild Wigtownshire moor, on the edge of a gloomy lake … almost inaccessible by road or rail…' where he would 'rough' it with his cronies, into somewhere suitable to spend his honeymoon.[29] Schultz enlisted the help of his friends Ernest Gimson and the Barnsley brothers, leading exponents of the Arts and Crafts Movement, to complete the interiors and supply key pieces of furniture (Fig 10.8).[30]

The Bute family was enthusiastic about embracing new technology, Mount Stuart being the first house in Scotland to be lit electrically.[31] Dumfries House, however, was not electrified until 1909 although the first mention of installing electricity at the House[32] had been three years earlier in relation to the building of the Billiard Room.[33] The scheme not only entailed the delicate operation of threading electric cables through the historic building but also the building of an Engine and Battery House at the Mains Farm to supply the electricity. The electrification was later extended to include the Mains Farm, the Stables and the Coach House. There are very few references to the light fittings that were installed but a set of photographic views from the 1920s show, for example, a very simple circular fitting in the Entrance Hall (Fig 10.15) with four glass shades, and electrified chandeliers in the other reception rooms.[34] In a letter of 1927, Lady Bute's Secretary refers to 'Adams lanterns' that are to be

Fig 10.10 The Book Room created by the 3rd Marquess to provide a retreat from the main reception rooms was converted into a Gun Room by his son with the installation of cupboards, shelves and a chimneypiece. He later adapted the shelves to house his large collection of Toby Jugs. John Batty/NTS 1994

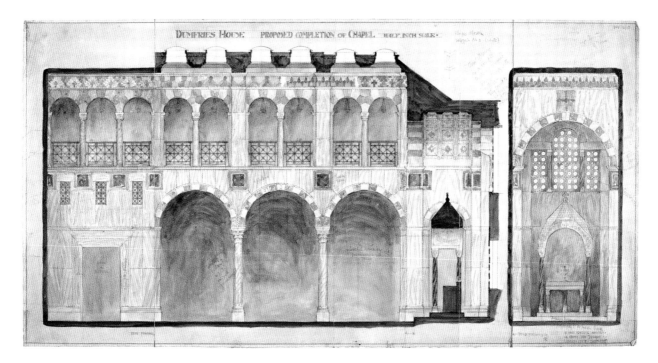

Fig 10.11 This detailed section of the proposed chapel by Robert Weir Schultz describes the expensive interior finishes with which the 4th Marquess was to complete his father's intention to incorporate a chapel into Dumfries House.
Bute Archives DHP/16/14

electrified; these are the presumably the glass lanterns that remain in the Stair Hall and Gallery at Dumfries House.[35]

A major scheme of alterations was begun in 1913 in order to improve the ability of the house to withstand a fire.[36] This involved the insertion of a reinforced concrete and steel floor on the first floor between the staircases and above the Entrance Hall during which time a temporary roof was erected over the main block and a large steel truss temporarily inserted on the first floor to support the 18th century plaster ceilings below. The attics were also rebuilt (Plan 14) to accommodate additional bathrooms, two water closets and seven new servants' bedrooms, whilst improving overall fire resistance through the use of concrete and steel. The anticipated increase in staffing was never achieved because, in common with country houses in general following the outbreak of war, the number of servants employed at the House began to decline and before long the new rooms were used for storage. The availability of clean, dry rooms that could be utilised for storing surplus furniture is perhaps one of the reasons why much of the House's historic furniture has survived. Early 20th century photographs show that relatively few pieces were in everyday use and that therefore much must have been in store.[37] Apart from the new rooms in the attic, alterations of this date included the removal of the columned screen in the south-west central bedroom, the insertion of a new timber floor in this and the adjacent room and the introduction of a new cornice in the Entrance Hall lobby between the two sets of doors to the staircases. These complicated and costly works are a testament to both architect and contractor who between them managed to preserve the external appearance of the House and the important

plasterwork within. Further improvements included the removal in 1923 of the magnificent central kitchen range (Fig 8.5), installed by Carron in the 1880s, and its replacement with a new range which was installed in front of the early 19th century range.[38] Four years later a telephone was installed to enable communication between the house and the garage.[39]

The west wing now provided comfortable accommodation that could easily be used without opening up the whole house.[40] In his otherwise exceptional design for this wing, Weir Schultz had not been able to resolve the different levels of the principal floor of the main block and the first floor of the pavilion and had therefore resorted to adding a step at the south end of the corridor. Lord Bute was obviously annoyed by this step (Fig 10.21), writing to Hendrie, his factor in 1933, 'Everybody trips over this step, especially when going down'[41] and proposing a rather drastic solution, 'I wonder if the floor in the small bedrooms could not be brought down to the level of the corridor, so as to do away with this step. This would mean, of course, bringing down the ceiling in the room I sit in level with the top of the windows.' (This refers to his Business Room at the south-east corner of the pavilion.) He continues, 'I don't think there is much in this, because, as far as I remember, the ceiling is made in bits and screwed on, and I suspect that the ceiling of the Library is the same. The real work would come in lowering the floors of the bedrooms. However Mr Mairns might look into this in the meantime.' This would have caused a major upheaval and been a very expensive solution but

Fig 10.12–20 A set of photographs were taken c1927 for Lord Bute prior to the creation of the new Dining Room as a record of the building before it was given to his son.

Dumfries House from the south, from the north, from the west, The Entrance Hall, The original Dining Room, The Drawing Room, North Parlour, The Tapestry Room, The Smoking/Billiard Room. The Bute Collection

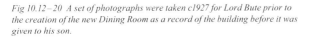

Fig 10.22 The Earl and Countess of Dumfries with their twin sons, John and David, around the time they moved into Dumfries House which they had been given to use as their principal residence. The Bute Collection

it illustrates Lord Bute's willingness to engage with the practical challenges of altering buildings. Hendrie came up with the eminently more practical solution for removing the step, explaining to Lord Bute,[42] 'Your lordship's proposal would entail a large expenditure, and I would respectfully suggest that the floor of the corridor be gradually raised from the Tapestry Room door to this step. The height of the step is 6 inches and the length from the Tapestry Room door to the step is 26' – i.e. there would be a gradual rise of 6" in 26' – this would scarcely be noticed and could be done at very little expense.' The oak floor was carefully lifted and re-laid as a shallow incline which, as Hendrie pointed out, was hardly perceptible.

The lack of a service pantry adjacent to the Dining Room had always been a problem at Dumfries House which suffered from the perennial country house challenge of keeping food warm during the journey from Kitchen to Dining Room.[43] The moving of the Dining Room from its original location in the south-east corner of the house to the North Parlour in the 19th century solved none of the service problems although it did enable the creation of a suite of Drawing Rooms facing south and a north facing Dining Room which was believed to be more conducive to good digestion.[44] The use of the House

as a secondary, more private residence meant that a formal Dining Room was not required in the way that it was at Mount Stuart. The North Parlour was still being used as the Dining Room when Lord and Lady Bute held a wedding anniversary luncheon there in 1930.[45]

In January 1934, Lord Bute gave Dumfries House to his eldest son John, Earl of Dumfries, and his wife Lady Eileen as their permanent residence although he continued to play a key role in the management of the Estate.[46] John had married Lady Eileen Forbes, daughter of the 8th Earl of Granard, two years before. The 2nd and 3rd Marquesses had died before their eldest sons had married but now a home was required for a young married couple and Dumfries House was the logical choice. Lord Bute continued to be involved with works at the House, adapting it to accommodate a young family which had expanded with the birth of twin sons in 1933, 'now the house is being regularly occupied, I feel it should be finished … The cost would be about £2,500 but it will greatly improve the house as the Dining Room will then be close to the kitchen.'[47] The Chapel that had been created in the upper portion of the east wing was now little used since the motor car allowed easy access to the more social experience of attending the

Fig 10.21 The change of floor level between the west pavilion and the Domed Corridor was problematic for Lord Bute and, after various alternatives had been explored, the oak floor of the corridor was tilted to eliminate the offending step, shown here. The Bute Collection

magnificent Catholic Church of St John in Cumnock. Lord Bute had been contemplating alterations to the east wing as early as 1928 in discussion with the architect Arthur Forman Balfour Paul with whom he had worked on the restoration of 5 Charlotte Square, Edinburgh.[48] In 1934, Lord Bute asked Balfour Paul to remodel the Upper Chapel as a new Dining Room, a relatively straightforward matter of converting the passage that was to have led to the family gallery into a service pantry with a new staircase linking down to the Kitchen. The main structural alteration required was the removal of the upper parts of the Chapel's arcades; the lower portions were retained to support the existing floor that subdivided the space and a new floor of Austrian oak was laid over this existing floor.[49] The staircase that was to serve the upper gallery was removed, plaster mouldings were applied to the walls as imitation panelling and a new oval 'Georgian' inspired roof light was installed (Plan 16). Balfour Paul appears to have reused the doors which served the Upper Chapel and also the extra doors that were listed as being stored in the Chapel Book Store in the Inventory of 1920. They are very similar to the design of the Tapestry Room doors and appear to be also the work of the Cardiff Workshops.

The main architectural feature of the new Dining Room was the chimneypiece, one of the five white marble chimneypieces that had been designed by James Byres of Tonley for Luton Park, Bedfordshire.[50] As in the case of the Tapestry Room chimneypiece, its

Fig 10.23 The spacious New Dining Room, photographed in 1994, was originally painted pale green. The dining table was acquired by the 4th Marquess from the Eglinton Castle sale and the Alexander Peter chairs by the 5th Earl. John Batty/NTS 1994

damaged mantle-shelf bears witness to its complicated history. It had previously been installed in the Morning Room at Mount Stuart before being transferred to Dumfries House. The large dining table was bought at the Eglinton Castle sale in December 1925 while the chairs chosen to accompany it were the 5th Earl of Dumfries' dining chairs, which had been made

Fig 10.24 The New Dining Room chimneypiece. The room was painted red after 1993. HES 2007 DP033729

Fig 10.25 From the 1920s onwards, Kames Castle, the towerhouse built for the Bannatynes of Kames, became Lord Bute's preferred residence on Bute, Mount Stuart having been closed up and unsuccessfully put on the market. HES 2006 DP010303

Fig 10.26 The Adam Bridge was reinforced by the Coal Board in the 1940s in order to support the weight of coal trucks while the Estate's coal measures were being mined as part of the war effort. HES c1944 SC1342634

by Edinburgh cabinet maker Alexander Peter. The creation of a new dining room meant that the North Parlour could be returned to its original function as a sitting room. The 18th century Dining Room remained as a secondary Drawing Room. New bathrooms were installed on the bedroom floor (Plan 17) as part of the same set of alterations and involved the creation of a bathroom in all four of the corner rooms. This meant the removal of the partitions erected c1900 by Weir Schultz and the insertion of new Shanks of Barrhead baths and wash hand basins set in Blanc Clair marble. New teak floors were laid over the existing boards in each bathroom.[51] Balfour Paul also installed a new heating system at this time.[52] The room below the new Dining Room was fitted out with bookcases in order to house some of the books transferred to the house from Loudoun Castle[53] and The Garrison on Millport and it became known as the Chapel Book Store.[54] The original Lady Chapel off this room was retained as an oratory and survives, complete with the stained glass window from St John's Lodge, Regent's Park, London.[55] This arrangement of the House survived until the death of the Dowager Marchioness of Bute in 1993. The new Dining Room was the 4th Marquess' last major intervention at Dumfries House. In much the same spirit that his father had approached the House, his alterations were intended to make it more practical without adversely affecting its Georgian character. In December 1920 Mount Stuart was put up for sale through John Baxter of Glasgow 'Conditional to its complete demolition and removal by the Purchaser'.[56] It may be that the new Dining Room at Dumfries House was intended to house some of the family portraits from Mount Stuart in the event that it became the principal family seat in Scotland.

Dumfries House had become the principal residence of a young family for the first time since the 18th century, rather than one of the Scottish homes of a Marquess. On taking up residence in 1934, Lady Dumfries played an important role in the redecoration and refurnishing of her new home. The removal of the Dining Room to the east wing meant that the main block now contained a suite of three Drawing Rooms around the Entrance Hall, which was itself also used as a sitting room and Lady Dumfries made the interior more comfortable and fashionable, with Afflecks of Ayr supplying carpets,[57] upholstery and pelmets as well as providing some new furniture and selling some pieces.[58] Her love of horses and racing is evinced by one of her first actions when moving to Dumfries House in January 1934 which was to remodel the Stables (Fig 5.16) with new stalls made by the Clydesdale Iron Works.[59] Her husband appears to have let his wife have control of domestic matters whilst he pursued his own interests. His enthusiasm for ornithology extended to acquiring the archipeligo of St Kilda in 1936.[60]

In 1942 parts of the Estate were requisitioned by the Army who built a camp known as the Pennyland Barracks to the north of the Lugar Water where the existing modern farm buildings lie. Initially used to house and train members of the Allied forces, it operated briefly as a Prisoner of War Camp, Auchinleck Camp 22, primarily for Italian Prisoners of War. Although de-requisitioned in 1944, the Camp was converted three years later into a Polish Repatriation Centre, evidence for which lies in the woods between the farm building and the Gothic Temple Lodge where a number of hut platforms remain.

The coal mining rights on the Estate were leased to support the war effort with the proviso that no Estate buildings were to be undermined.[61] The Adam Bridge was, however, affected by the mining of seven seams of coal in close proximity to it and had to be temporarily shored up with elaborate timber trusses. The lease stated that the Army were to completely replace the Bridge if it was affected by the mining,[62] but fortuitously, their inaction meant that the Bridge survived. The early 18th century Lady's Well (Fig 5.18) fared worse from the military occupation of the Estate, being destroyed during target practice on 10 April 1944 for which the

Figs 10.27–10.35 Set of photographs taken by John Batty 1994. John Batty/NTS
The Pink Drawing Room – originally the Dining Room, The west corridor, View through the front door, The North Parlour.
(Overleaf) The east corridor, The White Drawing Room, North-west or Blue Bedroom, North-east or Green Bedroom, The White Drawing Room.

Estate received only partial compensation.[63] The Gothic Temple Lodge (Fig 5.39) was damaged in the summer of 1942[64] and further problems were caused when a bomb accidentally exploded during manoeuvres at the east side of the House, breaking 48 panes of glass.[65] In response to the requisition of parts of the House, including rooms in both the wings and the Servants' Hall, detailed instructions were given as to what could and couldn't be used. In particular, Lord Bute was reluctant to allow the Lady Chapel to be used for Anglican worship.[66] The family moved out of Dumfries House during its requisition by the Army, dividing their time in Scotland between Edinburgh and Bute.

The extensive programme of redecoration that was required after the wartime occupation was supervised by the Lady Dumfries.[67] The tapestries were dispatched to the Dovecot Studio in Edinburgh for repair under the guidance of chief weaver Ronald Cruikshank.[68] The House and the family were beginning to return to some form of normality when Lord Bute died in 1947 at the age of 66. Lord Dumfries was now the 5th Marquess of Bute, and as such, he and his family moved to Mount Stuart; consequently the need to carry out improvement works at Dumfries House was less pressing. The new Marchioness set about attempting to tame some of the interiors of Mount Stuart bringing the House closer to her preferred 18th century character but the untimely death of the 5th Marquess at the age of 49 brought a halt to work on Mount Stuart and after only nine years his widow returned to Dumfries House.[69]

The Drawing Rooms flanking the Entrance Hall had been completely redecorated the previous year with '3 coats oil paint with flat enamel finish in selected shades'.[70] White was chosen for the West Drawing Room and pink for the East Drawing Room.

The colour schemes of all the interiors were simplified, the exuberant decoration in the west corridor was painted out as was the naturalistic painting of the plasterwork in the North Parlour. The Entrance Hall retained the 3rd Marquess' colour scheme for the plasterwork which was now offset by the hanging of a large collection of Dutch paintings[71] and Afflecks of Ayr were once again called in to provide new upholstery and curtains.[72] With the help of a variety of designers, including Jean Monro, the Dowager Marchioness created an extremely comfortable home which continued to celebrate both the Chippendale furniture and the 18th century interiors of the House. In the 1960s, Watson Salmond & Gray of Glasgow[73] were employed to carry out various maintenance jobs including the re-roofing of part of the House and the installation of new chimneypots. They also proposed extensive alterations to the new Dining Room that would have reduced it in size and, although this was not carried out, a coffered ceiling was inserted in the window recess. The use of coffering demonstrates an awareness of the drawings for the original chapel, which used the same sort of ceiling in this position, and respect for the history of the house.[74] Their other contribution to the interior was the addition of a series of glazed cabinets to the east corridor to hold Lady Bute's collection of Waterford Crystal. The firm was also responsible for the heaters in the window recesses of the principal rooms on the south front. In the early 1990s, Edinburgh architect Bob Heath was employed to carry out further repairs and maintenance.[75] Eileen, Dowager Marchioness of Bute, died at Dumfries House in the first week of July 1993 and was buried a week later at Mount Stuart. The untimley death of her son the 6th Marquess only two weeks later was what eventually led to the need to find a new future for Dumfries House.

Fig 10.36 Lady Eileen with her hunter in the 1930s. The Bute Collection

1   Letter from Lord Bute to Henry Heaton. Bute Archives, Mountjoy Ltd Correspondence

2   The 3rd Marquess is commemorated with a memorial crucifix overlooking the Lugar Water to the east of the House. The inscription reads 'HOEC SACROSANTA IMAGO JUSSU JOANNIS MARCHIONIS III BOTHAE ERECTA ESTPROPE LOCUM UBI IPSE ANIMAM DEO REDDIDIT DIE IX OCTOBR ANN MDCCCC' [This sacred image on the wishes of John the 3rd Marquess of Bute erected near to the place where his spirit returned to God on 9 October 1900].

3   The Toby-jug collection of 193 items was sold at Christie's, London, on 8 July 1996.

4   The 4th Marquess owned the Hotel El Minzah in Tangier, Morocco, which he opened in 1930. He also had extensive landholdings in Morocco. Conversation with Peregrine Bertie 13 November 2012

5   The Jerusalem properties were bequeathed to his daughter Margaret, the Falkland Estates to his son Ninian and the Morayshire estates to his son Colum.

6   Hunter Blair 1921, 241

7   R W Schultz photograph of the Tapestry Room without the frieze (no trace of the photograph can now be found), referred to in Maclean 2007, 28. Reference to the completion of the Tapestry Gallery, Bute Archives, The Lindsay Jamieson and Haldane Accounts of the 4th Marquess of Bute 1905–09. Schultz's balance of account in connection with Tapestry Room carving, £10 10s. Report by Lindsay, Jamieson & Haldane On accounts of cashiers and factors for most Hon. John Crichton-Stuart fourth Marquess of Bute 30 May 1910–1913

8   Dumfries House Inventory, 1900. Bute Archives, DH Inventories

9   Stamp 2001, 36

10 The Loudon Castle book collection is now at Mount Stuart.

11 The split level billiard room at Ardkinglas, Argyll, was described in glowing terms by Lawrence Weaver, 'The players are thus saved from the distraction of having people walking about on the same level near the table, and spectators can draw up chairs to the railing that guard the edge of the raised floor and look down on the table … A plan of this type is not always possible as it depends naturally on the disposition of the other rooms: but when it can be contrived it makes a pleasant and convenient room.' Weaver 1912, 38

12 The Smoking Room chimneypiece is listed as completed in Robert Weir Schultz's Journals; Contract Journal 1903–33, 1904/5. HES, NMRS Survey of Private Collections, P109, 37–49

13 The standing of Turner is clearly shown by his commissions for the tombs of both William Morris at Kelmscott and Norman Shaw at Hampstead. His carving was described by Lawrence Weaver as 'admirable in its bold lusciousness'. Weaver 1912, 29

14 Bute Archives Report by Lindsay Jamieson & Haldane On accounts of Cashiers and Factors for Most Hon. John Crichton Stuart Fourth Marquess of Bute 1905–1909, 31

15 Ibid

16 Full list of Payments in connection with alterations on Dumfries House:

'1 Aug 1904 Mitchell Taylor for plasterwork £20;18 Aug P & W MacLellan for Steel joists £7.13/5

26 Sep 1904 James Boyd & Sons for alts to heating £17; 12 Oct 1904 Galbraith & Winton for marble work to gunroom £32.2/-; 13 Jan 1905 D White account for joiner work £130.14/11; 23 Jan 1905 Mitchell Taylor for Plaster and cement work £5.19/3; 23 Jan 1905 H & T Morrison for plumber work £110.8/5; 25 Jan 1905 Morton & Kerr mason work £308.19/8; 1 Feb 1905 Dumfries Estate for labour & materials £17.11/8; 13 Mar 1905 Hayward Brothers & Echstein Ltd for wrought steel doors £3.3/-

29 Apr 1905 Mitchell Taylor for plaster and cement works £14.4/3; 30 Jun 1905 Mitchell Taylor for plaster and cement works £30; TOTAL £697.17/7'

Work on 5 Charlotte Square, Old Place of Mochrum, Mount Stuart Chapel and Dumfries House all concurrently:P. 31 Payments in connection with alterations on Dumfries House 1905:

'7 Aug Galbraith & Winton for marble chimney piece carving etc

£85.14/8; 7 Aug Mrs Keightley for tiles etc £11.9/6; 8 Aug RW Schultz Architect on account of his fees £50; 8 Aug RW Schultz Architect on account of proportion of outlays from Sept 1903- December 1904 £17.4/3; 19 Aug D Whyte third instalment for joiner work £350; 2 Sept L A Turner for ceiling cornice, frieze etc & for wood carving to bookcases £206; 15 Sept Henry Nelmes & Co for billiard table £183.8/-; 15 Sept Pennycook Glazing Co for glazing roof light lead capping ridge etc £16.5/8; 15 Sept Mitchell Taylor for plasterwork £29.5/6; 15 Sept H & T Morrison for plumber work on Billiard Room roof £127.16/8

15 Sept H & T Morrison for general plumber work £34.12/7; 3 Nov Stuarts Granolithic Co for suspended roof and floor to Billiard Room £160.13/10; 3 Nov Stuarts Granolithic Co for fire proof partition slabs £3.15/-; 4 Nov C Pratt & Sons for stoves and fire irons £15; 4 Nov Daniel Whyte for joiner work £272.8/5; 4 Nov William Dodds for making lead clock dial £10.7/6; 6 Nov R & A Allan for repairing turret clock £35.10/-; 7 Nov Morton & Kerr on account of mason work £195.1/3'

Payments in 1906

'12 Feb James Boyd & Sons for heating apparatus to Billiard Room £23./4; 12 Feb J Elsey for stoves etc for smoking and gun rooms £52.8/3; 12 Feb Dumfries Estate for building materials etc £27.5/-

12 Feb J M Mackay & Co for electric light work in Billiard Room £23.8/10; 23 May RW Schultz architect balance of his account for period from October 1903- October 1905 £212.10/-; 23 May RW Schultz architect balance of account from Dumfries House Record Plans £26.5/3; 23 May RW Schultz architect balance of proportion of outlays for year 1905 £25; 26 July James E Sayers & Caldwell their charges in connection with proposed electric lighting of Dumfries House £214.16/6; 26 July Lavers and Westlake for glazier work £33.12/-; 15 Sep H Nelmes & Co for supplying pyramid & pool outfit £41.13/-; 15 Sep H Nelmes & Co for making pool & billiard marking board £18.10; 29 Dec RW Schultz architect on account of work done since October 1905 £50; Total £2,553.2/-'

Bute Archives Accounts of Messrs J & F Anderson WS for the most Hon John Crichton Stuart Marquess of Bute with reports by Messrs Lindsay, Jamieson & Haldane thereon from 9 October 1900 – 31 July 1905'.

'Marble work in gun room' described as completed in the Robert Weir Schultz Contract Journal 1903–33. HES, NMRS Survey of Private Collections, P109, 37–49

17 '13 March 1905 Hayward Brothers & Echstein Ltd for wrought steel doors £3.3/-.' Bute Archives, Accounts of Messrs J & F Anderson WS for the most hon. John Crichton Stuart Marquess of Bute with reports by Messrs Lindsay, Jamieson & Haldane thereon from 9 October 1900–31 July 1905. Bute Archives DHP/13/5

18 George Jack was paid £4.00 for a sketch of frieze for gun room £4. Accounts of the executors with reports by Messrs Lindsay, Jamieson, & Haldane, CA thereon from 9 October 1900 (the date of his lordship's death) to 31 July 1902 Marquess of Bute's Executary.

19 Stamp 1981, 34. '3 January 1907, Galbraith & Winton for erecting sample pieces of marble work in chapel £153.10.' Bute Archives, Accounts of cashiers and factors for most Hon John Crichton-Stuart fourth Marquess of Bute 1905–1909.

20 Bute Archives, Inventory & valuation of the furniture & china etc at Dumfries House Old Cumnock Ayrshire Scotland October 1920 taken for insurance.

21 These were probably the doors made by the Cardiff Workshops for the new Chapel but later utilised in the New Dining Room.

22 Bute Archives inventory, 108

23 Plan of attics as existing with chapel shown at head of west staircase, servants' rooms only in the mezzanine with the attic rooms used only for storage, March 1913. Ayrshire Archives, Darley Hey Collection; Allen Stevenson drawings.

24 'Lady Bute tells me that when the electric light was installed in dh five Adams lanterns were taken down … they should be in the house somewhere and were for a time in the chapel before it was cleared up for use.' Letter from Sibyl Dowling, Secretary to Lady Bute to Mr Hendrie, 13 June 1927. Bute Archives, Dumfries Estate Box 139, 1923–27

25 See Chapter 3, note 75

26 Bute Archives 'Statement for year to 31 July 1903 Page 5, Price of House No 5 Charlotte Square, Edinburgh and Expenses £9,567.1/4. Accounts of Messrs J & F Anderson WS for the most Hon John Crichton Stuart Marquess of Bute with reports by Messrs Lindsay, Jamieson & Haldane thereon from 9 October 1900–31 July 1905'.

27 Original Adam designs for Luton Park. Bute Archives BHP/2/S

28 Lord Bute's ancestor, the 3rd Earl of Bute, had commissioned Robert Adam to design Luton Park and various other buildings.

29 Hunter Blair 1922, 126

30 Greenstead, M 1980, 176–7

31 The New Mount Stuart, Gavin Stamp *Mount Stuart Guide Book* 2001,14

32 'J M Mackay & Co for electric light work in the Billiard Room, 12 Feb 1906, £23.8/10.' Bute Archives, Reports by Messrs. Lindsay, Jamieson & Haldane on Accounts of cashiers and factors for most Hon John Crichton-Stuart fourth Marquess of Bute 1905–1909

33 In 1909 James E Sayers and Caldwell of Glasgow were appointed as consulting engineers to design the lighting system, J M Mackay & Co were the contractors who installed it. Remitted by DW Shaw for the following sums paid in connection with the Electric Light installations 1909:

'17 July J M Mackay & Co Contractors first instalment per Engineers certificate £2,000
17 July Sawers & Caldwell consulting engineers on account £75
29 July J M Mackay & Co Contractors further instalment £1,500
29 July H & T Morrison Plumbers for work in Engine and Battery rooms fitting in new water supply etc £90.17/6
29 July D White for general joiner work £85.4/8
29 July D White for painting electric tubing £8.17/2
29 July D White to account of joiner work of Engine House £70
29 July Morton & Kerr raggling for electricians £53.25/-
29 July Morton & Kerr to account of building Engine and battery room £300
29 July M Taylor for general plaster work £10.12/4
29 July M Taylor for cementing in battery room £8./2
29 July A & J Main & Co for beams etc £2.3/6
29 July Macleod Bros for general joiner work £59.13/-

TOTAL £4,264.3/'

Bute Archives, Reports by Lindsay, Jamieson & Haldane on Accounts of cashiers and factors for most Hon John Crichton-Stuart fourth Marquess of Bute Accounts for 1909, 16

34 Bute Archives, An uncatalogued album of professional photographs taken in the 1920s.

35 Letter from Sibyl Dowling, Secretary to Lady Bute, to Mr Hendrie, Estate factor, 13 June 1927. 'Lady Bute tells me that when the electric light was installed in Dumfries House five adams lanterns were taken down … three in the gallery, one outside her bedroom and one outside the nursery … and others replaced these. she wonders where these Adams lanterns are … she wants the lanterns put up again … they should be in the house somewhere and were for a time in the chapel before it was cleared up for use.' Letter from Hendrie to Dowling 16 June 1927, 'the Adams lanterns are to be fitted with electric lights'. Bute Archives, Dumfries Estate Box 139, 1923–27

36 The total cost of the works was over £4,000 The Plans include 'Undated Plan of corridor on first/bedroom floor showing steel beams 5'x 3" x 11lb steel beams. Section showing temporary truss inserted over Entrance Hall while reinforced concrete with steel beams inserted steel beams at 3'6" centres; Elevation of Hall shows columned screen; 26 January 1915 Steel lattice of beams over the Entrance Hall and running N–S on the long landing.'
13 July 1913 New plan of the attic
The central section of the attic with two light wells is original, all the rest was inserted including new roof lights. Only the main structural walls were retained, the mezzanine rooms remain unaltered.
April 1913 New steel roof section and plan
August 1913 Shows new plan of attic with servants bathroom
March 1913 Plan of attics as existing with chapel shown at head of west staircase, servants' rooms only in the mezzanine with the attic rooms used only for storage. Section shows temporary roof over whole building
December 1914 Plan of first floor showing proposed fireproof floor
Temporary truss along south wall of first floor landing across archway

plan showing existing retained wooden beams and proposed steel beams
December 1913 Plan of roof showing chimneys and roof lights
Undated Roof construction
14 x 2 ½ Wood kerb bolted to concrete beam for fixing lead work
16 x 5 ½ concrete beam
1 ½ inch thick 'breeze' concrete for fixing slates
16″ x 8″ slates all to be nailed with a single nail at top and two nails at bottom as in old roof.
3″ concrete slab
December 1913 Sections of new roof
February 1915 Detail drawing of new cornice for whole corridor between both staircases on principal floor (appears to have been carried out)
25 July 1914 James Boyd and Sons plumber adaption of heating with new mains supply and notes.'
Ayrshire Archives Darley Hey Collection; Allen Stevenson drawings

37 Photographic views of the principal rooms c1927, Bute Archives, Photograph Album uncatalogued

38 Repairs 'proposed to the central range in the kitchen which was originally supplied by Carron and who are to restore it, 8 October 1923; decision made to remove the central range, 16 October 1923.' Bute Archives, Dumfries Estate Box 139, 1923–27

39 'Cowan & Linton Ltd, Quote for fitting a telephone connecting the House and garage located in the original coach house £7.10/2 overland or in a trench £19.18/6, 5 September 1927.' Bute Archives, Dumfries Estate Box 139, 1923–27.

40 There are various references in the archives to making the bedrooms beyond the Tapestry Room ready Telegram from Lord Bute about arriving at Dumfries House asking the housekeeper 'to prepare … two rooms off Tapestry Room', 27 July 1925. (These rooms, a bedroom and Dressing room, lie to the west of the Tapestry Gallery). Dumfries Estate Box 139, 1923–27

41 Letter from Lord Bute to Mr Hendrie the factor, 3 September 1933. Bute Archives Dumfries Estate Box 144

42 Letter from Mr Hendrie the factor to Lord Bute, 5 September 1933, Bute Archives Dumfries Estate Box 143

43 This problem was resolved at Arniston with the installation of an internal railway system to speed the movement of food from the kitchen to the Dining Room.

44 Franklin 1981, 49

45 The table plan used for the luncheon held by Lord and Lady Bute for their 25th wedding anniversary shows that the North Parlour was used as a Dining Room on 18 August 1930. Bute Archives Dumfries Estate, Box 140, 1923–7

46 Letter from Lord Dumfries to Hendrie saying that his father has given permission for him and Lady Dumfries to live at Dumfries House and that they will be there mid January, 16 December 1933. Bute Archives Dumfries Estate Box 147, 1934–5

47 Letter from Lord Bute to Henry Heaton. Bute Archives, Mountjoy Ltd Correspondence

48 2 October 1928 letter to Hendry from Balfour Paul of Rowand Anderson & Paul 16 Rutland Square 'In connection with the plans that are now being prepared, for Lord Bute's consideration, of the rearrangement of the east wing.' Bute Archives, Dumfries Estate Box 142

49 Letter from Mr Hendrie to Lord Bute, 12 June 1935, 'The flooring of the new Dining Room is Austrian Oak'. Bute Archives Dumfries Estate Box 144.

50 See Chapter 9, 193

51 Letter from Mr Hendrie, factor, to Lord Bute, 12 June 1935 regarding the choice to be made between oak and teak for the new flooring for the bathrooms on the bedroom floor. In the reply from Lord Bute to Mr Hendrie, 15 June 1935, it is agreed that teak should be laid over the existing floor.

13 July 1935 Letter from Lord Bute to Mr Hendrie regarding the choice of Blanc Clair marble for the wash hand basin stands in the bathrooms. Bute Archives, Dumfries Estate Box 144

52 Letter from Mr Hendrie to Lord Bute, 28 March 1935, in which he quotes from a letter from Balfour Paul about rationalising the heating system from two central heating boilers and three independent hot water boilers to one boiler in the boiler room that would link to the boiler in the west wing; he recommends the retention of the small boiler in the kitchen

for use when the house is only occupied by the staff. Bute Archives Dumfries Estate Box 144

53 The 3rd Marquess helped out his maternal cousin Henry Rawdon-Hastings 4th Marquess of Hastings, when he got into financial difficulties in the late 1860s. This included taking over the responsibility for the heavily mortgaged Loudoun Estates. Henry's sister Edith became the 10th Countess of Loudoun in her own right and Lord Bute gave her and her husband the Loudoun Estate while keeping a significant portion of the extensive Loudoun Castle library for himself. Her son Charles Rawdon-Hastings, 11th Earl of Loudoun,went onto to marry Lady Bute's sister Alice in 1880. The Loudoun books were partially housed in the Book Room in Dumfries House by the 3rd Marquess consciously keeping an Ayrshire collection of books in the county and later moved into the Billiard Room Library by the 4th Marquess. Report by Messers Lindsay Jamieson & Haldane on The Accounts of the Cashiers & Factors for The Most Noble The Marquess of Bute From 31 July 1869 – 31 July 1870. Maclean 2007, 26

54 Books transferred from The Garrison Millport to Dumfries House. Bute Archives, Dumfries Estate Accounts for the year 1921

55 Letter from Lord Bute to Mr Hendry, 12 June 1936, 'Yes the woodwork in the chapel should be painted white I noticed that the covering to the radiator there took up a good deal of room, so that perhaps the step and the altar may have to be brought forward a little – I want room to move about behind the altar.' Bute Archives Dumfries Estate Box 145

56 There was never any intention to sell the estates on Bute, only the house which by this time had become extremely unfashionable but it was eventually taken off the market because a buyer could not be found. Lord Bute used Kames Castle, a 16th century towerhouse with later additions, near Port Bannatyne as his main residence on Bute after his younger daughter Lady Jean's marriage in 1928. Conversation with Peregrine Bertie 13 November 2012

57 Afflecks of Ayr to supply a Grey Wilton stair carpet 45″ wide £102.10/-.8 July 1937.Tender accepted. Bute Archives Dumfries Estate, Box 148

58 'Afflecks Ltd quotation to supply a Library desk in mahogany for 2x 6′ 4 ½″ cabinets in Spanish mahogany £48.10/- each take off carcase backs of present cabinets and replace alder plywood panels with African walnut £3.10/- each, 14 June 1937.

Afflecks valuation of various furniture at Dumfries House, 10 June 1937 includes Chippendale Mahogany Display Cabinet,Chinese design, astragal doors and sides on square legs with carved scroll feet £90

Set of 6 mahogany shield back chairs on fluted legs with under stretchers £40

Display cabinet marked as retain in pencil retained.

Sale of furniture through Afflecks agreed and also the supplying of stair carpet, mahogany cabinets and a Library desk made in four equal separate sections with one adjustable shelf dividing the extreme right. 8 July 1937.'

Bute Archives Dumfries Estate Box 150 1937 – 9

59 'Proposal for alterations to the stables at the behest of the Countess of Dumfries, new stalls to be fitted out by the Clydesdale Iron Works, Possilpark, 19 January 1934. Work agreed on 10 February 1934 and carried out for £70.00.' Bute Archives Dumfries Estate Box 147 1934 – 5

60 5th Marquess of Bute gifted St Kilda to the National Trust for Scotland in 1956.

61 Letter from Mr Hendrie to Lord Bute regarding 'pillars of coal to be left under various farm steadings and cottages', 18 June 1942. Bute Archives, Dumfries Estate Box 152.

62 Proposal to strengthen the Adam Bridge with steel supports by Bairds of Glasgow, Bute responds that it was in the terms of the lease to replace the bridge not prop it up as lease is for coal mining. Proposals approved as a temporary measure but all to be made good by the leases, 27 December 1941. Bute Archives, Dumfries Estate Box 152.

63 Claim for compensation for the 'destruction of the well made in 1955…' reported as partly destroyed on 10 April 1944. Bute Archives Dumfries Estate Box 156.

64 Letter from Lord Bute to Mr Hendrie, 19 July1942, in which he explains that he is not happy about the Church of England using the Roman Catholic Chapel and also that damage to the Temple (Lodge) should be dealt with. Bute Archives Dumfries Estate Box 152.

65 Letter from Lord Bute to Mr Hendrie, 4 October 1945, 'also there are the 48 panes of glass which were broken by the bomb on the east end of the house to be renewed'. Bute Archives Dumfries Estate Box 153.

66 Letter from Mr Hendrie to Lord Bute, 15 July 1942, regarding a request by Capt Stevens to use the chapel and from Lt Col R T Ransome for permission to use the east wing excluding the Library from 28 July to 10 August 1942. Also regarding the permission granted to military authorities to use the Servants Hall from 28 July to 10 August 1942 provided that access to the main building is cut off by brick partitions and the partitions removed immediately after. Bute Archives Dumfries Estate Box 152

67 Copy of specification for painter work proposed at Dumfries House, 28 February 1945, comprising the Dining Room, two recesses off and the small room off, patching and washing, decorating as existing. Also includes back stair from kitchen passage. J B Bennett & Sons carried out the work 20 November 1944. Bute Archives Dumfries Estate Box 153

68 October 1946 Tapestries from Dumfries House sent back to Dovecot Studios for repair, Ronald Cruikshank the chief weaver. Bute Archives, Dumfries Estate Box 154 1946 – 9. Cumming 2011, 8 – 10

69 Notes from a conversation with Jennifer Dowager Marchioness of Bute

70 W G Mackie & co decorators estimate for redecorating Dumfries House, 16 November 1955. Bute Archives, Dumfries Estate Box 156

71 See photograph Bute Archives, DSC 1802

72 Afflecks quotation of 8 December 1956 for:

'Drawing Room new damask curtains, recovering 6 easy chairs, one settee, one stool and two roll cushions in damask as selected. Dining Room recovering 16 Chippendale chairs in damask as selected. New Red Room (Bedroom) Including 2 festoon curtains, bed re up holstered and hangings, recover easy chair & red dressing room including curtains and fitted bedspread Green Room and Dressing same extent as Red rooms 16 Ecru holland blinds work also in nurses room, Fullarton's Room (central bedroom), Drawing Room, work on various carpets total cost £1,367.16/6'

Bute Archives Dumfries Estate Box 157

73 Watson Salmond & Gray Collection, Mitchell Library, Glasgow, Special Collections Reference/Job Number 550 Boxes A, B & C

74 See Bute Archives DHP/17 1 – 6 and DP106914

75 Bob Heath repaired the Adam Bridge in 1990 and moved the Auchinleck Gates to Hill of Tarvit as a gift from the 6th Marquess in 1993. He was also the architect for repairs to the roof of the Billiard Room and other more minor repairs. Information from Bob Heath.

Bibliography

Abbreviations

DSA
Dictionary of Scottish Architects
http://www.scottisharchitects.org.uk/

HES
Historic Environment Scotland

NGS
National Galleries of Scotland

NRS
National Records of Scotland

NTS
National Trust for Scotland

RCAHMS
Royal Commission on the Ancient and Historical Monuments of Scotland

RIAS
Royal Incorporation of Architects in Scotland

RIBA
Royal Institute of British Architects

Bibliography

Adam, W 1811
Vitruvius Scoticus Facsimile Edition, Simpson J, 1980: Paul Harris

Allardyce, A 1888
Scotland and Scotsmen in the Eighteenth Century, Ulan

Arnold, D 1996
The Georgian Villa, Alan Sutton

Bamford, F 1983
Dictionary of Edinburgh wrights and furniture makers, *Furniture History* 19

Beard, G and Gilbert, C 1986
Dictionary of English Furniture Makers 1660–1840, Furniture History Society

Bessborough, Lord 1950
Lady Charlotte Guest: extracts from her journals 1833–1852, John Murray

British Geological Survey Report 2010
Report on the Building Stones of Dumfries House held at Dumfries House

Brown, M 2012
Scotland's Lost Gardens, From the Garden of Eden to Stewart Palaces, RCAHMS

Buxbaum, T 1987
Scottish Doocots, Shire Publications

Buxbaum, T 1989
Scottish Garden Buildings, From Food to Folly, Mainstream

Charlton, J 1984
A History and Description of Chiswick House and Gardens, Department of the Environment

Cheape, H 1995
Tartan The Highland Habit 2nd edn: National Museums of Scotland

Christie's 1996
Works of Art from the Bute Collection, Christie's Sale Catalogue 3, July 1996

Christie's 2007
Dumfries House: A Chippendale Commission, Christie's Catalogue, volumes 1&2: Christie's

Clifford, T & Gow, I 1995
Duff House, NGS

Close, R & Riches, A 2012
Buildings of Scotland Ayrshire and Arran: Yale

Close, R 1992
Ayrshire and Arran, an Illustrated Architectural Guide: RIAS

Coke, M 1970
Lady Mary Coke, Letters and Journals 1756–74, London

Coleridge, A 1960
Chippendale, the Director and some Cabinet-makers at Blair Castle, *Connoisseur*, Dec, 252–6

Coleridge, A 1966
James Cullen, cabinet-maker, at Hopetoun House I and II, *Connoisseur*, Nov, 154–60, Dec, 231–4

Coleridge, A 1968
Chippendale Furniture, London

Colvin, H 1995
Biographical Dictionary of British Architects 1600–1840 3rd edn: Yale University Press

Cosh, M 2003
Edinburgh The Golden Age, John Donald

Cosh, M 1984
The Adam Family and Arniston, *Architectural History* 27, 214–30

Crouther, G T 1936
The History of Clackmannan, Civic Press

Cruft, C, Dunbar J & Fawcett R 2006
Buildings of Scotland, Borders: Yale University Press

Cumming, E 2011
The Art of Modern Tapestry: Dovecot Studios since 1912, Ashgate

Davies J 1981
Cardiff and the Marquesses of Bute, *Studies in Welsh History* 3

Dunbar, J 1972
The building of Yester House 1670–1878, *Transactions of the East Lothian Antiquarian and Field Naturalists' Society*, 13, 20–42

Fleming, J 1962
Robert Adam and his Circle: Harvard University Press

Franklin, J 1981
The Gentleman's Country House and its plan 1835–1914: Routledge & Kegan Paul

Friedman, T 1984
James Gibbs: Yale University Press

Gibbs, J 1728
Book of Architecture

Gifford J, 1989
William Adam 1689–1748: Mainstream

Gilbert, C 1978
The Life and Works of Thomas Chippendale: London

Girouard, M 1978
Life in the English Country House A Social and architectural history: Yale University Press

Glasgow Corporation, 1967
The Stirling Maxwell Collection Pollok House

Glendining, M & Wade Martins, S 2008
Buildings of the Land: RCAHMS

Gomme, A 2000
Smith of Warwick, Francis Smith Architect and Master-Builder, Shaun Tyas

Gow, I 1984
Sir Rowand Anderson's National Art Survey of Scotland, *Architectural History* 27, 43–54

Gow, I 1997
Scottish Houses and Gardens from the archives of Country Life: Aurum

Graham, E 2010
The 18th century British bath house, unpublished PHD thesis, University of Edinburgh

Greenstead, M 1980
Gimson and the Barnsleys, Wonderful Furniture of A Common Place Kind: Amberley

Greig, J 1926
The Diaries of a Duchess. Extracts from the Diaries of the First Duchess of Northumberland (1716–1776), Hodder and Stoughton

Hannah, R 2003
St Sophia's Church, Galston: 'The Vast Space of the Interior' *Architectural History* 46, 255–268

Hannah, R 2012
The Grand Designer: Birlinn

Harris, E 2001
The Genius of Robert Adam The Interiors: Yale University Press

Harris, J 1994
Chiswick Villa, The Palladian Revival Lord Burlington, His Villa and Garden at Chiswick: Yale University Press

Harris, J 1995
The Palladians, RIBA Drawings Collection: Trefoil

Hewlings, R 1988
A palmyra ceiling in Lincoln, *Architectural History* 31, 166–70

Hunter Blair, D 1921
John Patrick 3rd Marquess of Bute 1847–1900: A Memoir: Longmans

Hunter Blair, J 1922
New Medley of Memories: Longmans

Hussey, C 1955
English Country Houses: Early Georgian 1715–1760: Country Life

Joy, E T 1977
English Furniture 1800–1851: Sotheby Parke-Bernet

King, D 2001
The Complete Works of Robert and James Adam: Butterworth

Leach, P 1988
James Paine: Zwemmer

Lees-Milne, J 1970
English Country Houses Baroque: 1685–1715: County Life

Lindsay, I & Cosh, M 1973
Inveraray and the Dukes of Argyll: Edinburgh University Press

Loudoun, J 1822
Encyclopedia of Gardening

Macaulay, J 1987
The Classical Country House in Scotland 1600–1800: Faber and Faber

McClure, D 1994
Tolls and tacksmen: 18th century roads in the county of John Loudon McAdam, *Ayrshire Archaeological and Natural History Society 6*

McKerlie, P 1906
History of the Lands and their Owners in Galloway: Edinburgh

McWilliam, C 1978
Buildings of Scotland, Lothian: Yale University Press

Maclean, A 2007
Dumfries House: a history, *Dumfries House: A Chippendale Commission* Christie's Catalogue, volume 1: Christie's

Millar, A H 1885
The Castles and Mansions of Ayrshire

Mordaunt Crook, J 1981
William Burges and the High Victorian Dream: Francis Lincoln

Mowl, T 1985
Trumpet at a Distant Gate: The Lodge as a Prelude to the Country House: Waterstone

Paterson, J 1852
History of County of Ayr, Ayr: J Dick

Paterson, J 1863
History of the Counties of Ayr and Wigton, Vol I Kyle part II, Ayr: J Dick

Pryke, S 1992
Furniture Designs at Hopetoun House, *Furniture History* 27, 35–41

Pryke, S 1994
Pattern Furniture and Estate Wrights in Eighteenth-Century Scotland, *Furniture History*, 30, 100–4

Pryke, S 1995
The eighteenth century furniture trade in Edinburgh, unpublished PhD Thesis, St Andrews University

Rowan, A 1984
The building of Hopetoun, *Architectural History* 27, 183–209

Ruddock, E 1979
Arch Bridges and their builders 1735–1835: Cambridge University Press

Russell, F 2004
John Stuart 3rd Earl of Bute, Patron and Collector, London

Rykwert, A&J 1985
The Brothers Adam, the Men and the Style, Collins

Sambrook, P 2003
A Country House at Work, Three Centuries at Dunham Massey: National Trust Enterprises

Scots Magazine 1754
July 1754 16, 353

Schultz R W 1909
Reasons in Building parts I–III, lectures published in *The Arts Connected with Building*, ed. Raffles T Davison, London: Batsford, 1–40

Shifrin, M 2011
Victorian Turkish Baths: their origins, development and gradual decline http://www.victorianturkishbath.org/

Simpson, J 1980
Vitruvius Scoticus: A Study: Paul Harris

Simpson & Brown 2008
Dumfries House & Landscape Draft Conservation Plan, July 2008 (unpublished)

Stamp, G 1981
Robert Weir Schultz Architect and His Work for the Marquesses of Bute: Mount Stuart

Stevens, H 1899
The Cumnocks Old and New Cumnock: Town Council of Cumnock

Stillman, D 1966
Decorative Works of Robert Adam: Academy Editions

Stillman, D 1988
English Neo-Classical Architecture volume 1, Zwemmer

Stirling Maxwell, J 1938
Shrines and Homes of Scotland: W & R Chambers

Strang, C 1994
The Borders, an Illustrated Architectural Guide: RIAS

Strawhorn, J 1966
The New History of Cumnock: Town Council of Cumnock

Summerson, J 1969
Architecture in Britain 1530–1830: Yale University Press

Swan, A 1987
Clackmannan and the Ochills, an Illustrated Architectural Guide: RIAS

Tait, A 1980
The Landscape Garden in Scotland 1735 – 1835: Edinburgh University Press

Taylor, K & Peel, R 2012
Passion, Plants and Patronage: 300 years of the Bute Family Landscapes: Black Dog

Torrie & Coleman 1988
Historic Cumnock: Scottish Burgh Survey

Turberville, F A 1958
The House of Lords in the Age of Reform: Faber and Faber

Walker, FA 2000
Buildings of Scotland Argyll and Bute: Yale University Press

Ware, I 1731
Designs of Inigo Jones and Others: London

Ware, I 1756
A Complete Body of Architecture: London

Weaver, L 1912
The House and Its Equipment: Country Life

Warrick, J 1899
History of Old Cumnock: Town Council of Cumnock

Williamson, E Riches, A & Higgs, M 1990
Buildings of Scotland Glasgow: Yale University Press

Wilson, R & Mackley, A 2000
The Building of the English Country House: Hambledon

Wood, R 1753
The Ruins of Palmyra otherwise Tedmor in the Desart: London

Worsley, G 1995
Classical Architecture in Britain the Heroic Age: Yale University Press

Worsley, G 2005
The British Stable: Yale University Press

Index